THE
POETRY
OF
FREEMASONRY

Rob Morris

ISBN 0-7661-0032-4

THE

POETRY OF FREEMASONRY.

BY

ROB MORRIS, LL.D.

WRITER AND LECTURER ON FREEMASONRY FOR FORTY YEARS, AND BY UNIVERSAL CONSENT
MASONIC POET-LAUREATE.

WITH PORTRAIT AND AN AUTHENTIC BIOGRAPHY WRITTEN BY
HIS SON ROB MORRIS.

Jamque opus exegi, quod non Jovis ira nec ignis,
Nec poterit ferrum, nec edax obolere vetustas.—OVID.

MACOY PUBLISHING AND MASONIC SUPPLY CO.,
34 PARK ROW, NEW YORK.

Rob. Morris

(From his latest photograph)

R.W. WILLIAM JAMES HUGHAN,

OF TORQUAY, ENGLAND,

AUTHOR OF VARIOUS WORKS ILLUSTRATING THE EARLY HISTORY OF FREEMASONRY IN
GREAT BRITAIN, PAST SENIOR GRAND DEACON OF THE

UNITED GRAND LODGE OF ENGLAND, Etc., Etc.

WITH PROFOUND ADMIRATION FOR YOUR TALENT, INDUSTRY, AND AMIABLE
QUALITIES, AND THE MOST ARDENT GRATITUDE FOR YOUR
PERSONAL KINDNESS, I DEDICATE TO YOU THIS

LAUREATE EDITION.

INDUCTION.

INDEBTED as I am to a rare circle of intelligent friends for my title and my title page, and many of the prose thoughts interspersed through these pages, it is nevertheless thought best that I should write my own Preface and subscribe it with my own name. This counsel I the more readily accept, as it enables me to speak as if personally to the large number of Brethren, at whose request many of these pieces were composed. In former editions their names were attached respectively to the various odes and poems, but for good reasons they are omitted in this.

When in 1871, the disastrous fire in Chicago destroyed the plates of my Masonic Poems and many other works, I resolved never again to publish. The fire fiend had followed me so far and fast since 1837 that I felt too old and too indigent to challenge him further.

But the importunities of friends and the gentle yearnings of authorship were, after all, too much for me; and in 1875 I made a collection of some four hundred of my poetical productions, long and short, and gave them to the winds. They have been well received by the reading world, ten editions having been taken up, and an increasing demand appears now to exist. So I am induced to make one more contribution to Masonic literature (my last), in this large and tasty edition, and courteously commend the efforts of forty years to the patronage of the Masonic Craft.

Those who have honored my poems by perusal are aware that they were composed, for the most part, *upon the wing*. On horseback, on foot, in coach and in car, at wayside inns and on the sea, the genius of song has found me and inspired me in the modest way that appears in these pages. Emphatically, my contributions to the poetry of Masonry are *fugitive pieces*. What I might have done could I have had leisure,—could I have found kind friends to give me the means of leisure for half a year,—will never be known. Years, verging upon threescore and ten, blunting eye and ear and dulling the sense deeper than both, warn me to be content that "what is writ is writ."

Twenty years since, before a brilliant assembly of Masons and their lady guests at Indianapolis, Indiana, I expressed, in effect, the following thoughts upon "The Poetry of Masonic Literature":

If Masonic literature may justly be divided, like other branches of human knowledge, into departments, then we may style one of those divisions *Poetry*. The biographical, historical and ritualistic divisions, added to that which is termed *belles-lettres*, in which fiction is introduced by way of parable, make up the ordinary understanding of *Masonic literature*, to which I would add *Poetry* as the complement.

It is not too much to say that this branch of Masonic learning has been overlooked and neglected by Masonic writers. The Order has had among its votaries Walter Scott, Lamartine, Thomas Moore, William Cowper, James Hogg, Robert Burns, George D. Prentice, George P. Morris, Charles Mackay, James P. Percival, and many others of poetic fame,—men whose effusions will survive while sweet sentiments, wedded to melodious diction, have any value; but the united efforts of all these poets applied to Masonic themes scarcely fill a dozen pages. Burns wrote one Masonic ode, and rested. It is his "Adieu, a heart-warm, fond adieu," a piece so exquisitely affecting, so filled with Masonic imagery, that we cannot read it without sensations of regret that he *wrote* no *more*. Scott, Hogg, Moore, Mackay, none of them, so far as I know, ever contributed so much as a line to the poetry of Masonic literature.

George P. Morris composed at least one ode, " Man dieth and wasteth away," which is worthy the man and the theme. Giles F. Yates contributed a paraphrase of the 133d Psalm, which has gone into large use in our lodges, "Behold, how pleasant and how good." Thomas Smith Webb left one upon record, "All hail to the morning," abounding with poetic fire and Masonic imagery. David Vinton gave us "Solemn strikes the funeral chime," which has found extraordinary favor as a funeral hymn. With this our stock of Masonic poetry is exhausted. Not but that there is much jingle, mixed with stanzas of merit scattered through the pages of our books and periodicals, but they are not such as will be selected by future writers to exemplify this Masonic age.

And why is this? Does not the subject of Freemasonry suggest to the poetic mind a flight skyward? If religion, and especially that derived from the contemplation of the Holy Scriptures, constitutes so favorable a theme for poets because of its extraordinary array of imagery,—types, symbols, emblems and what not,—does not Freemasonry abound even more in such things? In fact, Freemasonry is *composed* of allegory, types, imagery, etc.; it is in itself a true "chamber of imagery." The very nature and purpose of the Order is to teach one thing by means of another,—to suggest an inward truth by an outward emblem. Yet the great writers whose names are given above seem never to have recognized this.

Robert Burns found in the murmur of a brook and the warbling of a bird the voice of his mistress. Walter Scott saw through the outlines of a rusty lance-head or broken pair of spurs the imagery of a well foughten field. Thomas Moore drew from the twang of a ricketty lute wails of lamentation for the decadence of his green old Ireland. All this is in the nature of suggestion, the very essence of poetry. Yet these men could look coldly upon the most pregnant images of Freemasonry, the G, the Broken Column, the Mystic Pillars, and a score of others; they could listen to a rehearsal of the Masonic covenants without once considering the inexhaustible mine of poetic thought of which these were only the surface.

As compared with any other theme, I would give the preference to Symbolical Masonry as the richest in poetic thought, and I can only hope that the day is not distant when a great poet will arise who will be to Freemasonry what Scott was to chivalry, Moore to patriotism, Burns to rustic love.

My attention was early turned, as a Masonic student, to the department of poetry, and whatever grade of merit may be attached to my own effusions, I may justly claim to have searched with assiduity the gems of poetic thought buried in the mines of Masonic literature, and brought them to the public eye.

For convenience of use I have arranged the pieces into divisions, as Templary, Symbolical Masonry, etc.; but the distinctions are not particularly obvious, for the aims and teachings of the Masonic Order are the same, whether enforced by the Gavel, the Scepter, or the Sword; whether embodied in emblems of Christ, Zerubbabel or Solomon. In the present edition I have omitted all my odes and poems not Masonic, and supplied their places with a number of productions, notably "The Utterances of the Sword," composed since the edition of 1878 was published.

As to the spirit in which these pieces were composed, I quote from a communication sent ten years since to Hon. James M. Howry (deceased 1884), who was my Masonic instructor forty years since: "I became early fascinated with the wonderful machinery of Freemasonry, and what I felt I spoke and wrote. I could no more check my thoughts than the tempest can silence the sounds it makes. Freemasonry appeared to me such a field for the reformer. Here was a body of selected men, united by indissoluble covenants, working out a few grand, simple principles of architecture, and having celestial wages in view! Was not this a perfect theory? I wrote because my heart burned within me, and silence seemed impossible. I found that the effect of Masonry properly appreciated was to render men lovely to their fellows, pleasing to their God. In my poems I said as much, and said it in the most forcible, the most tuneful words at my command. I have visited more than one lodge where learning, religion, the useful and liberal arts, law, polished manners, all that marks and embellishes the best society, and man as a constituent in the best society, is found, and of such I endeavored to be the reporter, tnat by their life I might aid in vitalizing other lodges that

'Lie in dead oblivion, losing half
The fleeting moments of too short a life.'"

But my preface is becoming verbose, and I will close. To the present generation I pray to commend the thoughts which pleased their fathers.

ROB MORRIS.

LA GRANGE, KENTUCKY, December, 1884.

y.

THE LEVEL AND THE SQUARE.

WE MEET UPON THE LEVEL, AND WE PART UPON THE SQUARE,—
What words of precious meaning those words Masonic are!
Come, let us contemplate them; they are worthy of a thought,—
With the highest and the lowest and the rarest they are fraught.

We meet upon the level, though from every station come—
The King from out his palace and the poor man from his home;
For the one must leave his diadem without the Mason's door,
And the other finds his true respect upon the checkered floor.

We part upon the square, for the world must have its due;
We mingle with its multitude, a cold, unfriendly crew;
But the influence of our gatherings in memory is green,
And we long, upon the level, to renew the happy scene.

There's a world where all are equal,—we are hurrying toward it fast,—
We shall meet upon the level there when the gates of death are past;
We shall stand before the Orient, and our Master will be there,
To try the blocks we offer by His own unerring square.

We shall meet upon the level there, but never thence depart;
There's a Mansion,—'tis all ready for each zealous, faithful heart;
There's a Mansion and a welcome, and a multitude is there,
Who have met upon the level and been tried upon the square.

Let us meet upon the level, then, while laboring patient here,—
Let us meet and let us labor, tho' the labor seem severe.
Already in the western sky the signs bid us prepare
To gather up our working tools and part upon the square!

Hands round, ye faithful Ghiblimites, the bright, fraternal chain;
We part upon the square below to meet in Heaven again.
O what words of precious meaning those words Masonic are,—
WE MEET UPON THE LEVEL, AND WE PART UPON THE SQUARE.

The above is the original form in which the poem, "We Meet upon the Level," etc., was written. Its history, as often told, is simple enough, and has none of the elements of romance. In August, 1854, as the author was walking home from a neighbor's, through the sultry afternoon, he sat upon a fallen tree, and upon the back of a letter dashed off, under a momentary impulse and in stenographic character, the lines upon this page.

Eighteen years since, Brother George Oliver, D.D., eminent above all others in English Masonry, and the Masonic historian for all time, said of the poem: "Brother Morris has composed many fervent, eloquent and highly poetic compositions, songs that will not die, but in 'The Level and the Square' he has breathed out a depth of feeling, fervency and pathos, with brilliancy and vigor of language, and expressed due faith in the immortal life beyond the grave."

THE LEVEL, PLUMB AND SQUARE.

We meet upon the LEVEL, and we part upon the SQUARE:
What words sublimely beautiful those words Masonic are!
They fall like strains of melody upon the listening ears,
As they've sounded *hallelujahs* to the world, three thousand years.

We meet upon the LEVEL, though from every station brought,
The Monarch from his palace and the Laborer from his cot;
For *the King* must drop his dignity when knocking at our door
And *the Laborer* is his equal as he walks the checkered floor.

We act upon the PLUMB,—'tis our MASTER's great command,
We stand upright in virtue's way and lean to neither hand;
The ALL-SEEING EYE that reads the heart will bear us witness true,
That we do always honor God and give each man his due.

We part upon the SQUARE,—for the world must have its due,
We mingle in the ranks of men, but keep *The Secret* true,
And the influence of our gatherings in memory is green,
And we long, upon the LEVEL, to renew the happy scene.

There's a world where all are equal,—we are hurrying toward it fast,
We shall meet upon the LEVEL there when the gates of death are past;
We shall stand before the Orient and our MASTER will be there,
Our works to try, our lives to prove by HIS unerring SQUARE.

We shall meet upon the LEVEL there, but never thence depart.
There's a mansion bright and glorious, set for the pure in heart;
And an everlasting welcome from the Host rejoicing there,
Who in this world of sloth and sin, did part upon the SQUARE.

Let us meet upon the LEVEL, then, while laboring patient here,
Let us meet and let us labor, tho' the labor be severe;
Already in the *Western Sky* the signs bid us prepare,
To gather up our Working Tools and part upon the SQUARE.

Hands round, ye royal craftsmen in the bright, fraternal chain!
We part upon the SQUARE below to meet in Heaven again;
Each tie that has been broken here shall be cemented there,
And none be lost around the Throne who parted on the SQUARE.

This poem has been subjected to so many alterations in its thirty years of active use that it is deemed proper to give it here with the last emendations. It is likely that older readers will prefer it in its first draft.

BIOGRAPHY OF ROB MORRIS, LL.D.

MASONIC POET LAUREATE.

[From official data furnished by his son, Robert Morris, Jr., of Franklin, Ky.]

"THE MASONIC DICKENS OF AMERICA."—ALLIBONE'S DICTIONARY OF AMERICAN AUTHORS.

DR. ROB MORRIS was born August 31, 1818, near Boston, Mass. His parents were teachers, and he, following in their footsteps, taught school the first ten years of his manly estate. He then wandered, like many others, from the New England shores to the cotton fields of the South, and settled down to teach at Oxford, Miss. There he met Miss Charlotte Mendenhall, whose parents resided near that place, and they were married August 26, 1841. About thirty-seven years ago Dr. Morris removed to La Grange, Ky., where he passed his remaining years until his death in 1888.

Through the means of the great amount of labor done by him, and the excellence, and, it might be called, genius of that work, or a great portion of it, Dr. Morris' name became more familiar throughout the Masonic fraternity through distant parts of this country, and the world, than it was to those outside of that order who lived within five miles of his home. His publications, numbering seventy-three works, his contributions to and in connection with the Masonic, the religious, the sectarian and the scientific press, which extended through half a century; his unparalleled industry as a lecturer upon many themes, all unite in surrounding his name with a halo of public respect.

He was a very large contributor to many Masonic periodicals, and various newspapers and magazines. Throughout all the world the name of the Poet Laureate of Masonry is known and loved next to the ancient order itself.

Dr. Morris' chief fame came to him through his poems. They are of a very high order, and are recognized as being the productions of a healthy brain, an erudite conception, a grand appreciation of the good, and a beauteous imagination. It was a circumstance commented upon in one of Dr. Morris' lectures that while there was an abundance of poets who belonged to the Masonic ranks, notably Thomas Moore Sir Walter Scott, James Hogg, Ferguson, George P. Morris, Percival, Robert Burns Duganne, Shilliber, Lamartine, Cowper and others, yet altogether they have scarcely written a score of Masonic poems. Percival and George P. Morris wrote two or three each, Robert Burns one, the greatest of them all, except Rob Morris' poems. while all the others named wrote none.

Robert Burns, over one hundred years ago, was crowned with the laurel wreath, which signified his elevation to the station of Poet Laureate of Freemasonry. This was for one poem he wrote, and he was the first to be so crowned. Upon his death no one was ever deemed fit to assume the high station until Rob Morris was so selected through the expressed wish of over 500,000 Masons throughout all the world.

The coronation took place in New York City, on December 17, 1884, in the presence of several thousand Masons who attended, many of them from distant points of the compass, to merely witness the one event. It was in a double sense the crowning point of a wondrous life.

It was the prediction of the venerable and learned Salem Town, LL.D., himself a Mason of great prominence, and an expounder of its grandest themes, that "Brother Morris' fame as a poet will outlast his memory as a writer in prose."

Out of more than three hundred pieces that make up his poetical collections, there are many of rarest delicacy and beauty. His poetical labors extended over every class of thought proper to the theme. Very many were written to be accompanied by music, and so have entered into Festival, Funeral and Work meetings ; some to be recited with emblematic accompaniments. The greater portion were composed "upon the wing" in stage coach, railway carriage, on steamboats, on horseback, and at Low XII hours after lodge-meetings.

It would seem that no man could perform the amount of labor accomplished by Rob Morris, unless he preserved all his faculties intact and attained nearly the number of years of life allotted to Methuselah. Yet that work was all done, unassisted, by Rob Morris, and the spring of inspiration which promoted it lay in the one source, "ambition."

When this ambition was gratified with his coronation as Poet Laureate he ceased his labors and dwelt nearly four years in the quiet lull before death came to claim him for its own. In speaking of him a number of Masons, among the most eminent in the land, said that he was not only the greatest Masonic poet and prose-writer, but he was the greatest Mason that had ever lived.

In fact, there have been few men who ever lived who have done more work with the pen for publication than Rob Morris. There has certainly been no writer of Masonic literature at any time in the world's history who has written half as much as he either of poetry or prose. The work he has done would seem too stupendous for any one man to perform in a lifetime, yet he has done it, and well. He has not only written all these works, songs, hymns, poems, addresses and essays, but furthermore he has done such other minor literary work as would require a couple of columns additional merely to enumerate.

It is of course chiefly as a writer that Dr. Morris is known to the Masonic world. He was not only the universally accepted Poet Laureate of Masonry, but in addition to this his prose works are of the first rank in Masonic literature. He wrote extensively on the subject of Masonic jurisprudence, produced several rituals and hand-books, many fugitive pieces, edited some Masonic journals, and published an important book of travel and research, "Free Masonry in the Holy Land," which appeared in 1872.

The Masons of this country raised between $9,000 and $10,000 as a fund to enable Dr. Morris to make his journey to the original seat of Masonry. He went to the Orient in 1868, and traveled very extensively there and in Europe. His researches confirmed many traditions as to Masonry, and enabled the author to contribute much valuable evidence as to the truth of what was before then little more than conjecture. Being learned in Masonic lore, the inscriptions, coins and customs of the people among whom he journeyed often had a meaning for him which was not apparent to others. His trip to the Holy Land discovered abundant testimony as to the great age of Masonry. His book is dedicated to His Excellency Mohammed Raschid, Governor-General of Syria and Palestine, who was an eminent Mason.

A profound admiration for the Bible, as the only inspired book in Masonry, led Dr. Morris early in his career to propose an exploration of the lands of the Bible in the interests of the order. In 1854 the grand lodge of Kentucky entered into the plan, and proffered a loan sufficient for the cost, but circumstances at that time forbade the journey. It was still, however, a favorite theme in his lectures and writings, and in 1867 he visited one hundred and thirty lodges, chiefly in the northern states, and proposed to them that he would donate the necessary time and labor if they would undertake the cost. The response was a practical one, for 3,782 brethren clubbed together to supply the necessary means.

He set out February 2, 1868; addressed the lodges at Smyrna, upon the way, on February 25, and reached Beyrout, Syria, March 3. At Damascus, through the influence of Brother E. T. Rodgers, H. B. M. Consul there (and master at the time of Lebanon lodge, at Beyrout), he made the Masonic acquaintance of the governor-general and of General Abdel Kader. He delivered addresses before the members of the Masonic fraternity in Damascus, Beyrout, Joppa and Jerusalem. In the latter city he opened a Lodge of Instruction, May 13, which, five years afterward, culminated in the Royal Solomon Mother Lodge, No. 293, upon the Canada Register of which he was first Master. He reached home early in August. The results of his industrious researches are seen in the large volume entitled "Freemasonry in Holy Land." At Jerusalem he made the personal acquaintance of that learned and zealous explorer, Captain Warren, himself a member of the Masonic brotherhood.

This oriental lodge has maintained a distinct and honorable existence, and has become the mother of a group of lodges in Palestine and the center of a grand lodge in Jerusalem. Dr. Morris made a second visit to Europe in 1878, at which time he was especially noticed by the Prince of Wales, who, being a Mason, departed from his habit of non-attendance so far as to attend lodge in London, and then to follow him to Oxford to attend lodge there, while Dr. Morris was at those places lecturing.

Dr. Morris was "brought to Masonic light," as the phrase is, in Oxford, Miss., March 5, 1846, when he joined Gathright Lodge, No. 33. At that time he was principal of the Mount Sylvan Academy, near Oxford. He at once became deeply interested in the subject of Masonry, and his progress thereafter was notable.

He was exalted to the degree of Royal Arch in Lexington, Miss., in 1848; accepted as R. and S. M. in 1849; made a Knight Templar at Jackson, Miss., in 1850, and received the Scottish Rite degrees to the Thirty-second degree in 1854. He received the Rite of Memphis, so far as the Ninetieth degree, in New York in 1864, and the encampment order of English Templary in Canada in 1857. He also received a very large number of the honorary appendages to Masonry, such as the three official orders of Royal Arch Masonry, Past Eminent Commander, Past Grand Commander, Grand High Priest, Past Grand Commander-in-Chief 32°. The Masonic and Military Orders of the Knights of Rome, and the Red Cross of Constantine, were communicated to him in 1857, and afterwards in 1873.

The Order of Past Grand Master was given him at his installation as Grand Master of Kentucky, in 1858, the Hon. Henry Wingate, Past Grand Master, presiding. Among his honorary degrees and complimentary memberships, which were nearly one hundred and fifty in number, that of Past Deputy Grand Master of the Grand Lodge of Canada was chiefly prized.

Dr. Morris was a member of Fortitude Lodge, No. 47, at La Grange, Ky., and of the Eminence Royal Arch Chapter. He was also a member of the Louisville Commandery, No. 1, Knights Templar, and was Past Grand Commander-in-Chief of the Grand Consistory of Kentucky, 32°.

He was the originator of a large number of special features, among them the most superior degrees of "Ladies' Masonry." The most popular of these with the order are "The Eastern Star," composed and communicated by him in 1850. This degree is divided into five sections, named from as many historical characters, namely: "Jephthan's Daughter," "Ruth," "Esther," "Martha" and "Electa." So popular has this degree become that there are now hundreds of organizations styled "Chapters of the Eastern Star." These societies extend throughout the entire world. In addition to this degree Dr. Morris also added "The Queen of the South," "The Cross and Crown," etc.

Of Masonic rituals and hand-books, the following is a list of his works: "Free Masons' Monitor," twelve degrees; "Miniature Monitor," three degrees; "Eastern Star Manual," "Rosary of Eastern Star," "Guide to High Priesthood," "Special Help for Worshipful Master," same for Senior Deacon, same for the Secretary, "Funeral Book of Freemasons," "Prudence Book of Freemasons," "Masonic Ladder," "Dictionary of Freemasonry," "Guide to the Consecration of Masonic Cemeteries," "Discipline of Masonic Offenders." He was the first writer, according to very high authority, in Masonic belles-lettres, his "Lights and Shadows of Freemasonry" being the pioneer work in that line.

Of all these and others, it may truthfully be said, as Lyttleton, in his eulogy of Cowper:

> "Not one immoral, one corrupted thought,
> One line which, dying, he would wish to blot."

His rule of life, from the commencement of labor as a Masonic journalist, was borrowed from Addison: "I promise never to draw a faulty character, which does not fit at least a thousand people, or to publish a single paper that is not written in the spirit of benevolence, and with a love of mankind."

By many Dr. Morris was considered the leading numismatist in America. In the science of historical numismatics in America he was one of the pioneers, his monograph, entitled "The Twelve Cæsars, illustrated by Readings of 217 of Their Coins and Medals," being the first issue of its class west of the Atlantic. He also published the "Numismatic Pilot," devoted to the explanation of ancient coins. He was Secretary of the American Association of Numismatists; honorary member of the Numismatic and Antiquarian Society, of Montreal, Canada; also of the Boston Numismatic Society and the New London, Conn., Historical Society, and an active member of the American Numismatic and Archæological Society, of New York.

Rob Morris gave us altogether, as from a perennial fountain, more than three hundred effusions in form of odes and poems; but none wear so well with old admirers, none secure so speedily the favor of the newly-initiate, as his conception of August, 1854, which has "gone out through all the earth" under the name of "The Level and the Square." It is the Masonic song of the age, tending to the immortal. Brother George Oliver, D.D., eminent above all others in English Masonry, and the Masonic writer for all time, said of this piece: "Brother Morris has composed many fervent, eloquent and highly-poetic compositions—songs that will not die,—but in 'The Level and the Square' he has breathed out his depths of feeling, fervency and pathos with brilliancy and vigor of language, and expressed his faith in the immortal life beyond the grave."

Periodically published in Masonic journals, quoted in a thousand orations, seen in fragments in innumerable epitaphs, musically wedded to sixteen airs, declaimed by traveling performers, and embodied in many "Gems of Reading," this effusion deserves best of all to live in his memory as one of his grandest efforts.

Of Masonic belles-lettres, he wrote "Life in the Triangle," 1853; "The Two St. Johns," 1854; "Tales of Masonic Life," 1860; "Lodge at Mystic," 1863; and "Masonic Poems," 1864 and 1876. In Masonic history and biography he wrote "Freemasons' Almanacs," 1860–'61–'62–'63–'64; "Masonic Reminiscenses," 1857; "History of Freemasonry in Kentucky," 1859; "Life of Eli Bruce," 1859; "Freemasonry in the Holy Land," 1872. He also published in thirty octavo volumes, under the general title of "Universal Masonic Library," fifty-six distinct works, including writings of Oliver, Mackey, Town, Portal, Preston, Hutchinson, George Smith, Morris, Anderson, Harris, Calcott, Ashe, Lawrie, De Vertot, Gourdin, Taylor, Creigh, Brown, Morton, Arnold and Towne. In addition to these, he published the

"American Freemason," 1853-'58; "Voice of Masonry," 1859-'67; "Light in Masonry," 1873, and "Kentucky Freemason," 1853.

In addition to these he has given to the Sunday-school literature of the world scores of odes, sketches, addresses and songs. In 1884 he published a new edition of his poems entitled the "Poetry of Freemasonry," which was a compilation of his best poetry. He also wrote a series of sketches for the "Courier Journal," entitled "Jesters with Whom I have Jested," published in 1886. One of his most famous songs was called "Blind Bartemus."

The beginning of official work of this zealous veteran was that of Grand Lecturer, first in the state of Tennessee; afterwards in Kentucky. On horseback, before the days of railways, he visited the lodges of those jurisdictions to the number of a hundred or more, and communicated to them rituals and general instructions in Masonry. The originality and thoroughness of his teachings are best described by a gentleman who accompanied him for a week or more in the spring of 1851:

"Brother M.'s marked trait was *industry*. He made little pretension to genius or talent of high order, but he always made *the best use of his time*. I never saw him idle for a moment. In the lodge or out of it he was *ever seeking* or *communicating* Masonic light. He visited sick brethren, if there were any, at their houses, and imparted comfort. He inquired for destitute brethren and tendered them aid. He looked up the graves of departed Masons and suggested better care of them. He set the secretary to making a list of the widows and orphans of the craft, that if any were needy they might not be overlooked by the brotherhood in future. His appearance in those days was very peculiar. Lank as a rattlesnake, and as swift at a witty stroke; nervous to the last degree; frightfully dyspeptic; extremely fond of nature, and an idefatigable collector of shells, arrow-heads and eccentric stones; a glutton for reading books; fluent as the river and generous as the sea; speaking in all things from the heart; amiable and generous."

In Dr. Morris' lodge lectures a beauty, grandeur and significance were apparent that impressed even the doltish mind. At that period American lodges were at a low ebb of information. The ceremonials were often wretchedly burlesqued by ignorant pretenders, and Rob Morris came among them as a reformer. Instead of an unmeaning tragedy the craft acquired a sublime symbol, and if the neophyte had a soul at all able to appreciate a grand thought, he received a permanent impression. On Sabbath days Dr. Morris addressed communities, wherever he might be, in their churches and school-houses, upon *Freemasonry as identified with Bible truth*. Once, at least, in every village, he invited a union of the ladies with their husbands, fathers and brothers in the lodge-room, and to the united assembly gave his beautiful system entitled *The Eastern Star*. Though the country was wild with political and sectarian strife (the mutterings of civil war) he talked of *nothing but Freemasonry*, and for all this service he accepted a compensation so meagre that the poorest lawyer or physician that sat in any of his audiences would have spurned it.

The system of itinerant lecturing upon Freemasonry, begun by Dr. Morris, has been continued to the present. The venerable Mentor of Masonry raised his voice in defense of the order and its covenants in the lodges of Indiana, Illinois, Iowa,

Wisconsin, Nebraska, Colorado, Wyoming, Utah, Nevada, California, New Jersey, Delaware, Ohio, Connecticut and New York, and other states. He once estimated that in thirty-two years of such *travel and travail* he climbed the stairs and entered the *adyta* of fifteen hundred lodges !

The growth of skepticism among American Masons has been too marked to escape the notice of any. Leading men among the craft have at one time and another publicly attacked the old principle of "faith in an inspired word as a fundamental belief in Masonry." To counteract this, the most dangerous foe that Masonry can have, Dr. Morris early made himself the champion of Biblical faith. To unsettle the minds of the craft as to *the object* their fathers venerated has been the first aim of the Masonic skeptic, and we see that while casting the Holy Scriptures out of the lodge-room was the first step of the French infidel, ignoring faith in God was the second and an easier step. Dr. Morris said in an oration in 1853 : "I repeat, with the great moralist Johnson, that there is no crime so great that a man can commit as poisoning the sources of eternal (Masonic) truth. Faith in God tends, in the only high and noble sense, to make Freemasons *one*."

So many of Dr. Morris' diplomas and official jewels were destroyed in the burning of his house, "The Three Cedars," at LaGrange, Ky., November, 1861, and in the terrible conflagration of Chicago, October, 1871, that no accurate list can now be given of them. It is within bounds, however, to assert that the number of honorary degrees and complimentary memberships with which his signal services were recognized in America and abroad exceeds *one hundred*. Dr. Morris at one time recalled a list of *one hundred and forty-three* regular degrees and orders in Masonry, whose covenants he has assumed. In 1856 he made this summary of them in a symbolical strain of thought:

"I have been *around*, *under* and *through* the temple of Masonry, searching out its foundations, its builders and its trestle board. With its builders I have handled, in turn, each of its implements; with the *Entered Apprentice*, trimming the rough ashler on the checkered pavement; with the *Fellow Craft*, moralizing upon the pillars of the porch, and the fifteen grades of the winding stairs; with the *Master Mason*, smoothing the indissoluble cement with silent awe; with the *Mark Master* I have penetrated the quarries, found my own best block, brought it up for a place in the walls, and claimed my penny with the rest; for I never have received, of salary or official emolument, to the value of one Jewish half shekel of silver. I have shared the responsibilities of the *Past Master*, seated in the Oriental Chair of King Solomon. As a *Most Excellent Master*, my hands have aided to rear the cap-stone to its place, while my lips have sung the triumphant strain, *All Hail to the Morning*, of Thomas Smith Webb, and my face was bowed to the pavement in acknowledgment of the descent of fire and cloud. As a *Royal Arch Mason*, returning from exile in Babylon, my feet have wandered, weary and sore, over rough and rugged ways, seeking the Sacred Hill. As a *Select Master*, I have wrought in silence, secrecy and darkness, upon the mystic arches within the Holy Mountain. I have stood as a *Knight Templar* with companions loyal and brave, wielding my brand, excalibur, two-edged and cross-hilted, while guarding the SHRINE where the body of MY

DEPARTED LORD was laid. In all my career as a Mason I have ever held that excellence is granted to man only in return for labor, and that nothing is worth having that is not difficult to acquire. My life has been, thus far, a contest with obstacles; but no man would be what he is, had he tamely suffered the difficulties of life to overcome him."

It has been claimed that Dr. Morris was the first to ever write a book upon the subject of Masonic Jurisprudence. The work upon that subject was published in 1855 and was entitled the "Code of Masonic Law." Doubtless there has been too much legislation among American Grand Lodges, too much of the whimsical, special and ephemeral, yet he conceived that there is a *basis of legal principles* to which all questions may be referred, and this is what he undertook to point out in his "Code of Masonic Law." All thoughtful Masons admit that

> " Law should speak
> Seldom, and never but as wisdom prompts,
> And equity."

The spirit of his writings upon jurisprudence is suggested by Hooker:
"It is easier a great deal for men to be taught by laws what they *ought* to do, than intrusted to judge as they *should*, of law: for the wisest are ready to acknowledge that soundly to judge of law is the weightiest thing a man can take upon him."

In his contributions to the periodical literature of Masonry since 1850 will be found replies to questions upon Masonic law and usage, and dissertations upon special subjects of this class. His studies in this branch gave him the facility seen in the various Constitutions drafted for Grand Bodies, Standard Forms of By-Laws, and in the Handbooks issued in great numbers for use in the workings of Masonry.

The custom of giving honors to our Masonic dead has become so intimately incorporated into our American Masonry that many continue their attachment to the order "even down to old age," that so they may not forfeit the funeral honors due the faithful departed. On the other hand, it is an attraction to a certain class of minds to unite themselves with a fraternity which follows its members lovingly to the grave's brink and lays them gently back upon the bosom of mother earth. In honoring this custom the practice of Dr. Morris was supplemented by his writings. His "Funeral Book of the Freemasons," a work of widespread celebrity, contains, in addition to copious and easy instructions, a long catalogue of epitaphs and forms of obituary notices, also of funeral songs suitable to such occasions; while no one was so often called upon to attend in person and preside over such ceremonials.

This passage was first published by Dr. Morris in 1852, and expresses his views upon the subject with much vigor:

"In all ages the bodies of the Masonic dead have been laid in graves dug due east and west, with their faces looking toward the east. This practice has been borrowed from us, and adopted by others, until it has become nearly universal. It implies that when the great day shall come, and He who is death's conqueror shall give the signal, *His ineffable light shall first be seen in the east;* that from *the east* He will make His glorious approach; will stand at the *eastern* margin of these graves, and with His mighty power—that grasp irresistibly strong which shall prevail—will raise the bodies which are slumbering therein. We shall have been long buried, long decayed. Friends, relatives, yea, our nearest and dearest, will cease to remember where they have laid us. The broad earth will have undergone wondrous changes, mountains levelled, valleys filled. The seasons will have chased each other in many a fruitful round. Oceans lashed into fury by the gales of to-day will to-morrow have sunk like a spoiled child to their slumber. Broad trees with broader roots will have interlocked them, hard and knobbed as they are, above our ashes, as if to conceal the very fact of our having lived; and then, after centuries of life, they, too, will have followed our example of mortality, and, long struggling with decay, at last will have toppled down to join their remains with ours, thus obliterating the last poor testimony that man has ever lain here. So shall we be lost to human sight. But the eye of God, nevertheless, will mark the spot, *green with the everlasting verdure of faith;* and when the trumpet's blast shall shake the hills to their very bases, our astonished bodies will raise, impelled upward by an irresistible impulse, and we shall stand face to face with our Redeemer."

Dr. Rob Morris closed his earthly career at La Grange, Ky., on July 31, 1888. He had been in bad health for a year or more, but was not seriously ill until about six weeks before his death, when he was stricken with paralysis, and after that time he steadily declined. For twenty-four hours preceding his death he was unconscious. His immediate family of six children and their mother were present during his last moments.

The surviving children were: John A. Morris; Charlotte F., married to Hon. H. J. Goodrich; Dr. Alfred W. Morris, Robert Morris, Jr., Sarah M., married to Latimer Hitt; and Ruth E., married to John Mount.

The Grand Master of Kentucky, upon receipt of the intelligence of the death of Dr. Morris, at once caused the issuance of the following circular letter:

GRAND LODGE OF KENTUCKY, F. AND A. M.

LEXINGTON, KY., July 31, 1888.

To the Free and Accepted Masons of Kentucky:

It becomes my painful duty to announce to you the death of our venerable and learned brother, P.˙.G.˙.M.˙.Rob Morris, which occurred at his home in La Grange, on the 31st day of July, 1888, after an illness of short duration, following years of ill health.

The fame of our eminent brother was not confined to our continent—he was a citizen of two hemispheres; for his learning and zeal made him known to Masons everywhere as a chieftain among the clans, a master builder among the workmen. His mark is upon the most beautiful stones of our Masonic edifice, and his designs remain upon our trestle board, for he both conceived and executed.

It is my order that this announcement be read in every lodge at its next regular meeting, that proper respect may be shown to the memory of our deceased brother until the Grand Lodge of Kentucky can, in ample form, testify its appreciation of his many excellencies.

J. SOULE SMITH,
Grand Master.

H. B. GRANT,
Grand Secretary.

The funeral ceremonies took place at La Grange, which had been his home for over thirty years, and were conducted by the Grand Lodge of Kentucky, Past Grand Master Hiram Bassett, an old and zealous Mason, and an intimate friend of Dr. Morris, acting as Grand Master.

A special train carried the brethren of Louisville up to La Grange on August 1st, the day of the funeral.

The Knight Templars were under command of E∴Sirs F. H. Johnson and John A. Stratton. The procession was in charge of Col. John B. Castleman, K. T., assisted by Capt. John H. Leathers, Grand Treasurer; Bro. W. H. Shaw.

The following officers officiated :

P∴G∴M∴Hiram Bassett, as Master, representing also the Grand Master.

Bro. J. R. Adams, Master of Fortitude Lodge, assisted Bro. Bassett as Deputy; Bro. L. M. LaRue, Senior Warden; Bro. H. R. Coleman (Grand Chaplain) as Chaplain; D. T. Carson, Junior Warden; William Manby, Secretary; J. W. Russell, Treasurer; R. D. Cassiday, Senior Deacon; Henry Egert, Junior Deacon, and J. T. Davidson (Grand Tyler) as Tyler. Bro. M. Cary Peter, Grand Junior Deacon, was present, but his jewel was worn by Bro. Kinkead, W. M. of Lodge 376.

At the residence a number of Pilgrim Knights (of the Palm and Shell—organized by Bro. Morris) performed the mystic ceremonies of that order about the remains. These were Bros. H. R. Coleman, Hiram Bassett, H. B. Grant, J. H. Leathers, Chas. Sauer, J. M. Hall, J. W. Hopper, W. H. Shaw, W. E. Woodruff, Wm. Moses and Alex. Evans.

A Guard of Honor, consisting of Past Commanders, viz.: E∴Sir Knights C. E. Dunn, C. L. Martin, C. C. W. Alfriend and Thos. H. Sherley (P. G. C.), of Louisville Commandery, No. 1; A. H. Gardner, Chas. C. Vogt, H. R. Mitchell and John Finzer, of DeMolay, conveyed the casket to the church, where a male choir, led by Bro. Smythe, assisted by a number of brethren, with Bro. Wm. T. Boden at the organ, rendered most solemn and beautiful music.

Rev. H. Calvin Smith delivered the discourse from the text: Psalms lxviii, 13—"Though ye have lain among the pots, yet shall ye be as the wings of a dove covered with silver and her feathers with yellow gold."

Rev. Bro. H. R. Coleman followed with a few remarks and P∴G∴M∴Eginton read a tribute prepared for Fortitude Lodge.

P∴G∴M∴James W. Hopper also read an original "song of lamentation."

Bro. H. B. Grant, Grand Secretary, being called upon, said:

"About four years ago I received from Bro. Rob Morris a paper containing these words, afterwards making verbal request that they be read at the first Masonic gathering after his death:

To my dear friend, H. B. Grant:

A MESSAGE FROM THE GRAVE.

I have composed this poem as under the shadow of impending death. I have made a few copies, and sent them to particular friends only, asking that they should not be published, or any public use made of them, until I am gone.

Brothers in June or in December,
　　Honoring the memory of the dear St. John,
Then let some kind participant remember
　　The name of him who wrote this, *but is gone;*
Let some kind brother rise, while all are silent,
　　And with deep pathos and fond friendship say:
He was a Mason, gentle, true, not violent,
　　And loved old things that do not pass away.

He loved his friends; in them his heart found anchor,
　　Bound in affection as with hooks of steel;
As for his foes, he gave few signs of rancor,
　　But bore their slanders patiently and well.
He loved to make in simple verse that rhyming
　　Where ancient signs and emblems smoothly lie,
Where deeds of brother-love and truth are chiming,
　　And Masonry is wed to poetry.

He loved the word of God; its hopes eternal
　　Grew sweeter as the end of life drew nigh;
A sinful man, but saved by Grace supernal,
　　Trusting in Christ, he dreaded not to die.
At times a cloud the promises disguising,
　　And deep humility obscured the scene,
But the bright Son of Righteousness uprising
　　Dispelled the gloom and warmed his soul again.

He gave the widows and the orphans duly
　　A portion of his hard-earned scanty store,
And though the amount might seem but trifling truly,
　　He gave so cheerfully it seemed the more.
His heart was in his work, to *Build the Temple,*
　　In fervency, he toiled through many years,
To " build the temple " spiritual and mental,
　　He triumphs now—is freed from toils and tears.

He's gone; the problem that so long he studied,
　　That mystery of " the world to come " profound
Is solved; his tree of life which only budded,
　　Bears now full harvest in Celestial Ground.
In the Great Presence, with the weaned resting
　　He has his wages and is well content.
Brothers, in silence stand; your love attesting—
　　This is the word your dying brother sent!

The Knights Templars commenced their beautiful service, which was concluded at the grave, E.˙.Sir Frank H. Johnson, Commander, and E.˙.Sir John Frank Lewis, Prelate, officiating.

The procession filed out of the church and, led by the band from Louisville, the Templars and the lodge were followed by the hearse and mourning family and friends to the village cemetery.

Bro. Bassett then took up the solemn Masonic services, which being concluded,

Bros. J. H. Leathers and H. B. Grant placed upon the grave a floral design, representing a Masonic level, about three feet across the base, and a square, referring to the popular poem by Bro. Morris,

"We meet upon the Level and we part upon the Square."

This was surrounded by a laurel wreath, suggesting that the deceased had been crowned "Poet Laureate of Freemasonry." Another floral tribute, by the Commandery, was a very large Roman cross. Other very pretty designs were laid upon the grave.

The attendance was very large, and represented the brain and zeal of Kentucky Masonry.

PART FIRST.

———

POEMS:

EMBODYING THOUGHTS OF THE BIRTH, LIFE, DEATH, RESURRECTION
AND ASCENSION OF

JESUS, THE CHRIST.

The first is a coin of John Zimisces I, Emperor of the Byzantine Dominions, A.D. 969 to 975. Upon the obverse is
the portrait of CHRIST in the style of the Middle Ages, with the inscription in Greek, EMMANUEL. The
reverse presents a Passion Cross *bent to the left*, with Greek letters and words cantoned in the spaces.
These are read " Jesus Christ, the King of Kings." This fine specimen was procured by Dr.
Morris at Gebal, on the Phœnician coast. The coin is copper. The Seal is that of
the *Militia Templi*, founded at Jerusalem by King Baldwin, A.D. 1118. Two
chevaliers upon one horse signify the extreme poverty of the Order.
The inscription, in Mediæval characters, is *Pauperes Commili-
tones Christi et Templi Salomonis.* " The Poor Fellow-
soldiers of Christ and of the Temple of Solo-
mon." Procured at Malta.

13

14

THE POETRY OF FREEMASONRY.

THE MASTER OF THE TEMPLARY ORDERS.

ONE is your Master, CHRIST, the Lord,
    And we are Brethren, true and strong,
Sincere in heart, exact in word,
    Abhorring vice and wrong.
Sir Knights, flash out the Cross-hilt Sword!
ONE is your Master, CHRIST, the Lord.

ONE word inspires the valiant Knight,—
    It is the cruel GOLGOTHA;
ONE star leads on with steady light,
    The bright, the Orient star.
Sir Knights, flash out the Cross-hilt Sword!
ONE is your Master, CHRIST, the Lord.

Where lines of Knightly legends flow,
    From Bethlehem to Olivet,
There do our warrior-longings go,
    There is our Master yet.
Sir Knights, flash out the Cross-hilt Sword!
ONE is your Master, CHRIST, the Lord.

And when is won this earthly strife,
    Laid by the SPEAR, assumed the CROWN,
We trust to share that peaceful life
    Which our GREAT CAPTAIN won.
Sir Knights, flash out the Cross-hilt Sword!
ONE is your Master, CHRIST, the Lord.

The term *Master*, which occurs so often in this volume, is of good lineage. Here are some inspired uses of this word : " Meet for the *Master's* use"; " Your *Master* is in Heaven"; " Ye call me *Master* and say well, for so I am"; " *Master*, we know that thou art true"; " One is your *Master*, even Christ." In the symbolical Lodge, with the respectful adjunct " Worshipful," the term *Master* denotes the ruler and law dispenser of the Lodge. " Sovereign Master" is a synonymous use of the word in the Commandery. This piece has been set to music.

THE KNIGHTS OF JESUS.

We meet *upon the naked blade*, we cross the glittering steel,
Opposing foot to foot we stand, our Knightly vows to seal;
Erect as men, with watchword high, of truth and victory,
The Templar Knight brings forth his blade to conquer or to die.
      We are the Knights of Jesus,—
      Our word — EMMANUEL.

We meet *before the Sepulcher*, and sheathe the blood-stained sword;
In awe-struck silence gaze we on the Rising of the LORD!
No earthly victory this, and yet the greatest battle's won,—
The FATHER triumphs over death through Jesus Christ, the SON!
      We are the Knights of Jesus,—
      Our watchword — GOLGOTHA.

We meet *around the tri-form*, Sir Knights, can we forget
The hour, the place, the scene? ah, no, they haunt our memory yet;
And while one spark of honor kindles in the Knightly heart,
We vow that in eternal scorn we'll hold the traitor's part.
      We are the Knights of Jesus,—
      Our line of labor — TRUTH.

The widow and the orphan hail the flashing of our steel;
The maid forlorn and innocent doth Knightly aid appeal;
Pilgrims, who seek Jerusalem, our timely succor greet,
And this is Christian work for which the Templar Masons meet.
      We are the Knights of Jesus,—
      Our word — BENEVOLENCE.

And when the bitter cup is quaffed, which flesh and sense abhor,
And banner cased and good swords sheathed, and words of parting o'er,
Then, by the Throne, beside the LAMB, whose service is so sweet,
We hope, Sir Knights, in endless *rest*, in endless *bliss* to meet,
      We are the Knights of Jesus,—
      Our word — CELESTIAL LIFE.

THE CROWN OF THORN.

O Crown of Thorn, by Jesus worn,
   Bedewed with heavenly gore;
If mine the pain be mine the gain
   To wear as Jesus wore.

O Crown of thorn, by Jesus worn,
 The badge divine, 'tis given;
And may it prove by Jesus' love
 A Crown of life in Heaven.

O Crown of thorn, His flesh was torn,
 His blood suffused for me;
The sin was mine, the grace divine,
 For oh, it sets me free.

O Crown of thorn, when breaks the morn
 That Christ shall come again,
Above the host that love him most
 This token will be seen.

O Crown of thorn, imposed in scorn
 And cruel mock and jeer,
Upon my brow I lay it now,
 And while I live, will wear.

A FIXED AND FRAGRANT MEMORY.

To the far-distant shore, the utter past,
He was our link ; he brought us all the good
There is in old-time things, and made them good
By his example. Now our bark has slipped
Its moorings, and we try the unknown sea,
Assured that when the Haven of Peace is found,
Where'er it be, we shall regain our lost !

O truest man, one in a thousand men !
O generous heart ! O trusty, faithful heart !
How in our hearts indelibly is drawn
The record of thy virtues, many and pure,
Twin record with the register in Heaven,
Whose penman is, O joy, the Omniscient God !
He made our Brother, made him of the clay,
So sacred hence to virtue and to us !

This token of "a fixed and fragrant memory" is to the honor of Salem Town, LL.D., for half a century Grand Chaplain of the State Grand Bodies of New York. His name appears in Masonic literature as a prolific author. Deceased 1864.

DIRGE OF THE TEMPLARS.

PRECIOUS in the sight of Heaven
  Is the place where Christians die;
Souls with every sin forgiven,
  To the courts of glory fly;
Every sorrow, every burden,
  Every CROSS they lay it down;
JESUS gives them richest guerdon
  In His own immortal CROWN.

Here, above our BROTHER weeping,
  Through our tears we seize the hope,—
He in Jesus sweetly sleeping,
  Shall awake in glory up;
He has borne his CROSS in sorrow,
  Weary pilgrim, all forlorn —
With the new light of to-morrow,
  He will have the sparkling CROWN.

Knights of Christ, your ranks are broken;
  Close your front, the foe is nigh;
Shield to Shield, behold the TOKEN
  As he saw it in the sky!
BY THAT SIGN, so bright, so glorious,
  YOU SHALL CONQUER, if you strive,
And like him, though dead, victorious,
  In the courts of JESUS live!

Composed in 1857 to accompany the beautiful Ritual of *Templars' Burial*, by Eminent Sir John L. Lewis, of New York. This song has entered into large use. The air to which it was written is Mozart's, ordinarily known as "Go, Forget Me."

THE GRAVE OF SIR OSSIAN E. DODGE.

Departed friend, by thy lone grave I stand,
Like thee, a pilgrim in this alien land;
And with a tribute tear, all mournfully,
I meditate, dear friend, in thoughts of thee.

I call the parted years,— they come no more
In fancy only can I tread that shore
Where mirth, and joy, and charming melody
Made up, dear friend, my intercourse with thee.

18

Thy home no more to know its master's tread;
Our genial comrades scattered, haply dead;
Youth, hopes all buoyant, genius bright and free,—
Gone, gone, forever gone, dear friend, with thee.

Midst London's dead I leave thee here to rest;
No mortal care can now distract thy breast;
But in a bright *hereafter* may I see
All earthly loss repaired, dear friend, with thee.

This sweet musician and genial brother, the author of the music commonly sung to "The Level and the Square," died in London, England, October 17, 1876. I spent a Sabbath day in August, 1878, searching for his grave. It is in one of those enormous *Cities of the Dead* that form such prominent features in the periphery of the great circle occupied by London. The place is Paddington Cemetery, Willesden Lane, Kilburn, about six miles from St. Paul's Cathedral. The burying ground contains thirty-six acres, the same extent as Mount Moriah, Jerusalem, and embosoms more than half a million graves.

SORROWING, YET NOT WITHOUT HOPE.

Composed and inscribed to the fragrant memory of Thomas J. Corson, by special request of M.E. Companion I. Layton Register, Grand High Priest.

No! though the grave hath claimed our best,
No! though the green sprigs mark his rest,
Weeping we cry with chastened faith,
Trust in the Lord, and conquer death.

No! though a seat is vacant here,
No! though his voice no more may cheer,
Upward we cast the eye of love,
Lost to the earth, but safe above.

How through long years of wasting pain
Bright burned his soul and fired his brain;
In this dear place he loved to be —
Here keep his name eternally.

Brethren, be strong, for life's demand
Boldly endure and bravely stand;
From his bright life example take —
From his blest grave let hopes awake.

THE COMING OF THE MASTER.

A Metrical Composition, Arranged for a Recitation of Five Templars, as Rendered in Various Grand and Constituent Commanderies in the United States and Canada.

Why is his chariot so long in coming? why tarry the wheels of his chariot? . . . A holy one coming down from Heaven. . . . Who may abide the day of his coming? and who shall stand when he appeareth? . . . They shall see the Son of Man coming in his kingdom. . . . The coming of the Just One. . . . The coming of the Lord draweth nigh. . . . The Master of the house cometh.

This metrical composition first given to the world in Philadelphia, Pa., at a convention of the four city commanderies, 1873, is a paraphrase of St. John xi, 28, which contains the words of Martha addressed to her sister Mary, "The Master is come and calleth for thee." The Templars' Master, as suggested on page 12, is Jesus Christ, King of Kings and Lord of Lords. "When He had led his disciples out as far as to Bethany, He was taken up and a cloud received Him out of their sight. And while they looked steadfastly toward Heaven as He went up, behold two men stood by them in white apparel, which also said, Ye men of Galilee, why stand ye gazing up into Heaven? this same Jesus, which is taken up from you into Heaven, shall so come, in like manner as ye have seen Him go into Heaven." It has been the steadfast belief of pious Templars in all ages that this Master will come again!

When that illustrious day shall rise, and the Great Captain of our Salvation demands of each of us, "What hast thou done, Sir Knight, for me?" the intelligent Frater will have ready his response. In the following poem I have suggested four different forms of reply. While one may humbly submit to the divine Inquirer that he has cared for the widow and orphan, another may claim that his sword has been drawn in defense of injured innocence, and yet another that he has pointed the contrite and broken-hearted sinner to the Lamb of God that taketh away the sins of the world. These three classes of Christian performances, almsgiving, courageous aid and religious instruction occupy the field of our duty as applied to others. What, then, is left to the fourth? Why, that he has performed *the duty to himself*, by giving himself to Jesus Christ to work in Him, to will and to do of His good pleasure.

Such is the line of thought that pervades this poem. Delivered by a group of five Templars, the first speaker recites the two opening stanzas, and makes the solemn demand,

> Servant of Jesus, bold and free,
> What hast *thou* done, Sir Knight, for me?

The second Knight in his response declares that he has labored zealously in the field of Christian Benevolence.

Then the demand is repeated by the first speaker, and addressed in turn to the respondants. Successive replies come from the third, fourth and fifth Sir Knights, as will appear in the stanzas severally apportioned to him. The poem then concludes by the first speaker reciting the last four stanzas.

The effect of this dramatic composition has been most encouraging. It has entered into the *repertoire* of those Knights who prepare themselves to give interest to banquetry occasions, both in the red and black. It has been quoted in orations and addresses, and it may be supposed that but few who see these pages are not in some degree familiar with it.

The following lines, whose authorship is to us unknown, afford a proper colophon to this preface:

The lance is rusting on the wall,
    No laurel crowns are wove;
And every Knightly strain is hushed
    In castle, camp and grove.

No manly breast now fronts the spear,
    No strong arm waves the brand,
To vindicate the rightful cause,
    Or stay oppression's hand.

The minstrel pilgrimage has ceased;
    Chivalric days are o'er,
And fiery steeds bear noble men
    To Palestine no more.

Rejoice in beauty more than gain;
    Guard well the dreams of youth,
And with devoted firmness true
    Crusaders for the truth!

THE EXORDIUM.

Oh gallant Knights, in fitting garb arrayed,
With crested helm and Cross and trenchant blade,
Brave Warriors in a warfare not to cease,
Till wearied hearts shall find eternal peace.
    While in this broad Asylum meet,
        Where wisdom, beauty, strength rejoice,
    Let's gather at the MASTER's feet,
        And listen to the MASTER's voice:
            The MASTER, Prince Emmanuel,
            The voice His Word we love so well.

If to this Conclave our dear Lord *would* come,
If here and now, JESUS *would* grace this room,
If face to face, we *might* behold that head,
Once scarred with thorns, once humbled with the dead,
If in our hands those hands *were* laid, once torn
With spikes, alas! on cruel Cross tree borne,
What startling question, gallant Templars, might
The GRAND COMMANDER make to us to-night.

THE FIRST DEMAND AND REPLY.

" Servant of Jesus, bold and free,
What hast *thou* done, Sir Knight, for Me?"

21

I saw the Widow's tears, I heard the cry,
Her little ones in rags and misery,
Her household lamp gone out, her firelight sped,
In utter loneliness and lack of bread;
　　Then MASTER, in Thy place I stood! my hand
　　Was opened wide to that unhappy band.
　　I fed them, clothed them, and the Widow's prayer
　　Named my poor name who saved her from despair.
　　　　This, oh LORD, I did for THEE,
　　　　Thou hadst done so much for me.

THE SECOND DEMAND AND REPLY.

"Servant of Jesus, bold and free,
What has *thou* done, Sir Knight, for Me?"

I found a good man compassed round with foes,
On every side reproaches, threats and blows.
In innocence he bravely strove, and well
And many a foeman to his good sword fell;
But, nature fainting, soon his arm were numb
Had not my cross-hilt sword, relieving, come.
　　Then, MASTER, in THY place I stood! my blade
　　Flew swiftly from its scabbard to his aid!
　　I shielded him; I smote till close of day,
　　And drove them all, discomfited, away.
　　　　This, O LORD, I did for THEE!
　　　　Thou hadst done so much for me.

THE THIRD DEMAND AND REPLY.

"Servant of Jesus, bold and free,
What hast *thou* done, Sir Knight, for Me?"

I saw a stricken Knight — his youth had fled;
Friends of his manhood, age, were with the dead;—
Leaning upon a monumental stone,
A mourner, broken-hearted and alone;
　　Then, MASTER, in THY place I stood! I showed,
　　In all THY life divine, the love of God;
　　Pointed THEE out upon THY radiant throne,
　　And lo, he made THY promises his own!
　　　　This, O LORD, I did for THEE!
　　　　Thou hadst done so much for me.

THE FOURTH DEMAND AND REPLY.

"Servant of Jesus, bold and free,
What hast *thou* done, Sir Knight, for Me?"

MASTER DIVINE, in all life's weary round
Naught so unhappy *as myself* I found;
Blind, naked, sin-polluted, wholly lost,
A wreck upon the ocean, tempest-tost;
Naught could *I do* to win THY gracious smile,
For all *my doings*, like myself, were vile;
    Then, MASTER, to THYSELF I flew! I plead
    That righteousness that triumphed o'er the dead;
    Placed my eternal trust within THY hand,
    And evermore will bow at THY command.
        This, O LORD, I did for THEE!
        Thou hadst done so much for me.

THE LAUDATION.

Sir Knights, well done! the high award is given.
    Yon open book assures you of HIS praise!
It is not far from grateful heart to Heaven,—
    Almost we see HIM by faith's earnest gaze;
        Sir Knights, well done! in golden letters see,—
        "Ye did it unto them and unto ME!"

It is but little any man can do,
    So insignificant is human power,
But as on earthly pilgrimage we go,
    There are occasions, every day and hour,
        When sorrow's voice is heard, and be our care
        To do as JESUS would were JESUS there!

The Widow's tears are HIS, for JESUS wept;
    The imperiled Knight is HIS,— leap forth, ye blade!
The broken heart is HIS,— while others slept
    How, in Gethsemane, HE wept and prayed!
        Sir Knights, HE left this sin-struck world to us,
        To teach its comfort and remove its curse.

Leap forth, good Swords! stand, Templars, on your feet!
    In serried ranks bear one another up!
BY THIS SIGN CONQUER,— it is full, complete,—
    You need no other faith, no other hope;
        And when from dying hands the sword shall fall,
        Fear not, the MASTER will redeem us all!

23

The following is sung in full chorus at the conclusion of the Recitation·

HOSANNA.

Now Hosanna, Son of David,
  Blessed be Thy name to-day!
Shout Hosanna in the highest,
  Born to everlasting sway!
    Lift your head, ye golden gate,
    Jesus comes in royal state;
    Shout Hosanna, shout and sing,
    Jesus Christ, the Lord is King!

Blessed be the King of Judah,
  Peace and glory in the sky!
In the name of God he cometh,
  Here to rule eternally.
    Mighty doors, your bolts unbrace,
    Let the Lord of Glory pass;
    Shout Hosanna, shout and sing,
    Jesus Christ, the Lord is King!

Glory to the Conquering Hero;
  Not with strength of warrior swords,
His the might of earth and Heaven,
  KING of KINGS and LORD of LORDS.
    Hearts of stone your hinges move,
    Open to the Lord of love;
    Shout Hosanna, shout and sing,
    Jesus Christ, the Lord is King!

Praise to God, the Glorious Father,
  Praise to God, the Gracious Son,
Praise to God, the Loving Spirit,
  God Eternal, three in one
    Powers of sin no more restrain,
    God is come on earth to reign;
    Shout Hosanna, shout and sing,
    Jesus Christ, the Lord is King!

And I heard as it were the voice of a great multitude, and as the voice of many waters, and as the voice of mighty thunderings, saying ALLELUIA! for the Lord God Omnipotent reigneth.—REVELATION xix, 6.

THE TEMPLARS OF CALIFORNIA.

In your own bright California, along this golden slope,
Is set by bounteous Providence each emblem of our hope ;
The giant trees, the placid sea, the pure and virgin snow,
And golden fruits unrivaled that in your gardens grow.

Yes, this is like the *Palestine* upon whose soil I've trod,
Where man first learned his brother-man, first learned his father God ;
The same bright fruits, the seasons, and the same pacific sea,
Bring back from Judah's storied hills best memories to me.

Your mountains call from history that grand, heroic time
When David's son, the Mason king, reared up a wall sublime ;
When gold in countless measure by the willing hand was spent,
And Ophir to Jerusalem her wealth of treasure lent.

Your sea recalls that "utmost sea" of which the Prophet wrote,
That bore upon its billows such a cedar-laden flote,
And Parian stone and porphyry that by the skillful hand,
Assumed exquisite symmetry to answer God's command.

But most of all, most admirable, most memorable to me,
These cross-hilt swords and banners high of Knightly imagery ;
The soldiers of EMMANUEL, the Templars strong and rare,—
Yes, these recall the holiest thoughts that stirred my spirit there.

Sir Knights, I've stood within the cave where first HE saw the light
Whose NAME inspires, in Heaven and earth, the gallant Templar Knight;
I've bowed with head uncovered, bowed with bent and willing knee,
Beside the spot that drank HIS blood, the hateful Calvary.

I've followed Jesus, step by step, all through the Holy Land,
And *here*, said I, HE healed the sick, and *here* the withered hand,
Here brought the clamorous blind to sight, *here* cursed the barren tree,
Here fed the starving multitude along the stormy sea.

I've sat where the great Preacher sat when breathing words of love,
And read, in solemn silence, what HE said of things above.
Never in all my life, Sir Knights, stood Jesus Christ so nigh,
As in that land where Hiram taught Freemasons how to die.

Therefore, though in this withered arm is spent the manly force,
Nor spear nor falchion can I wield, nor guide the fiery horse,
Yet with an unchanged soul I gaze upon this Blazonry,
And lend a gladsome voice to yours, and join your battle cry.

Beauseant, Beauseant, 'twas uttered on that dark, ensanguined field
Of Hattin, where the Knights went down with shivered spear and shield;
"God wills it," *Dieu le veut,* and this, Sir Knights, shall be our cry
When in HIS own good time it is appointed us to die.

Then hail, dear Templar Knights, all hail! your warfare is of God,
And naught but what's *celestial* has the service of your sword;
If Charity, and Gentleness, and Chastity inspire
The warfare of the Templar Knight,—*this is the Christian fire.*

And when you sheathe the cross-hilt sword, and lay the helmet down,
May the COMMANDER wreathe your brows with the immortal crown;
In the Asylum where HE waits, may each the MASTER view,
And in eternal peace enjoy the wages that are due!

This poem was composed and read at a Lecture delivered by the writer before California Commandery, No. 1, at San Francisco, Cal., April, 1876. The similarity of soil, climate and productions between this state and the "Holy Land" is too striking to escape the notice of a traveler familiar with both.

THE KNIGHT TEMPLAR AT REST.

Resting in calm repose,
The fiercest blast that blows
And bows yon sturdy oaks on Bashan's height,
Can yield no influence here;—
For many and many a year
Hath "slept in Jesus" this our stalwart Knight.
While rust corrodes his great cross-hilted sword,
The toil-spent Templar rests before the Lord.

He heard an inward call,—
"Leave home, leave country, all
That love you or are loved,—leave wealth and fame,
And with this ruddy Cross,
Count other things but dross,
To go and battle in your Master's name!
There, where I walked in early days with men,
Go, I will meet you, striving there, again!"

Meekly he rose and went;
His hard-earned fortune spent
In the high cause for which he took the sword;
He chose the lowliest place;
For nothing can abase
The servant when he imitates his Lord.

Yet where the strokes fell thickest midst the din
He listened, yearning for that voice again.

And here the Templar fell ;
Battling full long and well ;
He fell beneath the point of Paynim spear ;
But to his dying eye
The Master's form drew nigh,
The Master's whisper blest his dying ear ; —
"Well done, true Knight, inherit thy reward !
The servant is not greater than his Lord !"

In a cave near Jericho there was found, in 1867, a skeleton distinguished as the relic of a Knight Templar by the armor, sword, spurs, and silver badge of the "valiant and magnanimous Order."

AT LAST.

At last — all things come round at last ;
Long years and strange events have past,
And some are dead we hoped to greet,
Since first these friends proposed to meet.
Blow, stormy winds, your utmost blast,
For here kind Fraters meet, *at last!*

Tyled closely from the world without, —
Inspired by faith unmixed with doubt, —
We bare our hearts to friendship's eye,
And every mortal care defy.
Drop, murky clouds, the sky o'ercast,
For here good Fraters meet, *at last!*

With glowing precepts old and dear ; —
With songs to move fraternal tear, —
And story quaint, and witty flow,
Our night shall sweetly, swiftly go :
Roar, angry stream, thou volume vast,
For here brave Templars meet, *at last!*

And when the parting prayer is given,
Which scales the inner walls of Heaven, —
When silent hand-grasps speak the grace
No language ever can express,
We'll hope, though happy night be past,
Within the veil to meet, *at last!*

THE PASTORAL IMAGE.

O Lamb of God, O, Lamb that once wast slain,
 We walk among the pastures of Thy land,
 Thy meads and founts spread out on every hand,
And long to see Thee feeding here again.

Thou art our Shepherd — Thou the expert, the bold —
 Thy mighty rod defends the gentle flock;
 The erring Thou restrainest with Thy crook;
At eventide Thou leadest them to the fold.

At noon, Thou guidest unto cooling springs;
 Sultry the blazing sun may heat the hills;
 In quiet meadows, by the singing rills,
We lie refreshed, while our sweet Shepherd sings.

And O, beloved Pastor, lest the harms
 Of the rude rocks should wound their tender feet,
 Thou, strong to save, and in Thy mercies sweet,
Dost take our little Lambs within Thine arms.

Thou art the door, the entrance to the fold;
 Through Thee we joyful pass: we know Thy voice;
 Yet *call us*, Lord ! O, how we will rejoice !
There is no hunger there, no pinching cold.

Where Thou art, all is safety, all is rest;
 Harmless the ravening wolf may seek his prey;
 The robber vainly haunts the midnight way,
While we repose in safety on Thy breast.

O, tender One ! and did our Shepherd bleed —
 Bleed for *our* sorrows ? when, midst galling storm,
 And blows, and sweat, and scourge, and poisonous thorn,
Thou, Jesus, died — *was it for us, indeed?*

Yes, yes, *for us:* then let us follow on;
 No more to lag, unwilling, on the way;
 No more from thy dear person, Lord, to stray;
But close and loving, till life's day is done.

The image of the Lamb, as a suggestion of Jesus, is common on the coins of the Knights of Malta, successors of the Templars. The Paschal Lamb, or lamb of sacrifice, is a type of the sufferings and death, the expiation and atonement taught in the Easter Services of the Templar Commanderies of the present day. This was in the writer's mind when he penned the above, amidst pastoral scenes of Bethlehem and Galilee.

THE EARNEST PLEA.

Lord, why can I not follow now?
Where'er Thou goest let me go;
    Of Thy dark cup, oh, grant a share,
    And of Thy burdens let me bear;
Only do Thou acknowledge me,
Then, with full heart, I'll follow Thee!

Death — no, I do not fear his name;
Cross — yes, I covet all its shame;
    Friends go and leave disconsolate;
    Foes crush me down with cruel hate;
Only do Thou acknowledge me,
Then, with full heart, I'll follow Thee!

Jesus, I've found in Thine employ,
Still some new source of holy joy;
    Pilgrim, and sad, when shall I come
    Glad unto Thine eternal home!
Only do Thou acknowledge me,
Then with full heart, I'll follow Thee!

FAITHFUL UNTO DEATH.

PALM LEAVES to strew o'er our dead,
    Trump notes to grace his last way.
Gems to bedeck the fair head,
    Crowned for death's glory to-day;
Weep not midst triumphs like these,
    Give him with joy to the tomb;
Wages of promise are his,
    Soon shall he rise from its gloom.

Green live the deeds of our friend;
    Sweet is his virtue's perfume;
Prayers from his soul did ascend,
    Pure as the dewy-washed bloom;
Open his heart as the day,
    Prompt to yield Heaven its due;
Strong to give virtue the sway,
    Heart-warm his pity, and true

Used, as set to music by various composers, at the Templar demonstrations associated with the obsequies of Sir James A. Garfield, President of the United States.

THE BRIGHT AND MORNING STAR.

THE GLEAMING OF THE ORIENT.

The ORIENT gleams with starry beams, the STAR OF CHRIST is up;
It guides us on our pilgrimage, it points the NATION'S HOPE;
It points the flowery way of life, there's joy in every beam,
And we shall surely find at last the BABE OF BETHLEHEM.

The generations of the dead have gone this way before;
The STAR to them, as unto us, immortal tidings bore;
They bade farewell to earthly things, they counted all things dross,
And found immortal glory in the burden of the CROSS.

And we have seen the EASTERN STAR break through the shadows dim;
And, led by this, have hastened here to serve and worship HIM,—
The LAMB OF GOD, th' ETERNAL WORD, the LILY and the SUN,
And the strong LION, that shall raise the dead when all is done.

We follow fast, we follow far, we follow while we live,
We never cease, through weariness, the WORSHIP that we give.
We only crave to find at last, beyond the shadows dim,
Our Rest and our Salvation in the BABE OF BETHLEHEM.
        Then gleam, O STAR, forever,
        And lead us on to GOD!

THE GRAND ADVENT OF THE TEMPLARS.

Hark to the din of drums !
    List to the bugles' blare !
And lo, the cross-hilt column comes,—
    Was ever sight so fair?
See on the archèd sky,
    Hear in the murmuring wave.
How nature joins us joyously
    To meet the Templar brave !
        The NORTH sends forth her legion long,
        The EAST her tide compact and strong,
        The WEST her best of warrior throng,
            The SOUTH her Templars rare;
            Was ever sight so fair?

CHRIST rules the earth to-day,—
    Light of the CROSS illumes.
His *Beauseant* on high display,
    And stir the rolling drums !

Host of the martyred LORD,
　　Knights of the Orient Star,
O spread His name, His praise abroad,—
　　Was ever sight so fair?
　　　　The NORTH sends forth her legion long,
　　　　The EAST her tide compact and strong,
　　　　The WEST her best of warrior throng,
　　　　　　The SOUTH her Templars rare;
　　　　　　Was ever sight so fair?

The coming of the Commanderies to Chicago, Illinois, in the summer of 1880 was an event never to be forgotten by an eye witness. It demonstrated the strength and zeal of Templar Masonry with a force that has put to silence the cavilings of our opponents. The above lines were set to martial music by Frederic W. Root.

FOR JESUS' SAKE.

For Jesus' sake,—for O, a weary road
　　O'er hill and valley Jesus trod for me;
My gentle Shepherd, with the love of God,
　　In mercy sought and found and set me free.
I was a prisoner in the thrall of sin,
　　I was a wanderer on the mountain bleak,
And since my Saviour now hath brought me in,
　　I'll guide and pity such *for Jesus' sake.*

For Jesus' sake,—for O, He died for me!
　　It was *my sin* that drove him to the tomb;
In ghastly horror, on the accursed tree
　　He bore them all while Heaven was draped with gloom;
I cannot keep my tears—they fall like rain
　　While thinking how that loving heart did break;
And since he has removed sin's galling chain
　　I'll consecrate my life *for Jesus' sake.*

For Jesus' sake,—for O, in whisperings low
　　His Holy Spirit tells me—I am His!
My spirit bounds to meet Him, and we go
　　In sweet communion to the Land of Bliss!
Come weal, come woe—it matters not to me;
　　Fast speeds the hour when angel wings I'll take.
One with the saints in glory I shall be—
　　Lift high your gates, ye Heavens, *for Jesus' sake.*

31

SEARCH THE SCRIPTURES.

O *early* search the Scriptures; 'tis the dew
   On tender leaves; 'tis the young rose's bloom;
'Tis the bright tinge of morning; 'tis the hue
   That doth on cheek of conscious virtue come;
     'Tis all that gratifies the sight.
     To *see* this precious BOOK aright.

O *fondly* search the Scriptures; 'tis the voice
   Of loved ones gone forever; 'tis the song
That calls to memory childhood's perished joys;
   'Tis the blest accents of the angelic throng;
     'Tis all that gratifies the ear,
     This holy Book aright to *hear*.

O *deeply* search the Scriptures; 'tis the mine
   Of purest gold, and gems of richest sort;
'Tis life's full sustenance of corn and wine;
   'Tis raiment, clean and white, from Heaven brought;
     'Tis wealth beyond all we can crave,
     This Heavenly Book aright *to have*.

For here, O here, the fond departed,
   The MAN OF SORROWS, slain for us,
Speaks to the worn and broken-hearted,
   And tells us, " I have borne the curse !
     Redeemed thee from the power of death,
     And sanctified thy parting breath ! "

That in bright lands depictured here,
   Are many mansions, ample room,
Where parted ones, of all most dear,
   Will bid us welcome from the tomb;
     Where many a friend we counted lost
     Is singing with the heavenly host.

This is the one appointed way
   Through which the Holy Ghost doth speak;
O search the Scriptures through life's day,
   And treasures of salvation seek;
     Assured there is no other ford
     Through Jordan's billows save the WORD.

THE CHOICE OF DUKE GODFREY

"Not where the Saviour bore
 Thorns on His brow;
Not where my King upon
 Cross tree did bow;
Not where the Prince of Life
 Sorrowed and groaned,
Godfrey shall ever be
 Homaged and crowned.

"Mine be the humbler name,
 Fitter by far,
'Warder of Tomb Divine,
 Christ's Sepulcher';
Mine at its portal
 In armor to lie!
Mine in death's ministry
 When I shall die."

Knight of Christ's Sepulcher,
 Christ's Chevalier,
Good Sword of Jesus,
 Oh, live grandly here!
Ashes of Godfrey, there's
 No place like this,
Crowned in Christ's glory
 And reigning in bliss!

This redoubtable hero, Godfrey de Bouillon, when crowned as the first King of Jerusalem, August, 1099, refused to wear the emblem of gold and jewels, averring that "King Jesus had worn a crown of thorns." The writer visiting the site of his tomb in 1868, laid upon it a wreath of the *spina-christi* from the Jordan Valley, in commemoration of the story.

RISE UP: HE CALLETH THEE.

HE calleth us to words and deeds of love,
 As spring calls forth from wintry crust the flowers;
He breathes within us spirit from above
 As zephyrs breathe within the sunny bowers;
He saith, Arise, shake off the dust, and go
 Where duty calls, where sorrow hath its sway;
He points our feet the proper path, and lo,
 He promiseth to be with us alway!

THE SERVICE OF THE TEMPLAR.

I SERVE, and my wages are ample,
  I watch by the gate of my Lord;
The innermost joy of his Temple
  Not yet does the MASTER afford.
    But I SERVE at His will
    And all patiently still,
    At the Mystery gate
    I wait, I wait.

I SERVE, and my service is holy,
  Though raiment be scanty and torn;
The crumbs of the feast to the lowly,
  The rags to the watcher forlorn.

I SERVE, and if sometimes o'er weary,
  Impatient at moments so slow,
My Master sends messages cheery,
  "Be vigilant, gallant and true!"

I SERVE, but the long watch is ending,
  The waning stars hint of the morn,
My LORD from His palace is bending,
  Oh, joy to the watcher forlorn!
    For I SERVE at His will
    And all patiently still,
    At the Mystery gate
    I wait, I wait.

The motto for the Prince of Wales, *Ich Dien* (" I serve "), is peculiarly applicable to the relations borne by the Templar Knight to his Heavenly Master. As expressed in the Templar's Rituals and shadowed in the armorials of the Order, the position of a Templar is that of a servant, the servant of Christ. His time of service is marked out in the mind of his Master, and his wages are "laid up in store for him," to be paid over at the proper time.

Inscribed, under brotherly memories of many years, to Sir Theodore S. Parvin, Grand Recorder of the Grand Encampment of the United States.

INVITATIONS TO PILGRIMAGE.

COME then, dear followers of Christ, your hand;
Together, Pilgrims, to the Holy Land!
Climb nimbly now, along the sacred hills;
Drink joyously the cool, refreshing rills;
Tread the same pathway in this later age
That Jesus trod in early pilgrimage.

All well known things are there; from flowers that bloom
And trees that soar, down to His empty tomb;
And all things speak in nature's chorus true,
Of Him who lived, and loved, and died for you.

Come, and when *Holier Land*, where Christ hath gone,
Breaks on your sight,—when breaks the expectant Morn
O'er heavenly hills, and faith and hope shall die,
The deepest secrets of the upper sky
Shall be revealed; the humblest emblem here
Shall have its antitype celestial there,
And earth, with all its imagery be given
A school to fit us for the perfect Heaven.

NEVER FORGET.

Never forget, dear Comrade, while you live,
The ties of which the Templar's vow is wound;
Never forget a Templar to forgive,
If in his breast a kindred heart is found;
    Never forget, though rust and sin may soil,
    And lewd desires your bosom's tablet stain,
    There is *full pardon* after life's turmoil,
    If we but trust in HIM "who rose again."

Never forget the sad, sad story told
This hour, of treason in Gethsemane;
Never forget the good Cyrenian bold
Who bore the SUFFERER's cross so manfully;
    Never forget the taper quenched in night,
    The darkened room, the silent group around;
    Never forget the jubilant delight
    When in his place a worthier was found.

Never forget to live the Templar's life,
Though hard it may be, rough, and fraught with care;
Our work, we told you, is a constant strife,—
We promised you but coarse and scanty fare;
    Not long the weary arm, the moldy crust,—
    See on Celestial plains our camps are set!
    Strike and press on, brave Comrade, as you must,
    "By this sign conquer!" do thou *ne'er forget!*

This piece is extensively used in the American Commanderies as an exhortation to the newly created, immediately following the accolade. For this use it admits of esoteric changes and interpolations *ad libitum.* It has been set to music.

THINKING OF JESUS.

REFLECTIONS UPON THE LIFE AND WORK OF THE LORD JESUS CHRIST, WHILE EXPLORING THE HOLY LAND IN 1868. IN NINE PARTS.

That which we have seen with our eyes, and our hands have handled . . . . declare we unto you.— I JOHN i, 1–3.

I. BETHLEHEM : THE PLACE OF HIS BIRTH.

I thought of JESUS on the Hill
  Of BETHLEHEM, fair BETHLEHEM:
    The Shepherds watching through the night,—
    The angelic songsters clothed in light,—
The promised CHILD so humbly born
For pilgrimage of toil and scorn;
    Then, as I mused on them,
      This voice from BETHLEHEM I heard,—
      The Hill is Holy to our new-born Lord!

The city of Bethlehem, five miles south of Jerusalem, is charmingly situated upon an eastern spur of the ridge that composes the land of Palestine. It is 2,700 feet above the Mediterranean, and 4,100 above the Dead Sea. It covers the hill, terraced on every side from the valleys, and is thus embowered in groves of mulberry, fig and olive trees, and grape vines that produce marvelous clusters. *The Shepherds watching through the night.* There were shepherds abiding in the field, keeping watch over their flocks by night.— LUKE ii, 8. *The angelic songsters, clothed in light.* And lo, the angel of the Lord came upon them, and the glory of the Lord shone round about them. And there was with the angel a multitude of the heavenly host praising God.-- LUKE ii. 9–13. *The promised child.* Behold, a virgin shall bear a Son, and shall call his name EMMANUEL.— ISAIAH vii, 14. —— *so humbly born.* She wrapped him in swaddling clothes and laid him in a manger, because there was no room for them in the inn.— LUKE ii, 7. *For pilgrimage of toil and scorn.* I gave my back to the smiters, and my cheeks to them that plucked off the hair, hid not my face from shame and spitting.— ISAIAH i, 6. " He went about doing good."

II. NAZARETH : THE HOME OF HIS YOUTH.

I thought of Jesus in the Vale
  Of NAZARETH, sweet NAZARETH.
    His name is murmured in its Fount,—
    His praises sweep along its Mount,—
His youthful feet have trodden there,—
His earliest thoughts distilled in prayer;
    Then, as I bowed in faith,
      This voice from NAZARETH I heard,—
      The Vale is Holy to our youthful Lord!

36

His name is murmured in its Fount. The fountain which supplies the people of Nazareth with water is one-half mile east of the city. Thither the mother of Jesus must have gone often with water jar on shoulder, and the prattling boy by her side, as the mothers of Nazareth are yet seen to do, morning and evening. *His praises sweep along its Mount.* Above the city of Nazareth, on the west, is the overhanging mountain described in Luke iv, 29. The view from its top is one of the broadest and most interesting in all Holy Land, and as such must frequently have met the eye of the divine Nazarene. *His youthful feet have trodden there.* From the day of his learning to walk, to his departure upon his divine mission at the manly age of thirty, Jesus made his principal labors and journeys in and around Nazareth. *His earliest thoughts distilled in prayer.* As we read in Luke ii, 52, that Jesus, at Nazareth, grew "in favor with God," and as he was emphatically a man of prayer during his ministry, often withdrawing in solitude for that purpose, we may safely conclude that his mind was absorbed in this sacred abstraction, even from early youth.

III. JORDAN: THE SCENE OF HIS BAPTISM.

I thought of Jesus in the rush
  Of JORDAN'S waters, cool and good;
    How cheering was that noontide draught!
    Never such healthful cup I'd quaffed;
So CHRIST, whose presence blest its wave,
Health and refreshing coolness gave;
  Then, as well cheered I stood,
    This voice from JORDAN'S wave I heard,—
    The Stream is Holy to our baptized Lord!

Of Jordan's waters, cool and good. The water of this swift-flowing river is much cooler than the atmosphere in the hot valley through which it flows, and being pure and wholesome, it is extremely grateful to man and beast. All the wild beasts and birds of the Jordan Valley throng to these waters as to a banquet God hath prepared for them. *Never such healthful cup I'd quaffed.* The writer had gone down from Jerusalem to the Dead Sea, bathed there, tarried there for some hours, and then traversed the burning plain six miles before he reached the Jordan, and this made his first draught of its cooling waters so delicious and refreshing that "the good cheer of Jordan" will abide in his memory so long as life shall last. *So Christ, whose presence blest its wave.* Then cometh Jesus to Jordan to be baptized.— MATTHEW iii, 13. Jesus was baptized of John in Jordan. — MARK i, 9. *Health and refreshing coolness gave.* All the happiness of the body, as well as the spirit, is primarily due to Jesus, CREATOR of all things. This fact is realized with peculiar force by the traveler following up the traces of the divine feet.

IV. GALILEE: THE CENTER OF HIS LABORS.

I thought of Jesus by the Sea
  Of GALILEE, blue GALILEE:
    His sermon blessed its peaceful shore,—
    He stilled its tempest by His power,—
His mightiest deeds He wrought and drew
From fishermen there His chosen few;
  Then, as I bowed the knee,
    This voice from GALILEE I heard,—
    The Sea is Holy to our laboring Lord!

——— *Blue Galilee.* The purity of the atmosphere in Palestine, giving a deep cerulean hue to every object, is peculiarly observable around the Sea of Galilee, as it lies in the bottom of a deep basin of basaltic mountains. All travelers remark " How blue is this charming lake ! " *His ser-mon blessed its peaceful shore.* The " Sermon on the Mount " was delivered, it is believed, upon the hills that overhang the Sea of Galilee on the west. In that clear atmosphere, the sound of his voice would readily reach the sea shore, and mingle with the singing tones of the waters as they ripple along the sand. *He stilled its tempest by his power.* He rebuked the winds and the sea; and there was a great calm.— MATTHEW viii, 26. The Sea of Galilee is subject to sudden storms like the one described in the Scripture. *His mightiest deeds he wrought.* Some twenty out of the thirty-five of the recorded miracles of Jesus, including the cleansing of the leper, restoring the blind to sight and raising the dead, were performed around or in the vicinity of the Sea of Galilee. ——— *drew from fishermen there, His chosen few.* Jesus walking by the Sea of Galilee saw Peter and Andrew, fishers, and James and John, in a ship mending their nets, and he called them.— MATTHEW iv. 18–21. It is thought that all the Apostles, save, perhaps, Judas Iscariot, were residents of the vicinity of Capernaum.

V. GETHSEMANE: THE GARDEN OF HIS AGONY.

I thought of JESUS, in that Grove
Of agony, GETHSEMANE :
Its hoary leaves around me sighed,
Its dewdrops wept ; my spirit vied
With nature's grief, till I forgot
All time, all space, in that sad spot ;
Then, as my thoughts came free,
This, from GETHSEMANE I heard,—
The Grove is Holy to our sorrowing Lord!

——— *that Grove of agony, Gethsemane.*— The present inclosure of Gethsemane, a scanty half acre, is marked by the presence of eight large olive trees, to which were applied by the writer of this poem the names of eight pious song writers of America. *Its dewdrops wept.*— The writer visited the Garden of Gethsemane at the close of the day, as the cool olive leaves began to con-dense from the superheated atmosphere the refreshing dews of evening. *I forgot all time, all space in that sad spot.*— Cold must be the heart that can meditate under the trees of Gethsemane without tears. The writer reading there " of the agony " and " the sweat," as recorded in Luke xxii, was fain to yield to an uncontrollable gush of emotion.

VI. JERUSALEM: THE CITY OF HIS DEATH.

I thought of JESUS, as I walked
A pilgrim through JERUSALEM.
What memories does its history trace !
His living *love ;* His dying *grace ;*
The bread ; the wine ; the coming doom ;
The Scourge ; the Crown ; the Cross ; the Tomb ;
Then, in the Paschal hymn,
This, from JERUSALEM I heard,—
City most Holy to our dying Lord!

——— *I walked a pilgrim through Jerusalem.*— Jerusalem is, of all the cities upon earth, the nucleus of pilgrimage. The Jews crowd there as to the capital city of their fathers ; the Mohammedans visit Jerusalem in multitudes, as a noted place in the history of their own lawgiver; and Christians "walk about Zion," as to the place of "the death and rising again" of the Son of Man. Mount Moriah, the site of the Jewish temple, is equally holy to both. *His living love.*— Jesus having loved his own which were in the world, He loved them unto the end.— JOHN xiii, 1. —————— *His dying grace.*— Then said Jesus, Father, forgive them, for they know not what they do.— LUKE xxiii, 34. Greater love hath no man than this, that a man lay down his life for his friends. — JOHN xv, 13. *The bread,* ————.— He took bread, and gave thanks and brake it, and gave unto them.— LUKE xxii, 19. ————— *the wine* ————.— He took the cup and gave it to them and they all drank of it.— MARK xiv, 23. ————— *the coming doom.*— Jesus knew that his hour was come that he should depart out of this world.— JOHN xiii, 1. *The Scourge* ————.— He scourged Jesus. — MATTHEW xxvii, 26. Pilate therefore took Jesus and scourged him.— JOHN xix, 1. ————— *the Crown* ————.— The soldiers therefore platted a crown of thorns and put it upon his head.— JOHN xix, 2. ————— *the Cross* ————.— He bearing his Cross went forth.— JOHN xix, 17. ————— *the tomb.*— Joseph laid him in a sepulcher.— MARK xv, 46. A new sepulcher wherein was never man yet laid.— JOHN xix. 41.

VII. OLIVET: THE MOUNT OF HIS ASCENSION.

I thought of JESUS, on the Mount
  Of OLIVET, gray OLIVET ;
    'Twas there He led His weeping band,
    Within their group they saw Him stand,
His parting promises were given,
He blest them, rose and went to Heaven;
    Then, as I turned my feet,
      This VOICE from OLIVET I heard,—
    The Mount is Holy to our ascended Lord !

————— *gray Olivet.*— The character of the stone which composes the country around Jerusalem is calcareous, producing a thick, caustic and grayish dirt. The general impression made upon the traveler's mind is grayishness. *Within their group they saw Him stand.*— No painter has succeeded in embodying this event. The KING about to exchange His earthly for His heavenly throne; the waiting DISCIPLES accompanying Him to the very confines of His promised possession ; the solitary place; the awful expectation standing out upon the countenances of HIS OWN,— the idea is too grand for mortal pencil to delineate. *His parting promises were given.*— Behold I send the promise of my Father upon you.— LUKE xxiv, 49. This Jesus shall so come in like manner as ye have seen him go.— ACTS i, 11. *He blest them* ————.— He lifted up his hands and blessed them.— LUKE xxiv, 50. ————— *rose, and went to Heaven.*— While he blessed them he was parted from them and carried up into Heaven.— LUKE xxiv, 51. He was received up into Heaven and sat on the right hand of God.— MARK xvi, 19. He was taken up and a cloud received him out of their sight. .— ACTS i, 9.

VIII. THE FIRST SUMMARY OF CHRISTIAN TESTIMONIES.

Thus Holy Land, on every side
Tells of the ONE, the CRUCIFIED !
  Its *Hill tops* sacred witness bear,
  That HE, the homeless, slumbered there ;
Its *Plains* HIS footsteps still imprint,
Who o'er their thirsty pathways went ;

Its *Waters* HIS blest image trace
That once reflected JESUS' face;
Its *Stars* on Heaven's broad pages write
That JESUS prayed beneath their light;
Its *Flowers* in grace and perfume tell
That their CREATOR loved them well;
And e'en its *Thorn tree* bears HIS Name
Whose platted Crown was woven of them.

That He, the homeless, slumbered there. — Jesus said, Foxes have holes and the birds of the air have nests, but the Son of Man hath not where to lay his head. — LUKE ix, 58. *Who o'er their thirsty pathways went.* — Jesus, wearied with his journey, sat on the well and said, Give me to drink. — JOHN iv, 6, 7. The Holy Land is emphatically a "thirsty land" to travelers, who require frequent draughts of water at every stage of their journey. *That once reflected Jesus' face.* — In visiting the fount of Ain Kanterah at Sarepta, where Jesus healed the daughter of the Syro-Phœnician woman, the writer was moved by this thought: "Could the unconscious fountain speak, it would describe the lineaments of the Son of Man." And he there wrote this stanza:

"How looked the Saviour? Oh to see
His face divine! was it in grief
At human pain, and misery,
And want, and sin, and unbelief?"

How Jesus prayed beneath their light. — He went up into a mountain to pray. — MATTHEW xiv, 23; MARK vi, 46. He continued all night in prayer to God. — LUKE vi, 12. *That their Creator loved them well.* — Consider the lilies of the field. — MATTHEW vi, 28. *And e'en its Thorn tree bears His Name whose platted Crown was woven of them.* — The Spiny tree, from which the twigs were taken that formed "the platted Crown," were unquestionably those of the Nubk (*Zizyphus spina-christi*), or "Thorn of Christ." It grows in the valleys around Jerusalem, and abundantly in the Jordan Valley, and is a vegetable production of portentous character.

IX. THE FINAL SUMMARY OF TESTIMONIES.

Its *Breezes* sigh; its *Tempests* roar:
Its wild *Waves* break along the shore:
Its *Fruitage* ripens in the Sun:
Its *Song Birds* tell the day begun:
Its *Hills* in snowy grandeur rise:
Its *Storm Clouds* vex the peaceful skies:
In every sight the Christian's eye
Something of JESUS will espy!
In every sound the Christian's ear,
Something of JESUS CHRIST will hear!
One testimony all afford,—
THE LAND IS HOLY UNTO JESUS CHRIST OUR LORD!

Its breezes sigh, ———. — The morning and evening breezes in the hill country are regular, and in the sultry season peculiarly grateful and wholesome. As they come surging up the mountain slopes they seem to sigh of the waves they have just left. ——— *its tempests roar.* — The writer encountering a terrible storm of hail and rain in Lebanon, near the Nahr-el-Kelb near Beyrout, was deeply impressed by the splendid imagery in which the Psalmist describes such an elementary strife. *Its wild waves break along the shore.* — The coast line of Palestine undergoes steady abrasion from the heavy rollers that move in upon it with irresistible power from the broad expanse of the Mediterranean. Many wrecks meet the eye along the beach. *Its fruitage ripens in the sun.* — The immense variety and abundance of Holy Land fruits have been the marvel of all ages. Fruit constitutes much of the living of the natives. *Its song birds tell the day begun.* — A burst of nightingales (*bulbuls*), doves and many other varieties of song birds hails the approach of day, particularly along the water streams. *Its hills in snowy grandeur rise.* — Hermon, 10,000 feet high, and Sunnin, even a little more elevated, exhibit snowy caps all through the season of summer. *Its storm clouds vex the peaceful skies.* — As intimated, the strife of elements at certain seasons is indescribably grand, especially through the mountain region of Lebanon. *In every sight the Christian's eye something of Jesus will espy.* — The traveler who reads "the coming Messiah" through all the narratives and predictions of the Old Testament will discover that every visible object is made use of by the Holy Spirit as an emblem to suggest the character or mission of the COMING ONE. *In every sound the Christian's ear something of Jesus Christ will hear.* — The Messianic imagery embraces as well the sounds of nature as its sights. The very birds give tongue to HIM who framed them and intrusted them with the sweetest notes in the scale of earthly music. *One testimony all afford,* — *The Land is Holy unto Jesus Christ our Lord.* — This is the only conclusion that renders the Land of the Bible a worthy place of pilgrimage. All others degrade it to the class of ordinary resorts. Unmitigated despotism, supplementing the waste and horror of protracted war, leaves nothing else to the country save glorious memories and its power to illustrate "the Word of God and the testimony of Jesus Christ."

EAT AND BE FILLED.

A RECITATION FOR A RED CROSS BANQUET.

Eat and be filled, no scarceness here;
Welcome, brave Knights, to ample cheer!
The hand divine hath blessed our bread,
Freely partake — for you 'tis spread!

Eat and be filled, come thickly now,
"The more the merrier," we vow!
This night to us is blest and bright —
Praise God for such a goodly sight!

Eat and be filled, let merry jest
Betray the joy of every guest;
Let mirth abound, and lightsome song
Our glad festivities prolong.

Eat and be filled, may HE who fed
Ten thousand with His fish and bread
Enlarge our Knightly store to feed
Earth's starving millions in their need.

"And they did all eat and were filled." — MARK vi, 42.

FAITHFUL UNTO DEATH.

Faithful to the trust imposed,
    Holding in an honest heart,
Secrets to the true disclosed,
    Laws from which we ne'er depart—
Be thou faithful unto death,
And thou shalt have a Crown of Life.

Active as the Master was
    In all deeds of charity;
Sowing as the farmer sows,
    Freely o'er the fruitful lea—
Be thou faithful unto death,
And thou shalt have a Crown of Life.

Chaste and pure in virtue's way,
    Spotless as the lambskin worn
By the mystical array,
    Pure as dewdrops of the morn—
Be thou faithful unto death,
And thou shalt have a Crown of Life.

Honest with a neighbor's store;
    Wronging none, o'erreaching none;
Timely warning him before
    Danger falls and hope is gone—
Be thou faithful unto death,
And thou shalt have a Crown of Life.

Bearing up an earthly Cross,
    Patient, humble, meek and true;
Taking cheerfully the loss,
    Gratefully the wages due—
Be thou faithful unto death,
And thou shalt have a Crown of Life.

Soon the Sabbath will appear,
    End of sorrow, pain and wrong;
Only six days' labor here;
    Can ye not endure so long?
Be thou faithful unto death,
And thou shalt have a Crown of Life.

SHAME NOT THE CROSS.

Shame not the Cross, dear Templars! word and deed
  Be holy while you bear the mystic sign!
The Master's wounds, alas! too freshly bleed
  Whene'er His votaries unto sin incline.
The All-seeing Eye is ever bent to catch
  Each deviation from the Templar's vow,—
In constant vigil, therefore, wait and watch,
    Nor shame the Cross which marks the Templar now.
    Shame not the Cross — Shame not the Cross.

Shame not the Cross! a host of witnesses
  Eager to slander, waiting to decry,
Is gathered round, and shall we pleasure these
  To be their byword and a mockery?
Ah, no; be true, brave Templars! By the sword
  Which speaks of Calvary from its very hilt,
Resolve to honor JESUS as the LORD,
  Nor foul His emblem with a stain of guilt.
    Shame not the Cross — Shame not the Cross.

For if we sin willfully after that we have received the knowledge of the truth, there remaineth
no more sacrifice for sins.— HEBREWS x, 26.

THE LAND THAT IS VERY FAR OFF.

To that *far* land, far beyond storm and cloud,—
  To that *bright* land, where sun doth never set,—
To that *life* land which has nor tomb nor shroud,
  And Brothers meet again who oft have met,
    Joyful we go! why should we not be glad?
    Joys that had lost their joy await us there,
  And nobler mansions than our Craft have made,
  And all is permanent, and all is fair.

There we shall see the MASTER; here, indeed,
  Sometimes we see Him, dimly, doubtfully,
But O, His lineaments we scarcely heed,
  So clouded is the soul, so weak the eye!
    But there, in Heaven's Orient displayed,
      His faithful all around Him we shall meet,
  Shall hear, shall see, shall evermore be glad,
    Thronging and singing at the MASTER's feet.

Thine eyes shall see the King in His beauty; they shall behold the land that is very far
off.— ISAIAH xxxiii, 17.

THE TEMPLARS' LINKS OF LOVE.

Flaunting our Banners on the breeze,
  Flashing the mystic steel above,
The Knights of GOLGOTHA are these,
  And linked in holy links of love.

Stained with the dust of many a clime,
  Weary and travel-worn we are,
But see how gleams the Cross sublime !
  In CHRIST we make the Holy War.

Ah, who can speak our warrior bliss,
  Bound in a blood-cemented chain !
Our life has had no scene like this,
  And few will see the like again.

Hands, in a mighty union grasp,—
  Voice, take the courteous Knightly tone,—
Let hearts in love of CHRIST enclasp,
  For soon this happy time is gone !

THOU, who on cruel cross tree died,
  THOU, who from rocky tomb arose,
O be in life the Templar's GUIDE,
  In death his crown and sweet REPOSE !
    The links of love, the links of love,
    The Knights of GOLGOTHA are these,
      Linked in the holy links of love.

The music to this was composed by Brother H. S. Perkins. The song is inscribed to Sir Theodore T. Gurney, of Chicago, Illinois.

THE WORD WE GIVE YOU.

Off gauntlets, Boys ! show naked palms !
  Left foot in front ! come nearer still !
The Order takes you to her arms
  And holds you with a will.
Off gauntlets ! hand in hand combine !
Left foot in front ! you know the sign !
Low breath,—no cowan must divine,
  The word we give you !

MASONIC BALLADS OF THE CIVIL WAR.

The writer begs to include in the *military department* of the volume a few pieces suggested by the awful scenes of the civil war of 1861–5. Among the dead upon every battle field were men whose feet had hastened upon the loving errand, whose knees had knelt in the availing prayer, whose breasts had pressed kindred breasts in the interchange of holy secrets, whose hands had sustained the falling brother, whose instructive tongues had whispered the generous counsel to attentive ears. Out of his own band of Masonic acquaintance the dead were reckoned by hundreds, perhaps thousands, and it is not strange that, without venturing to intrude any political views upon the reader, he should ask to insert a few of the poetic suggestions of that darksome period, when death reigned supreme over the land.

WE SWEAR TO BE TRUE TO A BROTHER.

Dear Friends of the Square, *let us cherish the faith,*
  Though broken and torn every other!
REMEMBER THE VOW;— we swore unto death
  We would cling, *hand and heart,* to a Brother!
Then raise up to God, up to God the left hand!
  With mine join, with mine join the other!
Though war blow the blast, and with death strew the land,
  WE SWEAR TO BE TRUE TO A BROTHER!

The EAST lends its light, though the world is at war;
  The SOUTH shines in glory and beauty;
The WEST gently smiles o'er fields drenched in gore,—
  They teach to the Mason his duty!

The Badge of the Craft is unsullied as yet —
  From war's dust and blood let us fold it!
The Page of our History, brilliant with light;
  Let's swear thus in honor to hold it!

GREAT GOD! from Thy Throne view the nation at strife!
  THY GAVEL must heal this disorder!
Send Peace o'er the land! give Refuge and Life!
  Be THOU, LORD, our Saviour and Warder!

Through all the strife which deluged our land in blood, while other bonds and covenants were nullified, the BOND OF FREEMASONRY remained intact. Composed at the opening of the war and set to the music of Bradbury, this song was scattered by tens of thousands through the knapsacks both of the gray and the blue, and sung in every variety of voice. May we not believe that the animosities of war were in some degree softened by the influence of these sentiments?

WORDS OF PEACE AND LOVE.

Now, while the thunder peal of battle is heard,
Earth with the tramping of legions is stirred,
Turn from the battle, Brothers, take from above,
    WORDS OF PEACE AND LOVE!

Hearts of consolation, bide ye the vow!
Hands, never weary in charity now!
Tongues rich in sympathy, oh, take from above
    WORDS OF PEACE AND LOVE!

Blood like a river flowing, smokes o'er the plain;
Tears, bitter weeping,— oh, who can refrain!
Stay, stay the slaughter, Brothers, stay this distress,
    Speak the WORDS OF PEACE!

Thus speaks the TROWEL, Brothers, thus speaks the LINE,
Thus speaks the COMPASS and the SYMBOL DIVINE;
Each bears its message on the white wings of Peace,
    Bids all warring cease.

Composed at an early period of the war, when hopes (alas, how illusory!) were entertained that compromises might be effected and the strife closed.

NEVER SLIGHT A HAILING BROTHER.

Never slight a hailing brother —
    Be it *Blue* or *Gray* he wear;
Never ask his creed or country,
    So he's *faithful to the Square;*
Only know he's true and faithful
    To the solemn vow he swore,
And then a generous hand extend him
    As in peaceful days of yore.

Sad the strife, and fearful, Brother,
    Almost hopeless seems the end;
Some have felt its utmost horror,
    In the loss of home and friend;
Yet the fire and shot have left us
    Even stronger than we were —
And oh! this day Freemasons conquer,
    Faithful, faithful *to the Square.*

46

When sweet peace shall bless us, Brother,
     And the fire and shot have ceased,
Then we'll strive not to remember
     All the cruel things that passed;
But there's one thing we'll forget not,
     While a memory we bear;
It is the sacred tie so cherished
     By the Brothers of *the Square.*

Composed and sung at an assembly of Masons held at Memphis, Tennessee, in the summer of 1863, in which both Federal and Confederate soldiers were present. The air is Mr. Root's "Just Before the Battle, Mother."

THE WASTINGS OF WAR.

How many a strong right hand that grappled ours
     In truest faith;
How many a generous heart, with mercy filled,
     Lies low in death!
How many a beaming eye, that caught the light
     From the better shore;
How many a tongue that thrilled our inmost chords
     Will speak no more!
How many a seat where sat the good and true
     Is vacant now!
How many a foot in mercy's quest that flew
     No more shall go!
How many a knee that bent with ours in prayer,
     Or prayed alone,
Has vanished from our mystic brotherhood,
     And gone — and gone —
To the Celestial Lodge, the Land of Peace,
     And Light, and Song,
Where war and bloodshed have no entering,
     Nor vice, nor wrong!
Where the Supreme GRAND MASTER wise presides,
     No blight, nor curse,
And keeps, in holy welcome, crowned and blest,
     A place for us!

The will of God is done —
Their mortal race is run —
Beneath the circling sun

47

They're seen no more;
Their bright and genial word
Can never more be heard
    On earthly shore.
Remains there naught of them except the dust
Wherewith is mingled Masons' dearest trust.

Oh, brave and true, farewell!
Though south winds make your knell,
And sprigs of cypress fell
    Upon your grave—
In memory shall abide
The gallant ones who died
    Our land to save;
No better *place* to die beneath the sun,
No better *time* than where our duty's done.

In reply to a copy of this sent to President Lincoln, a most complimentary letter was received.

COMING HOME TO DIE.

The war-worn soldier leaves
The camp where comrades lie;
    Alas, his cheeks, how deathly pale!
    Alas, his limbs, they bend and fail!
    He's coming home to die!
The last tattoo yet lingers on his ear,
The last command the dying brave shall hear.

The heavy, mournful look,—
The melancholy eye;
    He's thinking of his comrades now
    Who went with him a year ago,
    Who went with him to die.
Their joyful shouts yet linger on his ear,
Their songs and revelings he seems to hear.

Meet him with cheering words—
Hands full of sympathy;
    Throw wide your doors in welcoming;
    Let woman's love her graces fling
    Around him ere he die.
He dies for woman's love and woman's faith;
Her honor lives in that brave patriot's death.

48

Now go with trumpets forth,
Let drum and fife reply;
　　Join, oh, ye patriots, round the grave
　　Of him, the generous and the brave,
　　　Who homeward came to die.
The last tattoo has beat upon his ear,
The last command the fallen brave shall hear.

Set to music, and largely used in the funeral services of the heroes whose returned bodies were made occasions of public honors.

HYMN OF THE MASON SOLDIERS.

Brothers, met from many a nation,
　　Far away from home,
Men of every rank and station,
　　Round this altar come.
Bring your hearts, so full of feeling;
　　Join your hands, so true;
Swear, ye sons of truth and honor,
　　Naught shall sever you.

CHORUS.

War's dark cloud will vanish,—
　　Joy to EAST and WEST,
　　　Oh, Brothers!
Though the land is full of weeping,
　　Masons, Masons still are blest.

Come, forgetting every sorrow,
　　LEVEL bring, and SQUARE;
Leave all trouble to to-morrow;
　　Each the COMPASS bear;
Pass a TROWEL o'er the discord;
　　Wear the LAMBSKIN white;
Brothers, one more happy meeting
　　In our Lodge to-night.

In the circle here extended,
　　Shadowy forms appear;
With our loving spirits blended,
　　Dead ones, ah, how dear!

49

Dead on many a field of battle
    Lost to friends and home,
Yet in Mason's love surviving,
    Round this altar come.

When to distant homes returning,
    We shall say farewell,
And shall cease the tender yearning,
    Now our bosoms feel.
Prattling lips and sweet caresses,
    All the joys of home,
Will bring back the loving circle,
    Round this altar come.

In camp, hospital, and on the march, the " Friends of the Square " in both armies, were wont, during their campaigns, to enliven the sad hours by singing this " Hymn of the Mason Soldiers," as arranged to Brother Henry Tucker's melody, " When this Cruel War is Over."

THE SHORTENING CHAIN.

War's hand has sorely tried our Brotherhood;
    They sleep on every hard-fought battle plain,
They who around our Altars loving stood,
    Shall never stand at Mason's side again.
The sinewy grip's relaxed, the tongue is mute,
Death's heavy fetters clog the willing foot.

The Chain is shortening, where they once were found;
    Close in, close up! the Gavel calls in vain;
The song has lost, ah, many a well known sound —
    Brothers, the louder sing the mystic strain!
Though we and all our works shall pass away,
Freemasonry must never know decay!

Thank God, and yet again thank God, a few
    Of the old love-warmed Brotherhood abide!
A few whose charitable hands will do
    Whate'er their hearts may prompt of generous deed.
For such as I have found on life's hard road,
I humbly, and yet gratefully, thank God!

Written in 1863.

THE COLOR GUARD.

Hurrah, the noble color guard,
    How grandly they are led!
Though many fall by steel and ball,
    Right gallantly they tread!
Hurrah, the eagle points the way,
    And never be it said,
That living soldier fought to-day,
    Less bravely than the dead.

Hurrah, through storms of shot and shell
    The colors proudly fly,
The patriot marks their progress well,
    And follows, though he die;
The dead behind, the foe before.
    Above, the pitying sky,
And hark, o'er all the cannon's roar,
    Hurrah,—*'tis victory!*

The colors that so proudly flew
    Are blackened now, and torn;
The color guard, alas, how few
    Of all who hailed the morn!
But yet, hurrah, the foemen fly,
    The bloody day is won,
And other gallant forms supply
    Their place whose deeds are done!

MASONIC REFLECTIONS IN A MILITARY PRISON.

Pining in the prison cell,
Those we cherished long and well;
Brothers of the mystic light
In the dungeon's gloom to-night;
Brothers of the perfect square,
On the damp ground, cold and bare,
Far from home and hope removed,
Brothers fondly, truly loved.

Prisoners, as they sadly muse,
Do they ever think of us?
Do the memories of the tie
Woven strong by Masonry,

Enter in the dungeon's gloom
Bearing thoughts of Masons' *home*,
Masons' song, and Masons' light?
Is it so with them to-night?

We can almost hear the sigh
And the groan of the reply;
Listen to the dungeon's voice:
"Memories of mystic joys,
Sweet illusions of my cell,
Emblems prized and pondered well,
Words of sweetest, sunniest cheer,
Signs expressing truth so dear!"

While we *pray*, then be our prayer
Fervent for the prisoner;
While we *sing*, let every note
Name the absent, not forgot;
While refreshment hours we join,
To their memory drink the wine;
And the toast of all the best
Be, "Our captives, soon released!"

This effusion was a marked favorite of Brother General Stephen A. Hurlburt, of Illinois.

THE UTTERANCES OF THE SWORD.

A DRAMATIC POEM,

EMBODYING, IN NINETEEN DEMONSTRATIONS, THE AUTHORIZED MOVEMENTS OF THE SWORD EXERCISE OF KNIGHTS TEMPLAR.

And the king said, Bring me a sword.— I KINGS iii, 24. Nation shall not lift up sword against nation, neither shall they learn war any more.— ISAIAH ii, 4. Take the sword of the Spirit which is the word of God.— EPHESIANS vi, 17. Galeatum serò duelli pœnitet.— JUVENAL.

☞ The Tactical works authorizing these movements are those most in favor among American Knights Templar, such as the Manuals of Grant, Meyer, Welch, Loder, Ruckels, Garfield, Eddy, Robinson, etc.

GENERAL DIRECTIONS FOR USE.

1. It is well to have some officer (the Eminent Commander, for instance) to give the word of command, but if it is not convenient the Demonstrator himself may do so.

2. The word "Sword" (not "Swords") is used in the words of command.

3. The time necessary for the full recital of the poem is from twelve to fifteen minutes.

4. A slight delay is necessary after the word of command, to give proper effect to the lines.

5. In several instances two or three movements described in the Tactics are embodied here in one motion, that greater effect may be given to the words.

THE UTTERANCES OF THE SWORD.

The favor with which my poem THE MASTER COMETH (1873) was received, awakened in me the ambition to do something better. I longed to produce a work worthier the FELLOWSHIP OF THE SWORD, whose white tents are dotting the Masonic arena in every jurisdiction of our country. I thought to compose something nearer the exalted theory of " The Freemasonry of Christ the Lord,"—a poem, to be elaborately wrought, and demonstrated in nineteen parts by those picturesque movements of the Sword which are the chief attractions of the Templar's Exercise. Leisure was afforded me in the summer of 1882, and here is the result.

My concept will appear upon perusal of the composition. Before me I set an image of a healthy, sober, soldierly figure, standing squarely before an audience of Templar Knights, and so expanding the lessons of the cross-hilt Sword, so intimating, by tone and gesture, the esotery of the Templar rituals, that the initiate will gain *more light* and the uninitiate *more desire for light* in the magnanimous branch of Freemasonry. The test has been applied in the delivery of the piece in Boston, New York, Chicago and elsewhere, also before the Grand Commandery of Kentucky, which courteously accepted the Dedication. I only add that in using the word " Demonstration," at the head of each of the nineteen parts, I refer to the definition of the term, "an expression of feeling by outward signs."

The finest historical figure of a Sword is that of Arthur's EXCALIBUR, and I cannot more worthily close this page than to copy Mr. Tennyson's lines describing it. The passage is from " The Idyls of the King," "The Passing of Arthur," where the dying warrior directs Sir Bedivere to restore the noble weapon to the waters whence it came :

> . . . . " Take my brand Excalibur,
> Which was my pride . . . . take Excalibur
> And fling him far into the middle mere ;
> Watch what thou seest, and lightly bring me word."
> Then quickly rose Sir Bedivere, and ran,
> And leaping down the ridges lightly, plunged
> Among the bulrush beds, and clutched the Sword,
> And strongly wheeled and threw it. The great brand
> Made lightnings in the splendor of the moon,
> And flashing round and round, and whirl'd in an arch,
> Shot like a streamer of the northern morn,
> Seen where the moving isles of winter shock
> By night, with noises of the northern sea ;
> So flashed and fell the brand Excalibur.
> But ere he dipt the surface, rose an arm
> Clothed in white samite, mystic, wonderful,
> And caught him by the hilt and brandished him
> Three times, and drew him under in the mere.

The sword exercise of itself is an elegant and manly accomplishment, developing gracefulness and activity, while it imparts suppleness to the limbs, strength to the muscles and quickness to the eye ; and it is a source of surprise to many, as well to Masons as non-Masons, that while the marches and evolutions of the Templar Commanderies are so thoroughly taught that no further improvement seems possible, *the use of the sword* is comparatively little regarded. In earlier days the manner of a skillful swordsman was grave, graceful and decorous. The most undaunted and energetic courage was marked by the greatest modesty, and never until the moment of trial arrived was the full man made manifest.

THE FIRST DEMONSTRATION (in Eight Motions).

DRAW SWORD.

Come out,[1] come out,[2] thou glittering brand ![3]
Obey a Christian Knight's command ![4]
　　Inspire a Templar's hand !
Celestial signs, thou sword, reveal[5]
In cut[6] and flash[7] of sacred steel,
　　As in the ancient Band![8]
As when, before the SAVIOUR's shrine,
Each Templar breathed his countersign !

FIG. 1.

FIG. 2.

EXPLANATORY NOTES.— 1. With the left hand seize the scabbard near the top, and press it against the thigh; with the right grasp the hilt and bring it a little forward. Draw the sword until the right forearm is horizontal, as in *Figure 1.* (In some Manuals it is directed to begin with the HAND SALUTE, which is made by extending the right hand its full length, palm upward, finger forward, and then grasping the hilt as above; a graceful performance.)

2. Complete the sword drawing with a quick motion, raising the right arm to its full extent, at an angle of forty-five degrees, with the body ever square to the front.

3. Turn the sword and bring it to the PRESENT, as in *Figure 3*, explained in DEMONSTRATION II.

4. Come to the CARRY, as in *Figure 2*, the sword being vertical against the right shoulder, edge in front ; the grip inclosed with thumb and forefinger; the left side of the grip and the thumb against the thigh ; left arm nearly extended ; the other fingers extended and joined in rear of the grip, the elbow near the body. This is the most natural and manly of all military positions. (The English method of *drawing the foil*, which is much like the Templar's Sword, is to advance the right foot slightly to the front, take the scabbard with the left hand, raise the right elbow as high as the shoulder, seize the hilt with right hand, nails turned inward, and having drawn the foil, pass it with vivacity over the head in a semicircle, and bring it down to the guard.)

5. Raise the sword vertically above the head, executing the movement with spirit.

6. Flourish the sword to the left.

7. Flourish the sword to the right.

8. Return to the CARRY as in *Figure 2.*

THE SECOND DEMONSTRATION (in Three Motions).

PRESENT SWORD.

Oh, Prince Emmanuel, Son of God,[1]
From this far-off and humble sod,
Once by thy gentle footsteps trod,
　　Thee, JESUS, we salute![2]
Omniscient KING, behold our Band
As with this emblematic brand,
　　Our work we execute!
Each movement of the Knightly Sword
Shall tell of THEE, thou Templar's LORD![3]

FIG. 3.

FIG. 4.

EXPLANATORY NOTES.— 1. Come from the CARRY to the PRESENT, as in *Figure 3*. This brings the sword to the front, the hand so high that the cross hilt is opposite the chin and six inches in front of it; the back of the hand to front; right forearm resting along the side and breast; elbow against the body; end of hilt nearly against the breast; thumb on the back of the grip to the right; the blade inclined to the front at an angle of twenty-five or thirty degrees from the perpendicular.

2. Make the OFFICER'S SALUTE as *Figure 4*, by dropping the point of the sword near the ground (not touching it), and on a line with the right foot, the arm extended so that the right hand is near the right thigh with the back to the rear; arm extended; flat of the sword to the front; body plumb and square to front.

3. Come to the CARRY. DEMONSTRATION II should be made with a subdued and reverential voice and manner. If any Christian Knight objects, upon Unitarian principles, to the expressions "Son of God" and "Omniscient Christ," he is at liberty to substitute others more in harmony with his views.

THE THIRD DEMONSTRATION (IN THREE MOTIONS).

SUPPORT SWORD.

FIG. 5.

Embattled hosts are pressing
    Along the serried line,
Their venomed darts distressing
    The Guardians of the SHRINE.
Support, brave Knights,[1] with dauntless mind![2]
    What though the foemen's banner flaunt!
Little *we* reck, upon the wind,
    Blasphemous word and taunt![3]

EXPLANATORY NOTES.— 1. First motion from the CARRY: Bring the sword vertically to the front of the center of the body, the cross six inches from the breast.

2. Second motion: Bear the sword to the left side, the cross opposite the hollow of the elbow; with the left hand grasp the right elbow, the thumb over and resting on the forearm of the right; the blade perpendicular (*Figure 5*). (Some Monitors give PORT SWORD, as in *Figure 6*, for the SUPPORT.)

3. Seize the blade without deranging its position, with the thumb and forefinger of the left hand, the left elbow remaining close to the body as a pivot. Carry the sword vertically, with both hands, to its place at a CARRY, fingers extended, pressing the sword gently against the hollow of the shoulder, hand at the height of the shoulder, its back to the front, elbow near the body. Then drop the left hand to the side.

Guardians of the Shrine. The Templars were appropriately styled Guardians of the Shrine, for they sentineled the highways that led to it, they stood as watchmen at every gate opening to it and day and night kept guard upon the Sepulcher of their Lord.

Upon the wind. The word *wind* in the seventh line, is made, by poetic license, to rhyme with *mind*.

As remarked before, the exercise of the sword is an elegant and manly accomplishment, developing gracefulness and activity, while it imparts suppleness to the limbs, strength to the muscles, and quickness to the eye. There are few sights in *Disciplina*, ancient or modern, more attractive than a line of Knights upon the position indicated in *Figure 5*. They seem to be awaiting in the calmness and strength of Christian faith, whatever fate has marked out for them. In the early allusions to the Order of Rhodes and Malta, this figure was often used. Upon this isolated rock at Rhodes, cut off from all the Christian world, a position thrust, as it were, into the very face of their implacable enemy, the Moslem, the little group of "Chevaliers of Jesus" held their lines steadily. All true hearts must honor a lofty and fearless spirit that seeks no selfish end, but braves all opposition from the noblest impulse.

> With force of arms we nothing can;
> Full soon were we downridden;
> But for us fights the proper MAN,
> Whom God Himself hath bidden.
> Ask ye who is this same?
> CHRIST JESUS is His name,—
> The Lord Sabbaoth's Son;
> HE, and no other one,
> Shall conquer in the battle.

THE FOURTH DEMONSTRATION (IN THREE MOTIONS).

PORT SWORD.

FIG. 6.

> To the ardent Pilgrims journeying from afar,[1]
> Warriors enlisted in Jesus' Holy War,
> 'Neath the Cross the sacred WORD,[2]
> Speaks the one effulgent LORD.
> Purged from slavery and sin,
> IN HOC SIGNO, we come in;
> Open, Warder, at the gate,
> Wide to admit this conquering Band!
> Thou, the KING of earthly state,
> Thou, the KING of Heavenly Land![3]

EXPLANATORY NOTES.— 1. Seize the blade by the thumb and forefinger of the left hand, the left elbow remaining as a pivot, close to the body.

2. Bring the sword diagonally across the front of the body, flat of blade to the front and resting in the hand at the height of the breast, thumb extended in rear along the blade toward the point, the right hand grasping the hilt and nearly in front of the right hip, the edge of the sword down (*Figure 6*).

3. Return to CARRY by bringing back the sword with both hands, the left coming as high as the right armpit, and pressing the blade to its place; the fingers extended at the height of the shoulder; the elbow near the body, the back of the hand to the front. Drop the left hand to the side.

Neath the Cross the sacred Word. The *Cross* and *Word* here refer to objects on the Baldric. In declaiming, the speaker should give point to this passage by casting his eye upon the *Cross* and the inscription, *In Hoc Signo Vinces*, below it.

How far we may put faith in the legend of Constantine concerning "the Cross in the sky" will not be argued here. It is certain, however, that this emblem, the *Cross*, was seldom found in use before his time, and whatever motive may have actuated that astute monarch, he placed it in the form of the Greek XP upon the legendary standards in place of the eagle. The motto *In Hoc Signo Vinces*, both in its Latin and Greek forms, is seen upon the coins of the immediate successors of Constantine, as early as A.D. 340. The history of the Cross itself is full of interest to the Templar. Thousands died to rescue it from the infidel. Kings and Knights fought side by side to rescue it, and dying, were buried at its foot.

THE FIFTH DEMONSTRATION (in Four Motions).

ORDER SWORD.

But who is this,[1] in humble weeds, with Cross and Cord and
    Scrip,
This man impetuous, resolved to share our fellowship?
With "pure ablutions" thoroughly washed, with "patience
    sorely tried,"
Waiting to have instructions from the one unerring GUIDE!

Welcome the stranger,—give him bread,—his water cruse
    supply;
Cheer him with comfortable words; his tears of weakness dry;
'Tis written in Heaven's Chancery[2] that they who help the poor
Shall find their deeds remembered when they knock at Heaven's
    door.[3]

FIG. 7.

Then cover ye their nakedness, who, poor and friendless, come!
Fling wide your Asylums, NOBLE KNIGHTS, and give the homeless home!
Strike manfully, BRAVE HEROES, when the defenseless call,
And with your comrades conquering *stand*, or with your comrades *fall*.[4]

EXPLANATORY NOTES.—1. Take position of ORDER SWORD, viz.: bring the sword point to
the ground, one inch from the point of the right toe and on a line with it; the sword vertical, the
right hand resting on the top, back of the hand up, first three fingers in front touching the grip, the
thumb and little finger partially embracing it (*Figure 7*).

2. Raise the sword impressively, and point as if to some object in the sky above, following the
movement with the eye.

3. Return to ORDER SWORD, as in *Figure 7*.

4. CARRY SWORD, as in *Figure 2*.

(In some tactical Manuals the movement called "Order Sword" is omitted.)

'*Tis written in Heaven's Chancery*, etc. The reference is to the sublime description of the Final
JUDGMENT, divulged in Matthew xxv:

"Then shall the King say unto them on his right hand, Come, ye blessed of my Father,
inherit the kingdom prepared for you from the foundation of the world;

" For I was an hungered and ye gave me meat; I was thirsty and ye gave me drink; I was a
stranger and ye took me in;

''Naked and ye clothed me; I was sick and ye visited me; I was in prison and ye came unto
me.

"Then shall the righteous answer him, saying, Lord, *when* saw we thee an hungered and fed
thee? or thirsty and gave thee drink?

"When saw we thee a stranger and took thee in? or naked and clothed thee? . . . And the
King shall answer and say unto them, . . . Inasmuch as ye have done it unto one of the least of
these my brethren ye have done it unto me."

THE SIXTH DEMONSTRATION (IN FOUR MOTIONS).

CHARGE SWORD.

Speed the spoil, the booty hasten,
    Templars *charge*[1] along the lines !
See the opposing forces shaken,
    Victory to us inclines ![2]
Innocent maidens, helpless orphans,
    Widows destitute, forlorn,
Will you leave them all to scorn ?
By the power of Christ's religion,
    Templars charge,[3] nor be forsworn.[4]

FIG. 8.

EXPLANATORY NOTES.— 1. Take position of CHARGE SWORD. This is to bring the right heel in rear of left; bend the left knee slightly; incline the body forward, supported principally by the left foot; at the same time drop the point of the sword forward to the height of the belt, the right hand firmly grasping the handle, the thumb against the hip (*Figure 8*). This DEMONSTRATION, with necessary modifications, can also be taken on the march.

    2. Return to position of CARRY SWORD, as in *Figure 2.*

    3. CHARGE SWORD, as in *Figure 8.*

    4. CARRY SWORD, as in *Figure 2.*

Speed the spoil, the booty hasten. This is a close translation of one of the most suggestive expressions in the Templars' Ritual.

The declarations in the Templars' Monitor concerning the three classes of bereaved ladies named above are among the finest portions of our Service. " To wield the sword in the defense of innocent maidens, destitute widows and helpless orphans " comes near to St. James' definition of " pure religion and undefiled before God and the Father." The reader cannot fail to notice the application, " To visit the fatherless and the widows in their affliction, and keep . . . unspotted from the world." It recalls the nervous injunctions of the Hebrew moralist six centuries earlier: " Learn to do well; seek judgment, relieve the oppressed, judge the fatherless, plead for the widows."

Oh pity, LORD, the widow, hear her cry!
Lonely her household lamp burns through the night;
    He who possessed her heart's young sympathy
No longer lives, her portion and delight.
      She looks from earth, raises her heart on high,—
      Pity, oh Lord, the widow, hear her cry!

Pity, oh Lord, the orphan, hapless child !
Father and mother mourning,— view her tears,—
    Abandoned, lost upon earth's dreary wild;
What can relieve her anguish, what her tears?
      Walking with Thee, the just, the undefiled;
      Pity, oh LORD, the orphan, hapless child !

THE SEVENTH DEMONSTRATION (IN FOUR MOTIONS).

RIGHT-SHOULDER SWORD.

FIG. 9.

Here let us muse awhile on far-off scenes,
Where Templars won their earliest renown;
This very dust of Palestine was once
Bone, sinew, *heart* of Christian chivalry,
That fell to win CHRIST'S HOLY SEPULCHER;
O'erborne by arrogant infidels they fought,[1]
All through that summer day, on Hattin's plain,
But when the night came down they slept in death;
Never GOD'S glittering stars looked on such men !

At Acre's siege[2] how strove their matchless Band !
How flew their BEAUSEANT on the morning breeze,
When wall and tower surmounted, in her streets
They sung their hymn, NON NOBIS DOMINE,
And worshiped GOD, to whom the victory is !

Banished from Palestine,[3] the centuries flew,
And lo, at Rhodes and Malta, in the might
Of the INVINCIBLE they held their lines,
And in their island forts kept back the foe,
While nations at their prowess stood amazed !
Honor, infinite honor, to each Knight,
Upon whose lance head gleamed such grand heroic light ![4]

EXPLANATORY NOTES.— 1. Make the RIGHT-SHOULDER SWORD by bringing the flat of the sword to the right shoulder, the cross as high as the armpit, the thûmb nearly touching the side of the right breast, the point of the sword up to the left and rear, so as to clear the chapeau (*Figure 9*).

2. Change to SUPPORT SWORD, first by returning to the CARRY, as in *Figure 2;* then by two motions to the SUPPORT, as described in DEMONSTRATION III.

3. Return to the CARRY, as described in DEMONSTRATION III; and then to RIGHT SHOULDER, as above.

4. CARRY SWORD, as in *Figure 2.*

All through that summer day. This commemorates that awful scene, the battle of Hattin, July 3, 1187, when Saladin and his Saracens exterminated the Christian forces, making a second Golgotha of the beautiful plain. *At Acre's siege* recalls the capture of that strong city by the Crusaders, July 12, 1191. They held it to May 20, 1291. *At Rhodes and Malta.* The Knights Hospitaller settled Rhodes, A.D. 1309, after their banishment from Holy Land, and held it until 1522. They occupied Malta from A.D. 1530 to 1798, when the Order was finally destroyed. During those 489 years they were indeed a *bulwark* against the Mohammedan powers which otherwise threatened to overthrow the Christian world. The *Templars' Chronology*, on later pages, gives the proper dates.

THE EIGHTH DEMONSTRATION (in Two Motions).

REAR REST SWORD.

Eloi,[1] 'twas said on Cavalry,
Eloi, lama sabachthani,
Why hast thou, Lord, forsaken me?
 Oh, when these Templar Knights shall die,
 Not this their last despairing cry,
 But rather, midst death's thickening gloom,
 Exultant at the very tomb,
 "Hail, CHRIST, EMMANUEL, we come!"[2]

FIG. 10.

EXPLANATORY NOTES.— 1. Make the REAR REST SWORD by taking, first, the position of RIGHT SHOULDER, as in DEMONSTRATION VII; then drop the sword point to the left and rear, letting the flat of the blade rest upon the shoulders, in the rear of the neck, at the same time raising the left hand, palm in front, and grasping the blade near the left shoulder with the fingers and thumb, holding the grip in like manner with the fingers and thumb of the right hand, elbows close to the body. Be cautious to preserve the head and shoulders square to the front (*Figure 10*).

2. Return to the CARRY.

The voice in this DEMONSTRATION should be held slow, deep and impressive. The speaker may bear in mind some image of that awful scene on Calvary, when "there was darkness over all the land unto the ninth hour. And about the ninth hour Jesus cried with a loud voice, saying, *Eli, Eli, lama sabachthani?* that is to say, My God, my God, why hast thou forsaken me? . . . And Jesus cried with a loud voice, and gave up the ghost. . . . And the sun was darkened, and the veil of the temple was rent in the midst."

In contrast with this death, most terrible when viewed in its relations to the illustrious SUFFERER, the declaimer may cast his thoughts upon another scene, which occurred near the same spot, in which the protomartyr was stoned to death, "calling upon God, and saying, Lord Jesus receive my spirit! and he kneeled down and cried with a loud voice, Lord, lay not this sin to their charge. And when he had said this he fell asleep."

THE NINTH DEMONSTRATION (in Three Motions).

REVERSE SWORD.

By the deep booming of the Templar's knell,[1]
By the slow march that endeth with the grave,[2]
By funeral badge, and sign, and sorrowful brow,
We mark *a Templar fallen;* swords reversed,
And trumpets sounding, let the dead go on!
He that hath fallen is *Conqueror,* while we,
The battle heat must challenge, and the strife,
Until the MASTER calls to everlasting life.[3]

FIG. 11.

EXPLANATORY NOTES.— 1. Take position of REVERSE SWORD by two motions. First, raise and carry the sword vertically to the front, the elbow advanced and forming an obtuse angle (*Figure 11*). Then bring the point down to the front and rear, turning the sword by a wrist movement completely round, so that the edge will be down and the blade inclined to the rear at an angle of forty-five degrees; the hilt at the height of the shoulder, and the sword held across at the right side.

2. Take two or three steps forward slowly, as if in deep meditation.

3. CARRY SWORD, as in *Figure 2*, by reversing the motions first described.

The effort of turning the sword gracefully and securely, as in *Note 1*, is the most difficult of those described in these Demonstrations. The hilt must play smoothly between the thumb and two fingers, yet with a grip strong enough to preserve the sword from falling to the ground; a thing mortifying to a sensitive Knight. The second engraving required to complete the study of this movement was not at hand when this page was made up. (In some Manuals, it is required to carry the left forearm horizontally behind the back, the left palm out, clasping the blade.)

> Hush, the *Dead March* wails in the people's ears ;
> The dark crowd moves, and there are sobs and tears ;
> The black earth yawns, the mortal disappears ;
> Ashes to ashes, dust to dust.

THE TENTH DEMONSTRATION (IN FIVE MOTIONS).

SWORD-ARM REST.

> When JESUS doth marshal [1]
> His ranks in accord,
> He blesses each sword
> With *Justice* impartial, [2]
> With *Valor* undaunted, [3]
> With *Mercy* adored ;— [4]
> What Templar can falter
> When CHRIST is his LORD ? [5]

FIG. 12.

EXPLANATORY NOTES.— 1. Take the SWORD-ARM REST by bringing the right hand in front of the body, the arm extended, the blade resting along the right forearm and diagonally across the body, the palm of the left hand embracing the back of the right, as in *Figure 12*. (In some Monitors it is required to leave the left hand at the side.)

2. Glance at the hilt of the Sword.

3. Glance at the blade of the Sword.

4. Glance at the point of the Sword.

5. Return to the CARRY, as in *Figure 2*, by reversing the first motion.

With Justice impartial, etc. These three qualities of the Christian's blade are familiar to all Templars. Not only is the Sword endowed with Faith, Hope and Charity, obvious principles, and suggesting only common thoughts, but in the hand of a valiant and magnanimous Knight it is endowed with three *most excellent* qualities. Its *hilt* is associated in the Templar's respect with JUSTICE impartial ; its *blade* with FORTITUDE undaunted ; its *point* with MERCY unrestrained.

Upon another page reference is made to that most renowned Sword of all history, the blade *Excalibur* of King Arthur. In Tennyson's poem one is saying :

> "There likewise I beheld Excalibur,
> Before him at his crowning borne, the Sword
> That rose from out the bosom of the lake,
> And Arthur rowed across and took it ; rich
> With jewels, elfin Urim, on the hilt,
> Bewildering heart and eye : the blade so bright
> That men are blinded by it ; on one side

Graven in the oldest tongue of all this world
Take me : but turn the blade and ye shall see
And written in the speech ye speak yourself,
Cast me away." . . .

THE ELEVENTH DEMONSTRATION (IN TWO MOTIONS).

CROSS SWORD.

Lift up your golden heads, ye gates,[1]
Lift up, ye everlasting doors,
And let the KING of GLORY pass,—
KING of the upper world and ours !
   How strong and mighty HE in war !
   The victory HE will surely win,—
   Lift up your golden heads, ye gates,
   And let the KING of GLORY in ![2]

FIG. 13.

EXPLANATORY NOTES.— 1. Take position of CROSS SWORD, by first coming to the PRESENT, as in *Figure 3 ;* then plant the right foot sixteen inches straight to the front, the right knee slightly bent, at the same time raising the right hand, the arm extended, the wrist as high as the head, the Sword in prolongation of the arm, the thumb extended along the left of the grip, the back of the Sword up. Cross the Sword, as if with an opponent's, six inches from its point, at the same instant planting the foot with a very light shock (*Figure 13*).

2. Return to the PRESENT, as in *Figure 3*, bringing back the foot to its former place, and then to the CARRY, as in *Figure 2*.

Lift up your heads, etc. This is suggested by these passages in the Twenty-fourth Psalm : " Lift up your heads, O ye gates ; and be ye lift up, ye everlasting doors, and the King of glory shall come in. Who is this King of glory ? The LORD, strong and mighty ; the LORD mighty in battle. Lift up your heads, O ye gates ; even lift them up, ye everlasting doors ; and the King of glory shall come in. Who is this King of glory ? The LORD of hosts, HE is the King of glory."

The style of speech in this DEMONSTRATION should be spirited, cheerful and triumphant. The eyes may be cast above, as with an exultant expression.

THE TWELFTH DEMONSTRATION (IN TWO MOTIONS).

PARADE REST.

Our MASTER, journeying o'er the hill,
   Rested in noonday heat,[1]
So we, the servants of HIS will,
   Rest at our MASTER's feet.
How gracious bends His loving gaze
   Upon the faithful Band,
Whose strength and joy and hopes are His,
   The expectancy of future bliss,
When we exchange the toils of this,
   For rest in heavenly land.[2]

FIG. 14.

EXPLANATORY NOTES.— 1. Carry the right foot three inches to the rear, the left knee slightly bent, resting the weight of the body principally on the right foot. *Second*, drop the sword point to the ground to the right, and on a line with the great toe of the left foot, parallel to the front; the sword vertical in front of the body; the fingers and thumb holding the end of the hilt, which rests in the palm of the right hand, the back of the hand up and covered by the left hand, as in *Figure 14*.

2. Return to the CARRY, as in *Figure 2*, bringing the right foot to its former position. The references in the first line is to John iv, 6: "Jesus, being wearied with his journey, sat." . . . "And it was about the sixth hour."

THE THIRTEENTH DEMONSTRATION (IN ONE MOTION).

SIR KNIGHT, KNEEL.

Knee, in worship at the throne
Where EMMANUEL rules alone;[1]
And the service of the *tongue*,
By celestial chorus sung,—
"Glory in the highest be,
Peace, good will eternally!"

EXPLANATORY NOTES.— 1. Kneeling is done by three motions. *First*, come from the CARRY to the PARADE REST, as in *Figure 14*. *Second*, draw back the right foot about twenty-eight inches to the rear. *Third*, kneel on the right knee so that the front of the knee and the rear of the left heel will be on a line parallel with the front, the head erect *Figure 15* gives this position, save that the head in that engraving is bowed, where in the present DEMONSTRATION it should be erect.

The reference in the lines is to Philippians ii, 10, 11. "At the name of JESUS every knee should bow, of things in Heaven and things in earth, and things under the earth; and that every tongue should confess that JESUS CHRIST is Lord, to the glory of GOD the Father."

THE FOURTEENTH DEMONSTRATION (IN ONE MOTION).

REST ON SWORD.

Rejected,[1]— HE who came to save,
Despised,—the LORD of all,
Embittered in HIS very grave
With wormwood and with gall:
A man of sorrows, and acquaint
With grief's most agonizing plaint.

Fig. 15.

EXPLANATORY NOTES.—.1. Incline the head forward as in *Figure 15*. In place of the lines given above a solo singer may introduce Handel's music from *The Messiah* to the words of Isaiah: "He was despised and rejected of men; a man of sorrows and acquainted with grief." The effect of this is beautiful.

THE FIFTEENTH DEMONSTRATION (IN THREE MOTIONS).

SIR KNIGHT, RISE.

Would we, Sir Knights, be freed from care,—[1]
The storm cloud vanishes in prayer:[2]
One true petition, fervent, deep,
Is, to the soul, refreshing sleep;
Prayer animates the arm and heart;
Prayer points anew the Templar's dart;
And binds his powers in sweet accord
To do the bidding of the Lord.[3]

EXPLANATORY NOTES.— 1. Raise the head and assume the position indicated in DEMONSTRATION XIII.

2. Rise up with a dignified movement, and bring the right foot to the side of the left, as in *Figure 14*.

3. Take the CARRY, as in DEMONSTRATION XII.

THE SIXTEENTH DEMONSTRATION (IN SIX MOTIONS).

RETURN SWORD.

Perish every sword in rust,[1]
Crumble, emblems, into dust,
Be our very flag accursed,
   And our names forgot,
Ere we *draw* in evil strife,—[2]
Ere we *use* in evil life,—
Ere we *flaunt* where sin is rife,[3]
   And the Lord is not!

Templars, thorny was the road
That the MAN OF SORROWS trod,[4]
But, returning back to God,
   Peace HE left, and love:[5]
Follow peace! the way is short,
Cherish love! this life is naught,
And the last great battle fought,
   Find THE LORD above![6]

FIG. 16.

EXPLANATORY NOTES.— 1. Seize the scabbard as in *Figure 16*, near the top with the left hand, inclining it a little forward, as in *Figure 1*. Then bring the sword, with the blade vertical, to a point six inches in front of the left shoulder, the lower part of the hand to the height of the chin. Lower the blade across and along the left arm, the point to the rear. Turn the head slightly to the left, fixing the eyes upon the opening of the scabbard, and insert the blade, assisted by the thumb and forefinger of the left hand, until the right forearm is horizontal (*Figure 16*). Finally, return the blade, turn the head to the front and drop the hands to the sides. (In some Manuals it is ordered that the *eyes be not cast down*.

2. DRAW SWORD, as directed in DEMONSTRATION I, and come to the CARRY.
3. Raise the sword vertically, and wave it right and left as in DEMONSTRATION I.
4. REVERSE SWORD, as instructed in DEMONSTRATION IX.
5. CARRY SWORD, as in *Figure 2.*
5. RETURN SWORD, as above.
The manner of recitation of this part should be bold and forcible as possible.

THE SEVENTEENTH DEMONSTRATION (IN ONE MOTION).

SECURE SWORD.

PRAYER OF THE TEMPLARS.

FIG. 17.

Groaning in Gethsemane,—[1]
Crowned from Jordan's thorny tree,—
Scourged, alas! with Roman lash,
Gory streams from every gash,—
Mocked with purple robe and reed,—
Nailed, and dying,— MASTER, heed,
    And hear the TEMPLARS' PRAYER!

Now on high-exalted throne,
See THY Templars marching on!
May we feel THY presence near,
May we never, never fear!
Though we linger, though we bleed,
Though we falter, MASTER, heed,
    And hear the TEMPLARS' PRAYER.

While THY Templars faithful live,
Shield, and arms, and courage give!
When THY toil-spent Templars die,
Crowned with glorious victory,
In THY presence, by THY side,
Us eternal rest provide!
Then, thou omnipresent LORD,
By the utterances of the sword
    Grant the TEMPLARS' PRAYER!

EXPLANATORY NOTES.— 1. The sword being in the scabbard, as at the close of DEMONSTRA-
TION XVI, seize the scabbard with the left hand, palm in front, thumb to the left, arm extended,
and raise it, bringing the left hand in front, nearly as high as the belt, and a little to the left of the
buckle, as in *Figure 17.* The scabbard rests along the left forearm, the back of the hand down,
the cross at the hollow of the elbow.
The recitation of the Templars' Prayer should be deliberate, reverential, and intoned in the
manner of cathedral service. Solemn music would give effect to this DEMONSTRATION.

THE EIGHTEENTH DEMONSTRATION (IN ONE MOTION).

DROP SWORD.

No more the trenchant blade to wield,[1]
No more the helmet and the shield,
　　The Templar's strife is o'er;
The sepulcher where Christ hath lain,
That holiest place is ours again,
　　To be bereft no more.
In peace we lay our weapons by,
And chant the hymns of victory.

EXPLANATORY NOTES.— 1. Drop the scabbard to the side and place the left hand upon it, as before advised.

The allusion in the fourth line is to the nominal purpose of the Crusades, viz.: to rescue the Holy Sepulcher from the hands of the enemy. This attempt cost the Christian world millions of human lives, and the impoverishment of all the business interests of Europe.

THE NINETEENTH DEMONSTRATION (IN ONE MOTION).

SIR KNIGHT, YOUR VALEDICTORY.

The earth may reel from trembling pole to pole,
The fiery billows in their fury roll,
But, fixed on CHRIST, the Templar Host will stand,
And brave the terrors of the burning land:—
　　　Hail and Salute![1]

Winter may bind the earth in icy chain,
Spring may unloose the laughing streams again;
Summer may heat, and autumn heap the land,
While fixed on CHRIST the Templar Host will stand:—
　　　Hail and Salute![1]

The enemies of law may rouse their ire,
And threaten us again with rack and fire,—
We laugh to scorn the persecuting hand,
And, fixed on CHRIST, the Templar Host will stand·—
　　　Hail and Salute![1]

God speed you, Brothers of Golgotha's Cross!
God keep you from all detriment and loss!
Ever, by gates Celestial be ye fanned,
And, fixed on CHRIST, your Templar Host shall stand:—
　　　Hail and Salute![1]

1. Take the chapeau (or cap) by the front piece with the left hand; raise it from the head and place it on the right shoulder, slightly inclined to the front; then replace it on the head and drop the hand to the side.

This completes the Poem. It is courteously offered the devotees of Masonic chivalry as a combination of declamation and military exercise, uniting the glorious hopes of Christian Knighthood with the graceful, heathful and suggestive movements of the cross-hilt Sword. To render it with due effect demands much practice, considerable suppleness of tongue and limbs, and a knowledge of the ritualistic allusions pervading every line. Its preparation has cost much labor, both at midnight and at noon, but in the conclusion the writer feels a glow of satisfaction in the hope that Templars, after he has left the field, will find in it a reference to the adage:

Placeat homini quidquid Deo placuit.

REMARKS CONCERNING THE TEMPLAR'S SWORD.

(From an Address delivered at Washington, D. C., March 28, 1860, on the reception of the Honorarium of a Templar's Sword from the Grand Encampment of the United States.)

There is a romance, if I may so express it, in all past time attending the SWORD. Scarcely do we enter upon the Mosaic account of the Creation ere we find that " the Lord God placed at the east of the garden of Eden cherubim, and a flaming sword which turned every way to keep the way of the tree of life "; showing that as an implement of war or defense, the SWORD was the earliest weapon known.

Throughout the Old Testament, the SWORD is conspicuous as a weapon. We find mention of that most mythic of all mythical SWORDS, inasmuch as it doth not appear at all, and is only known in the interpretation of a dream as the SWORD of Gideon the son of Joash, and is afterward proclaimed as the SWORD of the Lord and of Gideon.

As an evidence of the careful manner in which that weapon, when the property of any noted individual, was preserved, we see that the SWORD of Goliath was wrapped up in cloth, and kept behind the ephod by the priest of the Most High. In modern times the Swords of Frederick, of Charlemagne, of Napoleon, etc., have been carefully preserved. Even among the disciples of Jesus one was armed with a SWORD which he used most valorously in defense of his Master.

In the history, real and fanciful, of past heroes, the SWORD bears no insignificant part. That chivalrous leader of the olden Knighthood, King Arthur, bore a SWORD, whose miraculous reception is told in many ways, the SWORD EXCALIBUR.

From the days of the patriarchs, through the whole range of history both ancient and profane, we see standing out in bold relief the Hero and his SWORD. We have all seen the SWORD of Washington as preserved in our national archives by the care of his grateful countrymen.

Every true Templar holds his SWORD under certain solemn conditions; no true patriot can receive one without attaching to it duties sacredly to be regarded.

The word SWORD in its original signifies *to lay waste*, and this meaning is forcibly shown in the account of the assassination of Abner, disemboweled by one stroke of the Jewish sword. "To gird on the sword " implies the declaration of war ; "to smite with the edge of the sword " signified a passage of arms *to the hilt.*

68

CHRONOLOGY OF TEMPLAR MATTERS.

These tables have been condensed at great labor by the writer, and are offered as a useful digest of Templar Chronology :

323, July 3, decisive victory of Constantine over Maxentius.
615, Feast of Holy Rood (or Cross) instituted.
1096, December 23, Godfrey's army reached Constantinople.
1097, June 20, Nice captured by Crusaders.
1097, July 4, Crusaders' great victory at Dorylæum.
1098, June 27, Antioch captured by Crusaders.
1099, March, Crusaders left Antioch for Jerusalem.
1099, June 10, Crusaders' first view of Jerusalem.
1099, June 15, Crusaders' first assault on Jerusalem.
1099, July 15, Jerusalem captured by Crusaders.
1099, July 23, Godfrey elected King of Jerusalem.
1101, Baldwin I crowned at Bethlehem.
1107, King Sigurd, of Norway, visited Holy Land.
1118, Hugh de Payens installed Grand Master.
1187, July 3, 4, disastrous battle of Hattin.
1191, July 12, Acre captured by the Crusaders.
1192, January 11, Crusaders captured Ascalon.
1199, April 6, King Richard I (Cœur de Lion) died.
1249, June, battle at Damietta, Egypt.
1291, May 20, Acre finally lost to Christians.
1307, October 13, De Molay arrested in France.
1309, Rhodes captured by Knights of St. John.
1310, May 12, fifty-four Knights Templar burnt at Paris.
1312, April 3, Order of Knights Templar extinguished in France.
1313, March 18, De Molay burnt at the stake.
1314, July 25, battle of Bannockburn.
1376, June 8, Edward the Black Prince died.
1522, December 25, Rhodes captured by the Turks.
1530, May 24, Knights of Rhodes occupied Malta.
1530, September 8, Turks retired, defeated, from Malta.
1769, March 2, De Witt Clinton born.
1771, October 30, Thomas Smith Webb born.
1798, June 12, Malta surrendered to the French.
1798, November 24, Paul, Emperor of Russia, Grand Master Malta.
1800, September 4, Benjamin B. French born.
1804, May 6, Grand Encampment Massachusetts and Rhode Island organized.
1814, June 18, Grand Encampment New York organized.
1816, June 22, General Grand Encampment United States organized.
1817, January 15, Theodore S. Parvin born.
1819, September 16, Second Conclave General Grand Encampment United States, New York.
1819, July 6, Thomas Smith Webb died.
1823, November 27, Grand Encampment Virginia organized.
1826, June 13, Grand Encampment New Hampshire organized.
1826, September 18, Third Conclave General Grand Encampment United States, New York.
1827, September 13, Grand Encampment Connecticut organized.
1828, February 11, De Witt Clinton died.
1829, September 4, Fourth Conclave General Grand Encampment United States, New York.
1832, November 29, Fifth Conclave General Grand Encampment United States, Baltimore, Md.
1835, December 7, Sixth Conclave General Grand Encampment United States, Washington, D.C.
1838, March 4, Theodore S. Parvin initiated.
1838, Sept. 12, Seventh Conclave General Grand Encampment U. S., Boston, Mass.

1841, January 5, reëstablishment Knights Malta by Emperor of Austria.
1841, September 14, Eighth Conclave General Grand Encampment United States, New York.
1843, April 1, Jonathan Nye died.
1843, October 24, Grand Encampment Ohio organized.
1844, Sept. 10, Ninth Conclave General Grand Encampment United States, New Haven, Conn.
1847, Sept. 14, Tenth Conclave General Grand Encampment United States, Columbus, Ohio.
1847, October 5, Grand Encampment Kentucky organized.
1850, Sept. 10, Eleventh Conclave General Grand Encampment United States, Boston, Mass.
1851, May 5, Grand Encampment Maine organized.
1851, August 14, Grand Encampment Vermont organized.
1853, Sept. 13, Twelfth Conclave General Grand Encampment United States, Lexington, Ky.
1854, April 4, Grand Encampment Indiana organized.
1854, April 12, Grand Encampment Pennsylvania organized.
1855, January 19, Grand Encampment Texas organized.
1856, Sept. 9, Thirteenth Conclave General Grand Encampment United States, Hartford, Conn.
1856, October 6, James J. Loring died.
1857, January 21, Grand Commandery Mississippi organized.
1857, October 27, Grand Commandery Illinois organized.
1857, April 7, Grand Commandery Michigan organized.
1858, August 10, Grand Commandery California organized.
1859, September 13, Fourteenth Conclave Grand Encampment United States, Chicago, Ill.
1859, October 12, Grand Commandery Tennessee organized.
1859, October 20, Grand Commandery Wisconsin organized.
1860, February 4, Grand Commandery New Jersey organized.
1860, April 25, Grand Commandery Georgia organized.
1860, May 20, Grand Commandery Missouri organized.
1860, December 1, Grand Commandery Alabama organized.
1861, September 9, Charles Gilman died.
1861, December 24, Samuel G. Risk died.
1862, September 5, Fifteenth Conclave Grand Encampment United States, New York.
1864, February 12, Grand Commandery Louisiana organized.
1864, June 6, Grand Commandery Iowa organized.
1865, September 5, Sixteenth Conclave Grand Encampment United States, Columbus, Ohio.
1865, October 25, Grand Commandery Minnesota organized.
1865, December 22, Archibald Bull died.
1866, January 5, William B. Hubbard died.
1868, September 15, Seventeenth Conclave Grand Encampment United States, St. Louis, Mo.
1868, December 29, Grand Commandery Kansas organized.
1870, August 12, Benjamin B. French died.
1871, January 23, Grand Commandery Maryland organized.
1871, September 19, Eighteenth Conclave Grand Encampment United States, Baltimore, Md.
1871, December 28, Grand Commandery Nebraska organized.
1872, March 25, Grand Commandery Arkansas organized.
1874, February 25, Grand Commandery West Virginia organized.
1874, September, Nineteenth Conclave Grand Encampment United States, New Orleans, La.
1876, March 14, Grand Commandery Colorado organized.
1876, August 10, National Grand Priory Canada organized.
1877, August 28, Twentieth Conclave Grand Encampment United States, Cleveland, Ohio.
1878, March 21, Orrin Welch died.
1880, August 17, Twenty-first Conclave Grand Encampment United States, Chicago, Ill.
1883, August 21, Twenty-second Conclave Grand Encampment U. S., San Francisco, Cal.
1886, September 21, Twenty-third Conclave Grand Encampment U. S., St. Louis, Mo.
1889, October 8, Twenty-fourth Conclave Grand Encampment U. S., Washington, D. C.
1892, August 9, Twenty-fifth Conclave Grand Encampment U. S., Denver, Colo.
1895, August 27, Twenty-sixth Conclave Grand Encampment U. S., Boston, Mass.

Rob. Morris

(At the age of fifty-four)

PART SECOND.

SYMBOLICAL MASONRY.

IN THIS PART IS GIVEN

A SERIES OF ODES AND POEMS,

Embodying emblems and symbols of Masonry, the technical phrases, the myths and traditions, the festival pieces, the references to Lodge nomenclature and numerous offerings concerning death and the dead.

In so great variety of productions will be found appropriate hymns for cornerstone and capstone ceremonials, for the consecration of halls and cemeteries, for the semi-annual feasts of the Order, and for all other incidents that agitate the Lodge.

Many of the shorter pieces in this division of the book have been made subjects of musical compositions by famous song writers, among whom may be named without impropriety, H. R. Palmer, Mus. Doc., of New York, Geo. F. Root, of Illinois, A. C. Gutterson, of Minnesota, Prof. Butterfield of Illinois, Ossian E. Dodge, of Minnesota, M. H. Morgan, of Chicago, Ill., Henry C. Tucker, of New York, J. T. Baker, of Massachusetts, H. S. Perkins, of Chicago, Ill., and others of our own country, with some in England.

A few pieces, such as "Our Vows," etc., written only for recitation in tyled assemblies, are properly omitted here.

And yet the world goes round and round,
    And the genial seasons run,
And ever the truth comes uppermost
    And ever is justice done.
                —*Brother Charles Mackay.*

THE SYMBOLISMS OF THE LODGE.

THE LODGE FOCUS.

Oh, when before the Lodge we stand,
  Its walls hung round with mystic lines,
And for the loving, listening band
  Draw truth and light from those designs; —
See ON THE RIGHT the Open Word,
  Which lendeth grace to every thought!
See ON THE LEFT the Mason's lord,
  'Tis chosen well, the sacred spot.

For there our youthful minds received
  The earliest impress of that light,
Whose perfect radiance, believed,
  Will lead the soul to heavenly height.
Around the spot there clusters much
  Of Masons' lore; and dull were he
Who, standing in the light of such,
  Cannot unveil our Mystery.

If in instruction's voice there come
  A tone of hatred ; if, alas,
The love and music of our home
  Be changed to discord and disgrace, —
'Tis that the speaker has forgot
  The solemn words first uttered there, —
His feet have left the sacred spot,
  His heart and tongue no wisdom bear.

But when the soul is kindled high
  With love, such love as angels know —
And when the tongue trips lightly by
  The truth and love our emblems show; —
When round the Lodge, the eye and cheek
  Prove how congenial is the theme,
No further need the speaker seek —
  Good spirits stand and speak with him!

It is admitted by lecturers that the true acoustical focus of the Lodge is near the northeast corner. This is attributed to the fact that it was there each of us received those first impressions on which to build our future moral and Masonic edifice. Certainly in no other part of the room can the speaker give utterance, so truly and eloquently, to the genuine sentiments of the Order; and the unhappy debates which sometimes disturb the harmony of our meetings would be obviated were the speakers required to take their stand at the focus of the Lodge!

THE SQUARE.

In the Holy Land, Oriental Masons teach that while the SUPREME ARCHITECT used the Gauge, Gavel, Plumb, Level, and other working tools in building the earth, yet when HE built the heavens HE used the SQUARE alone.

'Twas in Damascus on an April day;
In the bazars where pilgrims congregate
I met an aged Mason; on his head
The turban of Mohammed, large and green;
In his right hand the mystic almond rod,
Such as wise Jacob bore, and Moses bore
When the Red Sea was cleft beneath his hand.

Mustapha was his name; tall, gaunt and gray,
Yet his black eye, undimmed, flashed into mine;
And his strong hand exchanged the mystic grip
With sinewy force.

He was my senior by some forty years,
And sixty years a Mason. He had thought
More deeply than the most of the intent
Of Solomon's wise imagery so quaint and old,
And how it makes its impress on the soul.
I asked him which of all these emblems wise
That glorify our Trestle Board, is best?
Which gives divinest light? which points to us
Most surely the Great Master of the Craft?

In quick reply, he laid that sinewy hand
Upon the SQUARE. It is my favorite type,
One that in a thousand Lodges I have loved
To moralize upon the Trying Square.

He took it up, and with great reverence
Raised it toward the Throne. "By this," he said,
"The Heaven of Heavens in perfect order fell,
When God took out the Master's implements
From His own chest, and built the universe!
By THIS the radiant Throne—by THIS the Courts
Of His own glory were constructed sure!

"Earth and the stars were fashioned well by THESE,
The Gavel, Trowel, Level, Line and Rule;
The Lodge Celestial by the SQUARE alone!"

This was the legend that the Arab told.
I partly do believe it, for I see
In this full angle and these perfect lines
What in no other working tool appears.
And noting that you choose this honored type
To give your Lodge a name, I charge you now,
Dear brethren, KEEP WITHIN IT! Do your work,
Your praise, your counsels to the listening Craft,
And oh, your daily walk before the world,
WITHIN THE SQUARE.

PERFECT ASHLARS.

The sunbeams from the eastern sky,
Flash from yon blocks, exalted high,
And on their polished fronts proclaim
The framer and the builder's fame.

Glowing beneath the fervid noon
Yon marble dares the southern sun,
Yet tells that wall of fervid flame,
The framer and the builder's fame.

The chastened sun, adown the west,
Speaks the same voice and sinks to rest,
No sad defect, no flaw to shame
The framer and the builder's fame.

Beneath the dewy night, the sky
Lights up ten thousand lamps on high;
Ten thousand lamps unite to name
The framer and the builder's fame.

Perfect in line, exact in square,
These Ashlars of the Craftsmen are,
They will to coming time proclaim
The framer and the builder's fame.

THE WORKING TOOLS.

Let us be *true*,—each Working Tool
    The Master places in our care
Imparts a stern but wholesome rule
    To all who work and journey here;
The Architect divine has used
    The Plumb, the Level and the Square.

Let us be *wise; the Level* see!
    How certain is the doom of man!
So humble should Freemasons be
    Who work within this narrow span;
No room for pride and vanity—
    Let wisdom rule our every plan.

Let us be *just;* behold *the Square!*
    Its pattern deviates no part
From that which, in the Master's care,
    Tries all the angles of the heart.
O sacred implement divine,—
    Blest emblem of Masonic art!

Let us be *true; the unerring Plumb,*
    Dropped from the unseen Master's hand,
Rich fraught with truthfulness has come,
    To bid us rightly walk and stand;
That the All-seeing Eye of God
    May bless us from the heavenly land.

Dear friend, whose generous heart I know,
    Whose virtues shine so far abroad,—
Long may you linger here below,
    To share what friendship may afford!
Long may the Level, Plumb and Square,
    Speak forth through you the works of God.

THE APRON.

This fair and stainless thing I take
To be my badge for virtue's sake;
Its ample strings that gird me round
My constant cable tow are found;
And as securely they are tied
So may true faith with me abide;

76

And as I face the sunny *South*
I pledge to God my Mason's truth,
That while on earth I do remain
My Apron shall not have a stain.

This fair and stainless thing I raise
In memory of Apprentice days,
When on the checkered pavement wide,
With gauge and gavel well supplied,
I keep my garments free from soil
Though laboring in a menial toil;
And as I face the golden *West*
I call my MAKER to attest
That while on earth I do remain
My Apron shall not have a stain.

This fair and stainless thing I lower,—
Its 'Prentice aid I need no more;
For laws and principles are given
The Fellow Craft direct from Heaven;—
To help the needy,— keep a trust,—
Observe the precepts of the just;
And as I face the darkened *North*
I send this solemn promise forth,
That while on earth I do remain,
My Apron shall not have a stain.

This fair and stainless thing I fold,—
A Master Mason now behold !
A welcome guest in every land
With princes and with kings to stand;
Close tyled within my heart of hearts
I keep all secret arts and parts,
And try to walk the heavenly road
In daily intercourse with God;
And as I face the mystic *East*,
I vow by Him I love the best,
That while on earth I do remain,
My Apron shall not have a stain.

This fair and stainless thing I doff;—
But though I take my Apron off
And lay the stainless badge aside,—
Its teaching ever shall abide;

For God has given Light Divine
That we may walk opposed to sin;—
And sympathy and brotherly love
Are emanations from above;—
And life itself is only given
To square and shape our souls for Heaven,
The glorious temple in the sky,
The grand Celestial Lodge on high.

GAVEL SONG.

Through the murky clouds of night,
Bursts the blaze of Orient light —
In the ruddy East appears the breaking Day.
Oh, ye Masons, up ! the sky
Speaks the time of labor nigh,
And the MASTER calls the quarrymen away.

CHORUS.

One, Two, Three, the Gavel sounding,
One, Two, Three, the Craft obey;
Led by holy Word of Love
And the fear of One above,
In the strength of God begin the Opening Day.

Oh, the memory of the time
When the temple rose sublime,
And JEHOVAH came in fire and cloud to see !
As we bowed in worship there
First we formed the PERFECT SQUARE,
And the MASTER blessed the symbol of the free.

While the Mason craft shall stand,
And they journey o'er the land,
As the golden sun awakes the earth and main,
They will join in mystic ways
To recall the happy days
When on Zion's mount they built JEHOVAH's fane.

Life is fleeting as a shade,—
We must join the quiet dead,
But Freemasonry eternal life shall bear;
And in bright millennial way
They will keep the Opening Day
With the Sign and Step that make the PERFECT SQUARE.

THE LEVEL.

We love to hear the *Gavel*, to see the silver *Square*,
But the moral of *the Level* is best beyond compare,—
Is best beyond compare for it guides us to the West,
Where the shades of evening cover the islands of the blest.

When the weary day has parted and starry lights appear,
We miss the faithful-hearted, the brother-forms so dear,—
The brother-forms so dear, of all the world the best,
But *the Level* points their mansions in the islands of the blest.

And we again shall meet them within the sunset band,
And face to face shall greet them, the Unforgotten Band,—
The Unforgotten Band, whose emblem is the best,
The Level, for it points us to the islands of the blest.

THE TROWEL.

The Perfect Ashlars, duly set
Within the walls, need mortar yet —
A Cement mixed with ancient skill,
And tempered at the Builder's will ;
With this each crevice is concealed —
Each flaw and crack securely sealed,—
And all the blocks within their place
United in one perfect mass !

For this *the Trowel's* use is given,—
It makes the work secure and even ;
Secure, that storms may not displace,
Even, that beauty's lines may grace ;
It is the proof of *Mason's* art
Rightly to do the Trowel's part !
The rest is all reduced to rule,
But this must come from God's own school !

We build the " House not made with hands ";
Our Master, from Celestial lands,
Points out the plan, the blocks, the place,
And bids us build in strength and grace :
From quarries' store we choose the rock,
We shape and smooth the perfect block,
And placing it upon the wall,
Humbly the Master's blessing call.

But there is yet a work undone,—
To fix the true and polished stone!
The Master's blessings will not fall
Upon a loose, disjointed wall;
Exposed to ravages of time,
It cannot have the mark sublime
That age and honor did bestow
Upon the FANE on Sion's brow.

Brothers, true Builders of the soul,
Would you become one perfect whole,
That all the blasts which time can move
Shall only strengthen you in love?
Would you, as Life's swift sands shall run,
Build up the Temple here begun,
That death's worst onset it may brave,
And you eternal wages have?

Then fix in love's cement the heart!
Study and act the Trowel's part!
Strive, in the Compass' span to live,
And mutual concessions give!
Daily your prayers and alms bestow,
As yonder light doth clearly show,
And walking by the Plummet just,
In God your hope, in God your trust!

THE PUBLIC GRAND HONORS.

I.

Bear on your souls, dear friends, the blest departed;
    Engrave on memory his beloved name;
Gone to his wages, gone, the faithful-hearted,
    Write on heart tablets his deservèd fame,
His spotless truth, his boundless charity,
His trust in God, his love for Masonry.

II.

Look to the Lodge floor where he now is walking!
    Angel and spirit, he is clothed in white;
Hark, of what mysteries he now is talking;
    Too bright, too dazzling for our mortal sight!
There his undying nature has its rest,
In the communion of the good and blest.

III.

Honor the grave, honor the open earth,
    Honor the body that we give to clay ;
'Twas an immortal structure from its birth,
    And it shall have its resurrection day ;
Tenderly give to mother earth the prize,
And let her keep it till God bid it rise.

In recitation, these lines are pointed by the three appropriate movements of the Public Grand Honors as practiced in this country.

THE PILLARS OF THE PORCH.

The Old is better : is it not the plan
    By which the WISE, in by-gone days, contrived
To bind in willing fetters man to man,
    And strangers in a sacred nearness lived ?
Is·there in modern wisdom aught like that
    Which, midst the blood and carnage of the plain,
Can calm man's fury, mitigate his hate,
    And join disrupted friends in love again ?

No ! for three thousand years the smiles of Heaven,
    Smiles on whose sunbeams comes unmeasured joy,
To this thrice-honored CEMENT have been given,
    This BOND, this COVENANT, this sacred TIE.
It comes to us full laden ; from the tomb
    A countless host conspire to name its worth,
Who sweetly sleep beneath th' ACACIA's bloom ;
    And there is naught like Masonry on earth.

Then guard the venerable relic well ;
    Protect it, Masters, from th' unholy hand ;
See that its emblems the same lessons tell
    Sublime through every age and every land ;
Be not a line erased ; the pen that drew
    These matchless tracings was the PEN DIVINE · —
Infinite Wisdom best for mortals knew —
    GOD will preserve intact the GRAND DESIGN.

An innovation upon the Masonic landmarks is like removing one of the emblems from the Pillars at the entrance of the Temple.   It is Masonic sacrilege.

THE FIVE POINTS OF FELLOWSHIP.

Joyful task it is, dear Brothers
    Thus to take upon the lip
With full heart, and fitting gesture,
    All our points of fellowship.
Foot and knee, breast, hand and cheek
Each a measured part shall speak :
    Speak of answering mercy's call ;
    Speak of prayer for Masons all ;
    Speak of keeping secrets duly ;
    Speak of stretching strong hand truly ;
    Speak of whispering the unruly.

FOOT TO FOOT : 'tis Mercy's mandate,
    When is heard the plaintive sigh,
Hungry, thirsty, homeless, naked,
    On the wings of aid to fly ;
Hasten, mitigate the grief,—
Hasten, bear him quick relief !
    Quick with bread to feed the hungry ;
    Quick with raiment for the naked ;
    Quick with shelter for the homeless ;
    Quick with heart's deep sympathy.

KNEE TO KNEE . in silence praying,
    LORD, give listening ear that day !
Every earthly stain confessing,
    For all tempted Masons pray !
Perish envy, perish hate,
For all Masons supplicate.
    Bless them, Lord, upon the ocean ;
    Bless them perishing in the desert ;
    Bless them falling 'neath temptation :
    Bless them when about to die !

BREAST TO BREAST : in holy casket
    At life's center strongly hele,
Every sacred thing intrusted,
    Sealed by faith's unbroken seal ;
What you promised GOD to shield
Suffer, die, but never yield.
    Never yield whate'er the trial ;
    Never yield whate'er the number ;
    Never yield though foully threatened,
    Even at the stroke of death.

HAND TO BACK : A Brother falling,—
  His misfortune is too great,
Stretch the generous hand, sustain him,
  Quick, before it is too late.
Like a strong, unfaltering prop,
Hold the faltering Brother up.
    Hold him up ; stand like a column ;
    Hold him up ; there's good stuff in him ;
    Hold him with his head toward Heaven ;
    Hold him with the lion's grip.

CHEEK TO CHEEK : O, when the tempter
  Comes, a Brother's soul to win,
With a timely whisper warn him
  Of the dark and deadly sin.
Extricate him from the snare,
Save him with fraternal care.
    Save him, — heavenly powers invoke you,— .
    Save him,— man is worth the saving,—
    Save him,— breathe your spirit in him
    As you'd have your God save you.

This completes the obligation ;
  Brothers, lest you let it slip,
Fasten on tenacious memory
  All our points of Fellowship ;
Foot and knee, breast, hand and cheek,—
Foot and knee, breast, hand and cheek.

The above was a favorite poem of Brother Andrew Johnson, late President, and is one that has entered largely into popular use, during the twenty years since it was written. The paraphrase embodies the following ancient form of injunction. "*Foot to foot* [teaches] that we will not hesitate to go on foot and out of our way to aid and succor a needy Brother ; *knee to knee*, that we will ever remember a Brother's welfare, in all our applications to Deity ; *breast to breast*, that we will ever keep, in our breast, a Brother's secrets, when communicated to us as such, murder and treason excepted ; *hand to back*, that we will ever be ready to stretch forth our hand to aid and support a falling Brother : *Cheek to cheek, or mouth to ear*, that we will ever whisper good counsel in the ear of a Brother, and in the most tender manner remind him of his faults, and endeavor to aid his reformation ; and will give him due and timely notice that he may ward off all approaching danger." These sentiments seem to express the whole charitable scheme of Freemasonry. In the succeeding poem the same thought is wrought out to correspond with the English form of injunction.

  Men and brethren, hear me tell you
    What we Masons vowed to do,
  When, prepared at mythic altar,
    We assumed the Masons' vow :

Hand and foot, knee, breast and back,
Listen to the charge they make.
Men and brethren, God be with you
While you keep the charge they make !

Hand to hand, in mystic meeting,
   Thrills the Masons' cordial clasp,
Telling of a deathless greeting
   Linked in this fraternal grasp :
While upon God's earth we stand
Truth and love go hand in hand.
Men and brethren, God is with you
While in loving grasp ye stand !

Foot to foot, he stands before you
   Upright in the plummet's line !
Share with him your manly vigor,
   Be to him the power divine.
While he keeps the unerring law,
Never let your foot withdraw.
Men and brethren, God be with you,
While ye keep the unerring law !

Knee to knee, in earnest worship,
   None but God to hear and heed,
All our woes and sins confessing,
   Let us for each other plead.
By the spirit of our call
Let us pray for Brothers all.
Men and brethren, God be with you,
While ye pray for Brothers all !

Breast to breast, in sacred casket,
   At life's center let us seal
Every truth to us intrusted,
   Nor one holy thing reveal.
What a Mason vows to shield
Die he may, but never yield.
Men and Brethren, God be with you,
While your mysteries you shield !

Hand to back, no base-born slander
   Shall assail an absent friend ;
We from every foul aspersion
   Will the honored name defend,

Warding from a Brother's heart
Slander's vile, envenomed dart.
Men and Brethren, God be with you,
Warding slander's venomed dart !

Let us, then, in earnest ponder
What we Masons vowed to do,
When prepared at mythic altar
We assumed the Mason's vow.
Hand and foot, knee, breast and back,
Heed the solemn charge they make.
Men and Brethren, God be with you,
While you heed the charge they make !

The author employs the following expressions as a preface to the recitation of this piece : "If there is real antiquity in Freemasonry, as I sincerely believe ; if this Order has come to us from the remote period of David and Solomon, as I am convinced it has, then this 'Five points of Fellowship' is the nucleus around which the whole structure was formed. Nothing in Masonry exhibits the master mind of Solomon like this symbol. How practical thus to teach the principles to Masons by these selected portions of the human body, the foot, knee, breast, hand, cheek ; as no one can lawfully be initiated who is deficient in these parts, they become the most undeniable object-lessons, always in sight, always in front !"

THE SACRED CORD, THRICE WOUND.

Bind it once, that in his heart,
He may surely hold
All the mysteries of the Art,
As did the Craft of old ;
Bind it once, and make the noose
Strong, that sin shall not unloose.

Bind it twice, that Masons' law,
Faith and Charity,
Ever may his spirit draw
In one resistless tie;
Bind it twice, and make the noose
Stronger,— death alone shall loose.

Bind it thrice, that every deed,
Virtuous and chaste,
On the heavenly page be spread,
Worthy of the best ;
Bind it thrice, and make the noose
Strongest,— death shall *not* unloose.

These lines were highly complimented by Brother George D. Prentice.

THE HOLY SCRIPTURES.—A RECITATION IN FIVE PARTS.

I. EXORDIUM.

(Bible closed.   Position west of the altar, facing the east.)

The Landmarks of Freemasonry are graven on God's Word;
It tells the WISDOM and the STRENGTH and BEAUTY of the Lord;
These tapers three, in mystic form, reveal to willing eyes
The freest, purest, grandest light of Masons' mysteries.
  O Wise and Good GRAND MASTER,
    Reveal this Law to us!

(Position north of the altar, facing the south.)

As lies the mightiest oak within the acorn's fragile shell,
So, with the secrets of the Craft, they in this VOLUME dwell;
King Solomon, directed here by the Omniscient JUDGE,
Drew forth the ashlars from their place, and built the Mason's Lodge.

(Position east of the altar, and facing the west.)

The golden Law unfolds itself, mysterious, by degrees;
At first comes *sunrise*, then *high twelve*, then *sunset* gilds the trees;
So, by three grades, we see our Ladder up to Heaven ascend,
And rising stronger, clearer, holier to the very end.

II.   THE ENTERED APPRENTICE.

(Bible open at the 133d Psalm.   Through the rest of the recitation, the speaker stands west of the altar, facing the east.)

"Behold how good and pleasant 'tis,—read it on yonder page,—
For brethren in true harmony of labor to engage!
'Tis like the dew of Hermon, yea, 'tis like the holy oil.
It sweetens all life's bitterness and mitigates the toil."
  O Wise and Good GRAND MASTER,
    We bless Thee for this light!

We must work in FIDELITY; no mystic thing, reposed
Under the sacred seal of faith, should ever be disclosed;
This, *this* is the foundation stone King Solomon did lay,
And curses on the traitor's heart that would the trust betray.

We must not take the HOLY NAME, the awful NAME *in vain;*
God will not hold us guiltless, if we dare that WORD profane;
But all our trust must be in HIM, sole source of living faith,
From our first entrance to the Lodge till we lie down in death.

86

III. THE FELLOW CRAFT.

(Bible open at the 7th Chapter of Amos.)

The Master stood upon the wall, a plumb line in his hand,
And thus in solemn warning to the working, listening Band:—
"By this unerring guide," he said, "build up your edifice,
For I will blast your labors as ye deviate from this!"
O Wise and Good GRAND MASTER,
We bless Thee for this light!

We must preserve the Landmarks olden, that our fathers set;
Approved of God, hoary with age, they are most precious yet;
Our brothers over the river worked within their mystic bound,
And for a six days' faithfulness, a full fruition found.

We must relieve the destitute, disconsolate and poor;
For 'tis our Master sends them to our hospitable door;
And HE who giveth all things richly, to His children's cry,
Will mark, well pleased, our readiness His bounty to supply.

IV. THE MASTER MASON.

(Bible open at the 12th Chapter of Ecclesiastes.)

Remember our Creator now, before the days shall come
When all our senses failing point to nature's common doom;
While love and strength and hope conspire life's pilgrimage to cheer,
We'll give our Master grateful praise whose goodness is so dear.
O Wise and Good GRAND MASTER,
We bless Thee for this light!

We must in honor shield the pure, the chaste ones of the Craft;
Ward off the shaft of calumny, the envenomed, horrid shaft;
Abhor deceit and subterfuge, cling closely to a friend;
And for ourselves and others at the shrine of mercy bend.

We must inter in everlasting hope the faithful dead;
Above their precious forms the green and fragrant 'cacia spread;
'Tis but a little while they sleep, in nature's kindly trust,
And then the Master's Gavel will arouse them from the dust,

V. PERORATION.

(Bible closed.)

And thus exhaustless mine of truth this holy Volume lies,
As open to the faithful *heart* as to the inquiring *eyes;*

Here are no dark recesses, but Freemasons all may see
The Landmarks of the ancient Craft, beneath the tapers three.
    O Wise and Good GRAND MASTER,
      This Law shall be our guide!

In every place, at every hour, this constant friend we have,
In quarry and in forest, on the mount and on the wave;
At toil and at refreshment, in youth, manhood, and old age,
Let's draw our inspiration from its bright and holy page.
    O Wise and Good GRAND MASTER,
      This Law shall be our guide.

Thus *laboring*, all our six days' burdens cheerfully we'll bear,
In hopes of wages ample, golden, held in promise there;
Then *resting* with the faithful, wait the MASTER's gracious will,
The summons to the Lodge above that crowns the heavenly hill.
    O Wise and Good GRAND MASTER,
      Desert us not in death!

STRONG FOUNDATION.

Craftsmen, this lesson heed and keep,
Lay your foundations wide and deep!
When the appointed time had come,
And Israel from allotted home,
    Came up, by Solomon's command,
To lay in state the corner stone,
    And build the Temple high and grand,
Such as the Lord would crown and own,
    The Monarch by a just decree
    Thus set the law eternally:

" Lay your *foundation* deep, the fane
  Will not eternally remain;
  For tooth of time will gnaw its side
  And foe deface its golden pride;
  Pillar, pilaster, height, and base,
  May mingle in the foul disgrace;
  But with *foundation* deep and wise,
  Other and nobler works may rise.
  And till the earth in ruin fall
  Some structure crown Moriah's wall."

The people bowed obedient head;
　Hiram, the Architect, began,
By long and wise experience led
　(How sadly to our spirits come
　The memories of the good man's doom!)
　To justify the Monarch's plan.
From mighty quarries raised, the rock
　In ashlars huge and weighty, drew;
　See yet they rise upon the view
In spite of time and earthquake's shock!
　Until there stood, as yet there stands,
　The grandest pile of human hands;
A *sure foundation*, deep and wise,
On which the noblest works may rise.

The underpinning of Solomon's Temple, intact to the present day, is the heaviest piece of stone masonry ever constructed.

THE TESSERA.

Parting on the sounding shore
　Brothers twain were sighing;
Mingle with the ocean's roar,
　Words of love undying;
A ring of gold was severed then
　And each to each the giver,
His faith renewed in mystic sign
　Which bound the heart forever.

"Broken thus THE TOKEN be,
　While o'er the earth we wander;
One to thee and one to me —
　Rudely torn asunder;
But though divided, we are one —
　This scar the bond expresses,
When all our painful wandering's done,
　Will close and leave no traces!

"Warmly in thy bosom hide,
　The golden voice, *I love thee!*
Keep it there whate'er betide,
　To guard thee and to prove thee!
And should THE TOKEN e'er be lost,
　The ring that now is riven,
I'll know that death hath sent the frost,
　And look for thee in Heaven!"

89

Parted on the sounding shore,
　　Each THE TOKEN keeping,
Met these Brothers nevermore —
　　In death they're widely sleeping.
But yet love's victory was won,—
　　The scar that bond expresses,
Their long and painful wanderings done —
　　Has closed and left no traces!

The ancient practice of sealing devoted friendship between parting friends, by separating some metallic substances, as a ring, a coin, and the like, and dividing the fragments between the parties, is not altogether disused. In the rural districts of England and Scotland it is a custom of lovers, and many a poor laborer, whose body lies buried in the soil of the western continent, bore upon his person at his dying hour this token of betrothal with one who shall never again meet him on earth.

THE DOOR OF THE HEART.

Tyle the door carefully, Brothers of skill,
Vigilant workers in valley and hill!
Cowans and eavesdroppers ever alert,
Tyle the door carefully, door of the heart.
　　Carefully, carefully, tyle the door carefully,
　　Tyle the Door carefully, door of the heart.

Guard it from envyings, let them not in;
Malice and whisperings, creatures of sin;
Bid all unrighteousness sternly depart,
Brothers in holiness, tyling the heart.
　　Holily, holily, tyle the door holily,
　　Tyle the Door holily, door of the heart.

But should the Angels of Mercy draw nigh,
Messengers sent from the Master on high —
Should they come knocking with mystical art,
Joyfully open the door of the heart!
　　Joyfully, joyfully, ope the door joyfully,
　　Ope the door joyfully, door of the heart.

Are they not present, those angels, to-night,
Laden with riches and sparkling with light?
Oh, to enjoy all the bliss they impart,
Let us in gratitude, open the heart!
　　Gratefully, thankfully, ope the door thankfully,
　　Ope the Door thankfully, door of the heart.

THE BEAUTIFUL STONE OF THE MASONIC ARCH.

If I were the Master Grand,
   If I were the King of Judah now,
And of that sage Tyrian band
   Who wore the cockle shell on the brow,
   I'll tell you what I'd do :
I'd choose my brightest Parian rock,
No flaw or crevice in the block,
     And right above the ivory throne,
     I'd set the beautiful stone,—
     The beautiful, beautiful stone.

I'd take from Lebanon the trees,
   The cedars fragrant, tall and fair,
And hardened by the centuries.
   And them to the Mount I'd bear ;
   Hiram should them prepare.
From Ophir's golden sands I'd drain
The yellow, choice and glitt'ring grain,
     And these in mystic form should crown
     The white and beautiful stone,—
     The beautiful, beautiful stone.

Then unto every shrine I'd go,
   To every lorn and humble grave,
And all the prayers and tears that flow
   From women meek, and manhood brave,
   And orphan lone, I'd have ;
Prayers for sweet incense should arise,
And holy tears for sacrifice ;
     I'm sure that God Himself would own
     And bless the beautiful stone,—
     The beautiful, beautiful stone.

This beautiful stone, its name should be —
   Each loving Mason loves it well,
'Tis writ in glory,— CHARITY,—
   Best word the earth can tell,
   Best word the heavens can tell ;
Above the ivory throne so bright,—
Were I the MASTER GRAND to-night,—
     Where God and man alike would own
     I'd set the beautiful stone,—
     The beautiful, beautiful stone.

THE CHECKERED PAVEMENT.

I on the WHITE SQUARE, *you* on the BLACK ;
I at fortune's *face, you* at her *back;*
Friends to *me many,* friends to *you few;*
What, then, dear Brother, binds me to you ?
    This, the GREAT COVENANT in which we abide —
      HEARTS charged with sympathy —
        HANDS opened wide —
      LIPS filled with comfort,
        And GOD to provide.

I in life's *valley, you* on its *crest;*
I at its *lowest, you* at its *best;*
I sick and sorrowing, you hale and free;
What, then, dear Brother, binds you to me?
    This, the GREAT COVENANT in which we abide —
      HEARTS charged with sympathy —
        HANDS opened wide —
      LIPS filled with comfort,
        And GOD to provide.

They in death's slumber, *we* yet alive ;
They freed from labor, *we* yet to strive ;
They paid and joyful, *we* tired and sad —
What, then, to us, Brother, bindeth the *dead?*
    This, the GREAT COVENANT in which we abide —
      HEARTS charged with sympathy —
        HANDS opened wide —
      LIPS filled with comfort,
        And GOD to provide.

Let none be comfortless, let none despair ;
Lo, round the *Black* grouped the *White Ashlars* are !
Stand by each other, black fortune defy,
All these vicissitudes end, by and by.
    Keep the GREAT COVENANT wherein we abide —
      HEARTS charged with sympathy —
        HANDS opened wide —
      LIPS filled with comfort,
        And GOD *will* provide !

There is no emblem that teaches a more practical every-day lesson to a Freemason than the Mosaic pavement, denoting human life checkered with good and evil.

THE CORNER STONE.

The thought embodied in these lines is one of the most charming fancies in Masonic symbolism; for the use of *the trowel* is admittedly the best work of the best Masons, and the Lodge that exists in peace and harmony is the model Lodge. To disturb this harmony by substituting clamor, calumny, and harsh judgment for the mild voices of peace is what is implied in the following lines under the idea of *robbing* the corner stone !

Here is a legend that our fathers told
When Mason toils were done, and round the board
The Craftsmen sat harmonious, in the glow
Of Brotherly Love ! I heard it long ago
From lips now silent; and by this corner stone
I fain would tell it as 'twas told to me.

'Tis said that SOLOMON, in the vast array
Of nine score thousand workmen who came up
From Lebanon's foot, to build the temple, found
Discord and strife, contentions harsh and sharp,
Even to murder; hands that wielded best
The peaceful Trowel, black with human gore;
Aprons, worn to protect them from the soil,
Bloody with horrid stain; and in their speech,
Instead of gentle memories of home,
And children's prattle and sweet mother love,
Dire curses, threats, the very speech of Hell,—
Such base *materials* came up from Tyre.

KING SOLOMON all humbly took the case to GOD,
And in deep visions of the night the VOICE
DIVINE came to his soul in sweet response.
From the great PEACE LODGE, where the patriarchs sit,
Wisdom descended, and his soul was glad.
The WISEST gave *our* wisest such a warmth
Of LIGHT celestial that the fire has burned,
Steady, undimmed, lo, these three thousand years.

'Twas this. I was but young in Masonry
When first I heard it; and 'twas told to me
By one of four score, long since gone to Heaven;
And he did testify unto his truth;
And now, I add the experience of my life
To its strict verity, and it was this:—

The MONARCH bade prepare a corner stone,
Vastly more large than this, than ten of this;

I saw it in my visit to the place —
A monstrous ASHLAR, beveled on the edge,
Phœnician emblem, standing plumb and firm
Within the mountain, standing, as we say,
Respected friends, "trusty, deep-laid and true!"
And on the under side of this large stone,
KING SOLOMON gave orders to scoop out
A *Cavity*, as you have done with this;
And when with mighty enginery, the Block
Was raised, as yours, dear Craft, just now was done,
He placed, with his own hands, within the Crypt,
What think you? newspapers? and current coins?
And names of honored men? No, no, he placed
All those damned vices, that discolored so
The spirits of his workmen, *hatreds*, all
That stained their Aprons, fouled their Trowels, cursed
The air of Palestine with notes of Hell!
These things by his great power, KING SOLCMON took
From out the hearts of that Freemason band,
Placed them within the Crypt and ordered *quick*,
The mighty stone let down, and closed them there,
And stamped his Mystic Seal upon the stone!
And there they lie intact, unto this hour!

Henceforth *the Work* all peacefully went on;
The giant stones were laid within the walls
Without the sound of ax or iron tool.
Pure Brotherly Love sublimely reigned, and so
The Temple of KING SOLOMON was built!

Honored and well beloved Grand Master! see
This mighty Order you so justly rule,
For thirty centuries has given respect
To SOLOMON'S SEAL! his corner stone abides
Right where he planted it, the strange contents
Festering dishonored in their dark repose.
Oh, may they *never* rise to plague the Craft!
No blood is on our Aprons, on our Tools
No trace of human gore; upon our tongues
No unfraternal epithets; thank God!
Thank God! And to the latest day of earth,
When the last trump shall call the blest above,
May PEACE, sweet PEACE, celestial PEACE, abide
In Masons' lodges and in Masons' souls.

94

THE GRAND HAILING SIGN.

Shipwrecked, nigh drowned, alone upon the sands,
    Chilled with the flood and with the frosty air
Hungry and wounded, lo, a Mason stands,
    And looks despairingly on nature there.

Her coldest frown the face of nature wears;
    She offers to the shipwrecked but a grave!
No fruits, sustaining life, the forest bears,
    No cheering flowers nor yet a sheltering cave.

The brake impenetrable closes round;
    Thence the dense clouds of stinging insects come,
Maddening with venom every cruel wound,
    Vexing the spirit with their ceaseless hum.

No hope, no hope! the soul within him dies;
    He seeks a sepulture within the sands,
Once more unto his mother's breast he flies,
    And scoops a self-made grave with bleeding hands.

The river moans in solemn strains his dirge;
    The unfeeling birds upon the tree tops sing,
Or in the distant skies their pinions urge,
    Southward to regions of perpetual spring.

He bids farewell to life; its joys so sweet;
    Children and mother,—happy, happy home,—
But yesterday, ran out his steps to greet,
    And bless his coming who no more shall come.

He bids farewell, and seals it with a prayer;
    That lonely beach resounded with the word:
"Keep them, All Gracious, in thy tender care,
    Thou art the widow's, Thou the orphans' God."

Then downward lying on earth's kindly lap,
    He draws the sand as a thick blanket o'er,
And strives in dreamless quietude to sleep,
    Vexed by life's fears and hungerings no more.

But hark, O joy! the voice, the voice of man!
    Springing with heart elastic from his bed,
Life's strong desires in him revive again,
    And hopes that seemed but now forever fled.

A gallant boat doth down the river come,
  A hundred men upon its margin crowd;
Surely among the many there are some
  Who know the Mystic Sign, the Holy Word!

He makes the Signal and the Signal Cry;
  The pitying crowds his frantic gestures see;
The echoing shores his solemn words swept by,
  "O, God, is there no help, no help for me?"

Alas, no help! 'tis thus that traitors work;
  Ay, even so full many a gallant boat,
Decoyed by pirates, as they grimly lurk,
  Has met the brand, or the destructive shot.

Yearning to stop and save him, how they gaze!
  Some answering who know not what they do,
Some weep, some turn away in sheer amaze,
  And so the vessel vanishes from view.

All then is death and solitude again;
  Months pass; a wary hunter hurrying by,
Sees on the beach the sad decay of man,
  And gives a grave for kind humanity.

And in the silence of the winter night,
  A voice from that poor skeleton is heard:
"The heart of man is smitten with a blight,
  There is no help but in the pitying God!"

This incident occurred in 1862, on the lower Mississippi.

LETTER G.

Referred to the emblem of Deity that marks the Lodge-East. *Deo optimo, maximo* [To God, all good, all great].

THAT NAME! I learned it at a mother's knee,
  When, looking up, the fond and tearful face
Beaming upon my eyes so tenderly,
  She prayed that GOD her little son would bless!

THAT NAME! I spoke it when I entered here,
  And bowed the knee, as each Freemason must;
From my heart's center with sincerity,
  I said, "In GOD, in GOD is all my trust!"

THAT NAME! I saw it o'er the Master's chair,
"The Hieroglyphic bright," and, bending low,
Paid solemn homage at the emblem there,
That speaks of GOD, before whom *all* must bow!

THAT NAME! In silence I invoked its power
When dangers thickened and when death was nigh!
In solemn awe I felt the death clouds lower,
And whispered, "GOD be with me if I die!"

THAT NAME! the last upon my faltering tongue,
Ere death shall still it, it shall surely be;
The PASSWORD to the high celestial throng,
Whose Lord is GOD in truth and majesty!

THAT NAME then, Brothers, always gently speak,
Before your father's, mother's name revered!
Such blessings from His gracious hand we take,
O be His honor to our souls endeared!

QUARRY.

Darkly hid beneath the quarry,
Masons, many a true block lies;
Hands must shape and hands must carry
Ere the stone the Master prize.
Seek for it,— measure it,—
Fashion it,— polish it!—
Then the OVERSEER will prize.

What though shapeless, rough, and heavy,
Think ye God His work will lose?
Raise the block with strength He gave ye;
Fit it for the Master's use.
Seek for it,— measure it,—
Fashion it,— polish it!
Then the OVERSEER will use.

'Twas for this our Fathers banded,—
Through life's quarries they did roam,
Faithful-hearted, skillful-handed,
Bearing many a true block home.
Noticing,— measuring,—
Fashioning,— polishing!
For their glorious Temple home.

THE PERFECT BRICK.

Come, ye that strongly build,
    And deftly wield
The Level, Plumb and Square!
Ye whose hard, girding toil,
God's Corn and Wine and Oil
    Were made to cheer!
Ye clothed in aprons white,
Whose uttermost delight,
    All through life's toilsome week,
Is, from the quarry, to perfect a stone,
That the CHIEF O'ERSEER will own,
And bless from His exalted Throne,—
    Come, and I'll tell you of a PERFECT BRICK!

Fit for the inclosing Wall
Of Hiram's royal Hall;—
    Fit for the Pavement that Queen Sheba trod;—
Fit for the Capstone high,
Or in the Depths to lie,
Hid from each prying eye,
    In the Mount of God,—
This PERFECT BRICK, whose *shape* delights the view,
Whose *polish* charms us, too,
Whose *angles* all are true,
By examination due,—
    This MASON fair and meek,
This son of Light and eke the son of Love,
Whose pattern is *the Sun and Dove,*—
    Rare are the virtues of our PERFECT BRICK!

See, on its six-fold face
    This PERFECT BRICK displays the things of light !
Turn it about, about, and trace
    The ancient symbols as they catch the sight !
The Trowel,—ah, it speaks of spreading peace,
Causing all wars and bickerings to cease !
The Compass,—ah, it serves to warm the soul,
To circumscribe the passions and control
The appetites within the due and honest bound !
The G,—can any view that mystic round,
    Nor feel like bending reverent knee,
    As if in presence of the Deity ?

It is the Signet of a King,
    Greater than Babylonian bard did sing!
The Square,—its trumpet tongue proclaims
    Great virtue's power to Square the heart,
    Upon the perfect angles of our Art!
The Broken Column, whose white marble gleams
    Above the grave of Hiram; and *the Spray*
Of everlasting Green that bade them seek
"Where he lay buried"; and through countless years
    Of sin and strife, and mortal agony,
Hath taught the sorrowing spirit to *look up,*
Amidst its tears, and fondly hope,
In Immortality to lose its cares,—
    These are the Emblems of our PERFECT BRICK!

At last life's powers fail;
The Silver Cord is loosed, the Wheel
    Of Life, and Golden Bowl are broken;
The sunny days return no more;
    There comes through every avenue, the Token,
That Death is knocking at the Door!
    The Grinders cease; the Eyes grow dim;
Gray Hairs are blossoming above;
    The Ear no more receives the happy hymn,
The Heart no more is kindled up with love;
The ruffian Death his work completes,—
The Mourners go about the streets,
Our souls with Sympathy to move!
Beneath the green Sprigs we entomb
Him the delight of the Mason's Home!
What, then, is there for all his toil
    Through life's long, weary week,
No Corn and Wine and Oil?
    Ye unseen, hovering Spirits, speak!
Hath the Grand Master a reward
For him who sleeps beneath the sod?
    I tell you yes! and when the wick
Of life's poor taper all is spent,
And the *body* goes to banishment,
The Soul, the Soul, the white-robed Soul,
All earthly dross off throwing, finds its goal;
The Column finds its place in Temple high,
To *stand* in honor to Eternity,—
    Then God Himself will claim our PERFECT BRICK!

The expression " Perfect Brick," is but another form for that of " Perfect Ashlar."

QUARRY, HILL AND TEMPLE.

Thine in the Quarry, whence the stone
For mystic workmanship is drawn ;
    On Jordan's shore,
    By Zarthan's plain,
Though faint and weary, *thine alone.*
The gloomy mine knows not a ray,—
The heavy toil exhausts the day,—
    But love keeps bright
    The weary heart,
And sings, *I'm thine without decay.*

Thine on the Hill, whose cedars rear
Their perfect forms and foliage fair ·
    Each graceful shaft
    And deathless leaf
Of Masons' love the emblems are ;
Thine when a smile pervades the heaven,—
Thine when the sky's with thunder riven.—
    Each echo swells
    Through answering hills,
My Mason prayer, *for thee 'tis given.*

Thine in the Temple, holy place,—
Where silence reigns, the type of peace ;
    With grip and sign,
    And mystic line,
My Mason's friendship I confess.
Each block we raise, that friendship grows,
Cemented firmly ne'er to loose ;
    And when complete,
    The work we greet,
Thine in the joy my bosom knows.

Thine at the midnight in the cave ;—
Thine in the floats upon the wave,—
    By Joppa's hill,
    By Kedron's rill,
And *thine* when Sabbath rest we have.
Yes, yes, dear friend, my spirit saith :
I'm thine until and after death !
    No bounds control
    The Mason's soul
Cemented with the Mason's faith.

TRUE CORNERSTONE.

What is the Mason's cornerstone?
  Does the mysterious temple rest
  On earthly ground — from east to west —
From north to south — and *this alone?*

What is the Mason's cornerstone?
  Is it to toil for fame and pelf,
  To magnify our petty self,
And love our friends — and *this alone?*

No, no; the Mason's cornerstone —
  A deeper, stronger, nobler base,
  Which time and foe cannot displace —
Is FAITH IN GOD — and *this alone!*

'Tis this which makes the mystic tie
  Loving and true, divinely good,
  A grand, united brotherhood,
Cemented 'neath the All-seeing Eye.

'Tis this which gives the sweetest tone
  To Mason's melodies; the gleam
  To loving eyes; the brightest gem
That sparkles in the Mason's crown.

'Tis this which makes the Mason's grip
  A chain indissolubly strong;
  It banishes all fraud, and wrong,
And coldness from our fellowship.

Oh, cornerstone, divine, divine!
  Oh, FAITH IN GOD! it buoys us up,
  And gives to darkest hours a hope,
And makes the heart a holy shrine.

Brothers, be this your cornerstone;
  Build every wish and hope on this;
  Of present joy, of future bliss,
On earth, in Heaven — and *this alone!*

CORN, WINE, OIL.

It is the Master's province to communicate light to the Brethren.

They come from many a pleasant home —
To do the Ancient Work they come,
  With cheerful hearts and light;
They leave the world without, apace,
And gathering here in secret place,
  They spend the social night;
They earn the meed of honest toil,
Wages of CORN, and WINE, and OIL.

Upon the sacred Altar lies,
Ah, many a precious sacrifice
  Made by these working men:
The passions curbed, the lusts restrained,
And hands with human gore unstained,
  And hearts from envy clean;
They earn the meed of honest toil,
Wages of CORN, and WINE, and OIL.

They do the deeds THEIR MASTER did;
The naked clothe, the hungry feed —
  They warm the shivering poor;
They wipe from fevered eyes the tear;
A Brother's joys and griefs they share,
  As ONE has done before;
They earn the meed of honest toil,
Wages of CORN, and WINE, and OIL.

Show them how *Masons*, Masons know,
The land of strangers journeying through;
  Show them how Masons love,
And let admiring spirits see
How reaches Masons' charity
  From earth to Heaven above;
Give them the meed of honest toil,
Wages of CORN, and WINE, and OIL.

Then will each Brother's tongue declare
How bounteous his wages are,
  And Peace will reign within;

Your walls with skillful hands will grow,
And coming generations know
   Your Temple is DIVINE;
Then give the meed of honest toil,
Wages of CORN, and WINE, and OIL.

Yes, pay these men their just desert,
Let none dissatisfied depart,
   But give them full reward;
Give LIGHT, that longing eyes may see;
Give TRUTH, that doth from error free:
   Give them to know the LORD!
Give them the meed of honest toil,
Wages of CORN, and WINE, and OIL.

THE HOUR GLASS.

Life's sands are dropping, dropping,—
   Each grain a moment dies;
No stay has time, nor stopping—
   Behold how swift he flies!
He bears away our rarest—
   They smile and disappear;
The cold grave wraps our fairest—
   Each falling grain's a tear.

Life's sands are softly falling,—
   Death's foot is light as snow;
'Tis fearful, 'tis appalling,
   To see how swift they flow;
To read the fatal warning
   The sands so plainly tell;
To feel there's no returning
   Through death's dark, shadowy dale.

Life's sands give admonition
   To use the moments well;
Each grain bears holy mission,
   And this the tale they tell:
"Let zeal than time run faster,
   Each grain some good afford,
Then at the last THE MASTER
   Shall double our reward!"

CEDAR TREE.

Droops thy bough, oh Cedar tree,
    Like yon dear, yon aged form,—
Droops thy bough in sympathy,
    For the wreck of life's sad storm?
Sad, indeed, his weary age,—
    Lonely, now, his princely home,—
And the thoughts his soul engage,
    Are of winter and the tomb!

'Twas for this, oh Cedar tree,
    Verdant midst the wintry strife,
'Twas for this he planted thee,
    Type of an immortal life,—
That when round his grave in tears
    Brothers in their ART combine,
From the store thy foliage bears
    Each may cast a portion in!

Lo! he comes, oh Cedar tree,
    Slowly o'er the frosted plain;
Pauses here the signs to see,
    Graven with a mystic pen;
How does each some hope express!
    Lighter gleams the wintry sky,
Lighter on his furrowed face
    Smiling at the mystery!

Soon to rest, oh Cedar tree,
    Soon the veteran shall be borne,
There to sleep, and patiently
    Wait the resurrection morn.
Thou shalt perish from the earth;
    He in sacred youth revive,
Glorious in a better birth,—
    Truths like these the emblems give.

In the lawn that graces an aged Mason's residence stands a Cedar tree, planted in 1836, "for Masonic purposes." Still (in 1853) the withered hand that placed it there to furnish sprigs of evergreen for burial use was strong enough to do the MASTER'S WORK at each Lodge meeting, and still at an age passing the Psalmist's utmost computation, he who planted it waited patiently for the day when its limbs should be bared of their foliage to bestrew his coffin.

EAR OF CORN.

Of the water fall 'tis born,
In the nodding fields of corn,
Blest type of Masons' love and plenty;
And the hymn of our delight
Shall be this symbol bright,
Singing the type of love and plenty.

CHORUS.— The emblem of plenty,
The rich, GOLDEN EAR,
Gift of a Father of grace ever dear,—
Oh, the hymn of our delight,
Shall be of this emblem bright,
Singing the type of love and plenty.

Of the bliss of earth it tells,—
Every blessing in it dwells,—
Sunshine is on its treasure golden ;
And the cooling drops of morn
Have bedewed the nodding CORN,—
Ripe in the field of treasure golden.

In the nodding EAR OF CORN,
Finds the spirit, weary, worn,
Hopes, hopes of better days in Heaven ;
When the harvest toil is done,
And the feasting is begun,—
Joy, joy, the Sabbath day of Heaven !

Let the golden symbol be
Where the toiling Crafts may see,
Toiling, and never quite despairing ;
Of the water fall 'tis born,
In the nodding fields of Corn,
Meet for the soul in its despairing.

The Masonic emblem of the EAR OF CORN, though rarely commented upon by our writers, is, in fact, one of the most expressive of all the designs upon our Trestle Board. It is generic, embodying all those symbols that refer to refreshment, rest, holidays, and the slumbers of the grave. In every Lodge the Ear of Corn should constitute one of those conspicuous objects which, like the LETTER G, by attracting the eye, instruct the mind. Its place is over the station of the Junior Warden.

WEARING THE EMBLEMS.

You wear the SQUARE! but have you got
   That thing the Square denotes?
Is there within your inmost soul
That principle which should control
   Your actions, words, and thoughts?
The Square of Virtue,—is it there,
Oh, you that wear the Mason's Square?

You wear the COMPASS! Do you keep
   Within that circle due
That's circumscribed by law divine,
Excluding hatred, envy, sin,—
   Including all that's true?
The Moral Compass draws the line,
And lets no evil passions in!

You wear the TROWEL! have you got
   That mortar, old and pure,
Made on the *recipe* of God
Divulged within His ancient Word,
   Indissoluble, sure?
And do you spread, 'twixt man and man,
That precious mixture as you can?

You wear the ORIENTAL G!
   Ah, Brother, have a care!
He whose All-seeing Eye surveys
Your inmost heart, with open gaze,
   Knows well what thoughts are there!
Let no profane, irreverent word
Go up t' insult th' avenging God!

You wear the CROSS! it signifies
   The burdens JESUS bore,
Who, staggering, fell, and bleeding, rose,
And took to Golgotha the woes
   The world had borne before!
The Cross,—oh, let it say, *Forgive,*
Father, forgive, to all that live!

Dear Brother! if you will display
   These emblems of our Art,

Let the great *morals* that they teach
Be deeply graven, each for each,
    Upon an honest heart!
Then they will tell, to God and man,
Freemasonry's all-perfect plan!

FOUNDATION STONE.

When the SPIRIT came to Jephtha,
    Animating his great heart,
He arose, put on his armor,
    Girt his loins about to part,
Bowed the knee, implored a blessing,
    Gave the earnest of his faith,
Then, divinely strung, departed,
    Set for victory or death.

If a rude, uncultured soldier
    Thus drew Wisdom from above,
How should we, enlightened Laborers,
    Children of the Sire of Love,—
How should we, who know " the Wisdom
    Gentle, pure and peaceable,"
Make a prayerful preparation
    That our work be square and full!

Lo, the future!   ONE can read it,—
    HE its darkest chance can bend.
Lo, our wants, how great, how many!
    HE abundant means can lend.
Raise your hearts, then, Pilgrims, boldly
    Build and journey in His trust;
Square your deeds by precepts holy,
    And the end is surely blest.

Vainly will the builders labor
    If the OVERSEER be gone;
Vainly gate and wall are guarded
    If the ALL-SEEING is withdrawn;
Only is successful ending
    When the work's begun with care;
Lay your blocks, then, Laborers, strongly,
    On the Eternal Rock of Prayer.

THE VETERANS' GATHERING.

Composed for a gathering of Masons at the Grand Union Hotel, New York city, February 15, 1883, in compliment to Brother Rob Morris, of Kentucky.

'Tis well nigh forty years ago,
　This gallant company set forth,
A warmer-hearted set, I trow,
　Hath never graced the earth ;
And here we are,— a veteran ring,—
　A remnant old and gray,—
Resolved, whate'er the morn may bring,
　To-night we will be gay, dear Boys,
　　Oh, very glad and gay.
Then close the ranks, touch elbows, Boys,
　Old friends are dropping fast,
Close up, close up a manly front,
　'Twill all come right at last, dear Boys,
　　Sure to come right at last.

What's three score years to men like you?
　The spirit scorns a base control,—
Old Time your sturdy *backs* may bow,
　He cannot bend the *soul ;*
The eye that scans an honest life
　Nor age nor clouds may dim ;
The heart with generous promptings rife
　Sings a perpetual hymn, dear Boys,
　　A bright, perpetual hymn.

Shall we begrudge the tender tear
　To those who've stemmed the Lethean wave?
Ah, no, 'twill cast no shadows here
　To name them in the grave ;
We loved them, "there's no fear in love,"
　Then reach across the sea,
And hail them in their homes above,
　Bright forms of memory, dear Boys,
　　Best forms of memory.

A moment longer,— he whose name
　To-night goes round your festive board,
In stammering words and couplets tame
　Thus pledges heart and word ;
"We may not meet again 'till death
　Unite us 'neath his power,

But while I draw the vital breath
　　I'll not forget this hour, dear Boys,
　　　　Never forget this hour!"
Then close the ranks, touch elbows, Boys,
　　Old friends are dropping fast ;
Close up, close up a manly front,
　　'Twill all come right at last, dear Boys,
　　　　Sure to come right at last.

GAVEL.

"We meet upon the Level," is the Senior Warden's word,
　　As he lifts his mystic column in the West,—
"We act upon the Plumb"—is the Junior's quick accord,
　　And to work the brothers hasten with a zest.
　　　　But the *Gavel* is my fancy
　　　　　　Over Level, Square and Plumb,
　　For it marks the very spirit of command,
　　　　In its ringing notes methodic
　　　　　　Every dissonance is dumb,
And a willing spirit hovers o'er the band.

"We part upon the Square" is the fiat of the East
　　When the hour of ten commands us to depart,—
And the Junior lifts his column, and the Tyler is released,
　　And we hurry to the welcome of the heart.
　　　　But the *Gavel* is my fancy,
　　　　　　I shall never cease to cry,—
'Tis Celestial music dropping to the earth;
　　　　　'Tis a memory of the angels
　　　　　　As they heard it in the sky,
When the KING from chaos called creation forth.

In the weird and mystic circle, solemn silence brooding round,
　　There's a something all invisible but strong,
Maybe summoned from the Highest by the *Gavel's* holy sound,
　　And it brings the better spirit to the throng.
　　　　Oh the *Gavel*, Master's *Gavel*,
　　　　　　It shall ever have my praise
While the Book and Symbol whisper "God is love";
　　　　　In His mighty NAME it speaketh,
　　　　　　All contention it allays,
Till the Lodge below is like the Lodge above.

THE EMBLEMS OF THE CRAFT.

Who wears the SQUARE upon his breast
Does in the face of God attest,—
   And in the face of man,—
That all his actions will compare
With the divine, the unerring SQUARE,
   That squares great Virtue's plan.
And he erects his edifice
By *this* design, and *this*, and *this*.

Who wears the LEVEL says that pride
Does not within his soul abide,
   Nor foolish vanity ;
That man has but a common doom,
And from the cradle to the tomb
   An equal destiny.
And he erects his edifice
By *this* design, and *this*, and *this*.

Who wears the PLUMB, behold how true
His words and walk ! and could we view
   The chambers of his soul,
Each hidden thought, so pure and good,
By the stern line of rectitude
   Points up to Heaven's goal ;
And he erects his edifice
By *this* design, and *this*, and *this*.

Who wears the G,— that mark divine,—
Whose very sight should banish sin,
   Has faith in God alone ;
His Father, Maker, Friend, he knows ;
He vows and pays to God his vows
   Before the eternal throne ;
And he erects his edifice
By *this* design, and *this*, and *this*.

Thus life and beauty come to view
In *each design* our fathers drew,
   So glorious and sublime ;
Each breathes an odor from the bloom
Of gardens bright beyond the tomb,

Beyond the flight of time,
And bids us ever build on *this*,
The walls of God's own edifice.

In reciting this popular piece it should be marked with full esoteric accompaniments to give it due effect.

SETTING A MEMORIAL.

We'll set a green sprig here to-night,
To rescue, from the days to come,
Each bright and joyous memory
That henceforth gilds this festive room;
And should occasion e'er require
A token, to recall the place,
THESE LEAVES will bring to clearest view,
The cheerful thought and sunny face.

We'll set a green and deathless sprig —
Each leaf a BROTHER'S NAME shall have;
And fragrant will th' acacia bloom
When one has left us for the grave;
When one in Temple labor fails,
And golden bowl is broken quite,
How grateful to the sense will be
The green sprig that we set to-night!

We'll set the sprig with every hand,—
Come round, and plant the deathless tree!
There is not one in all this band
But what is marked by destiny;
Death comes to all — how well to know
There is a life beyond this scene,
Whose deathless limit may be read,
O, Brothers, in this sacred green!

We'll set the green sprig deep in love;
We'll water it with sympathy;
We'll give it fond and faithful care,
Nor shall a single leaflet die;
And when the last of this true band,
Death's mighty puissance shall attest,
May those who follow after say,
FAITHFUL AND TRUE, HOW SWEET THEY REST.

These lines embody an expression familiar to the Masonic reader: "Setting a green sprig that the place may be known should occasion ever require it."

SHOE.

Take this pledge! it is a token
Of a truth that ne'er was broken,—
Truth which binds the Mystic Tie,
Under the All-seeing Eye.

Take this pledge! each ancient Brother,
By this gift bound every other
Firmly, so that death, alone,
Rent the bonds that made them one.

Take this pledge! no pledge so holy;
Though the symbol seem but lowly,
'Tis divine! It tells of ONE,
Of the raindrops and the sun.

Take this pledge! the token sealeth
All that judgment day revealeth;
Honor, truth, fraternal Grace,
Brother, in thy hands I place!

THE GREEN SPRIG.

FROM ME TO THEE, FROM ME TO THEE,
Each whispering leaf a missive be,
In mystic scent and hue to say,—
This green and fragrant spray,—
In emerald green and rich perfume,
To teach of FAITH that mocks the tomb,
And link the chain FIDELITY,
'Twixt, Brother, thee and me!

In distant land, in olden time,
The ACACIA bore the mark sublime,
And told to each discerning eye
A deathless constancy.
So may these green leaves whisper now,
Inform the heart, inspire the vow,
And link the chain FIDELITY,
'Twixt, Brother, thee and me!

It was the practice of the members of the now dissolved Order of Conservators, to inclose in all their correspondence with each other a sprig of evergreen.

THE SWEEP OF SYMBOLISM.

In the conception and arrangement of the following pieces, the writer has imagined himself conducting an intelligent inquirer around and through a well ordered Lodge room, whose lights, furniture, jewels and ornaments are complete in *number*, appropriate in *pattern*, and systematic in *arrangement*.

The neophyte is supposed to enter at the visitor's portal in the southwest, and stand, for a moment, taking in the imagery of the Lodge with a comprehensive look. Then the hierophant addresses him in these fifty-two forms of instruction:

I. THE MICROCOSM.

" The Freemasons' Lodge is a *microcosm* of symbolic forms and colors; a chamber of imagery; a school of moral truth, developed through ancient forms."

Bright Microcosm of high celestial types,
World of rare form and color, quaint,
Instructive in eternal laws which bind
All creatures,— yield us now thy truth!

Bear us above the sordid things of time,
For one brief hour; and let us see *above*,
Below, around this secret chamber, what
The Sages wrote upon the mystic tombs
That yawn in emptiness along the Nile.

II. BLUE — The Celestial Color.

The cerulean sky, nowhere so deeply blue as in the land of Hiram, affords fitting color for the Masonic Lodge.

The o'erarching sky around our busy sphere
Looks down alike on every race of man;
Where'er our feet may wander, there appears
With morning blush and evening's crimsoning,
The sober BLUE prevailing over all.
So should a Mason's charity extend,
To every needy soul, unchecked by clime,
By nation unrestricted, and by tongue!
For where the destitute, there, too, is GOD,
Calling us thither with an open hand,
To do His charity upon the poor.

III. APRON — No Degeneration.

No person can become *worse* for being a Mason. "Let every man abide in the same calling wherein he was called," says the most philosophical writer of the sacred canon, and the injunction is made practical in Masonry.

White, only *white*, the badge of truth,
Type of unspotted innocence,
The virgin *color*, lily-white,

The hue that marks the sheeted dead.
The Lodge Celestial, round the Throne,
The raptured choir, all enrobed in white,
Sing high salvation unto GOD !
Cleansed of all gross impurity,
We toilers in the Moral Fane,
So, humbly wear our garments, *white.*

IV. E., W. AND S.—NORTH, THE PLACE OF DARKNESS.

In all systems of ancient rites, the Borean has been stigmatized as the quarter of "frigid cold and cheerless dark."

Why tread in gloomy shades, when paths
Of light await the willing steps ?
Leave the dark Borean to the feet
Profane — to cowan's feet profane —
To shapeless monsters of the night
That hate the glories of the noon,
Marauders of the dark;— but we,
The ways of pleasantness and paths
Of peace will seek, where Wisdom dwells,
And find her form exceeding fair.

V. BEEHIVE—INDUSTRIOUS APPLICATION.

A society whose motto is, " *Travel and travail,* walk and work," sees practical suggestions to duty in the beehive. Well said the poet, " To do nothing, is to serve the devil and transgress the law of God."

None idle here ! look where you will, they all
Are active, all engaged in meet pursuit;
Not happy else. No, for the MASTER'S voice
That called them first, is ringing in their ears;
Go build! go build! a brief six days of toil
I have allotted, arduous toil, but brief;
The burden and the heat ye must endure
All uncomplainingly,— such is my will,
In darksome quarry, and on toilsome mount,
And heated wall;— *go build!* not happy else !

VI. HOUR GLASS—FLIGHT OF TIME.

" So teach us to number our days that we may apply our hearts unto wisdom."

Voice of the ages, wisdom ever new,
Speaking to Masons, in simplicity,
Soon thy last sand must leave the glass of time;
For while we contemplate them, they grow less,
And even now still less as yet we muse;

The Hour Glass bids us gauge the unfinished work
That meets the eye, and sum the amount, and so
With double assiduity to toil;
Each grain recorded in celestial scroll,
Demands of all a corresponding deed.

VII. BOOK OF THE LAW — The Mind of God.

As when we turn a vessel upward, during a shower of rain, the drops from Heaven are caught therein, so in the written Word have been caught and retained, in the descent from Heaven, the very thoughts, purposes and will of Him who ruleth all. " In keeping of them there is great reward." " The Bible is the lamp which God threw from his palace down to earth to guide his wandering children home."

And can we know the mind of God ?
A window to the will Supreme !
And is His purpose all exposed
To human eye, so faint and dim ?
Look ! open upward broadly lies
The Word of God,— the unerring Law,
Threatening and promising by turns,
As Masons yield to fear or love.
Oh, be it ours to walk therein,
And at the end have sure reward !

VIII. ALL-SEEING EYE — Sovereign Inspection.

That we are never lost to the direct inspection of God is a doctrine as consoling to the faithful workman as alarming to the man servant, the idle and the shirk.

Watch me, oh, Master, at my work,
And note my diligence of zeal !
Through the long day my handstrokes fall,
For thou shalt have my utmost strength;
So in the midnight horror; so
In the worst terrors of the storm;
And midst the assassin's thrust, and in
The hour and article of death,
Thy vigilant Eye will surely note,
Thy Hand avert, Thy Love abate !

IX. CHECKERED PAVEMENT — Human Vicissitudes.

The lesson of human vicissitudes is too obvious to require repetition. Uncertainty and change pervade all the affairs of men.

From purest white to deepest black;—
Despair and rapture, fear and joy,—
Misfortune's gloomy discipline,
The happy troop of good success,
Stern hue of death, sweet hue of life,

Coldness of winter, summer's heat,
Oh, who can walk from West to East,
Along this mystic floor, nor feel
His deep dependence on the Hand
Invisible that guides his steps?

X. CABLE TOW—BONDAGE OF DUTY.

To the faithful laborer in the speculative Temple, the four-fold cord, which "is not easily broken," is like the wing of the bird, which incumbers, yet uplifts: *strong* indeed, yet its restraints are altogether *wholesome.*

A *gentle* bond, soft as the filmy thread
That strings the dew drops on the sunny morn,
Or gossamer that floats upon the air;
A *mighty* bond stronger than anchor chain,
Or brazen fetters to the honest soul;
A chain of *length*, reaching as *high* as Heaven,
As *deep* as to the very mountains' roots;
A chain of *strength* that holds the wayward heart
From drift and danger; admirable bond,
Who would not be constrained with such as this?

XI. ARK—SAFETY UNDER DIVINE SHELTER.

In all systems of ancient mythology, the Ark is a type of refuge from danger—the resort in time of impending peril.

Type of serenity, we think of thee
When lightnings flout our unprotected heads;
So, when life's storms whip our unhappy souls,
And wild temptation rages in our hearts,
We turn, oh, Masons' Lodge, we yearn for thee,
Another ARK of refuge, tried and sure,
And in thy halls serene regain our strength;
In vain the storm at thy close portals beats;
Life's discords lag without; the voice within
Is music; doors secure, and keepers strong.

XII. GAVEL—OBEDIENCE.

There is no union of men so orderly as a Freemasons' Lodge. Submissiveness to rule is the *sine qua non* of the Mason. "The King's wrath," declares our first M. E. Grand Master, "is as the roaring of a lion."

As midst the incoherent clash and void
Of the new world, the voice of God rung out,
"Let there be LIGHT, and there was light!" so falls
This gentle monitor, and all is peace!
The clangor of debate, the heated breath,
The vow forgotten, and the sharp retort,
Yield sweetly to the GAVEL's strong "Be still!"

Reason returns with quiet, and she brings
That fine *reaction* which the generous heart
Moves to confess and heals the rankling wound.

XIII. CHARITY — THE GREATEST OF THE THREE.

"Now, there abideth faith, hope, charity, these three." This was the expression made, in unusually poetic mood, by a master of the human mind: "these three, but the greatest of these is charity!"

The soul serene, impenetrably just,
Is first in CHARITY; we love to muse
On such a model; knit in strictest bonds
Of amity with spirits like disposed;
Aiming at truth for her own sake, this man
Passes beyond the golden line of Faith,
Passes beyond the precious line of Hope,
And sets his foot unmoved on CHARITY.
"A soul so softly radiant and so white,
The track it leaves seems less of fire than light."

XIV. LILY — REMOVING THE STAINED.

The instinct of self-preservation compels Masons to expel from their Order the "found unworthy." "Put away from among yourselves that wicked person" is a divine injunction.

A wail of sorrowing hearts pervades the Lodge,
And flows and bears a volume of sad sounds;
O purity defiled! oh, soiled and smirched,
Who wert so fair! upon our Pillars twain
We hung thine emblem, gathered from the mead,
A modest flower, the LILY, virgin white,
White like the Apron, modest like the soul
That hides the left hand when the right hand gives.
Tear the smirched LILY from its place defiled,
And cast it out, alas, with bitter tears!

XV. TROWEL — SPREADING PEACE.

The fundamental idea of Freemasonry is *peace:* "He loveth transgression," declares the Preacher, the son of David, king in Jerusalem; "he loveth transgression that loveth strife."

Divinest privilege to trowel peace:
Strongest of cement, *peace*, the bond of Heaven,
Exalted on the everlasting hills:
This makes us fellow laborers with God,
And gives us best assurance of reward.
Peace, holy calm,— it broods within the veil
Where rests the golden Ark, and in the soul
Of gentle Craftsmen, infinite delight;
No sound of Axe discordant breaks the calm
In which the walls of Sion's Fane go up.

XVI. RULE — Unerring Truth.

This emblem — the Rule — teaches that the paths of truth are *straight*, the portals to her temple are *strait*, "and few there be that enter therein."

What voice, O simple RULE, hast thou to warn
And guide the willing toiler on his way?
" Better to journey with the humble few
Who walk the path unerring, than to crowd
Along the broad, meandering paths of sin;
Better in steadfastness to fix the gaze
On Truth's fair Temple where the MASTER sits,
And so, in shortest lines attain the prize,
Than gratify the lawless, roving eye,
In crooked highways ending in despair."

XVII. THE ACACIA TREE — Sacred Foliage.

The Acacia, or *Shittah*, is emphatically the Freemason's tree. The Burning Bush of Moses, the Ark of the Covenant and the Altars of the Temple were all of Acacia. It is sacred to the most affecting traditions of the Order. The sap of this tree is the well known *Gum Arabic*.

Thy very tears are precious, holy plant,
Dropt in sad recollections of the past;
The olden Builders knew thy merits well,
And prized, above the cedar, olive, palm,
The rare Acacia, offspring of the wild;
His feet the prophet bared before thy Bush,
Burning, and marvelous, and unconsumed;
Thy wood inclosed the tables of the Law,
In peaceful *Sanctum* resting; and the blood
Of countless victims on thine Altar flowed.

XVIII. EAR OF CORN — Bounty of Nature.

The term *Corn*, in all Biblical and Masonic passages, is to be read *Wheat*. This product of nature, in the abounding soil of Palestine, is the finest in the world.

Look, traveler, what name you this, that droops
In wondrous heaviness upon the stalk?
Look, traveler, old Canaan hath no gift
That equals this, to speak its MAKER's praise!
Abounding land! how lost to early truth
When EAR OF CORN is made the test of doom!
The rapid Jordan makes impetuous course,—
The lily specks the hills where Jephthah dwelt,—
The oleander scents the valley sweet
As in his time,—they wake the gloomy thought
Of SHIBBOLETH, the master key of doom!

XIX. SPANGLED ARCH — Nocturnal Splendors.

" When I consider thy heavens, the work of thy fingers, the moon and the stars, which thou hast ordained, what is man that thou art mindful of him?" In Palestine the stars shine with a brilliance unknown to more northern heavens.

Not stars alone, but windows unto Heaven,—
Not lights, affixed in glittering concave,
But chandeliers hung from invisible chains
Held by angelic hands beside the Throne !
O spangled roof, O feeble thought of Heaven,
How grand the night curtained so gloriously !
The watchers of Old Tyre beheld them thus,
And worshiped God ; sages of Babylon
Grew old, in study of thy splendors, and
The Bard of Israel sung, from palace roof, thy blaze !

XX. SQUARE — Implement of Proof.

The emblem of morality, in Masonry, is the implement of proof. " Prove all things ; hold fast that which is good," is an injunction cheerfully accepted by the Craft.

And who is this,— grave, reverend man,— who brings
With high command THE SQUARE ! whose practiced eye
Takes warily in the length and breadth and depth
Of the offered stone ! how, with this implement,
He proves the angles, tests the corners each,
Sternly rejects the ashlar reprobate,
Cheerful accepts if, to his scrupulous care,
The block responds ! not strange, if in the shock
Of earthquakes and the jarring elements
This wall, built up with such precision, stands !

XXI. BROTHERLY LOVE — The Spirit of the Craft.

" Bear ye one another's burdens " ; " Let brotherly love continue " ; " Tychicus, a beloved brother."

To suffer long, and yet be kind and true ;
To bear the slight and yet retain the love ;
To hope, whate'er betide, and still to hope
Through all the gloomy days that life may yield,—
This is *the love of Masons,*— BROTHERLY LOVE ;
This binds the old fraternity with brass
And iron fetters ;— while such Love endures,
The rage of foes assaults our fort in vain ;
The bigot's hate recoils ; palsied the arm
Which strikes a Brotherhood knit by such ties.

XXII. COMPASSES — Boundary of Passion.

The limit, within which the exercise of the passions of man is allowable, is clearly marked in the use of the ancient emblem, the Compasses.

> The grace of God directs this implement;
> His gracious hand so separates its limbs
> As to inclose a gracious boundary;
> He gives us ample scope for every bliss
> Of which our nature is susceptible;
> Let us, then, Craftsmen, keep within the sphere
> His wisdom marks, nor contravene his will:
> Lust and intemperance, the greed of gain,
> Anger and malice, envy, villainy,—
> All these outside *the Compass' points* are seen.

XXIII. G — Suggestiveness of Divine Presence.

This constant reminder to all Lodge attendants cannot fail to work happy effects in our age, so profane that the words of the prophet Jeremiah are literally verified : '' Because of swearing, the land mourneth.''

> As through an open window into Heaven,
> Through this strange symbol, golden, bright, we look,
> And muse upon celestial chamber; where
> "Upon His glorious throne God sits alone,
> Hath ever sat alone, and shall forever sit,
> Alone, Invisible, Immortal One!"
> The Master, o'er whose head the type impends
> Names it, awestruck and reverently, *God!*
> Then humbly as the creature should, the Craft
> In silent adoration, lowly bows.

XXIV. CLAY GROUNDS — Foundries of the Brazen Pillars.

'' In the plain of Jordan did the king cast them, in the clay ground between Succoth and Zarthan.''

> How once the furnace fires were heated here!
> Here the soft cooing of bright Jordan's dove,
> And nightingale's sweet song were silenced all
> By roar of Hiram's cupolas! the scent
> Of oleander buds, so exquisite,
> Lost in thick smoke and soot of molten brass!
> Now all is desolate; the poisonous thorn
> In matted thickets, guards the gloomy place,
> And Hiram's masterpieces are a myth.

XXV. MOON — Nocturnal Ruler.

The meetings of Lodges in hilly, woody, and unfrequented places, are mostly arranged with reference to the changes of the moon.

> Thy gentle face calls up the parted years,
> Guide of the evening, MOON, the Mason's sun.
> Led by thy light, the woodland paths were filled
> With cheerful voice — the stilly night was moved
> With feet fraternal, thronging to the Lodge.
> Sweet MOON, thou peered upon our mysteries,
> But saw no motion but what God could bless ;
> Bending toward the West thy silver light
> Admonished of the midnight hour, and led
> The happy Craftsmen to domestic joys.

XXVI. NETWORK — Interwoven Friendship.

The world observes the union of Masons, and marvels thereat. "A friend loveth at all times," observes the most shrewd observer of antiquity, "and a brother is born for adversity."

> This NET so strong, of thirty centuries,
> That gleams on high, in brazen imagery,
> Shows an artistic knot at every joint.
> Wonderful NETWORK ! whose the hand that first
> Taught us to tie thy fastenings intricate?
> The wants, and woes, and joys, and cares of men,
> So shared, so equalized,— whose work is this?
> None other than the Artificer's divine !
> 'Tis the same Unity that reigns in Heaven,
> Binding the angels to the throne of God.

XXVII. OBLONG SQUARE — True to Perfect Angles.

The form of Solomon's Temple, an oblong square, with no circular projections, suggests a whole class of symbolisms in the moral architecture of Freemasons.

> Blessèd the man who walks not by advice
> Of the ungodly, and who standeth not
> In the way of sinners, nor in scorner's seat
> Doth sit ; but in the law of God delights,
> And meditates thereon, both day and night ;
> He shall be like a fruitful, spreading tree,
> Planted on river's brink ; his fruit shall come
> In season, and his leaf shall never fade ;
> Such are the blessings promised in the Law,
> To those who duly form the OBLONG SQUARE.

XXVIII. PALM TREE—Water, Shade, Fruit, Gracefulness.

This far-famed tree, from which the land of Hiram, *Phœnicia*, was named, has many rare qualities. At its roots is *water ;* its shaft is the image of *gracefulness ;* its *shade* is inexpressibly grateful to the desert dweller; its *fruit* is the most nutritious grown in the Orient. On the walls of the Temple the palm tree was engraven.

Thou sealest up the sum of nature's gifts,
O grateful shaft, that send'st thy shade afar!
The royal sage adorned his olive gates
With thy fair image ; for it told of *food*
Delicious to the taste ; and grateful *shade*
Made by thy thickened foliage, while the sound—
No music in those eastern lands so sweet—
Of trickling *water* echoed at thy roots.
Perfect in beauty, and with bounty full,
Thou art the chief of Masons' imagery.

XXIX. ROUGH ASHLAR—Unformed Character.

" The earth was without form and void, and darkness was upon the face of the deep."

What changes must this quarry stone receive,
Ere the fair statue from its folds looks out !
Shapeless, unsightly—who can tell the form
May yet delight the eye from this rude block ?
So with the soul that comes beneath the edge
Of moral implements ; we cannot know
What treasure's hidden in that Ashlar Rough,
Until the forming, skillful stroke shall fall,
Divesting of all superfluities,
And leaving just the image God designed.

XXX. FORTITUDE—Safety of Esotery.

The coward merits no confidence, nor should he be made a Mason. Under the influence of terror he evinces the openness of the child.

In some far oriental land, they tell
Of one, a brave old man, who fairly died
His honor to maintain ; rude, violent hands
On him were laid in unexpected hour
And secret place, and he was given to choose
'Twixt vile dishonor and a cruel death.
He died ; in Fortitude he gave his life,
Redeeming thus the pledge made long before.
His high example for three thousand years
Has formed the model of true courage here.

XXXI. FAITH — Apprehension of Unseen Things.

" So it was with all the mysteries of faith; God set them forth unveiled to the full gaze of man, and asked him to investigate them." Our faith in God rests alone in the promises contained in His word.

Book of all Books, thou volume most profound,
Whose very words, majestic and sublime,
Excel all others ! see, we humbly lay,
And hopefully, undoubted FAITH on thee !
These good right hands we gladly rest on thee;
If thou art false, there is no truth on earth,
No God, no Heaven, no Hell, no lasting hope.
By FAITH we lightly pass beyond the grave,
O'erleap all present evils, and enjoy,
In fond anticipation, boundless good.

XXXII. WATER FORD — Remembrances of the Exploit of Jephthah.

The swiftness of the traditional river of Freemasonry explains the catastrophe of the fords :
" There fell at that time, of the Ephraimites, forty and two thousand."

So when we end this dreary tale of life,
And stand upon the river's edge, river of death,
Safe passage, needful aid, good cheer are all
Assured to him who has the needful *word*.
Dark stream ! we shudder at thy gulf profound ;
Bitter thy waters to sin's votary ;
All that a man hath he will give t' escape.
But to the righteous there awaits a guide,
Strong to uphold and gentle to console,
To him who, whispering, safely yields *the word*.

XXXIII. ANCHOR — Clinging to Assured Truth.

A true Mason may veer amidst tides and storms the length of his cable, but *he will never drift*.

Good anchorage our MASTER hath secured,—
Strong cable to the Master's bark is fixed,—
Brave ANCHOR, rooted firmly in the rock,—
What wreck, what peril can befall us now ?
The storms may break,— they enter every life ;
Foes may assault,— all good men live at war ;
Time may install harshest vicissitudes,
And threaten all that timid souls can fear ; —
Yet our good ANCHOR holds, will ever hold,
And we shall close our voyage in peace at last.

XXXIV. HERMON — MOUNT OF COOLING DEWS.

The elevation of this grand mountain, securing a cap of snows all through the sultry months, makes it a regulator of the atmosphere through its cooling dews. The expression "the dew of Hermon," in the opening of the Entered Apprentices' Lodge, is therefore an exquisite suggestion of *Brotherly Love.*

In sultry eve, oppressed with dust and toil,
The burning earth conspiring with the air,
The pilgrim waits, in deep suspense, the fall
Of Hermon's dews. It comes; like angel guest,
The cooling mist, down from the snowy crown,
Brings tone and gladness. The wanderer sleeps,
Devoutly grateful for the mountain joy;
So in the heat and dust of mortal strife,
The influence of Brotherly Love is seen,
Cooling and calming the o'erheated soul.

XXXV. BROKEN COLUMN — SUDDEN AND VIOLENT DEATH.

The application of this emblem is trite to every Mason.

Too soon, too soon, alas! for earth and us,
The temple yet unfinished, he is gone;
Weep, Craftsmen, not for him,— is not his fame
Secure?— but for the stricken mourners left.
Who, now, on tracing board, shall wisely draw
The strange device that binds the finished work
With the undone, making a perfect Fane,
By closing up in one the Grand Design?
Fallen the stroke, the inexorable blow,
Too soon, too soon, alas! for earth and us.

XXXVI. BOAZ — THE LEFT-HAND PILLAR.

"He reared up the pillars before the Temple, and called the name of that on the left, BOAZ." The terms *right* and *left* being reckoned from the position of a person looking east, BOAZ was on the *north* side of the porch. The word *Boaz* denotes *strength.*

Not strength for slaughter, strength to desolate
And strew the earth with legions of our race;
But strength to uphold the falling, strength to check
The erring, strength to build and not destroy.
In this our Craftsmen are confederate,—
Like network knotted, they're a web of strength,
Grand PILLAR, next the heart, thy gleaming cap
Looked out in glory toward the rising sun,
Bidding our souls be strong! "BOAZ, in strength
God will establish all His promises!"

XXXVII. SPADE — Tillage and Interment.

The same implement that opens the bosom of mother earth in the operations of the husbandman turns up the sod for the interment of the dead.

Are graves of man indeed a hopeless night,
That has no morn beyond it, and no star,
Wherein life's music ends forevermore?
Then, whence these transformations? Lo, the root
And tiny seed cast in the self-same earth,
Escape entombment! see them burst above,
With power irresistible, and clothe
The conquered earth with leaves and blossoms fair!
Have comfort, then, ye sons of heavenly hope,
The voice of God shall call our buried up.

XXXVIII. CORN — Emblem of Nourishment.

The wheat of Palestine is the heaviest and most productive that is cultivated. It was, therefore, one of the three conserving elements of Solomon's Temple, chosen as a representative of the country's best products.

We feed and worship, Author of our life,
Nourished by Thee. All through the changing year
Thou guid'st the seasons that we may not want.
The yielding furrow Thy command obeys,
And gives its CORN to consecrate our Lodge.
Oh, bounteous source of food, this precious grain,
Thus scattered on our altars, let it bring
Blessings of *nourishment* to after years,
Strength'ning the generations that shall fill
These chambers, when our pilgrimage is done!

XXXIX. WINE — Emblem of Refreshment.

The grapes of Palestine form the heaviest clusters of any known, and their wine is extremely sound and wholesome. It was, therefore, with corn and oil, one of the three conserving elements of Solomon's Temple, chosen as a representative of the country's best products.

We drink and worship, Author of our life,
Refreshed by Thee. All through the changing year
Thou guid'st the seasons that we may not want;
The stony hillside Thy command obeys,
And gives its WINE to consecrate our Lodge.
Oh, bounteous Source of good, this precious WINE
Thus sprinkled on our altars, let it bring
Refreshment's blessings to the coming years,
Gladdening the generations that shall fill
These chambers, when our pilgrimage is done!

XL. OIL — EMBLEM OF JOY.

The olive oil of Palestine is of the heaviest and purest. It was, properly, one of the three conservating elements of Solomon's Temple, chosen as a representative of the country's best products.

With OIL anointed, Author of our life,
Joyful we worship; through the changing year
Thou guid'st the seasons that we may not want;
The rocky cleft Thy great command obeys,
And gives its OIL to consecrate our Lodge.
Oh, bounteous Source of good, this precious OIL
Thus dripping on our altars, let it bring
Blessings of joy to all the coming years,
Cheering the generations that shall fill
These chambers, when our pilgrimage is done!

XLI. PLUMB LINE — UPRIGHTNESS.

The duty of rectitude, "Upright standing in the presence of God and man," is strongly suggested by this emblem: "Walk honestly toward them that are without."

We cannot hear His voice or see His face,
Yet, looking up along the unerring LINE,
We see it points HIM on His radiant throne.
Earth's center is beneath the foot of God,
And they will please Him best who bear the head
Erect, and walk uprightly on the earth.
'Twas thus with Hiram, widow's son,— he stood
Among the Builders like a polished shaft,
Along whose sides the PLUMB LINE vainly sought
A trace of deviation from the proof.

XLII. POT OF INCENSE — OVERFLOW OF GRATITUDE.

The ascending smoke, composed of the exquisitely compounded spices required by the Jewish ritual, afforded the best type of grateful prayer ascending from pious hearts.

"For He is good,"— went up the exultant cry
Of Israel's millions on their faces bowed.
"For He is good,"— our grateful hearts respond,
When at the morn we pray, and at the eve.
What dues we owe Him, creatures of His care!
What treasures from His liberal hand we take,
Of Corn and Oil and Wine! oh, at the close
May our enraptured tongues in Heaven be heard
At God's right hand, in glory evermore,
Hymning forever the Creator's praise!

XLIII. CEDAR TREE — Emblem of Endurance.

So enduring is the wood of the Lebanon cedar, that it is not extravagant to assert, "had not the Temple of Solomon been *burned*, its cedar beams would yet be found undecayed, after three thousand years."

Type of endurance, child of the mountain tops,
Companion of the eagle, born midst snows
And desolation, tree of Lebanon!—
With toil and weariness thy trunks were brought
Seaward, by Joppa, to this honored site.
Here, with the olive and acacia strong
Wedded to marble, gold, and precious gems,
Thy wood was consecrate in work divine.
Time spared thy glory, time and gnawing worm
But left thee victim to the foeman's torch.

XLIV. TRUTH — Foundation of Every Virtue.

"Oh, truth, divinely sweet and fair,
    The crystal springs of life are thine!
The light of years thy garments bear,
    The stars of ages o'er thee shine;
Inwrought with every circling sphere
Born of a heavenly atmosphere."

And so, at last, we find the basis stone,
The sure foundation of all virtues, TRUTH.
Through layers of materials select,
All rich, and rare, and gathered from afar,
And prized alike by angels and good men,
And hated by all those who hate the light,
We come to this, the deepest and the best!
This holds them all, and well may hold them all;
For 'tis the richest gem in Crown divine,
And sparkles brightest on the Orient Throne.

XLV. HILL AND DALE — Local Security.

The character of Palestine, a country of lofty hills and intervening valleys, gives point to the legend that "our ancient brethren met on the highest hills and in the lowest dales."

What caution marked the early Craft who met
In Canaan's dale, or Canaan's mountain top!
They sought in nature their security.
And scared the eagle from his rocky crag,
And drove him screaming at their opening lays;
They dazed the darkness with intruding torch,
Whispering their secrets in the chilly cave,
Teaching their lore from all intrusion free;

Thus it befalls, this ancient land is filled
With myths of wondrous meaning, dim and quaint.

XLVI. COFFIN — Mansion of Undisturbed Rest.

There is a serenity pervades this emblem when we view it as a type of undisturbed rest.

No cares shall meet the silent sleeper here ;
No foes annoy ; kind mother earth, wherein
He lies, surrounds him fostering, in her arms ;
She plants fair flowers above him ; storms may beat
Her bosom, opened to the winter's rage,—
He is secure,—she is his sure defense ;
" Clods of the valley shall be sweet to him,
And friends shall come and with him make abode."
Mansion of rest, the stillness and the gloom
Can bring no horrors to thy quiet home !

XLVII. LAMB — Innocence.

The idea of the lamb runs throughout Scriptural and Biblical teaching ; everywhere it is reckoned the emblem of innocence.

Invested thus in garb of innocence,
Robed as the angels are who soar and sing,
We cast our yearning eyes to that sure time
When on Celestial Hills our happy feet
As in the lamb-like days of youth shall stray ;
Oh, freed from all defilements, freed from sin,
And from sin's sequel, children once again,
In knowledge *men*, but in transgression *babes ;*
Lamb of the happy springtime, 'twas from thee
The Sinless took His title,—*Lamb of God!*

XLVIII. GLOBES — Assurance of Tradition.

" Brethren, stand fast, and hold the traditions which ye have been taught." " Withdraw yourselves from every brother that walketh not after the tradition which ye received."

In Oriental memories there dwells
A store of truths, dropped out of history,
But precious none the less ; from sire to son,
From age to age a rich inheritance,
These grains of gold have passed ; in ballads some
Are sung, when village loiterers sit down
To while the evening hour ; in nurse's croon
Above a sleeping babe these myths are heard;
And when a fiery youth goes forth to war
His soul is kindled high with truths like these.

XLIX. OLIVE TREE — Uncounted Liberality.

" Who gives what others may not see,
    Nor counts on favor, fame or praise,
    Shall find his smallest gift outweighs
    The burden of the mighty sea."

The doors of King Solomon's Temple were constructed of olive wood, as being the most elegant wood of the Orient.

To oldest age the OLIVE yields its wealth
In streams of oil ; the oldest gives the most
And gives the best ; tree of a thousand years,
Ragged and gnarled, none worthier than thou
To close the entrance of the Holy Fane;
The worshiper who bowed adoring, read
The lessons of the OLIVE ; — secret grace
That gives divinely ; and unstinted grace
That knows no scant of flow ; and that best grace
That flows still faster, richer to the end.

L. HOPE — Fixed upon God.

The hope that Masonry teaches is *in God.* Seeking hope elsewhere is like " seeking mellow grapes beneath the icy pole, or blooming roses on the cheek of death."

To life's worst labyrinth there is a clew,
A thread of silk that leads the traveler
Through losses, crosses, sicknesses, and deaths,
And gives him entrance to the central place ;
'Tis HOPE, the anchor of the soul,—'tis HOPE,
Steadfast and sure, a very gift of Heaven ;
How could our Temple ever be complete,
So great the work, so feeble we who build,
But for this aid ? the six days' work so long,
The summer's heat so strong, the toil so great !

LI. RAINBOW — Cheerful Hope.

The essential idea of refreshment after labor suggests cheerful hope. " The most Holy One requires a cheerful life." " There is joy in Heaven." " There shall be no more sorrow nor crying." The earth shall no more be destroyed by a flood.

Gorgeous in hue, a painted arch is drawn
Across the sky, late blackened and enraged,
A brilliant monitor, celestial cheer ;
From the bright picture falls the voice divine,—
After the thunder's roar how soft and low !
"The earth no more shall perish by a flood."

Oh, in the quiet of the Masons' Lodge
Where every emblem breathes of harmony,
How fit the iridescent bow to span
Our spangled arch, and bring its comfort home.

LII. RELIEF — The Divine Representative.

In the sublime allegory of "the Judgment Day" the TEACHER clearly expresses the thought that "a distressed human being is the representative of God."

We need not rise above this mundane sphere,
We need not 'neath the briny deep descend
To find the Deity; but on the path
Where blind Bartimeus begs, the Lord is seen;
Upon the fever couch He lies and burns;
He hungers in the dungeon's dreary cell;
He shivers naked, cold and shelterless;
Where sorrow dwells the MASTER too abides;
Builders of "house not made with hands" look out
At every window and behold the Lord!

THE BROKEN COLUMN.

"His WORK was not done, yet his Column is broken";
    Mourn ye and weep, for ye cherished his worth;
Let every tear drop be sympathy's token,—
    Lost to the Brotherhood, lost to the earth.

His WORK had been planned by a WISDOM SUPERNAL;
    Strength had been given him meet for the same;
Down in the midst he is fallen, and vernal
    Leaves fall above him and whisper his fame.

His WORK WAS TO BUILD; on the walls we beheld him,—
    Swiftly and truly they rose 'neath his hand;
Envious death with his Gavel has felled him,
    Plumb line and Trowel are strewn o'er the land.

His WORK thus unfinished to *us* is intrusted;
    MASTER OF MASONS, give strength, we entreat,
Bravely *to work* with these Implements rusted,
    Wisely *to build* till the Temple's complete!

A paraphrase of the well known expression found in the opening line.

THE ETERNITY OF THE ORDER.

ONO.

In the eleventh chapter of Nehemiah, the expression, "Ono, the valley of Craftsmen," occurs.

Where is the true heart's MOTHER LODGE?
　　Is't where, perchance, he earliest heard
The frightful voice, from rocky ledge,
　　Told of a horrid deed of blood?
Is't where his vision earliest saw
　　And hands enclasped that GOLDEN THING,
The symbol crowned, the wondrous LAW,
　　Noblest creation of our King?

No; though in fancy he may turn,
　　In pleasing reminiscence back,
As happy hearts at times will yearn
　　To tread again youth's flowery track,—
The true heart's MOTHER LODGE is found
　　Where truest, fondest hearts conspire
To draw love's deathless chain around,
　　And kindle up love's deathless fire.

Methinks that *here*, dear Friends, must be
　　ONO, the Craftsmen's happy VALE;
And *you*, true Laborer, brave and free,
　　The MASTER in the peaceful dale!
So let me fancy, and when bowed
　　In daily adorations due,
I will entreat the Masons' God
　　To bless the Craftsmen here, and *you!*

THE MASTER COMETH.

When the GREAT MASTER comes to view his own,
Reclaim his Gavel, and resume his Throne;
When through the Temple chambers rings the word
That Hiram and his willing Builders heard;
What will he find? in all this Brotherhood,
Where thousands stand, where myriads have stood,
What will he find?

By many a grave, the acacia boughs beneath,
He will detect the tokens of our faith;
The shining marble, and the humble stone,
Will the dead Mason's trust in triumph own.
The pointed Star, the Compass, Line and Square,
The acacia sprig will join in glory there;
These will he find!

By many a happy fireside, he'll see
And bless the fruits of Masons' charity:
The orphan's tear to merry laughter turned;
The widow's heart its cheerfulness has learned;
Blest households, round which groups of angels stand
And guard unceasingly the cherished band;
These will he find!

In many a Lodge, our MASTER's guest will find
The generous hand, large heart and cultured mind,
Engaged in toil, not upon walls of stone,
But squaring *hearts* for heavenly walls alone;
Builders of house eternal, mystic Craft,
Whose work is worthy, Ashlar, Keystone, Shaft;
These will he find!

Of every tongue on earth's extended bound,
In every land our Brotherhood is found;
Rising to *labor* with the awakening East,
Sinking to *slumber* with the darkening West;
Leading our sons as we ourselves were led;
Laying in honored graves our quiet dead;
These will he find!

Brothers! if here to-night our Chief were found,—
If now, at yonder door, were heard the sound,—
If, in the East, in Oriental hue,
Grand Master Solomon should meet the view,—
What welcomes, loud and loyal, should he have,
Absent and mourned so long in Sion's grave?
Would it were so; would it were mine to say,
"Behold, O King, thy Brethren! Day by day
Through countless years, our sires blew up the flame
Of love fraternal for thy honored name!
And we, obedient sons, have fanned the light,
And done the labor as we do to-night.

"Look 'round thee, Master! is there aught amiss?
Whence this mysterious image, this and this?
Who cast yon pillar with consummate cap?
Suggests this mournful emblem what mishap?
Look overhead! what golden arc is there,
Before which strong men bow as if in prayer?
What page is that, that lends unerring rays
To Mason groups who kneel and, reverent, gaze?"

*   *   *   *   *

Brothers, we may not see him, but we'll bind
The tie he gave us with unfailing mind;
His lessons, fraught with wisdom, we'll revere,
And keep his secrets with unwearied care;
The poor and sorrowing over land and sea,
To willing ears shall make their piteous plea;
The Holy Name we'll reverence and trust,
High over all, the Gracious and the Just;
And when death's Gavel falls and we must go,
This epitaph shall speak the general woe:—

"Honored and blest, his heart was given
To feel for sorrow and to aid;
On earth he made the unhappy glad,
His coming gives a joy to Heaven!"

A tradition among Oriental Masons affirms that the mighty *Suleiman Ben-Daoud* (Solomon, son of David), the Founder and Chief of Freemasonry, who deceased B.C. 975, and was buried upon Mount Sion, at Jerusalem, *will return again* to the earth in the last days, and inspect the work of the world-wide Brotherhood which he founded. Then he will pass upon the perjured and unfaithful. Then he will restore to the worthy the secrets forfeited by rebellious Craftsmen during the erection of his Temple upon Moriah.

LAST WORDS OF THE BUILDER KING.

'Twas in the years of long ago
The mighty task was done,
The waiting Craft in silence bow
And list to Solomon:

"Oh, bind the tie, Freemasons dear,
Where'er your feet may rove,
With *gifts* the empty hand to cheer,
The wounded heart with *love!*

133

"Whatever lands your skill reward
  With Level, Plumb and Square,
Oh, teach the Golden Rule of God,
  And be Freemasons there.

"The bread, the wine of quick relief,
  Have ready in your hand;
For tear and sigh of brother-grief
  Fulfill my last command.

"And though from Sion you depart,
  Still do your Master's will,
That you may build, with hand and heart,
  Upon the heavenly hill!"

When the Temple was finished, the monarch called the Craft together in the ample inclosure, and, standing between the glittering shafts J. and B., he exhorted them, as his last injunctions, to perfect themselves upon the sublime principles of *Brotherly Love* and *Relief*. The duty of Relief he applied to the column on his *right*, that of Brotherly Love to the column on his *left*.

THE EAST.

Yes, in yon world of perfect light,
  The fettered soul is now released;
No higher, farther wings its flight,
  Brought to the glories *of the East*.

There is the long-sought boon divine,
  'Tis worthy of the painful quest;
When evening shades of life decline,
  The day is dawning *in the East*.

Who feels this truth in fervent heart,
  May know his last hours are his best;
How joyful from *the West* to part,
  When calls the Master *from the East*.

Join hearts and hands in union dear,—
  Jesus has sanctified the test;
Life's chain is only broken here
  To join forever *in the East*.

Mourners, your tears with gladness blend!
  Joy, Brothers, joy, our faith's confessed!
The grave will yield our parted friend,
  When we with him *approach the East*.

LINGERING NOTES.

Lingering notes the echoes stir,
  Soft and sweet, these walls along;
Softly, sweetly they concur
  In the pleasant tide of song;
Night birds cease their plaintive lays
Listening to the hymn of praise.

Angels gliding through the air,
  On celestial mission bent,
Pause, the sacred hymn to hear,
  Fold their wings in soft content,
Join their notes divine to these,
Hymning Masons' mysteries.

Now the solitary room,
  Peopled with a countless throng,—
Now the stillness and the gloom
  Kindled with the tide of song,
Filling our delighted ears —
Music of three thousand years !

Every Emblem pictured there,
  On the ceiling, wall or floor,
GAVEL, TROWEL, APRON, SQUARE,
  COLUMN rent or open DOOR,
Blends a light and yields a tongue,
To this softly lingering song.

Now the anthem dies away;
  One by one the voices cease;
Birds resume their wonted lay;
  Angels on their mission press;
But the latest note that moves
In the mystic song is LOVE'S !

None of the ancient Masonic legends are more graceful, or convey a more charmingly esoteric meaning, than that which assures us there is for an hour after the Brethren disperse from their Lodge room a *mysterious echo of sounds*, which may be heard there, weird, lingering, fraternal in tone, made up, in fact, of all the brotherly expressions and divine acknowledgments that have passed about the group through the entire convocation! It is affirmed by those who have the gift to understand it, to be charming beyond expression, and that the last note, as it dies away upon the ear, is the echo of that spirit which filled the soul of our Patron Saint, the Evangelist John — " Love ! "

KING SOLOMON'S FAREWELL.

King Solomon sat in his ivory chair,
His chair on a platform high,
And his words addressed,
Through the listening West,
To a Band of Brothers nigh;
Through the West and South,
His words of truth,
To a Band of Brothers nigh.

"Ye Builders, go! ye have done your work—
The *Capstone* standeth sure;
From the lowermost block
To the loftiest rock,
The *Fabric* is secure;
From the Arch's Swell,
To the Pinnacle,
The *Fabric* is secure.

"Go, crowned with fame! old time will pass,
And many a change will bring,
But the *Deed* you've done,
The circling sun
Through every land will sing;
The moon and stars,
While earth endures,
Through every land will sing.

"Go build like this! from the quarries vast,
The precious stones reveal;
There's many a block
In the matrice rock,
Will honor your fabrics well;
There's many a beam,
By the mountain stream,
Will honor your fabrics well.

"Go build like this! strike off with skill,
Each superfluity;
With critic eye
Each fault espy,
Be *zealous, fervent, free.*
By the perfect *Square,*
Your work prepare,—
Be *zealous, fervent, free.*

"Go build like this! to a fitting place
Bring up the *Ashlars* true;
On the Trestleboard
Of your Master's *Lord,*
The *Grand Intention* view;
In each mystic line
Of the vast *Design,*
The *Grand Intention* view.

"Go build like this! and when exact,
The joinings scarce appear,
With the Trowel's aid,
Such cement spread,
As time can never wear;
Lay thickly round,
Such wise compound,
As time can never wear.

"Go, Brothers! thus enjoined, farewell!
Spread o'er the darkened West;
Illume each clime,
With *Art* sublime
The noblest truths attest;
Be *Masters* now,
And as you go,
The noblest truths attest!"

THE INVISIBLE WORKMEN.

And who are these, like shadows thin,
Heaving vast hammers without din,
Splitting in fragments huge the ledge;
Noiseless, with crowbar and with wedge,
In silence plying chisel's edge!

They bear the marks of steel and fire;
Upon each brow the impress dire
Of sin, and shame, and penalty,
As driven from the upper sky,
And doomed in God's rebuke to sigh.

It is the belief of the common people in the East, that the immense blocks seen in the ruined edifices at Baalbec, Gebal, Jerusalem, and elsewhere, were taken from the quarry, shaped, and set in place by the INVISIBLE ONES summoned through the influence of King Solomon's device (the five-pointed star) from the depths, and made thus to serve his irresistible will. Some of these ashlars weigh exceeding eight hundred tons.

THE VISIT OF KING SOLOMON

A TWENTY-FOURTH JUNE IDYL.

"Now the sun is burning dim, and the world is but a glim,
    And the race of man is loitering to its close,"
Quoth a phantom that I saw, weird and horrible with awe,
    In a vision that my very marrow froze.
          'Twas the phantom of the son
          Of King David, SOLOMON!

On the twenty-fourth of June, at the rising of the moon,
    In the year of Jesus eighteen seventy-five,
I was scurrying home at night, while the starry host was bright,
    Straight and sober, yes, as any man alive;
          I was hurrying home alone,
          When I met King SOLOMON!

All was silent save the frogs, hiccoughing among the bogs,
    And the katydids a-soloing through the trees;
When this fearful thing I saw, weird and terrible with awe,
    Even to tell it doth my very marrow freeze;
          'Twas the phantom of the son
          Of King David, SOLOMON!

First I took it for the devil, but I spied the Mason's gavel
    Held aloft, as Masters hold it in the East;
And the phantom let it fall, as we do the setting maul,
    With a clatter that the frogs their noises ceased.
          Such a *vim* have mortals none
          As Grand Master SOLOMON!

On his left hand and his right were his Wardens clothed in white,
    As we see in every mystic gathering;
Each a proper badge did wear, each displayed the silver Square,
    So I knew them,— Widow's Son and Hiram King;
          Hiram King and Widow's Son
          Walking with King SOLOMON!

"Why this meeting, I invoke?" Then the Prince of Masons spoke,
    "I have broken, I have broken death's repose,
For the sun is burning dim, and the world is but a glim,
    And the race of man is loitering to its close."
          Then a melancholy groan
          Shook the friends of SOLOMON.

"'Tis almost three thousand years since I left in doubts and fears,
    My great Brotherhood beneath Moriah's dome,
And I gave the working band, as my very last command,
    Not to alter nor to falter till I come;
        Now to judge them on my throne
        I will sit," said SOLOMON.

" Every tower and temple grand, built by their instructed hand,
    Every dwelling that displays my mystic seal,
Soon must topple to the ground, for the end of earth is found.
    And the cornerstone its secrets must reveal;
        Underneath the cornerstone
        Treasure's hid," quoth SOLOMON.

"When I left the weeping Craft, weeping round my Broken Shaft,
    I adjured them by this symbol *to be true!*"
Then the Monarch showed a *Name*, I had bowed before the same,
    Even when the mystic Winding Stairs I knew,
        " Bright as the meridian sun
        Is this name," quoth SOLOMON !

"*And they have been,*" I declared, while the attendant Wardens stared,
    " Yes, they have been faithful, earnest, and sincere !
Come, Grand Master, come, and see our world-wide Fraternity;
    This St. John's night, busy, closing up the year !"
        Then a smile, all sunny, shone,
        On the lips of SOLOMON !

How 'twas done I cannot say, but we scurried swift away,
    And we rattled round and round the world that night.
Where the Lodges were at work, Christian, Israelite, and Turk,
    Gavels sounding, Jewels gleaming, Tapers bright;
        Never Mason's road was run
        Like my trip with SOLOMON !

Many a query made the King of each mystic gathering,
    Many an answer prompt and honest they returned,
As the Craftsmen told of good they had done through Brotherhood
    And the plaudits of their first Grand Master earned;
        And I noticed, one by one,
        What they said to SOLOMON.

But as we went I said, " Both the living and the dead,
    Both the joyous and the sorrowing of our Band
Are the same to us in love, for we learn of God above,
    That we all shall meet again in Heavenly Land

139

Far beyond the glowing sun,"—
Were my words to SOLOMON.

But the moon had left the night; in the East a ruddy light
    Had awaked the early birds to morning strain;
And the Monarch disappeared, as my homeward course I steered.
    And I never met the Mason King again;
        But I've truly made it known
        What was said by SOLOMON.

SOWING OF THE SEED,

He that hath ears to hear,
    May listen now,
While he shall hear, in mystic words indeed,
Of a good husbandman who took his seed
    And went to sow.

Some by *the wayside* fell,
    On breezes borne;
The fowls of air flew down, a greedy train,
And snatched with hasty appetite the grain,
    Till all was gone.

Some fell upon *the rock ;*
    And greenly soon
They sprouted as for harvest, strong and fair;
But when the summer sun shone hotly there,
    They wilted down.

Some fell among *the thorns,*—
    A fertile soil,—
But ere the grain could raise its timid head,
Luxuriantly the accursèd plants o'erspread,
    And choked them all.

But some in *the good ground,*—
    God's precious mould,—
Where sun, breeze, dew and showers apportioned well;
And in the harvest, smiling swains could tell
    THEIR HUNDRED FOLD !

We are exhorted, in that Volume about which an OBLONG SQUARE is formed in the Masonic Lodge, " to sow beside all waters." In a Lodge of Freemasons, no more than in any other society, is there perfect sameness in sentiment and choice. While similarity in physical, mental and moral qualifications is needful in the construction of our social edifice, there are diversities of character sufficiently marked among us to justify the poet in offering the above paraphrase of Luke viii, 5-8.

THE THREE KNOCKS.

The Day has come:
Prophets and seers foretold it,— greatest day;
All secrets of this life to be exposed,
All prisoners and slaves to be released,
All darkness banished and all discord healed,—
Old time is ripe for this, and earth and Heaven
Wait with expectant ear and eye the call.

ONE!

A sigh, as from a sleeping host, begins to stir the air;
A voice from an awakening band whose numbers none compare;
The earth is to its center stirred, and on their crumbling base,
Old monuments are toppling down, in ruin and disgrace.

Upon the lower sky a gleam is reddening up the East,
As if the sun, ere early morn, would to his journey haste;
Strange faces, wondrous sweet, like those for which our torn hearts yearn,
Peer out, benignantly, from clouds that in the radiance burn.

In Mason Lodges, here and there, where taper light still burns,
Lo, every Brother from the open page of Scripture turns!
He turns, he looks beyond the East, beyond the Master's chair,
And wonders at the kindling blaze that stains the Orient there.

The Master drops his gavel now,— the OMNIPOTENT is heard;
The Tyler leaves his trust uncalled, resigns his useless sword;
The Scribe shuts up his volume, for the penman's work is done;
And all may see Eternity's great promised morn's begun.

TWO!

Now 'neath the heaving hillocks life descends;
    Now bone to bone conjoins, the sinews knit;
The coursing blood its vermeil brightness lends;
    The heart in rapture hastes again to beat;
Death and the worm are vanquished, and the grave,
    Stripped of its horrors, seemeth but a bed
Where tired ones come and sweet reposings have,
    And rise and go when eastern skies are red.

The Master joins his Craftsmen, and they link
    Their trusty hands in friendship's farewell chain;

As deeming, while they stand upon the brink
    Of Fate, that *Brethren faithful should remain;*
Nearer and nearer yet they gather in,
    And one, a gray-haired veteran, holds up
A green sprig gathered from an aged pine,
    Worn as memorial of Masons' hope.

What comfort now, that emblem of their faith!
    They pass it round, they press it to the lip;
Its sacred hue has often mocked at death,
    And lent new meaning to the Masons' grip.
Nearer and nearer yet, till foot to foot,
    And breast to breast, the moral builders stand,
While roar the unfettered elements without,
    And shudderings disturb the solid land.

Now on the left there starts from out the wall
    A *shadowy hand.* With occult character,
In light ineffable it fills the hall,
    Flashing till human vision scarce can bear.
It writes,— and well the joyful group can read:
    " You did it to the poor and the distressed;
Heaven's records show the generous word and deed,—
    Enter, ye faithful, to the promised REST ! "

THREE !

The drama ends,— the dead cast off their shrouds,
    And, all erect, in solemn awe await
The Message; earth in every ear attends,
    And Heaven is hushed while the Grand Master speaks.

'Tis not for man to look within the skies;
    Let pen prophetic all these words record:
"I saw the dead, both small and great, arise,
    And stand before the judgment seat of God;—

"I saw the grave deliver up its dead;
    I saw, amazed, the once remorseless sea,
The very dust the winged winds had spread,
    Collect and render up, all tenderly; —

"I heard one say, within the golden gate,
    The happy, happy dead, forever blest,
Who died in Jesus,— for their works do wait,
    And follow them to their eternal rest; —

"I heard one say, Depart, ye accursed, far
From Love Divine, and Light, and Heaven, depart;
The sick, the poor, the friendless prisoner,
Plead in my name, but vainly, to your heart; —

"I heard a multitude in sweetest frame,
Singing and harping to the All-Gracious God,
Who *is*, and *was*, and *will be*, aye, the same,
And never fails to man his plighted word!"

And reading this from the inspired hand,
May we not humbly hope, we Masons free,
That when before the Overseer we stand,
He will recall our deeds of charity?

Is it not written, from the widow's eye
We've wiped sad tears, — the fatherless have smiled, —
The homeless through our doors passed joyously, —
The hungry soul has been refreshed and filled?

We feel death's influence nearing, day by day;
In mother earth our hands must soon be stilled;
The evening shades to us seem cold and gray;
The night dews fall, our aching limbs are chilled.

Then let us hope, and hoping, labor yet,
Till the dread SIGNAL fall, and we shall rise;
Ample our wages, and divinely set,
In rest and peace and bliss beyond the skies!

Brother the Reverend John Newland Maffit, in a masterly discourse upon Freemasonry delivered at St. Louis, Mo., twenty-five years since, among various figures of surpassing elegance, describes the Omnipotent Judge calling up the "sheeted dead" from their places of sepulture on the Resurrection Day, *by the three symbolical knocks of Freemasonry*, This is in allusion to one of the oldest traditions of the Order, more fully expressed in the lines above.

VERDANT, FRAGRANT, ENDURING.

GREEN, but far greener is the FAITH
That gives us victory over death.
FRAGRANT, more fragrant far the HOPE
That buoys our dying spirits up.
ENDURING, but the CHARITY
That Masons teach will never die.

THE WISE CHOICE OF SOLOMON.

"In Gibeon the LORD appeared to Solomon in a dream by night; and God said, Ask what I shall give thee. And Solomon said, Give Thy servant an understanding heart to judge Thy people, that I may discern between good and bad."

When in the dreams of night he lay,
 Fancy led through earth and air,
Whispered from the heavenly way,
 The voice of promise met his ear;
Fancy ceased his pulse to thrill,—
 Gathered home each earnest thought,—
And his very heart was still
 Awhile the gracious words he caught:

"Ask me whatsoe'er thou wilt,
 Fame, or wealth, or royal power,—
Ask me, ask me, and thou shalt
 Such favors have as none before!"
Silence through the midnight air,—
 Silence in the thoughtful breast,—
What of all that's bright and fair,
 Appeared to youth and hope the best?

'Twas no feeble tongue replied,
 While in awe his pulses stood,—
"Wealth and riches be denied,
 But give me WISDOM, voice of God!
Give me WISDOM in the sight
 Of the people Thou dost know!
Give me OF THYSELF THE LIGHT,
 And all the rest I will forego!"

Thus, oh, Lord, in visions fair,
 When we hear Thy promise-voice,
Thus, like him, will we declare,
 That WISDOM is our dearest choice!
Light of Heaven! ah, priceless boon,
 Guiding o'er the troubled way,
What is all an earthly sun
 To His celestial, chosen ray!

Wisdom hath her dwelling reared,—
 Lo, the mystic pillars seven!

Wisdom for her guests hath cared,
    And meat, and bread, and wine hath given;
Turn we not, while round us cry
    Tongues that speak her mystic word;
They that scorn her voice shall die,
    But whoso hear are friends of GOD.

HARD SERVICE, GOOD WAGES.

Bow the back, ye Brothers dear !—
Pinch the flesh, the work's severe !
Come, while every workman sleeps,
View the City ! heaps on heaps !
See the Temple desolate !
Lo ! the burnt and shattered Gate.
To repair it is your wish ?—
Bow the back ! and pinch the flesh !

Bow the back ! — 'tis hopeful toil ;
Yours the Corn and Wine and Oil,
Emblems of reward, shall be,
Plenty, Peace, and Unity !
Pinch the flesh ! — not long you wait !—
Standing in the Golden Gate,
Lo ! your Lord ! and in his hand
Wages rich at your command !

Cheer to those who, long and late,
Meet and toil at Sion's Gate !
Cheer and courage ! — See ! on high
Beams the bright, ALL-SEEING EYE !
See ! the work goes bravely on ; —
Wall and Gate and Tower are won !
Grasp the Trowel ! — Wield the Sword !—
Cheer ! — And trust in Sion's Lord !

By the Hieroglyphics ten,—
Wisdom, Strength and Beauty's plan ; —
By the mystic Features seven,—
Surely by the MASTER given ;
By the covenant-woven faith,
Strong in life and strong in death ; —
Every hope of foemen crush !
Bow the back ! and pinch the flesh !

THE CULLING OF THE QUARRY

A POEM IN FOUR PARTS.

I. CULLING THE ASHLAR.

The Master to the Quarry came ;
The glittering Square bespoke his rank ;
An aged man — Phœnicia's swarthy race
Claimed him of birth ; his Apron, deftly turned,
Told of the mystic Ladder, up whose rounds
He had by faithful vigilance ascended

His thoughtful eye scanned all the busy scene ;
A thousand hammers ringing,
Ten thousand Craftsmen bringing
The Ashlars from their native bed
Where they had lain, deep hidden since creation,
To be inspected, trimmed, and shaped by rule,
And rendered worthy of the Sacred Fane.

Ah, faithful laborers ! no hand was stayed —
Yet sometimes upward glanced an eye,
Hoping to see the sun pause in the South ;
And sometimes stayed an ear to catch the sound
So longed-for, that would mark Refreshment Hour.
The Master's Gavel signaled a command.
Then every hand was stayed, and every ear
Opened to learn his will and pleasure.

  " Craftsmen, ho,
A Block, a perfect Stone, an Ashlar true,
To grace the Temple wall ! "
  Quickly the word
Passed through the quarries and the Warden brought
An Ashlar, laid it at the Master's feet,
And waited silently his bidding ; long
And earnestly the venerable man
Gazed on the polished stone,
As if to penetrate it to the core.
He sternly tried the angles, gauged the sides,
With measured steps *thrice round it walked*,
Then at low breath, as in a muse, he said :—
" This is such work as our Grand Master loves
The ages will not see this crumble ;

The morning rays, peeping o'er Olivet,
Will give it wondrous beauty, and the moon
Will kiss its pearly face with daintiest beams ;
Bear it, Apprentices, away, away
Up to the TEMPLE ?" Then loudly sung
The bearers, as they journeyed Sion-ward.

An Ashlar for the wall !
Sing praise, ye Masons all !
Give honor to the bright and perfect stone ;
A polished block and true,
Right worthy of the view
Of the CELESTIAL MASTER from his Throne.

The gnawing tooth of time,
The lightning flash sublime,
The penetrating frost, shall have no power,
Nor earthquake's mightiest shock,
To harm this chosen rock ;—
Of Wisdom, Strength and Beauty 'tis the dower.

We bear it proudly home —
Ye Masters, lo, we come !
Prepare the cement for this chosen block ;
Have by your Trowels bright,
And lay the Ashlar right,
In loving company with kindred rock.

Thus may the walls ascend,
And nearer, nearer tend
Unto that high Celestial Canopy,
Where, toil and travel ceased,
Beyond the gleaming EAST,
The UNIVERSAL BUILDER we may see !

II. CULLING THE PERFECT SQUARE.

Again unto the Quarry came
The Master ; for Phœnician hands had reared
The Temple walls ; the cedar beams beneath
The lofty roof high span the sacred spot;
And golden spires reflect the early rays
Flashing from Moab's hills.

For seven years
These zealous Builders had bestowed their strength,
While Wisdom planned and beauty graced their work.
For seven years, debarred the joys of home,
Strangers and pilgrims ; weeks sped wearily,
And Sabbath hours dragged cheerless ; seven years
To wrest th' unwilling blocks from cryptic bed,
To fell the groaning cedars on the heights,
To guide the flotes across the stormy wave,
And bow the back beneath oppressive loads

Such, oh ye moral Builders, who do ply
Your easy tasks on cushioned seats, such was
The apprenticeship of men in olden time !
What wonder Hiram's works do live forever ?

The Master's Gavel signaled a command ;
Then every hand was stayed, and every ear
Opened to learn his will and pleasure.

    " Craftsmen, ho,
A Square, a perfect Square, of firmest stone,
To grace the checkered pavement."
    Swift the word
Was passed from Warden unto Warden, through
The Lodges of the Fellowcrafts, and soon
Twelve stalwart men brought up a marble block
And proudly laid it at the Master's feet.

It was a milk-white stone, whose polished face
Reflected all the scene — the scaffolding,
The hammers, swung by brawny arms, the pick,
The keen-edged chisel, and that aged Man,
Whose glittering Square bespoke his rank.

        Within
Its glassy depths he peered, as though to read
The future ; had a prescience then been given,
What mourning through the ages had been spared !
Then had the Acacia's glory ne'er been shorn,
Nor Craftsmen ever blushed their fellows' sin !
He sternly tried the angles, gauged the sides,
With measured steps thrice 'round and 'round it walked ;
Then in commanding tones he said :

"Bear it, Apprentices, away, away,
Up to the TEMPLE!" Then loudly sung
The bearers as they journeyed Sionward :

Through the northern Gate we bear,
Joyfully the Perfect Square ;
Craftsmen, clear the way,
While the Checkered Pave we lay.
Where the Father stayed the knife
O'er the darling of his life;*
Be this marble laid,
Where the Avenger's Sword was stayed.†

O'er this consecrated stone
As a thousand years shall run
Their appointed ways,
Prophets, Kings and Priests shall trace.

Here the victim's blood shall flow
For a heritage of woe ;
Here in latest time,
ONE shall stand with power sublime.

Let the sunshine and the air
Warm and grace the Perfect Square ;
Craftsmen, clear the way,
While the Checkered Pave we lay.

III. CULLING THE COLUMN.

The Master to the Quarry came ;
The Temple walls are up, the Pavement laid,
The inclosing Courts spread broadly round,
The gilded Pinnacles displayed,
And Kedron's brook in song beneath
Murmurs the Temple's praise.

The Master comes, but not alone ;
Beside him walks his King ;
Monarch of wave-girt Tyre's Isle ;
The *Sea King*, whose broad sails
Whiten a hundred coasts ;
The *Mason King* whose wondrous skill has reared
The palaces renowned of the world's kings.

*Genesis xxii, 10–13.   † II Samuel xxiv, 16.

With bended knee and downcast eye
The Quarrymen in worship pause,
The echoes dying into silence.

The Master's Gavel then implies command,
And every form erect, and every eye
Intent, the laborers wait to hear
Once more his will and pleasure.

      "Craftsmen, ho !
A Block, a Stone of value —
One of ten thousand ! search the quarries through ;
'Tis for a Column, beautiful and true !
Search in the depths where light
Has never penetrated ;
Look for an Ashlar in whose heart is found
A figure polished, elegant and round,
Left on Creation's morn to serve
And glorify the Temple of the Lord !
Look North, look South, look East, look West,
Take no refreshment, seek no rest ;
Somewhere within the mine exists this stone,
Seek it and find it ere the sun goes down ! "

Quick and successful was the quest ;
Deep in the caverns had a veteran seen
That very morning such an Ashlar ;
Answering the might of nine score stalwart arms
It came to light, and lo, a perfect Block !
Divested of excrescences it stood
As the Creator made it,
Beautiful, strong and good.

The Master scanned it.   Seven times around
The glorious shaft he journeyed ;
With steady hand and eye applied
The line, the compass, and the unerring Square,
Then to the musing King he solemn said :
" This, Sire, will stand the ravages of time ;
The gnawing tooth of frost will vainly bite
To roughen its glossy face, nor till the foeman's wrath
Shall tread down Sion will it be o'erthrown ! "

Smiling the King responded ; then the arms
Of brawny Craftsmen swung the heavy shaft

Aloft, and bore it at good speed
Up to the Temple ; singing as they went
A fitting chorus :

Room for *the polished Shaft !*
Give way, ye Mason craft —
A fitting site for nature's gem prepare ;
Give it an eastern base,
That it may earliest grace
The Orient sun upon his golden car.

Room for *the Column bright,*
Rescued from nature's night,
Snatched from the cavern's loneliness and gloom ;
And let it signal here,
Through many and many a year,
To call the wandering worshipers all home.

Room for *the Pillar true ;*
How grandly on the view,
How like a speaking truth our treasure stands !
Never till time shall end
From rectitude to bend,
But ever pointing to the heavenly lands.

Alas, that we decay
And die from day to day,
While things inanimate thus grandly live !
Room for the polished Shaft !
Give way ye Mason craft,
And fitting site for Nature's treasure give.

IV. CULLING THE CAP STONE.

The Master to the Quarry came once more,
Two Mason kings attending — one of Tyre,
Pillar of strength through all the seven years' toil,
Whose fourscore thousands had the sacred Mount
With unexampled glory crowned ;
And one, great David's greater progeny.
The wise, the matchless SOLOMON,
The world-renowned, favorite of God and man,
For whom these thousands and this mystic plan.

Proudly between, the aged Master walked,
And all who saw the Architect declared :
" This is his triumph day, his crowning day,
To-day he seeks the cap stone ! "
            It was so —
Block upon block the walls had risen up,
North, South, East, West, the roof inclosing in,
And each in ghostly silence to its place;
Pillars and porch colossal faced the East;
The Checkered Pavement showed its mystic face.

Rich curtains veiled the portals of the Fane;
The glittering rays of diamonds displayed
Device of cherubim and Judah's palm
Graven on every wall;— the work was done;
Moriah from her deepest base to crown,
Was hidden 'neath this monument of God.

On bended knees the Quarrymen are grouped
Around the three Grand Masters, quick to hear
The final order; down — once, twice and thrice,
The Gavel falls upon a neighboring stone
And every ear intent, they cheerful wait
To hear the will and pleasure.

           " Craftsmen, ho !
A stone of matchless worth !
From deepest crypt bring forth the block to light,
A Cope Stone broad and beautiful and bright;
Ye veterans, seek it, ye can best attest
What prize of Nature crowns our Temple best ! "

'Twas found, 'twas wrought, and in an after day
(He whom they loved had passed from life away)
The exulting thousands looked aloft and sighed
To see his Signet on the stone; but now they sing:

    Hail, favorite of the skies,
    Hail, Sovereign great and wise,
Whose God hath answered thee in smoke and flame —
    This day the Scribe hath penned
    A record that shall lend
Thee and thy works to everlasting fame !

Hail, Hiram, builder king—
The cedars thou did'st bring
In princely state from snowy Lebanon,
Shall speak thy royal bloom
In beauty and perfume,
While vernal leaf shall catch the kindling sun!

Hail, thou departed one,
The loving WIDOW'S SON,
In life beloved and best beloved in death—
This Temple, through all time,
Shall speak in notes sublime
Thy *skill* unequaled and unshaken *faith.*

Hail to the finished Fane!
All hail, again, again—
Thy form magnificent our eye doth see,
Midst streaming fire and cloud
That vainly would enshroud
Its glories from th' Omniscient Deity!

Hail the MARK MASTER'S SIGN!
How from those letters shine
The mystic meaning that inspires the heart!
They speak of laboring days,
Of blessed rest and peace—
They prompt us each to choose the better part!

Jerusalem, farewell!
Fond memories shall tell
How we have builded, how fraternized here;
The might of Israel's God
Spread o'er thy hills abroad
To crown thee with all glory, year by year!

Hail now our long-hoped home!
Land of our birth, we come;
Ah, yearned for, prayed for, long and ardently!
Upon thy children now
A mother's gifts bestow,
In life a blessing and in death a sigh!

THE TEMPLE.

No human wisdom framed our halls,
No bodily sweat bedews our walls ;
The utmost ken of mortal eye
Fails its proportions to espy ;
Nor is it for a mortal's ear
Its songs at eve and morn to hear.

Our Temple crowns no earthly hill ;
The Turk profanes Mount Sion still ;
Siloam pours her hallowed stream
For those who spurn the sacred NAME ;
Yet fixed on an unshaken base
Is seen our Temple's resting place.

Unnumbered hearts and hopes prolong
The cadence of our votive song ;
The savor of our sacrifice
Ascends and gladdens up the skies,
Where BUILDERS, met from many lands,
Rear up "the House not made with hands !"

We would record some fitting phrase
Of those sublime, those mystic lays ;
Some names of the unnumbered host
Else 'neath the moss of ages lost ;
One episode in all those cares
Whose story marks three thousand years.

AUTHOR OF WISDOM, make us wise
To apprehend these Mysteries !
AUTHOR OF STRENGTH, the power impart
To build and cement from the heart !
AUTHOR OF BEAUTY, lend us grace,
The hue to paint, the line to trace !

The stones of the foundation
    In the Holy Mountain lie,
Brought from the sacred quarries
    By the hand of Deity ;
Each block "the perfect angle"
    Fulfills and gratifies,
And rests upon the level
    Acknowledged in the skies.

Each on its broadside graven
    Displays some mighty name ;
'Tis daily called in Heaven
    That roll of deathless fame ;
All ages, lands have yielded
    Their honored names to prop —
A glorious substructure —
    And bear our Temple up.

In such a sacred place,
On such a solid base,
Built on the pattern of the PLAN DIVINE,
    With time-defying walls,
    With love-o'erflowing halls,
Behold our Temple and come view our Shrine !

The mind would faint and fail
The multitudes to tell,
Of all the Ashlars that are here inwrought ;
    They're culled from every clime,
    Through long-revolving time,
And each bears token of the MASTER-THOUGHT.

Each bears the impress of MAN —
Such was the wondrous PLAN —
Of man in body, mind, and heart complete ;
    Each fills a stated place
    Of Wisdom, Strength or Grace,
By the GRAND MASTER designate and meet.

Many years since, the author projected a poem which, under the title, " The Nails of the Temple," should designate the names and services of those great men of the past and present generations to whose labor and sacrifices the Masonic Institution is chiefly indebted for its present high position in this country. These stanzas are but the opening of the design, which now, it is likely, will never be resumed.

HOURS OF PRAISE.

Morn, the morn, sweet morn is springing ;
    In the East his sign appears ;
Dews, and songs, and fragrance flinging
    Down the new robe nature wears.
Forth from slumber, forth and meet him !
    Who so dead to love and light ?
Forth, and as you stand to greet him,
    Praise to HIM who giveth night.

Noon, the noon, high noon is glowing;
   In the South rich glories burn ;
Beams intense from Heaven are flowing;
   Mortal eye must droop and turn.
Forth and meet him ! while the chorus
   Of the groves is nowhere heard,
Kneel to HIM who bendeth o'er us —
   Praise with heart and willing word.

Eve, the eve, still eve is weeping,
   In the West she dies away ;
Every wingèd one is sleeping —
   They've no life but open day.
Forth and meet her ! lo, she lends us
   Thrice ten thousand brilliants high !
Glory to HIS name who sends us
   Such night jewels from the sky.

Death, pale death, to all is certain ;
   From the grave his voice comes up —
" Fearless, raise my gloomy curtain —
   Find within eternal hope ";
Forth and meet HIM, ye whose duty
   To the LORD OF LIFE is given ;
HE will clothe death's garb with beauty —
   HE will give a path to Heaven.

THE REDDENING IN THE EAST.

Hopeful we look for the long-promised dawning,
Yearn for the light and the songs of the morning;
See how the shades pass ! the day is begun;
God soon will smile on the Land of the Sun.
Let the harp, let the trumpet make haste and rejoice;
Stand, O ye people, and join every voice !
Wake, holy mountains ! sing, tuneful fountains !
God soon will smile on the Land of the Sun !

God frowned on Judah,— His mercies withholding,—
Darkness He sent, all her glories enfolding,—
Blasting and blight on her meadows came down,
Olive and vine wilted under His frown.
But the curse is removed, the light is restored;
Stand, O ye people, give praise to the Lord !

THE SELF-EXAMINATION.

When placed before the throne,
Beyond the Orient sun,
Where the SUPREME GRAND MASTER sits as judge,
What record shall we show
Of all our works below,
We who have labored in the earthly Lodge?

Through life's hard travel come,—
It was our earthly doom,—
Through sin and sorrow suffering many a wrong,
When bowed in death at last,
And 'neath the trumpet's blast,
We've risen with th' innumerable throng; —

What answer shall we make?
Oh, brothers, for His sake,
Who died on Calvary to redeem us all,
Let's ponder while we may,
The questions of that day,
And have *the answer* ready for *the call.*

And this our answer be: —
"We strove to follow THEE,
In teaching truth and lessening human woe;
And scanty though our *deed*,
We ask Thee, Lord, to heed
Not what *we've done*, but what *we tried* to do."

Brothers, how brief is time!
But there's a world sublime
Eternal, blest, ineffably sincere;
And in this mystic place,
We can with surety trace,
His gracious purpose who has placed us here.

Then pledge anew each heart,
Ye, of the Royal Art,
To *labor* strongly and in truth to *love;*
And with the closing week,
Our eager hands will take
The *royal wages* waiting us above!

THE LADDER OF NINE ROUNDS.

I. THE ENTERED APPRENTICE.

Where two or three assemble round,
  In work the Lord approves,
His spirit with the group is found,
  It is the place He loves;
Be now all hearts to friendship given,
For we, the SONS OF LIGHT, are *seven.*

Bring here the *Gavel* and the *Gauge,*
  Those implements renowned;
And from each conscience disengage
  The faults that there are found;
Be now afar each folly driven,
For we, the SONS OF LIGHT, are *seven.*

Display the *Law*—the volume grace
  With *Compass* and with *Square;*
Illume the *Tapers* in their place,
  And all for work prepare;
We'll please our Master well this even,
For we, the SONS OF LIGHT, are *seven.*

Spread o'er us yon rich *Canopy,*
  Set up the *Ladder* high,
That angel visitants may see,
  And from their stations fly,
Where Faith, Hope, Charity are given,
And we, the SONS OF LIGHT, are *seven.*

II. THE FELLOWCRAFT.

This Lodge of *Five* from Tyre came,
Their leader one of matchless fame;
All through the toiling seasons seven,
Their time upon the work was given.

This Lodge of *Five* from Joppa's shore
To Sion's hill have journeyed o'er;
The quarry's inmost crypt have traced,
Whence many a stone the wall has graced.

This Lodge of *Five* have reared the shaft
That on the eastward hails the Craft;

And well they ken each mystic line
That sanctifies the great DESIGN.

This Lodge of *Five* with faith obey
The holy LAW and holy DAY;
They bow in reverence when they see
The emblem of the DEITY.

This Lodge of *Five*, for honest toil,
Good wages have — Corn, Wine and Oil;
And, should a brother be in want,
They ne'er forget the covenant.

This Lodge of *Five* have nearly done
The glorious work so long begun;
They, homeward bound, right soon will see
Their MASTER in eternity!

III. THE MASTER MASON.

O, Death, thy hand is weighty on the breast
    Of him who lies within thy grasp;
No power can raise the captive from his rest,
    When thy strong hand doth clasp!

The tears of broken spirits fall in vain;
    Their sighs are wasted o'er the grave;
Thou laugh'st to scorn the funereal strain,
    For " there is none to save."

From age to age mankind hath owned thy sway,
    Submissive bowed beneath thy hand;
The hoary head — the infant of a day —
    The loveliest of the land.

And thou hast struck the true and faithful now,
    Our model of Masonic faith;
It was a cruel and a dastard blow
    Thou stern, unpitying Death!

Yet, boastful Monster, he shall have release;
    Thy weighty hand, relentless power,
Shall be withdrawn, and all thy mockings cease,
    And all thy triumphs o'er.

The Lion of the Tribe of Judah comes —
　See in the heavenly East the sign!
To rend the sepulchers, disclose the tombs,
　And shut thee, Monster, in!

IV. THE MARK MASTER.

God trusts to each a portion of his plan,
　And doth for honest labor wages give;
Wisdom and time he granteth every man,
　And will not idleness and sloth forgive;
The week is waning fast — art thou prepared,
O Laborer, for the Overseer's reward?

Hast thou been waiting in the market here,
　Because no man hath hired thee? rise and go.
The sun on the meridian doth appear,
　The Master calls thee to his service *now;*
Rise up, and go, wherever duty calls,
And build with fervency the Temple walls.

Behold, within the heavenly home above
　One who hath done his life-tasks faithfully;
In the dark quarries all the week he strove,
　And "bore the heat and burden of the day";
So, when life's sun passed downward to the West,
Richest refreshment was his lot, and rest.

So shall it be with thee, O, toiling one!
　However hard thine earthly lot may seem;
It is not long until the set of sun,
　And then the past will be a pleasing dream;
The Sabbath, to the faithful laborer given,
　Is blest companionship, and rest, and heaven.

V. THE PAST MASTER.

O! raised to Oriental chair,
　With royal honors crowned,
High grace and dignity to bear,
　As in the days renowned!
With firmness guide the ruling hand,
　Nor Gavel fall in vain;
And kindness soften the command,
　And law the vice restrain.

The open WORD delight to read —
    That TRESTLE BOARD of Heaven —
And see that every Mason heed
    The deathless precepts given.
And let the *Trowel* truly spread
    Its cement so divine,
That all the Craft be duly paid
    Their corn, and oil, and wine.

The *Plumb Line*, hanging from the sky,
    In the Grand Master's hand —
Be this your emblem, ever nigh,
    By this to walk and stand;
Thus, grateful Craftsmen will conspire
    To sing your praises true,
And honors grant you, ever higher,
    Than now they offer you.

VI. MOST EXCELLENT MASTER.

Prostrate before the Lord,
    We praise and bless HIS name,
That He doth condescend to own
    The temple that we frame.

No winter's piercing blast,
    No summer's scorching flame,
Has daunted us; and prostrate here,
    We praise and bless His name.

From lofty Lebanon
    These sacred cedars came;
We dedicate them to Thy cause,
    And praise and bless Thy name.

Each noble block complete,
    Each pure and sparkling gem,
We give to build and beautify,
    And praise and bless Thy name.

With millions here below,
    With Heaven's own cherubim,
Prostrate before the fire and cloud,
    We praise and bless thy name.

VII. ROYAL ARCH.

O weary hearts, so worn and desolate !
Torn from their native land, from ruined homes,
From desecrated shrines.   O, hapless fate !
Better the solitude of Judah's tombs
Than all that Judah's foeman can bestow;
In the far land, where tuneless waters flow,
Along the sad Euphrates, as they sigh,
" Jerusalem ! "   " Jerusalem ! " they cry,
" When we forget thee, city of our love,
May *He* forget, whose city is above;
And when we fail to speak thy matchless fame,
May *He* consign us to enduring shame."

O, joyful spirits, now so bright and free
   Amid the hallowed palm trees of the West;
No more the exile's want and misery,
   The tuneless waters or the homes unblest;
Remember Sion now, her ruined shrine;
And take each manly form, the work divine;
Set up the altar, let the victims bleed,
To expiate each impious word and deed;
And tell the nations, when to Sion come,
" The Lord is God; *He* brought His people home !"

VIII. ROYAL MASTER.

We can predict, from day to day,
Some things will meet us on our way;
But who, of all that draw life's breath,
Can shadow *what is after death?*

When spring awakes, we look for flowers,
And leafy boughs and genial bowers;
The flowery spring rewards our faith —
What shall we look for *after death?*

When autumn spreads its sober skies,
With open lap we wait the prize;
We catch the showering fruits beneath —
For us what fruitage *after death?*

We trace the infant through each stage
Of youth, of manhood, and of age;
Each stage confirms our previous faith —
What grade awaits him *after death ?*

Such the reflections of this grade;
Such question here is freely made;
Life's secret lies *beneath, beneath* —
'Tis only yielded *after death!*

IX. SELECT MASTER.

At midnight, as at noon,
    The ancient worthies met;
The glances of the moon
    Beheld those laborers late;
Nor, till the glancing moon was high,
Did any lay his Trowel by.

Each felt a weight of care,
    A solemn charge o'erspread;
Each toiled in earnest there
    With busy hand and head;
And to the deep and faithful cave,
Those midnight craft a secret gave.

In whom the fire burns bright
    At midnight as at noon,
All secrets come to light
    Beneath the glancing moon;
Nor till the glancing moon is high,
Must any lay his Trowel by.

NOT BROUGHT TO LIGHT.

Not brought to light! when, ere your call
    At Masons' portals, you had given
All pledges that an honest soul
    Can give to earth or give to Heaven.

Not brought to light! that word you spoke,
    By man, by heavenly things adored,
The silence of the Lodge you broke,
    And loud averred, "I trust in God."

Not brought to light! when journeying round,
    Within the range of every eye,
Whole and unspotted you were found,
    Fit for the ranks of Masonry.

163

Not brought to light! when from that Book,
 That written Law by us adored,
Your dazzled glance its flight betook,
 To yonder type that speaks of God.

Then shame on them, "the sons of Night,"
 Thus blindly stumbling on their way,
Mistaking Masons' ancient Rite
 For childish jest or senseless play.

Shame on "the blind who lead the blind";
 Oh for an hour of HIM who drove
From temple courts the crowd that sinned,
 And taught the law of Light and Love!

OH, PITY, LORD.

Oh, pity, Lord, *the Widow;* hear her cry!
 Lonely her household lamp burns through the night,
He who possessed her heart's young sympathy
 No longer lives, her portion and delight.
She looks from earth, raises her heart on high,—
Pity, oh Lord, *the Widow,* hear her cry!

Oh, pity, Lord, *the Orphan*, hapless Child!
 Father and mother mourning, view her tears;
Abandoned, lost upon earth's dreary wild,
 What can relieve her anguish, what her fears?
Walking with Thee, the just, the undefiled,—
Pity, oh Lord, *the Orphan*, hapless Child!

Oh, pity, Lord, *the Lonely!* through the street
 Of crowded life, no friendly face she sees;
Turn *Thy* face to her graciously, and greet
 Her, Oh, blest Father, with the words of peace.
With Thee, Companion, solitude is sweet;
Oh, pity, Lord, *the Lonely* through the street.

Oh, pity, Lord, *Thine own ;* each hath a care,
 And we do lean in fondest trust on Thee!
Infinite mercy Thou canst justly spare,
 For JESUS died and rose, our souls to free.
Father of Jesus, answer now our prayer,
Oh, Lord, on Thee we lean, each hath a care!

THE DRUNKARD'S GRAVE.

I stood beside the grave,
  The last and dreamless bed ;
One whom I knew in other days
  Lay there amidst the dead ;
His head toward the setting sun ;
For O, his life and pilgrimage were done.

'Twas evening's pensive hour,—
  The rich and painted West
Had called earth's laborers,— weary ones,—
  To home delights and rest ;
Bird songs and voices of the day
Had melted all in evening's hush away.

Then came upon my soul
  A rush of memories ;
I seemed to see beside that grave
  My friend of other days ;
His beaming eye,— his generous hand,—
The largest, brightest, readiest of our band.

I seemed to hear once more
  His voice so full and free,—
My hand,— my heart,— my purse,— my life,
  I give from me to thee!
The scalding tears my grief confest ;
While night and darkness settled o'er the West.

For oh, I thought me then
  Of all his sad decline ;
He fell from honor's topmost height,
  The victim of one sin !
Yes, he, the generous and the brave,
Lay there dishonored in a *Drunkard's Grave!*

Long years and hard he strove
  Against the syren cup ;
Wife, Children, Brotherhood combined
  To bear him kindly up,
And cheer him midst that mighty woe
With which the unhappy drunkard has to do.

We plead by *this* and *this ;*
  We urged his plighted word ;
We told him what a shameful tale
  His story would afford ;
We gathered 'round him all our band
And warned and threatened with stern command.

In vain ; too strong his chain —
  Our cable tow too weak !
That cursèd thirst had burned his soul,
  He would no warning take ;
He broke the heart that leaned on his,
And brought himself, at last, at last, *to this.*

His sun went down at noon ;—
  His life expired in spring ;
His work undone, his column broke,—
  A ruined, loathsome thing !
Expelled from Masonry, his Grave
No emblems of the ancient Art can have.

I turned away in tears ;—
  The night had settled round ;—
I heard in cypress branches nigh,
  The owl's complaining sound,
Then homeward fled, amidst the gloom,
And left my Brother in the Drunkard's tomb !

THE VETERAN MASTER.

Worn, but not weary; stanch and true,
  Again the Master's Gavel bear,
And standing in the Eastern gate
  Display the bright and mystic Square.

Worn, but not weary; three score years
  Have marked your brow with lines of care,
Yet beats your heart as warm's the day
  When first you wore the mystic Square.

Worn, but not weary; when at last
  The slumbers of the dead you share,
May you be happy in His love
  Who wears *in Heaven* the mystic Square.

THE SPIRIT OF UNION.

In the settlement of long-pending difficulties among the Canadian Masons, the writer was called in, in July, 1858, with Philip C. Tucker, Grand Master of Vermont, to suggest proper terms of reconciliation. The pleasing task being performed, and the union complete, the following lines were read at a banquet that most agreeably terminated the meeting:

There never was occasion, and there never was an hour,
When spirits of peace on angel wings so near our heads did soar;
There's no event so glorious on the page of time to appear,
As the union of the Brotherhood, sealed by our coming here.

'Twas in the hearts of many, 'twas in the prayers of some,
That the good old days of Brotherly Love might yet in mercy come;
'Twas whispered in our Lodges, in the E. and S. and W.,
That the time was nigh when the plaintive cry our GOD would hear and bless.

But none believed the moment of fruition was at hand;
How could we deem so rich a cup was waiting our command?
It came like rain in summer drought, on drooping foliage poured,
And bade us look henceforth for help, in all our cares, to God!

The news has gone already upon every wind of Heaven;
The wire, the press, the busy tongue, the intelligence has given;
And everyone who heard it and who loves the *Sons of Peace*,
Has cried, "Praise GOD, the GOD of Love! may GOD this union bless!"

Vermont takes up the story,— her "old man eloquent,"—
Long be his days among us, on deeds of mercy spent,—
He speaks for the Green Mountains, and you heard him say last night,
"Bless God that I have lived till now to see this happy sight!"

Kentucky sends you greeting,— from her broad and generous bound,
Once styled of all the western wild, "the Dark and Bloody Ground;"
She cries aloud, "God bless you! Heaven's dews be on you shed,
Who first took care *to be in the right*, then boldly went ahead!"

From yonder constellation, from the Atlantic to the West,
Where the great pines of Oregon rear up their lofty crest,
From the flowery glades of Florida, from Minnesota's plain,
Each voice will say, "Huzza! huzza! this Craft is one again!"

Old England soon will hear it; not always will the cry
Of suffering Brothers meet her ear, and she pass coldly by;
There's a chord in British hearts vibrates to every tale of wrong,
And she will send a welcome and a *Brother's hand* ere long.

Then joyful be this meeting, and many more like this,
As year by year shall circle round, and bring you added bliss;
In quarry, hill, and temple, PEACE, nor cruel word or thought
Disturb the perfect harmony the gracious GOD has wrought.

But while your walls are thus compact, your cement strong and good,
Your workmen diligent and just, a mighty Brotherhood,
Remember, Brethren, o'er the earth, and on the raging sea,
How many a heart there is to-night that sighs, "Remember me!"

By the *sign* the world knows nothing of, but to our eyes so clear,—
By the *token* known in darkest hour, that tells a Brother dear,—
By the sacred *vow* and *word*, and by "the hieroglyphic bright,"
Remember all, the wide world round, who claim your love to-night.

TO THE SECRETARY.

Make thou the record *duly*,—
    Our Mason life is there;
Make thou the record *truly*,
    With close and anxious care.
The labors on the busy stage,—
At every step,—from age to age!

Make thou the record *plainly*,—
    How oft does error lurk!
Herein our children mainly
    Will read their fathers' work.
Herein will trace with joy or gloom
Our pathway to the closing tomb.

Make thou the record *kindly*,—
    Omit the cruel words;
The Mason spirit blindly
    A gentle shroud affords.
Oh, let thy record grandly prove
Freemasonry's a thing of love.

Make thou the record *swiftly*,—
    Time's scythe is sweeping fast;
Our life, dissolving deftly,
    Will soon, ah, soon, be past.
And may a Generous Eye o'erlook
Our record in the Heavenly Book!

THE PURSUIT OF FRANKLIN.

When Dr. Kane, the Arctic navigator, left New York in search of Sir John Franklin, he set the Masonic Square and Compass in large characters upon his foresail. He visited a Lodge in New-foundland at his brief call there. The flag taken *and left*, by his orders, nearest the North Pole, was the Masonic flag. It was an incentive to the zealous search made by our intrepid countrymen, that Franklin was reported to be a Freemason.

The following lines were written in 1853, upon his setting out upon his philanthropic errand. It is needless to say, however, that the writer's prediction failed in its fulfillment.

Midst polar snows and solitude,
    Eight weary years the voyager lies,
Ice-bound upon the frozen flood,
    While expectation vanishes;
Ah! many a hopeless tear is shed
For Franklin, numbered with the dead!

Midst joys of home, and well earned fame,
    Young, healthful, honored, there is one
Who pines to win a nobler name,
    And feels his glory but begun;
His heart is with the voyager, lost
Midst polar solitude and frost.

The voice from off the frozen flood
    Appeals in trumpet tones for aid;
'Tis heard, 'tis answered,— swift abroad
    The flag is hung, the sail is spread;
That sail on whose pure face we see
Thy symbol, honored Masonry!

Away, on glorious errand, now,
    Thou hero of a sense of right!
Success be on thy gallant brow,
    Thou greater than the sons of might!
Thy flag, the banner of the free,
Oh, may it lead to victory!

Is there some chain of sympathy
    Flung thus across the frozen seas?
Is there some strange, mysterious tie,
    That joins these daring men?— there is!
This, honored, healthful, free from want,
    Is bound to *that* in COVENANT!

For though these twain have never met,
  Nor pressed the hand, nor joined the heart,
In unison their spirits beat,
  Brothers in the Masonic art; —
One, in the hour of joy and peace,—
One, in the hour of deep distress.

And by the SYMBOLS, best of those
  Time-honored on our ancient wall,
And by the prayer that ceaseless flows,
  Upward from every Mystic Hall,—
And by thine own stout heart and hand,
Known, marked, and loved in every land,—

Thou shalt succeed,— his drooping eye
  Shall catch thy banner, broad and bright,—
That symbol he shall yet descry,
  And know a Brother in the sight!
Ah, noble pair! which happier then,
Of those two daring, dauntless men?

INSCRIPTIONS FOR A LODGE ROOM.

EAST.

Erect before Thee,
  A hand upon Thy WORD,
We thus adore Thee,
  And swear to serve Thee, Lord!

WEST.

So mote it be — each murmuring word
Speaks the soul's earnest, deep accord,
And echoes, from its inmost sea,
A deep AMEN, SO MOTE IT BE!

SOUTH.

Ye faithful, weave the chain!
  Join hand in hand again!
The world is filled with violence and blood!
  Hark to the battle cry!
  Hark to the answering sigh!
Come weave the chain admired of man and God!

GO ON THY BRIGHT CAREER.

Go on thy bright career, brave, faithful heart,
   Prayers of the faithful every step attending;
Go spread the triumphs of the MYSTIC ART,
   Wherever knee to DEITY is bending;
Raise up the landmarks, long in rubbish hidden ;
   Rear high the Altar on Moriah's brow;
Denounce all teachings by our rites forbidden,
   And LIGHT, MORE LIGHT, on yearning hearts bestow.

Crush all things that obstruct the cause of truth;
   How grand, how noble is the sacrifice !
How worthy of the brightest dreams of youth,
   To build a HOUSE like that within the skies !
Oh, when we lay thee, mourned-for, 'neath the sod,
   And cast the green and fragrant bough of faith,
How cheerful can we give thee to thy God
   Whose works defy the utmost power of death !

PRAYER—ORAL OR SECRET.

There is a prayer unsaid —
   No lips its accents move;
'Tis uttered by the pleading eye
   And registered above.

Each MYSTIC SIGN is prayer,
   By hand of Mason given;
Each gesture pleads or imprecates,
   And is observed in Heaven.

The deeds that mercy prompts,
   Are prayers in sweet disguise;
Though unobserved by any here,
   They're witnessed in the skies.

Then at the altar kneel —
   In silence make thy prayer;
And HE whose very name is LOVE
   The plea will surely hear.

The darkest road is light —
   We shun the dangerous snare,
When heavenly hand conducts the road
   Responsive to our prayer.

THE DEATH OF THE GRAND MASTER.

CRAWFORD, Grand Master of Maryland, died under the affecting circumstances here described :

His voice was low, his utterance choked,
　　He seemed like one in sorrow bound,
As from the ORIENT he invoked
　　God's blessings on the Masons round.

'Tis sad to see the strong man weep —
　　Tears are for sorrows yet untried ;
But who with sympathy can keep,
　　When age unseals emotion's tide ?

Reverently stood the Brothers round,
　　While their Grand Master breathed farewell,
And strove to catch the faintest sound
　　Of accents known and loved so well.

He told them of the zealous care
　　Of their forefathers of the Art ;
How valley-gloom and mountain-air
　　Bore witness of the faithful heart.

He conned the precepts, line by line —
　　Oh, that the Craft may ne'er despise
Precepts so precious, so divine,
　　That shape the Mason mysteries !

He warned them of a world unkind,
　　Harsh to the good, to evil mild,
Whose surest messengers are blind,
　　Whose purest fountains are defiled.

He told them of a world to come,
　　To which this life a portal is,
Where tired laborers go home,
　　To scenes of never ending bliss.

Then of himself he humbly spoke —
　　So modestly ! so tenderly !
While from the saddened group there broke
　　An answering sigh of sympathy :

" Now give me rest ; my years demand
　　A holiday, Companions dear !

My days are drawing to an end,
  And I would for my end prepare.

" Now give me rest ; but when you meet,
  Brothers, in this beloved spot,
My name upon your lips repeat,
  And never let it be forgot !

" Now unto GOD, the Mason's FRIEND,
  The GOD our emblems brightly tell,
Your dearest interests I commend —
  Brothers, dear Brothers, oh, farewell ! "

Down from the Orient, slowly down,
  Weeping, through that sad group he passed,
Turned once and gazed, and then was gone.
  That look — his tenderest and his last.

His last — for, ere the week had sped,
  That group, with sorrow unrepressed,
Gathered around their honored dead —
  Bore their Grand Master to his rest!

THE PYRAMID OF CHEOPS.

Not useless : cold must be the heart
  Can linger here in critic mood,
  And fail to recognize the good,
And look and sneer, and so depart.

Not useless : were it but to prove
  What aspirations are in man;
  Almost *divine* this mighty plan —
Almost an impulse from above.

Not useless : were it but to stir
  The sense of awe within the breast;
  What grandeur does the pile attest !
Is it a mortal's sepulcher?

Not useless : no; while life abide,
  The measure of the soul, to me,
  Its utmost stretch of thought shall be
My memories of the Pyramid !

THE DYING REQUEST.

The last request of Morgan Lewis, Grand Master of Masons in New York, is embodied in these lines:

The veteran sinks to rest;—
" Lay it upon my breast,
And let it crumble with my heart to dust —
Its leaves a lesson tell;—
Their verdure teacheth well
The everlasting greenness of my trust.

" Through three score years and ten
With failing, dying men
I've wept the uncertainties of life and time !
The symbols, loved of yore,
Have changed, have lost their power,
All save this emblem of a faith sublime.

" Things are not as they were;—
The Level and the Square,
Those time-worn implements of love, in truth,—
The incense flowing o'er
The lambskin, chastely pure,
Bear not th' interpretation as in youth.

" Their moral lore they lose;
They 'mind me but of those
Now in death's chambers who their teachings knew,
I see them — but they breathe
The charnel airs of death —
I cannot bear their saddening forms to view.

" But this, O symbol bright !
Surviving age's blight,
This speaks in honey tones, unchanged, unchanged !
In it I read my youth,
In it my manhood's truth,
In it bright forms of glory long estranged.

" Green leaves of summer skies,
Blest type of Paradise !
Tokens that there's a world I soon shall see,
Of these take good supply;
And, Brothers, when I die,
Lay them upon my breast to die with me ?"

'Twas done. They're crumbled now,
He lies in ashes, too;
Yet was that confidence inspired in vain?
Ah, no, his noble heart,
When death's dark shades depart,
With them in glory shall spring forth again.

FRAGRANCE OF A GOOD DEED·

Many years since, a poor sojourner through the wilds of Texas paused at a farm house on the lonely banks of the Brazos, to die. The owner, a Freemason, discovered the Masonic claims of his guest not too late to make the mystic tie available. All the consolations of brotherly sympathy and attendance were freely bestowed upon him, and when these could avail the pilgrim no longer, his remains were tenderly consigned to maternal earth, the generous planter reading the Masonic service and covering in the precious dust, *alone!*

Long years afterward, and when a populous village had sprung up upon the river banks, a Masonic Lodge was established there. The hall was built, and the Mount Moriah upon which it was erected was the green knoll beneath which the stranger's bones are moldering! Morton Lodge, No. 72, at Richmond, Texas, yet (1884) stands to perpetuate "the fragrance of a good deed."

On hallowed ground those walls are reared;
That roof incloses in
A spot to Masonry endeared,
To Sion's Mount akin;
Since Sion's Temple is bereft
And Judah mourns his God,
No holier site on earth is left,
Than this our feet have trod.

For here, inspired by truest faith,
Relief a Brother gave,—
Upheld a wanderer unto death
And blessed him with a grave;
Aye, with a grave whose portals closed
To that majestic song,
Which has to the fraternal host
Brought deathless hopes so long.

The EYE DIVINE approved the deed,—
'Tis graven as with steel;
And when the noble act we read
This fond desire we feel,—
That all *our* mystic work and word
Thus modeled well may be,
And so the Temple of our God
Rise fast and gloriously!

THE OBEDIENT DISCIPLE.

The ancient historian, Iamblichus, describes with unction the circumstance that forms the basis of the following piece. The two travelers therein named were disciples of Pythagoras. whose system of secret affiliation, if it was not FREEMASONRY, at least exhibited the benevolent features which make up so large a part of it.

A Brother, bound for distant lands,
  In sickness fell alone, alone;
And stranger care from stranger hands,
  Did the last rites of nature own.
But ere the trembling spirit passed,
He on a Tablet faintly traced

Some mystic lines—a spiral Thread—
  A Square—an emblem of the Sun—
A Checquered Band, that none could read—
  And then his work and life were done.
And stranger care from stranger hands,
Gave him kind burial in the sands.

Full many a year swept by, swept by,
  And the poor stranger was forgot;
While on an olive column, nigh,
  That Tablet marked his burial spot;
And many gazed at Square and Thread,
And many guessed, but none could read.

But then the sage Disciple came,
  Of one whose wisdom filled the land,—
Himself right worthy of the name,—
  The thoughtful head and ready hand;
He looked upon the mystic lines,
And read the Tablet's full designs.

It spoke of one long passed before,
  In quest of truth, like him, sincere;
Of one gone onward, never more
  To delve in mines deep-hidden here;
And solemn was the lesson traced,—
Lo, Pilgrim! 'tis your fate at last!

Awe-struck, yet wiser now, he strayed
  In solemn silence from the spot;
Repaid the debt his brother made,
  And eastward journeyed on his lot;

Yet never on life's shifting wave
Lost he the lesson of that grave.

How weighty is the charge we give,
    Brethren, in this short history read,—
To bless the living while we live,
    And leave some tokens when we're dead!
On life's broad Tablet let us trace
Emblems to mark *our* burial place!

PLEASANT MEMORIES.

It is the mercy of our Heavenly Friend
That memory clingeth most to *pleasant* things;
We may forget the ills and pains of life,
Its bonds and losses; we may forget the graves
Of best beloved ones early torn away;
But in our memory there is safely hid
A store of happy things — the social hours,
The genial smiles, brightest of earthly light;
The manly grip that thrills the soul within;
The loving " Farewell, farewell, brother dear!"
These things do lie so closely at the heart,
While pulses beat they never can fade out.

So, dearest Friend, in calling up the past,
We find *our* early friendship of that sort
That dwells in memory; for it was enshrined
With unforgotten names of friends now dead;
Kind-hearted, faithful, full of zeal and love,
In graveyard now is their abiding place;
Beneath the green sprigs they repose in peace;
While we, a little longer, toil and wait,
Cheered by the recollections of their love.

And so, in future years, should we be spared,
May we recall this one more happy hour,
This group of cheerful faces, every hand
Strong in the grip fraternal, every eye
Filled with the light fraternal, every soul
Softened and sanctified by brother love;
And when, at last, the summons we accept,
And join the Lodge Celestial, may we find
Amongst our very happiest memories,
The hour of social joy we now begin!

THE INHERITANCE OF FRIENDSHIP.

TO B. B. FRENCH, IN 1856.

When twenty years have circled round,
    The lads now standing at my knee
Will cherish one poor spot of ground
    Sacred to memory and me.
Gazing upon the humble sod,
Recalling each fond, loving word,
They'll keep one link in memory's chain
Bright, till the hour we meet again.

Such is the lesson I impart
    At evening's set when prayers are said;
The last sweet sentiment at heart
    Ere little eyes are closed in bed.
That when upon life's billows tossed,
In worldly selfishness engrossed,
A CABLE Tow the thought shall prove
To draw them by a Father's love.

When twenty years have come and gone
    They who shall fondly look for you
Must leave the scenes you now adorn,
    And seek the sodded hillock, too;
Tears will bedew the grass beneath,
Sighs will unite with nature's breath,
T' embalm within that hallowed bed,
A father loved, a father dead.

There's Brotherhood in honest sighs,
    There's Brotherhood in earnest tears;
Our sons, made kindred by such ties,
    Shall interchange their hopes and fears;
Yours to the WEST their steps will bend
To honor their dear Father's friend;
Mine to the EAST will make their way
A pious pilgrimage to pay.

Such was the dream that fired my brain
    Last night as 'mid my loved ones lying,
It came again, again, again,
    And traced itself in lines undying.

178

I dreamed we twain had joined the bands
Who live and love in other lands,
And from high seats beheld with joy
The step of each dear pilgrim boy.

I dreamed that on some sunny plain
    They, o'er whose couch we've bent at night,
Met, twined with eager hands the chain,
    The Chain of Love, the Chain of Light;
With glowing lips exchanged the Word,—
No fonder does our tongue afford,—
And covenanted by that faith
Their fathers pledged and kept till death.

Then be it so, dear Friend, and while
    For earthly labors we are spared,
Let's teach our sons to cherish well
    The friendship we've so freely shared.
Then at life's sunset we may die
And yet the power of Death defy;
Then by the Monster victor slain,
In our dear Children live again !

THE NARROW BOUNDARY.

So each one stands,— a narrow line
    Divides the future from the past,—
A little space to labor in,
    So brief for purposes so vast.

Those grand designs, whose tracing proves
    Their inspiration is from Heaven,—
Those boundless hopes,— those deathless loves,—
    'Tis but a day to these is given !

Then let us labor while we can,—
    Throw off the burdens that oppress,—
Redeem our poor and fleeting span,
    And trust in God to help and bless.

And should we seek, to give us cheer,
    Examples of the bold and true,
A cloud of witnesses is here,
    To prove what laboring man can do.

LANGUAGE OF FREEMASONRY.

Hark, 'tis the voice of the long-parted years!
An hundred generations, joining tongues
From every land to swell the choral song,
While angels bear it to the throne of God.

Where'er the patient dead lie waiting for
The Resurrection trump, their very graves
Are vocal with thy imagery divine,
That speaks the language of Freemasonry.

The living, loving groups in mystic round,
Whisper those words their fathers knew and loved;
While kindled eye and burning heart confess
That time but strengthens thee, Freemasonry.

Hark, 'tis the voice from vanished years, deep-toned
Like some cathedral chant, sounding the depths
Of human feeling, and awakening all
In one grand chorus to the God of love.

Hear it, ye nations! still the clash of arms!
The blood-flow stanch! no longer brothers' hands
'Gainst brothers' hearts be raised! but heed the voice
That speaks the Common Father of us all.

THE VETERAN'S LAMENT.

There's tenfold Lodges in the land,
    Than when my days were few;
But none can number such a band,
    The wise, the bright, the true,
As stood around me on the night
When first I saw the MYSTIC LIGHT,
    Full fifty years ago.

There's Brother-love and Brother-aid,
    Where'er the Craft is known;
But none like that whose twinings made
    The mighty chain that's gone —
Ah, none like that which bound my soul
When first my eyes beheld the goal
    Full fifty years ago.

There's emblems green to deck the bed
    Of Masons where they rest,
But none like those we used to spread
    Upon the Mason's breast,
When, yielding up to death, they fell,
Who'd battled with the monster well.
      Full fifty years ago.

Oh, how my heart is kindled now,
    When round me meet again
The shadows of the noble few,
    Who formed the mystic train
In which my feet were proud to tread,
When through admiring crowds we sped,
      Full fifty years ago.

They're fled, that noble train,— they're gone,—
    Their last procession's o'er —
And I am left to brood alone,
    Ere I, too, leave the shore ;
But while I have a grateful tear,
I'll praise the bright ones that were here,
      Full fifty years ago.

YEARNINGS.

Oh, might I live to see each Mason Lodge
    The abode of peace, the school of harmony,
    The place of prayer, the fount of charity,
The judgment seat of the Celestial judge !

Oh, might I know that, when I weep beside
    A dying brother, weeping for his loss,
    That loss is *all my own*, and he will cross
In light and ecstacy the rolling tide !

Oh, might I feel, when standing by the grave
    Where sleeps a Mason brother, that his soul
    Has gone on royal pinions to that goal
Where reigns the KING who died our souls to save !

Oh, that the day may come — it will, it must,—
    When Masons all shall live *upon the Square!*
    Brothers, be this our constant aim and care,
And we shall have the approval of the JUST.

TO THE DOUBTING.

Think ye that Masons, when they tyle the door,
    Excluding all unfriendly ears and eyes,—
Think ye they find no spirits hovering o'er,
    That bring bright blessings to their mysteries?
            With Bible at the feast,
            And God's Name in the East,
        And prayer and vow, true hearts to bow;
    Can holy ones absent themselves from these?

Think ye, when first are led our wandering feet
    About the mystic altar, slow and bare,
And priestly voice rehearses, as is meet,
    Of brotherhood all precious, fond and rare,—
            Think ye, in that dark hour
            There comes no inward power
        To bid us trust in God the Just,
    And waft full orisons on wings of prayer?

Think ye the long succession that have worn
    Our badges, understanding well their lore,—
Think ye when, to their resting places gone,
    They dropped the tools their fathers dropped before,
            The Level, Plumb and Square,
            So bright with moral rare,
        And Gavel full of mystic rule,
    That all their wisdom to the tomb they bare?

Think ye the dead, above whose face we flung
    Undying leaves that symbolize our faith,—
Think ye in honored graves that mighty throng
    Is silent utterly in sleep of death?
            When standing round their grave,
            Our weeping Craftsmen gave
        In sign and word, such full accord,
    With all they felt and hoped, who lie beneath?

Most wrongly judge ye, ye who judge us thus;
    We may not scorn the social word and smile,
For these are blessings God hath granted us,
    Life's weary heat and burden to beguile;
            But in our lightest thought
            A thousand types are wrought,
        Drawn from the Word and will of God,
    That link the heavenly to the earthly soil.

THE PRAYER OF DANIEL.

Now when Daniel knew that the writing was signed (forbidding any person praying for thirty days, except to King Darius), he went into his house, his windows being open in his chamber *toward Jerusalem ;* he kneeled upon his knees three times a day, and prayed, and gave thanks before his God, as he did aforetime.— DANIEL vi, 10.

If thy people sin against thee, and thou deliver them to the enemy, so that they carry them away captives into the land of the enemy, yet if they shall bethink themselves and repent, and make supplication unto thee, and *pray unto thee*, toward the city which thou has chosen ; then hear thou their prayer in Heaven, thy dwelling place, and maintain thy cause and forgive thy people.— I KINGS viii, 46.

As from the *Orient* the sun
Proclaimed his golden race begun,
And earth awoke in light and song,
Calling to toil the busy throng,
Upon his housetop, all abroad,
The exiled Hebrew plead with God,
And Sionward he breathed his prayer,
For Sion was his *morning* care :
" Hear the voice of supplication ;
Save our sinful captive nation ;
Lead us back to Sion's hill ;
Lord ! thou hast the power and will ! "

As in the *South*, the solar light
Mounted to his meridian height,
And man to cooling shelter fled
Shunning the fiery beams o'erhead ;
Upon his housetop, all abroad,
The exiled Hebrew plead with God ;
And Sionward he made his prayer,
For Sion was his *noontide* care :
" Hear the voice of supplication ;
Save our sinful captive nation ;
Lead us back to Sion's hill ;
Lord ! thou hast the power and will ! "

As in the *West* the sun withdrew
Midst zephyrs bland and healing dew,
While weary laborers homeward bent,
On evening cheer and sleep intent ;
Upon the housetop, all abroad,
The exiled Hebrew plead with God ;
And Sionward he made his prayer,
For Sion was his *evening* care :

"Hear the voice of supplication ;
Save our sinful captive nation ;
Lead us back to Sion's hill ;
Lord ! thou hast the power and will !"

If thus the exile bent his knee,
Fearless of spite and tyranny,
Shall Masons shrink to give their praise,
Through peaceful nights and happy days ?
No, no, in Lodge, at home, abroad,
Let Masons boldly plead with God,
And Sionward address their prayer,
Heaven is their Sion, God is there :
"Hear the voice of supplication ;
Save our proud and sinful nation ;
Lead us all to Sion's hill ;
Lord ! thou hast the power and will !"

A WELCOME INTO MASONRY.

Directed to one who subsequently acquired a distinguished name as a Masonic writer.

There were many with me were glad, Brother,
    When we read your latest thought,
And to one another we said, Brother,
    'Tis an omen of good import !
For the battle of law has begun, Brother,
    The strife for "the good old way,"
And we need just such an one, Brother,
    As we knew you of old to be !

Yes, one of the daring type, Brother—
    Such men as they had of yore,
With a head that in age is ripe, Brother,
    And a heart that is brimming o'er ;
To know what a LANDMARK is, Brother—
    In love to be warm and true—
Oh, how have we longed for these, Brother,
    And 'tis these we shall find in you !

In the day when your sands are spent, Brother,
    And the Craft shall your history tell,
They'll say, as their grief has vent, Brother,
    "He has done his labor well !"

For you know we have ARCHIVES, Brother,
   And a COLUMN rent in twain,
And a NAME that still greenly lives, Brother,
   Though the dust hath its dust again !

And these they'll give to you, Brother,
   As the guerdon of your meed ;
For the love that is warm and true, Brother,
   For the heart and for the head ;
For the battle of law has begun, Brother,
   The strife for "the good old way,"
And we need just such an one, Brother,
   As we know you of old to be !

LINES WRITTEN TO ACCOMPANY RECITATIONS.

Come, then, ye Masons wise,
Come with sound ears and eyes,
Join me in spirit, and with hand in hand,
Cross the broad waters o'er
Old Canaan to explore,
And make *our Crusade* to the Holy Land !

Honor to him who fills the EAST,
   For Wisdom's rule revered ;
Honor to him who fills the WEST,
   For Help and Strength endeared ;
Honor to him who fills the SOUTH,
Model of Beauty, Grace and Truth.

Oh, glorious task ! to dig in sacred soil
   'Neath ruined towers and temples where the hands
Of nine score thousand craftsmen wrought in toil
   Sublime ! Oh, to rehearse our Master's dread command
Amidst those scenes inspired ! oh, to join
   Around those altars loving hand and heart !
In all this Lodge terrestrial there's no shrine
   Like that where first was wrought Masonic Art.

What is the Mason's speech ?
How does the Master teach
The undying thoughts that we call *Masonry ?*
Mysterious dialect
Where sharpened souls detect
The inmost secrets of the mystic tie !

185

'Tis no mere local tongue
Informs our world-wide throng ;
No ! 'tis the hand, the lip, the face, the eye :
These make the unerring voice
That bids our souls rejoice
When hand in hand we form the mystic tie.

THE DECAYED LODGE.

These walls are tottering to decay,
　　There's dampness on the stair;
But well I mind me of the day
　　When two score men met here;
When two score Brothers met at night,
　　The full, round moon above,
To weave the mystic chain of light
　　With holy links of love.

But now the lightest of the train
　　In early grave is bowed;
The chain is broke, the holy chain,—
　　The MASTER's with his GOD !
The wailing notes were heard one day,
　　Where cheerful songs are best,
And two score Brothers bore away
　　Their MASTER to his rest.

The SOUTH, that pleasant voice, is still,
　　That spoke the joys of noon;
The WEST, that told the Master's will,
　　Has set, as sets the sun.
The sun may rise, may stand, may fall,
　　But these will stand no more,—
No more the faithful Craft to call,
　　Or scan their labors o'er.

I'll weep the rending of this chain,
　　As JESUS wept His love!
This haunted spot! what shall restrain
　　The tears these memories move?
Where two score Brothers met at night,
　　There's solitude and gloom;
Let grief its sacred train invite
　　To this old haunted room.

FREDSTOLE : THE SEAT OF PEACE.

FAR away in the West, where the savage is straying,
    His war path all gory, his visage begrimed,
Where man hates his fellow, betrayed and betraying,
    And nature alone breathes a spirit sublime —
There's a FOUNTAIN whose flow sweet as nectar inviteth,
    Embosomed in hills such as Eden adorn ;
Each sip of its waters to Friendship inciteth
    And PEACE is the song that its song birds return.

There met, drops the Savage his hatchet and arrow,
    There met, breast to breast, joins in fondest embrace ;
From the song birds the foemen sweet caroling borrow,
    And war paint the waters wash out from each face ;
The hills smile around — 'tis the approval of Heaven —
    Their light catches, glances in every eye,
And speaks of a host of foul insults forgiven,
    And pledges a Covenant that never can die.

THE LODGE is a peace fount ! come, Brothers, and taste it !
    O'erflowing with sweetness, to you it is given !
A ROCK its FOUNDATION, — what ages have placed it !
    Its COVERING, the starry-decked arches of Heaven.
Its LAW, 'tis inscribed in yon holiest Volume —
    Its CHAIN, every link is the soul of a Man !
Behold on the right hand and left hand its COLUMN !
    Behold in the East is its marvelous PLAN !

THE HEIMSKRINGLA.

SWEDISH FOR HOME CIRCLE.

Heimskringla, world circle,
    The sacred, the vast, —
The present and future
    Enlinked with the past, —
Great girdle fraternal
    That bindeth the earth,
Whose strands are all spirits
    Of virtue and worth, —
Thy name is Freemasonry, cherished and blest,
And thy light from the East ever tends to the West.

THE REPRESENTATIVE OF SOLOMON.

Ay, master of the true,
Urge on those hearts to do
A better testimony to the ONE
Who gave, all laws above,
The conquering law of LOVE,
And sealed it with the gracious name of JOHN.

Ay, hail his natal morn !
Fear not the winter's scorn,
The storm god will move leniently above;
Bring wife and child to hear
The word we so revere,
The key word of all Masons' music, LOVE.

Ay, round the Altar now
Let each one humbly Vow
Humbly but firmly, as beseems the wise,
That all that gracious Law
Which John in vision saw,
Shall be the essence of your mysteries !

Ay, thus will life afford
Its comfort and reward,
Its strengthening *corn*, its *oil*, its cheering *wine*,
And so to latest day,
Will coming craftsmen say,
" They loved each other with the LOVE DIVINE ! "

APPRECIATION.

'Tis good to feel ourselves beloved of men;
To know that all our anxious cares and sighs
For others' weal are given not in vain,
But treasured up in grateful memories;
How light the toil for those we fondly love!
How rich the wages grateful spirits prove!

But when those men are BROTHERS, strongly bound
By bonds indissoluble, sweet and true,—
When gratitude springs out of sacred ground,
And *prayers* are mingled with the praises due;
Ah then, toil is no burden, gifts no load !
We have full recompense for what's bestowed.

'Tis thus with you, my friend : the voice of all
    Yields willing tribute to your high deserts;
But from the CRAFT there comes a stronger call, —
    From that great Brotherhood whose chain begirts
The broad world round, the grateful wages come,
Whose price is HONOR and whose favor BLOOM.

Long may you live in Bloom and Honor, long,
    To show the CHRISTIAN in the MASON's guise!
In STRENGTH OMNIPOTENT may you be strong!
    In WISDOM HEAVENLY may you be wise!
And when to Death's dark portals you shall come,
May JESUS banish all the fear and gloom!

FELLOWCRAFT'S SONG.

HIS laws inspire our being —
    Our light is from HIS sun ;
Beneath the EYE ALL-SEEING,
    Our Mason's work is done ;
HIS Plumb line in uprightness
    Our faithful guide shall be ;
And in the SOURCE OF BRIGHTNESS
    Our willing eyes shall see.

THOU, FATHER, art the Giver
    To every earnest prayer !
O, be the GUIDE forever
    To this, our Brother dear !
By law and precept holy,
    By token, word and sign,
Exalt him, now so lowly,
    Upon this GRAND DESIGN.

Within thy Chamber name him
    A WORKMAN, wise and true !
While loving Crafts shall claim him
    In bonds of friendship due ;
Thus shall the walls extol THEE,
    And future ages prove
What Masons ever call THEE,
    THE GOD OF TRUTH AND LOVE !

Founded upon the Scriptural passage appropriate to this Degree, viz.: Amos vii, 7, 8, and used in American Lodges in the circumambulation in the Second Degree.

THE MASTER OF THE UPRIGHT HEART.

German authors describe the affecting incident given in the following lines.   The opening
verses allude to a journey up the Mississippi River in 1853, swollen at that time out of its banks,
during which the author related the incident to his three sons.

We journeyed up the western flood,
    My little boys and I,
And watched the drifts of ice and wood
    That floated swiftly by;
While banks and trees and dwellings, too,
Appeared like islands in the view.

We marked with sympathy and grief
    The general distress,
And fain the lads would give relief
    To every suffering case;—
But when a corpse came floating past
They fled the spectacle, aghast.

Then in our little room we met;
    They thronged the willing knee,
And listened to the various fate
    Of men by land and sea;
Of shipwrecked sailors, starved for food,
And lost ones wandering in the wood.

I told them of such noble deeds
    Where rescue had been given,
Such generous acts, that he who reads
    Is moved to worship Heaven.
But most I pleased them with the part
Of Julian of " The Upright Heart."

"'Twas on a stormy April day,
    The floods were at their height;
All Frankfort gather'd out, they say,
    To see a dismal sight:
A broken bridge — a swollen sea —
And oh, a drowning family!

" The Master of ' The Upright Heart '
    Was Frankfort's noblest son;
On many a field of high desert
    His laurels had been won

190

Not laurels wet with human blood,
But those acceptable to God.

"Smiles from the face of cold despair,
    The widow's grateful song,—
The orphan's praise,— the stranger's prayer,—
    These to his crown belong;
Ah! many such, thank God, there be
In our world-wide fraternity!

"Prince Julian galloped to the brink
    Of that tremendous flood;
The perishing about to sink
    Inspired his noble blood;
He called aloud, he called the brave
This wretched family to save!

"None answered him; again he cried:
    'Oh! have you hearts of stone,
To see them perish by your side?
    Look, look, they wave us on!'
He offered gold as water free,
To save the drowning family!

"But when the boldest shrank — deterred
    From such a desperate deed,—
He uttered not another word,
    But bowed his pious head,
Looked upward,— gave his soul to God,—
And plunged into the raging flood!

"That day the gates of Heaven were thrown
    To admit a spirit freed;
That day earth lost her noblest son,
    And gave him to the dead;
That day enshrined the Royal Art,
Her hero of 'The Upright Heart!'"

The lads sat thoughtful on my knee,
    Reflecting on the tale;
They loved to talk of Masonry,
    And knew its precepts well;
"*I know what made him take such pains;*
The signs they made were Masons' signs!"

THE GREATEST OF THESE.

The Word of God, the rule of faith to Masons true and free,
Sublimely says, "The greatest grace in man is Charity,"
To feel the sympathetic glow for souls in sorrow driven
And lend relief,—'tis this that brings the Mason nearest Heaven.

This broad-spread land, the Empire State, foremost in every art,
Hath lately shown in Charity the largest Mason heart ;
A Brother from a distant land came empty to their door,
And lo, the generous Brotherhood threw open wide their store.

All honor, praise, respect to them, the noblest in the land.
And honor their Grand Master, right worthy of command ;
And honor over all, to Him, the Sovereign King of Heaven,
Forever blest, who hearts to feel and hands to give, hath given.

EXHORTATION TO CHARITY.

'Tis but an hour—our life is but a span ;
No summer rose so frail as dying man ;
Did there no memory of *our deeds* survive,
Death were more welcome than the happiest life.

But the true heart shall live in mercy's deed ;
The *Record* stands where every eye can read —
Where countless myriads on the judgment morn
Shall see *each charity* our hands have done.

What wondrous mercy doth THE MASTER give,
That the true Workman *in his Work* shall live !
What wondrous power the dark grave defies —
The *Temple* stands although the *Builder* dies !

Bear me in memory then, kind Friends and true,
As one who loved the MASTER's cause and you !
Join my poor name with yours in Mystic Chain,
Although we may not, cannot meet again !

And when the stroke of Death, long-pending, falls,
And I no more shall work on Temple walls,
Wreathe the ACACIA green about my head
And give one memory to your faithful dead.

HAIL TO THE PEN!

"The pen is mightier than the sword."

HAIL TO THE PEN! the day is past,
    When man is governed by the sword;
    There is a principle abroad
Greater than bayonet or the cannon's blast.

HAIL TO THE PEN! the skillful Scribe
    Wields it, a scepter, o'er the world;
    From thrones of darkness it has hurled
The despot, spite of threatening and bribe.

HAIL TO THE PEN! perennial youth
    And power be with the hand that wields,
    Drawn from a Fount, divine that yields
Impartial Justice and unbiased Truth.

HAIL TO THE PEN! and hail to you,
    Illustrious Friend, whose pen has taught
    How light and truth may be inwrought,
And History writ that to all time is true.

A HEBREW CHANT.

Lonely is Sion, cheerless and still,
Shekinah has left thee, thou desolate Hill;
Winds sweep around thee, familiar their tone,
But trumpet, timbrel, song are gone.

Joyous was Sion on that glorious day,
When Israel beheld all thy Temple's display;
Heaven sent a token approvingly down,
But temple, altar, cloud are gone.

Foemen of Sion uplifted the spear,
The brand to thy Temple, the chains to each frère;
Pilgrims and strangers, thy children yet mourn,
But foemen, fetter, brand are gone.

Spirit of Sion, oh, hasten the day,
When Israel shall gather in matchless array!
Lord! build Thine altars, Thy people return,
For temple, altar, cloud are gone.

THAT VAPOR, LIFE.

Life is a *vapor*, how brief is its stay !
Vanishing, vanishing, passing away ;
Life is a *flower* that springs in the morn,
Fading, O, fading, no more to return ;
Life is an *arrow*, how swift is its flight,
Life is the *rose tint* that fades into night ;
Lord, may our lives in Thy service be given,
Fading on earth, but immortal in Heaven.

Teach us the worth of the vanishing time,
Make every life, in its purpose, sublime ;
Virtue and innocence, charity's dower,
Merciful Father, bestow us with power ;
Patient and strong to endure to the end,
Hopeful and faithful and true to each friend ;
Lord, may our lives in Thy service be given,
Fading on earth, but immortal in Heaven.

THE VISITOR'S WELCOME.

Composed to be read before The Friends in Council Lodge No. 1383, London, England, at a visit, September 3, 1878.

It is the pride of ancient Masonry,
  When Lodge fires blaze and Craftsmen gather round,
That in the East, upraised where all may see,
  An honored place is for the *Stranger* found.

Amid the *Friends in Council* then, I come,
  To claim the stranger's seat and welcome, too ;
For in my far-off, loved Kentucky home,
  There waits such welcome, Friends beloved, *for you.*

The Stranger represents *the absent Host ;*
  "The Universal Lodge" through him is here ;
Himself though lowly, he may proudly boast
  That in his person *all the Craft* appear.

Around me, though invisible, there stand
  The forms of Franklin and of Washington,
Of Clinton, Hubbard, Clay,— O, 'tis a Band,—
  No man can number 'neath the circling sun.

Rank upon rank they throng me, though I am
　　Not worthy to unloose the latchet-string ;
Such honor glorifies the Stranger's name,
　　When made the subject of your welcoming.

Then, as the spokesman of this mighty throng,
　　O *Friends in Council*, hear the Stranger's word :
His aims are yours, like yours his vows are strong,
　　His Overseer is yours, the Mason's LORD.

His word is *Fides* — Brethren, con it well,
　　And *Fides Incorrupta* your reply ;
Let it be with you while on earth you dwell,
　　Let it fly with you when you mount the sky.

BEING DEAD, YET LIVING.

Long, long ago, the man of Bethany —
He whom the Saviour loved — in sickness fell,
Died and was buried.　Yet he lives again;
He "being dead yet lives," to die no more.

Toiling and sorrowing, bending 'neath the yoke
Of age — gray hairs, dimmed eyes, enfeebled limbs —
What is there left, old friend, for me and thee?
Where are the joys of youth? where is the scorn
With which we mocked misfortune? where the hope
That beamed from every sky and lured us on?

Gone, gone, all gone ! the winter binds us now,
And in our life there's no returning spring !
Soon with our fathers thou and I must sleep;
And round our graves the busy world will surge,
Forgetting that we ever died or lived.

"Yet being dead we live !" if ever once
In genial mood we dropped the generous word
Or penned the loving precept; if in prayer
We sought the common Father, and besought
His aid to save the sorely tempted soul;
If from a scanty hoard we drew a mite
To help the poor and sorrowing, then, dear friend,
We have not lived in vain; we being dead,
Shall live forever in the life of God.

Be comforted; 'tis but a little while,
And the dark river that arrests our path
Shall roll behind us while we walk the fields
And climb the Mount Celestial; for we know
In whom we have believed, and rest secure ;
Be comforted; rejoice in hope; farewell.

BURNS' FAREWELL.

As sung by Professor John C. Baker, the vocalist, there is a pathos in Burns' celebrated Ode
that is irresistible. The occurrence is that of October, 1860.

Never since 'neath the daisies laid
Burns joined the cold and tuneless dead,
Were those sweet lines, his noblest flight,
Sung as you warbled them last night

They bore us, fancy-winged, above;
They thrilled the inmost soul with love;
And tears confessed "The fond Adieu"
As given so well, last night, by you.

Ah, what a thing is this to spread,
That binds the living with the dead,
And makes them *one fraternal throng*,
As you, last night, so justly sung.

How blest are we who rightly claim
The Mason's heart, the Mason's name,
And see "the Hieroglyphic bright!"
Of which you sung, so well, last night

Then as you journey sweetly sing;
Let Craftsmen hear that tuneful thing;
No better can the pen indite
Than those sweet words you sung last night!

Ah, what a power doth music give
To make the dead again to live,
And join with our fraternal throng
As you, last night, so justly sung !

And when your own HIGH XII has come,
And Craftsmen bear you, weeping, home,
May loving friends *your* requiem write
In those grand words you sung last night !

196

WHY HAVE THEY LEFT US?

They went out from us, because they were not of us; for if they had been of us, they would no doubt have continued with us; but they went out that they might be made manifest that they were not all of us.—I JOHN ii, 19.

Why have they left us? did we not impart
 Through Masons' ceremonials, noble thought?
Is there one doctrine, dear to generous heart,
 We have not, somewhere, in our system wrought?
Faith, Hope in God, a childlike Reverence,
High, brotherly Trust, a very strong defense,—
And patriotic Zeal, and love for Art,—
Such are the lines we printed on their heart.

Why have they left us? did they not receive
 Within our tyled retreats a holy thing?
Walls, floor, and ceiling, all combined to weave
 The pattern woven by Judea's king;
Bright types of truth immortal, old and quaint,
Things rare and common in strange union blent;
The Square, the Trowel, objects near and far,
The quivering Leaflet and the Orient Star.

Why have they left us? in yon hallowed graves
 Are there not buried friends for whom they mourn?
How can they look where yonder willow waves
 Nor long for those who've passed death's solemn bourne?
We laid them there with mystic signals, given
All earnestly, connecting earth with Heaven,
We'll join them there when the great WORD shall come,
And with them *rise* when bursts th' inclosing tomb.

Why have they left us? do they feel secure
 That trials and afflictions will not come?
Can they suppose that earthly things endure,
 That anything is *sure*, this side the tomb?
Health, Wealth, Prosperity are but a span,
That mocks with transient bliss deluded man;
When Sorrow shades us, Oh, how good to bend
Our steps toward the Lodge where friend meets friend!

Then let *the good* return and go with us;
 Their vacant seats wait to be occupied;
Our shattered ranks have long bewailed their loss —
 Worse the deserter than the faithful dead!

Return,— go with us in our generous toil ;
Return,— sleep with us in our hallowed soil ;
And when the well pleased Master calls his own,
Stand by our side before the Great White Throne !

THE DUELIST.

A Brother, known and beloved for his Masonic and general worth, and had in fraternal con-
templation for the highest honors of the Craft, was killed in a duel. His Lodge, though warmly
solicited, refused to bury him with Masonic honors, but accompanied his remains to the grave in
citizens' apparel.

Hark, how the air resounds with death !
    Lo, to the tomb a Mason comes !
But where is *the badge* the Mason hath —
    Type of a life beyond the tombs ?
Is there not one in all the band
    Owns him a Brother now?
Speak, ye that weep around the bier,
    And say where the honors were his due.

How he was loved these tear drops show —
    How he was honored midst our band ;
For he had a heart for every woe.
    For each distress a liberal hand.
Bright in the East our rising sun,
    Proud viewed we his career ;—
But now that to-day his race is run,
    We fling no Acacia on his bier.

Whispering low the cause we yield —
    History of his unworthy death —
False honor called him to the field
    And death the erring Brother met.
No dirge from us can o'er him swell,
    No banners round him wave ;
Emblem of faith we dare not strew
    Upon the sad, self-murderer's grave.

Ceases the knell of sorrow now —
    But long will the heavy sigh be drawn ;
Vacant the East ! ah, heavy woe !
    Our Wisdom, Strength and Beauty gone ;
But worst the grief this thought will bring
    To our fraternal home —
Brightest and dearest, thou art passed,
    Dishonored, to an early tomb !

198

THE STRAIT AND NARROW WAY.

We Masons walk along a road
　　Narrow and rugged, straight and rough,
But waymarks are laid down by God,
Whose discipline and rules afford
　　Guidance upon the road enough.

At every step we're called to warn
　　Some halting, erring, fainting friend ;
Some pilgrim from the road will turn
In paths forbidden — slow to learn
　　What sufferings such sins attend.

The poisonous cup allures the most,—
　　Alas, what havoc has it made !
What noble hearts therein are lost !
But few retrace of all the host
　　Who in this dangerous path have strayed.

The lust of flesh,— the speech profane,—
　　The tattling tongue, the thievish hand,—
The greed that craves unholy gain,—
And Sabbath breach and murder stain,—
　　Alas, the errings of our band!

At every step we're called to aid
　　The fallen of misfortune's host ;
The sick, in withering bondage laid,—
The mourner, sorrowing by his dead,—
　　The aged, destitute and lost.

Each waymark set by Hand Divine
　　Yet points unerring to the end,—
And we who seek life's crown to win
Must shun the glittering lures of Sin,
　　And the sure voice of GOD attend.

OUR MASTER thus we'll represent ;
　　HE walked in innocence life's road ;
To humbleness strange beauty lent,
In deeds of ceaseless mercy bent;
　　And gave to man the grace of God !

Departing to His Lodge above
  Thus to our willing hearts he said —
"Your faith by deeds of mercy prove,
Live in full exercise of love,
  And I will raise you from the dead!"

THE OLD TYLER.

The presentation of a beautiful set of Gavels to the Grand Lodge of Iowa, in 1869, by THEODORE SCHREINER, for many years the Grand Tyler, was the occasion of this poem.

  It was a happy thought
  To have these gavels wrought
By the old Tyler, for the honored Craft;
  Though placed without the door,
  To make the Lodge secure,
You know him as a bright and polished shaft.

  How many a year he's stood,
  Old Schreiner, brave and good,
And guarded you while secret works went on!
  How many a Brother's dead,
  Since first his honored head
Was seen amongst you in the early June.

  Can you forget him? No;
  His *earthly form* may go,
His kindly smile be hidden in the sod;
  But when those gavels ring,
  Fond memories they will bring
Of the old Tyler gone to rest with God.

  Then let his gavels sound
  At every annual round,
And when you hear them think of him that gave;
  'Tis but a fleeting day,
  And then the Craft will say,
"The Lodge has joined old Schreiner in the grave!"

  A knock will yet be heard,
  The sheeted dead be stirred,
With all that *are* and *have been* we shall rise;
  Oh, may each Brother come,
  Thus summoned from his tomb,
And share eternal glory in the skies!

HOLY LAND SPECIMENS.

I seem to see the heavenly Book
　　Ten thousand roots send down,
As though from out its native soil
　　To vindicate its own;
To rock and water, wood and earth,
　　The unerring fibers haste,
And draw such princely wisdom forth
　　As vivifies the waste.

The Book itself grows wiser, hence,
　　Its Lamp beams forth anew;
The Spirit's best deliverance
　　More plainly comes to view.
If He, our Wisest, deigned to use
　　Such objects for our good,
Oh, let us not their teachings lose,
　　So plainly understood.

NUNC DIMITTIS.

It is written of a venerable Craftsman of the past generation, that, having lived through all the trials and reproaches of the Anti-Masonic period (1826–36), and maintained his membership first in one Lodge and then in another, as the contiguous Lodges successively gave way under the pressure, he came peacefully to his death bed at last, and smilingly said to the friends who thronged about his bedside, "Now, Brothers, let me have my demit!"

"Now dismiss me, while I linger
　　For one fond, one dear word more;
Have I done my labor fairly?
　　Is there aught against my score?
Have I wronged in all this circle
　　One by deed, or word, or blow?—
Silence speaks my full acquittance—
　　Nunc dimittis, let me go!

"Let me go, I crave my wages;
　　Long I've suffered, long I've toiled;
Never once through work days idle,
　　Never once my apron soiled;
To the Chamber, where the Master
　　Waits with smiling to bestow
Corn, and wine, and oil abundant,
　　Nunc dimittis, let me go!

"Let me go, but *you* must tarry,
   Till the sixth day's close has come;
Heat and burden patient bear ye
   While you're far away from home;
But a little, for the summons
   Waits alike for each of you; —
Mine is sounding, spirits wait me,
   Nunc dimittis, let me go!

"Oh, the Sabbath day in Heaven!
   Oh, the joys reserved for them,
Faithful Builders of the Temple,
   Type of blest Jerusalem!
Oh, the rapture of the meeting
   With the friends 'twas bliss to know!
Strive no longer to detain me,
   Nunc dimittis, let me go!"

Hushed that voice its fond imploring;
   Faded is that eager eye;
Gone the soul of labor wearied,
   To repose eternally.
But the memory of his service
   Oft shall cheer me as I go,
Till the hour *I, too*, petition, —
   "*Nunc dimittis*, let me go!"

THE CELESTIAL RECORD.

An English Mason, whose name has never been made public, donated considerable sums of money about the year 1852, and made the Western Grand Lodges his almoners for its disbursement in Masonic charities. Kentucky received $500.

Written in Heaven
   What he has given!
Placed on the records in letters of gold;
   Read by the spirits,
   Judges of merits —
Some day the name to us all will be told.

   Meantime let silence,
   Free from all violence,
Drop its mute veil o'er the face of the man;
   Seek not to show it —
   Strive not to know it —
Go and do likewise, ye Brothers who can.

Blest was the offering;
Voices of suffering
Hushed under sympathy noble as that;
Tear drops were trailing—
Sighs and bewailing,
And tear drops and sorrow the orphans forget.

England, our Mother,
Toward thee each Brother
Reverently turns at this noble emprise,
" *This* makes the cable
Holy and stable,
Binding our Lodges forever," he cries.

A RESPONSE OF GRATITUDE.

Long may your Lodge fires burn!
Workmen in mystic labors, kind and good!
And many a year return
To shed new luster on your Brotherhood;
You, who the call of mercy heard and heeded,
And gave with cheerfulness as it was needed.

Men may your work defame,
And call your deeds the offspring of the night;
How often scorn and shame
Have stricken hearts in virtuous doings bright!
The LORD of all bore to his home of bliss,
In hands and feet and side the proofs of this.

But doubt ye not, dear friends,
There surely waits for you a FULL REWARD.
The Lord will give amends
At the great PAY DAY, for thus saith the Lord,—
" Because ye did it to the least, so free,
Come to my throne, ye did it unto me!"

A lasting blessing rest
Upon your labors prospering more and more;
God's largest gifts and best
Fill to the brim your basket and your store,
Till from hard service summoned by His voice,
You shall in LODGE CELESTIAL all rejoice!

THE TEACHER TO HIS PUPILS.

THE NATIONAL MASONIC SCHOOL OF INSTRUCTION, at Louisville, Kentucky, May, 1859, was a scene of great interest to the participants. The assemblage was large and enthusiastic, representing many portions of the country. The writer, as President, made the following his Valedictory of the School:

From the hills of old Virginia, from the meadows fat and rare,
From the banks of broad Ohio, and of others broad and fair,—
From the borders of our neighboring states, true neighbors each they stand,
You have come responsive, Brothers, and have gripped me by the hand.

You have brought me words of greeting,— words I never can forget;—
Have given me light my eyes will see till life's poor sun has set;—
You have told with signs significant, your messages so true,
And now, at parting, one kind word I offer, Friends, to you.

A goodly group around us! the thoughtful air of Greene —
The cheerful gaze of Webster,— and Williams' modest mien,—
The chivalry of Bullock, that courteous look and bow,—
The sterling sense, the honest voice, the gentleness of Howe.

These are the types of all who've sat unwearied 'neath the voice
That told of Masons' labors and of Masons' well earned joys;
Deep in the souls of these have sunk the unchangeable and true,
The mighty COVENANTS that bind, dear Brothers, me and you.

Here, too, those welcome lights have shone, ay, welcome as the sun,
Whose fame as skillful builders has in distant lands been won —
The veterans, Penn and Norris, Tracey, vigilant and leal,
And Hunt, the genial-hearted, and Bayless, true as steel.

To all who *work* as these work, to all who *love* like them,
To all who *build* as they build the NEW JERUSALEM,
Be *wages* such as they shall have, when, standing in the West,
They hear the Master call them, " Come, ye faithful, to your rest."

True, zealous, loving men ! on this tempestuous, rocky shore
I may not meet — ah, sad to think — not meet or greet you more;
Each day speaks louder in my ears the uncertainties of time,
And death amidst life's music louder peals his solemn chime.

Then each FAREWELL! bear homeward LIGHT our fathers well approved,
Set up the Pillars, rear the walls;—'twas work our fathers loved;
Time will your fond devotion to unending ages tell;
God will o'ersee and bless you ! Brothers, faithfully, farewell !

TIMELY WARNING.

Where is thy Brother, Craftsman, say,
Where is the erring one to-day?
We look around the festive band,—
What cheerful smiles on every hand!
The voice of laughter swells amain,—
Where is the brightest of the train?
The ready wit, the generous word,
The glee in music's best accord,
The bounteous gifts,— oh, where is he,
The prince of Masons' revelry?
Not left unwarned in death to fall,
To lapse without one friendly call!

Alas, the grave has closed above
So many objects of our love!
There is so many a vacant chair
In every group where Masons are!
Of some the drunkard's cup doth tell;
Tempted, yet sorrowing, *they fell;*
Day after day they saw the light
Recede, till day was turned to night;
Yet yearned and strove to pause, and stay
Their feet upon the slippery way;
They fell, and none so bright are left
As those of whom we are bereft.

A voice from out the grave demands,—
"Where is thy Brother? are thy hands
Quite guiltless of his priceless blood?
How often have ye kindly stood,
And whispered loving words and prayer
Within the erring Brother's ear?
How often counseled, plead, and warned,
And from approaching danger turned?"
The thoughtful tear, the heavy sigh,
Must speak for conscience a reply;
Quick, then, oh Craftsman, up and save
The living from untimely grave!

We whisper good counsel in the ear of a Brother, and in the most tender manner remind him of his faults, and endeavor to aid his reformation; such is the world-wide command.

ASK! SEEK!! KNOCK!!!

Ask, and ye shall receive;
　　Seek, ye shall surely find;
Knock, ye shall no resistance meet,
　　If come with ready mind;
For all that ask, and ask aright,
Are welcome to our Lodge to-night.

Lay down the bow and spear;
　　Resign the sword and shield;
Forget the arts of warfare here,
　　The arms of peace to wield;
For all that seek, and seek aright,
Are welcome to our Lodge to-night.

Bring hither thoughts of peace;
　　Bring hither words of love;
Diffuse the pure and holy joy
　　That cometh from above;
For all that knock, and knock aright,
Are welcome to our Lodge to-night.

Ask help of Him that's high;
　　Seek grace of Him that's true;
Knock patiently, the hand is nigh,
　　Will open unto you;
For all that ask, seek, knock aright,
Are welcome to our Lodge to-night.

THE LAST, LAST WORD, "FARE WELL."

The last, last word,—oh, let it tell
The inmost soul of love — *Fare well!*
　　Fare well in heart, in health, in store,
In going out, in coming in;
And when to slumber you incline,
May man's respect and woman's smile
And childhood's prattle to beguile,
　　Be yours, be yours, for evermore!
By every impulse that can swell
A loving heart, fare well, fare well!

Fare well,—the lights grow dim; the tear
   Lingers and sparkles in the eye;
"So mote it be!" I faintly hear
   Winged on the breath of answering sigh.
It is the voice of sympathy,
It tells of a fraternal tie
Once, twice and thrice about us wound
When first on consecrated ground
We walked the dark, mysterious round.
By all the secrets it doth tell
Of Bonds and Links and Ties, *fare well!*

Fare well! what other word besides
   Conveys the spirit of God's *Word,*
Around, above, beneath whose lids
   We tied the indissoluble cord?
Had I the tongue with power to say
   All that the hand expert can tell
Of signs and grips and mystic way
   I could but say, but say *fare well!*
I could but say, "May God *thus* do
By me should ever I prove untrue!"
And my choked utterance would prove
How weak are *words* to tell my love.

Then let the HAND speak what it should,
   And call to witness noblest things;
   The bounding heart responds and brings
Its godlike power to compass good.
The answering heavens admit the plea,
And vouch a present Deity;
Angels my loving wishes swell,
And God himself proclaims,—*fare well!*

EARNESTNESS OF COVENANTING.

Never will I break the Covenant
   Plighted, Brother, with thee now!
ONE between us stands attesting
   To the fervor of my vow.
In His name, *above* His Promise,
   By His honor, *for* His cause,
Here's my hand, the Lord confirm it,—
   I will surely keep my vows!

SO MOTE IT BE

So mote it be with us when life shall end,
And from the East the LORD OF LIGHT shall bend
And we, our six days' labor fully done,
Shall claim our wages at the MASTER's throne.

So mote it be with us; that when the Square,
That perfect implement, with heavenly care,
Shall be applied to every block we bring,
No fault shall see our MASTER and our KING.

So mote it be with us; that though our days
Have yielded little to the MASTER's praise,
The little we have builded may be proved
To have the marks our first GRAND MASTER loved!

So mote it be with us; we are but weak;
Our days are few; our trials who can speak?
But sweet is our communion while we live,
And rich rewards the MASTER deigns to give.

Let's toil, then, cheerfully, let's die in hope;
The WALL in wondrous grandeur riseth up;
They who come after shall the work complete,
And they and we receive the wages meet.

THE CHAMBER OF IMAGERY.

DECLAMATION PRIOR TO A LODGE LECTURE.

HAIL, workmen of the mystic labor, hail!
To-night let all things that have language speak,
Here in the image chamber of the Craft,
Where pure instruction beams on every hand;
Above — the spangled Arch, whose diamond rays
Twinkle sweet welcome on our road to Heaven;
Around — emblems of truth eternal, grand,
Quaint old imaginings of by-gone days;
Before — oh, blest eternally of God,
YON BOOK, whose secret is undying hope;
Beneath — the earth, our mother, whence we sprung,
And in whose bosom we shall sleep at last;
All these inspire and move the Poet's heart
To claim a welcome, Brothers, in your Band.

And let them speak ; those Pillars that look down
In brazen symbolisms on the scene ;
That golden G, that names the sacred Name ;
The Sheaf that marks His beauty and His love ;
The Gavel ringing in submissive ears ;
The Level, Plumb, and Square, on faithful breasts;
The Gauge, wise monitor of fleeting time,—
Of time, whose sands no mortal may recall ;
The Trowel, with its soothing tale of peace ;
Each has its voice, and let it speak to-night.

Craftsmen, we build but for a day,
Unless His precepts we obey !
How oft we see within our land
A structure reared upon the sand !
Its walls magnificently rise,—
Its turrets pierce the very skies,—
Crowds through its portals eager press,—
Beauty and rank its altars grace,—
And then the tempest falls, 'tis gone
From tower top to cornerstone !

Craftsmen, this lesson heed, and keep,—
Lay your foundations wide and deep !

THE THREE SALUTES.

I hail you, Brother, in the place
    Where none but those should meet
Whose *types* are bended knee and brow,
    And the uncovered feet;
I take you by the grip, expressing
    All that heart can feel,
And I pledge myself to be to you
    A Brother TRUE AS STEEL!

I've watched with real joy your quest,
    So ardent and so rare,—
Your bold, unflinching gaze upon
    The things we most revere;
I've seen that nothing daunts you
    In the paths our LIGHTS reveal;
And I pledge myself again to you,
    A Brother TRUE AS STEEL!

I think there's that within you
    Only needs for *time* to show,—
Will kindle up a flame, where others
    Only feel a *glow;*
I think the grave will claim you
    As a Mason ripe and leal;
And so once more I pledge myself
    A Brother TRUE AS STEEL!

WHITE-APRONED BROTHERS.

Come, cease from your labors,
Ye white-aproned neighbors,
    And answer my words —
Tells us *who are ye ?*
" We are friends of humanity,
Hating profanity,
Spurning all vanity,
    CHILDREN OF PEACE —
    Men who can feel
All our *own* need of kindness,
    And bless the GREAT GOD,
Who hath lightened our blindness."

Tell us, *what do ye ?*
" By precept, example,
We're building a temple,
Fair, lofty and ample,
    For HIM whom we serve —
    Following the plans
That our MASTER doth give us,
    And amply repaid
When His servants receive us."

And *what do you work with ?*
" The Gauge and the Gavel,
The Plumb, Square, and Level,
And then as we travel,
    The Trowel we hold —
    Skillfully these,
At first we're inducted —
    Obediently these,
In the way we're instructed."

Your timbers, what are they?
" The blocks that we quarry,
And timbers so heavy,
Our hands shape and carry,
    Those ashlars are MEN ;
    Rough ashlars they are —
But hewed, marked and garnished,
    By precepts divine,
Our task will be finished."

Your resting, when is it?
" We look for no leisure,
We sigh for no pleasure,
We covet no treasure,
    Till SATURDAY NIGHT —
Wages and joys,
And a rest without breaking,
    Wait for us then,
In the home that we're seeking."

"And he said unto me, What are these which are arrayed in white robes, and whence came they? And I said unto him, Sir, thou knowest. And he said unto me, These are they which came out of great tribulation, and have washed their robes, and have made them white in the blood of the Lamb."

ALL-SEEING EYE.

THERE is an eye through blackest night
    A vigil ever keeps ;
A vision of unerring light,
O'er lowly vale, o'er giddy height,
    The Eye that never sleeps.

Midst poverty and sickness lain,
    The outcast lowly weeps ;
What marks the face convulsed with pain?
What marks the softened look again?
    The Eye that never sleeps.

Above the far meridian sun —
    Below profoundest deeps,
Where dewy day his course begun,
Where scarlet marks his labor done —
    The Eye that never sleeps.

No limit bounds th' Eternal Sight ;
  No misty cloud o'ersweeps ;
The depths of hell give up their light —
Eternity itself is bright —
  The Eye that never sleeps.

Then rest we calm, though round our head
  The life-storm fiercely sweeps ;
What fear is in the blast ? what dread
In mightier Death ? An Eye's o'erhead,
  The Eye that never sleeps.

TOM BIGGS' BOTTOM DOLLAR.

He tapped his bottom dollar, Joe,
  When that poor barefoot child
Came moaning through the drifted snow,
  With cold and hunger wild;
Tom Biggs himself is old and poor
  And has a cough, you know,
But when he saw that wretched girl,
  He tapped his bottom dollar, Joe —
  Tom tapped his bottom dollar !

I don't believe he'll miss it, Joe,
  In that last, solemn rest
To which he's hurrying so fast,—
  He's shaky, at the best; .
I rather think the records there
  That very coin will show,
And God himself will keep the count
  Of Biggs' bottom dollar, Joe —
  Tom Biggs' bottom dollar !

THE OLIVE DOOR.

The two doors (of the Temple) were of olive tree. — I KINGS vi, 31.

No more to grieve for pleasures gone,
  For broken hopes no more,
We leave the outer world forlorn,
  And close the Olive Door.

The Tree of Peace, whose holy leaf
  The gentle Tyler bore ;
It ranked in Eden's bloom the chief,
  And made the Olive Door.

When brother-hands, on Aaron's head,
  The holy oil did pour,
The Olive of its fatness shed,
  And made the Olive Door.

So may we find unfailing Peace,
  .And Plenty's utmost store ;
May God His plenteousness increase,
  Within the Olive Door.

We gather round the Altar here,
  With spirits gone before,
And join the hand, in union dear,
  Within the Olive Door.

213

FESTIVAL SONGS.

FIFTIETH ANNIVERSARY OF A LODGE.

Two score and ten revolving years
Full charged with labors, sighs and tears,
    The Craft have brought
    Their tools, and wrought
Upon this temple old and vast,
A legend of the mighty past!
Now, Brothers, joyfully appear,
And celebrate our FIFTIETH YEAR!

One-half the century is spent,
But where the faithful ones who lent
    Voice, heart, and hand,
    A zealous Band,
To set aloft their Pillars twain
And dedicate the Holy Fane?
Not one is spared us to appear
And celebrate our FIFTIETH YEAR!

They sleep beneath th' Acacia green;
Their graves in solemn ranks are seen;
    And at the head,
    'Tis joy to read
The emblems full of hope and trust,
Which give a glory to their dust;
But yet, their names and lives are here
To celebrate our FIFTIETH YEAR!

What change has swept across this land
Since first their Gavels gave command!
    It is our boast,
    The countless host
Of Crafts, the living and the dead,
Where then a wilderness was spread;
In serried ranks our lines appear,
To celebrate our FIFTIETH YEAR!

Unchanged while all the world grows old,
We joy the ancient faith to hold,

Through centuries still
The task fulfill
That God intrusts to man below,
Freemasonry no change shall know !
Strike hands in this, ye Crafts, appear
And celebrate our FIFTIETH YEAR !

And when the century shall end
And over us th' Acacia bend,
The Craft will come
Within this home,
And speak our names with grateful thrill,
The loved, the unforgotten still ;
In such belief, dear friends, appear
And celebrate our FIFTIETH YEAR !

BROTHERLY LOVE.

By one GOD created, by one SAVIOUR saved,
By one SPIRIT lighted, by one MARK engraved,
We're taught in the wisdom our spirits approve,
To cherish the spirit of BROTHERLY LOVE.
Love, love, Brotherly love —
This world hath no spirit like Brotherly love.

In the land of the stranger we Masons abide,
In forest, in quarry, on Lebanon's side ;
Yon temple we're building, the plan's from above,
And we labor, supported by BROTHERLY LOVE.

Though the service be hard, and the wages be scant,
If the MASTER accept it, our hearts are content ;
The prize that we toil for, we'll have it above,
When the Temple's completed, in BROTHERLY LOVE.

Yes, yes, though the week may be long, it will end,—
Though the Temple be lofty, THE KEYSTONE will stand ;
And the SABBATH, blest day, every thought will remove,
Save the memory fraternal of BROTHERLY LOVE.

By one GOD created,—come, brothers, 'tis day !
By one SPIRIT lighted,—come, brothers, away !
With Beauty, and Wisdom, and Strength to approve,
Let's toil while there's labor in BROTHERLY LOVE.

ST. JOHN'S DAY.

Go now, dear friends, take fond farewell,
   Bear kindly cheer to Masons' home ;
The bliss of this bright morning tell
   In dews of memory to bloom.

Go now, dear friends, but ne'er forget
   That smiles and sunshine are of God ;
He makes the joys of life complete,
   And strews sweet flowers along the road.

Go, then, and serve Him all your days,
   Walk in His ways, obey His word ;
His ways are ways of pleasantness,
   And all His paths sweet peace afford.

Go, then, and hopeful look on high,
   There, where He sits on radiant Throne ;
He sees the tear, he hears the sigh,
   And waits to make our life His own.

MASONIC GREETING.

Lo, from the distant West,
Lo, from your honored guest,
The voice of greeting and the word of prayer;
Ye sons of cheer, all hail !
This grateful tongue shall tell
The tie that binds you and the joys you share !

There is a CORD of length,
There is a CHAIN of strength;
Around you each I see the sacred coil.
How long, ah, well I know !
How strong, your deeds do show,
The while you labor in the sacred toil.

In amplest share bestowed,
By Him you worship — GOD,
The joy of Friendship well you feel and prize.
'Tis HIS own best design,
'Tis perfect, 'tis divine,
It is the bliss diffused through upper skies.

Peace be within your halls !
The CEMENT of your walls
Be HOLY LOVE— pure, indestructible !
From the o'erarching Heaven
A gracious smile be given,
The favor of the DEITY to tell.

When each shall bow in death,
Joy to the parting breath !
Rich fragrance from a thousand generous deeds !
And where your ashes be,
Sacred to memory
The spot while man pure truth and honor heeds !

And me, oh loving Friends,
When life's poor story ends,
Me in your inner heart of hearts enshrine !
Humble, but oh, sincere,—
Erring and sorrowing here,
Write me as one who loved each Mystic line !

Builders of light, your hands !
Distant our several lands ?
No; for I see, I hear, I feel you now !
Bind once again the chain;
Again, dear Friends, again;
Hear, Gracious Lord, hear and confirm the Vow !

PSALM CXXXIII.

How pleasant is the scene
    Where Masons kindly dwell !
Where mystic tapers burn serene,
    And hymns fraternal swell.

How good the searching word
    That from the East descends !
It speaks the unerring Law of God
    And richest grace attends.

How strong the Mason tie,—
    It holds the willing band ;
'Tis wove in golden unity
    By God's mysterious hand.

How sacred is the place!
Behold, He dwelleth here!
His dews descend in nightly grace
Our loving Craft to cheer.

THE FREEMASON'S HOME.

Music of a very high character was composed for this by George F. Root.

Where hearts are warm with kindred fire,
    And love beams free from answering eyes,
Bright spirits hover always there,
    And *that's* the home the Masons prize.
The Mason's Home, the peaceful home,
    The home of love and light and joy;
How gladly does the Mason come
    To share his tender, sweet employ.

All round the world, by land, by sea,
    Where summers burn or winters chill,
The exiled Mason turns to thee,
    And yearns to share the joys we feel.
The Mason's Home, the happy home,
    The home of light and love and joy;
There's not an hour but I would come
    And share this tender, sweet employ!

A weary task, a dreary round,
    Is all benighted man may know,
But *here* a brighter scene is found,
    The brightest scene that's found below.
The Mason's Home, the blissful home,
    Glad center of unmingled joy
Long as I live I'll gladly come
    And share this tender, sweet employ.

And when the hour of death shall come,
    And darkness seal my closing eye,
May HANDS FRATERNAL bear me home,
    The home where weary Masons lie!
The Mason's Home, the heavenly home,
    To faithful hearts eternal joy;
How blest to find beyond the tomb
    The end of all our sweet employ!

THE GRAND, GRAND DAYS OF OLD.

Ye blithe and happy few
    Ye true, ye merry, merry men,
Come, now, I'll sing to you
    A good old mystic strain;
When the Rules and the Tools
    Made men free and bold;
And the Masons were like brothers —
They were not like any others
    In the Grand, Grand Days of Old!

How broad, how high toward Heaven
    Their Temple nobly, nobly soared!
And there 'twas grandly given —
    The PRESENCE OF THE LORD;
For his fire, on each spire,
    Did the craft behold;
When the Masons were like brothers —
They were not like any others
    In the Grand, Grand Days of Old!

The tears of kings and craft,
    Like drops of heavy, heavy dew,
Fell on our Beauteous Shaft
    That crime had rent in two;
And the dirge of the surge,
    Like a deep bell tolled;
And the Masons were like brothers —
They were not like any others
    In the Grand, Grand Days of Old!

They bore our Master then,
    With still and broken, broken heart;
No skill like his again
    Shall bless the Royal Art;
For His lamp, through death's damp,
    Cannot light our mold;
Though the Masons were like brothers —
They were not like any others
    In the Grand, Grand Days of Old!

But shall we not revive
    Those good, those happy, happy days?
Our MASTER bids us strive,

And all our toil repays.
We can trust,—He is just,
And will not withhold
While the Masons act like brothers,
And be not like any others,
As in Grand, Grand Days of Old!

TO MASONS EVERYWHERE.

In gladsome mood again we're met,—
How swiftly passed the year!
Begin the feast, and Brothers, drink
To Masons everywhere!
A Mason's love is unrestrained;
Each other's woes we share;
Then lift the cup, and, Brothers, drink
To Masons everywhere!

What would our Mystic Tie be worth,—
How little should we care
For Masonry, did not its links
Encircle everywhere?
With Masons' love so unrestrained,
Each other's woes to share,
Well may we fill the cup, and drink
To Masons everywhere!

Though some we loved have fallen on
The weary path of care,
What then? in Heaven they're yet our own!
To Masons everywhere!
For Masons' love, so unrestrained,
Eternity may dare!
Then, Brothers, fill, and fondly drink
To Masons everywhere!

And so, when death shall claim us, too,
And other forms be here,
May we in memory's heart be held
By Masons everywhere!
For Masons' love is unrestrained,
Nor death the chain may tear;
O'erflow the cup, and, Brothers, drink
To Masons everywhere!

THE OLD TYLER.

God bless the Old Tyler! how long he has trudged,
    Through sunshine and storm, with his "summonses due!"
No pain nor fatigue the Old Tyler has grudged
    To serve the great Order, Freemasons, and you.

God bless the Old Tyler! how oft he has led
    The funeral procession from Lodge door to grave!
How grandly his weapon has guarded the dead
    To their last quiet home where the Acacia boughs wave.

God bless the Old Tyler! how oft he has knocked,
    When, vigilant, strangers craved welcome and rest!
How widely your portals, though guarded and locked,
    Have swung to the signal the Tyler knows best!

There's a Lodge where the door is *not* guarded nor tyled,
    There's a Land without graves, without mourners or sin,
There's a MASTER most gracious, paternal and mild,
    And he waits the Old Tyler, and bids him come in!

And there the Old Tyler, *no longer outside,*—
    No longer with weapon of war in his hand,—
A glorified spirit, shall grandly abide
    And close by the MASTER, high honored, shall stand.

ST. JOHN'S DAY.

Ended now the Mason's labors,
Past the travel and the toil ;
Gather in, ye loving neighbors,
Share the Corn, the Wine, the Oil ;
Brethren now, of each degree,
Come in harmony and glee ;
    Happy meeting,
    Gentle greeting,—
'Tis the joy of Masonry.

Spirits of the blest departed,
As on earthly ways they roam,
Where are met the faithful-hearted
They to share our labors come ;
Though their forms we cannot see
They are here with you and me.

221

Love unites us with its cement ;
Truth inspires the Mason's breast ;
Ever faithful, ever clement,—
Thus our doctrines we attest.
Thus we come of each degree,
Come in harmony and glee ;
  Happy meeting,
  Gentle greeting,—
'Tis the joy of Masonry.

BUILDING THE FANE.

Come, Comrades, let us build !¹
Our Mason hearts are filled
With fond solicitude and keen desire,²
While musing o'er these heaps,
Whose every ashlar keeps
The stains of bloodshed and the marks of fire !³

What though some voice would say
"Leave Salem to decay !"⁴
Our Mason hearts were not instructed thus.
Let's work for Salem's Lord,—
And, Comrades, be assured
The God of Heaven, HE will prosper us !⁵

With goodly SWORD and bright,
With TROWEL in the right,
Each hand is sanctified to God's employ ;⁶
Let's build, nor doubt that soon —
This weary labor done—
Our Mason hearts will feel the BUILDER'S joy !⁷

¹ Come and let us build up the walls of Jerusalem, that we be no more a reproach.— NEHE-MIAH ii, 17. ² I sat down and wept, and mourned, and fasted, and prayed.— NEHEMIAH i. 4. ³ They slew with the sword young man and maiden, old man, and him that stooped for age, and they burnt the house of God and all the palaces with fire.— II CHRONICLES xxxiv, 17, 18. ⁴ Sanbal-lat and Tobiah and Geshem laughed us to scorn, and despised us and said, What is this thing that ye do ?— NEHEMIAH ii, 19. ⁵ I answered and said unto them, "The God of Heaven, He will pros-per us, therefore we His servants will arise and build."— NEHEMIAH ii, 20. ⁶ Every one with *one* of his hands wrought in the work, and with the *other* hand held a weapon.— NEHEMIAH iv, 17. ⁷ They sang together by course in praising and giving thanks, and all the people shouted with a great shout, because the foundation of the house of the Lord was laid.— EZRA iii. 11.

The cry of Nehemiah, when, on his return to Jerusalem, he saw the ROYAL CITY lying "heaps upon heaps," has, in every age, echoed upon the heart of the moral builder. Oh, the world in ruins ! oh, the wrecks of humanity, lying about us on every hand, and crying aloud for the MASTER BUILDER, who alone can reconstruct the edifice so fearfully cast down !

PERISHING ON THE RISE.

This *extravaganza* was written in ridicule of the tendency of the times to stiffen up Lodge work, and turn the Worshipful Master into a mere *martinet*.

Old Jephtha Hoys had drilled his boys
    With gavel, plumb and square, sir,
Till every craft a perfect shaft
    Stood perpendicular, sir.
Each Friday night 'twas his delight
    To call them to the hall, sir,
And catechise the willing boys,
    Till each could "cut and call," sir.

One evening late it was his fate,
    In leaning back his chair, sir,
The window glass right through to pass,
    And push the thing too far, sir;
In fact, he fled, heels over head,
    Clear down unto the ground, sir;
With mighty noise old Jephtha Hoys
    A broken neck had found, sir.

The neighbors there, with tender care,
    Prepared him for the tomb, sir,
And on the way, a long array
    Went out with grief and gloom, sir;
Yet many said, with whispering dread,
    "No Mason here is seen, sir!"
Strange to declare, not one was there,
    To cast the mystic green, sir!

I'll tell you where those Masons were,—
    Prepare for much surprise, sir,—
When Jephtha Hoys forsook his boys,
    He left them *on the rise*, sir!
The Brethren stood straight as they could,
    Till he should bid them sit, sir;
And as he's gone with no return,
    Why, there they're standing yet, sir.

The Tyler bore, outside the door,
    The pangs of cold and thirst, sir;
The Wardens twain do still remain,
    And will till they are dust, sir;

The Deacons stand with rod in hand,
  Not one will budge the least, sir;
And, strange to own, each skeleton
  Is *facing to the East*, sir.

Then be my task humbly to ask
  Each Master this to read, sir,
And beg and pray to them, that they
  The moral well may heed, sir;
When calling up the mystic group,
  To stand and catechise, sir,
Think of those boys of Jephtha Hoys,
  Who *perished on the rise*, sir.

WORLD-WIDE RECOGNITION.

Wherever man is tracing
  The weary ways of care,
Midst wild and desert pacing,
  Or lands of softer air,

WE SURELY KNOW EACH OTHER,
  And with true words of cheer,
Each Brother hails his Brother,
  And hope wings lightly there.

Wherever tears are falling,—
  The soul's dark, wintry rain,—
And human sighs are calling
  To human hearts in vain,

We surely know each other, etc.

Wherever prayer is spoken,
  In earnestness of Faith,
We're minded of the TOKEN
  That tells our MASTER's death.

We pray, then, for each other, etc.

Wherever man is lying
  Unknowing and unknown,
There's one yet by the dying,—
  He shall not die alone.

For then we know each other, etc.

ST. JOHN'S DAY.

We meet who never met before,
  And may not meet again;
Then fill the day with happy thoughts
  That memory will retain.

To-day the hand in honest grasp,
  To-day the tuneful voice,
Speak of the white-robed Brotherhood
  Who round the earth rejoice.

To-day be Sabbath to our God;
  His grace inspired this tie;
Honor to Him, the first, the last,—
  Lord of Eternity!

The day will come, oh, blissful time,
  The parted shall unite;
Be ours the hope, when life is done,
  To share the long delight!

NEW YEAR'S REFLECTIONS.

There is nothing esoteric in these initials. They are read, " The Celestial Lodge above, where the Supreme Architect of the Universe presides."

Shall we see it, loving Brothers,
  Ere another New Year's day?
Shall we join those loving others,
  Whom the past year tore away?
Shall we change this toil and drudge,
For the bright CELESTIAL LODGE,
      T. C. L. A. W.
    T. S. A. O. T. U. P.

Shall we tread that one more station,
  Take that last and best degree,
Whose consummate " Preparation "
  Is *to set the spirit free?*
Lay our bodies off, that then
Souls unburdened may go in,
      T. C. L. A. W.
    T. S. A. O. T. U. P.

Shall we find beyond the river,—
    Shall we find beyond the tomb,—
Those who left us, not forever,
    Left us till we, too, should come?
Shall we learn the long-lost WORD
That admits a man to GOD,—
       T. C. L. A. W.
      T. S. A. O. T. U. P.?

Then, be zealous, loving Brothers,
    While your lives so swiftly tend;
Emulate those faithful others
    In the prizes they have gained;
O'er the river, on the shore,
They are happy evermore,—
       T. C. L. A. W.
      T. S. A. O. T. U. P.

Toil,— your wages rich are ready;
    Bear,— your burdens all shall cease;
Give,— however poor and needy;
    Pray,— and God will give release
From this bitter toil and drudge
To the bright CELESTIAL LODGE,
       T. C L. A. W.
      T. S. A. O. T. U. P.

DUTIES OF THE CRAFT.

Come, and let us seek the straying,
    Lead him to the SHEPHERD back ;
Come, the traveler's feet betraying,
    Guide him from the dangerous track ;
Come, a solemn voice reminds us —
Come, a mystic fetter binds us —
Masons, here your duties lie,
Hark, the poor and needy cry !

Come and help the worthy poor,
    Starving for the needed bread ;
From your well replenished store
    Let your fellow-man be fed !
Bounties God to you supplieth,
To the poor He oft denieth.

Come where sorrow has her dwelling,
　　Comfort bring to souls distressed ;
To the friendless mourner telling
　　Of the Rock that offers rest ;
What would life be but for Heaven ?
Come, to us the WORD is given.

Band of Brothers, every nation
　　Hails your bright and Orient light !
Fervent, zealous, free, your station
　　Calls for deeds of noblest might !
Seek — the world is full of sorrow,—
Act — your life will end to-morrow.

To afford succor to the distressed, to divide our bread with the industrious poor, and put the misguided traveler in the way, are duties of the Craft, suitable to its dignity, and expressive of its usefulness.

OPENING ODE.

Begin the work of praise,
　　The joys of song begin;
And bid the mystical rays
　　To enter in.

The gleaming light, the guiding light,
　　The light that shines afar,
It yields a radiance pure and bright,
　　The beautiful, beautiful star.

It tells of deathless love,
　　And faith and hope sublime;
It lifts the soul above
　　All things of time.

It makes us free to die;
　　Since love has conquered death
No hopeful heart need sigh
　　To yield its breath.

Then let the song of praise
　　Our evening tasks begin,
And bid the mystical rays
　　To enter in.

227

MASONIC AULD LANG SYNE.

We do not sigh for pleasures past,
    Nor fondly, vainly pine ;
Yet let us give one memory
    To Auld Lang Syne.

With Gavel, Trowel, Gauge, we work,
    With Level, Square, and Line ;
Come, join the CHAIN OF LOVE, and sing
    Of Auld Lang Syne !

For Auld Lang Syne, my dear,
    For Auld Lang Syne ;
Ah, who like us can sing the days
    Of Auld Lang Syne ?

'Twas sweet when evening's shadows fell —
    How bright our Lights did shine !
Down from the East to hear the words
    Of Auld Lang Syne.

The 'PRENTICE knocked with trembling hand,
    The CRAFT sought Oil and Wine,
The MASTER stood, and nobly fell,
    In Auld Lang Syne.

With step so true, with form upright,
    We drew the GRAND DESIGN;
'Twas well we knew " to square the work "
    In Auld Lang Syne.

A tear to them, THE EARLY DEAD,
    Fond memory would consign ;
We dropped the green sprig o'er their head,
    In Auld Lang Syne.

And till the MASTER call us hence
    To join the LODGE DIVINE,
We sometimes give a grateful thought
    To Auld Lang Syne !

This piece in song or recitations is illustrated by the working tools named.

MODEL MASON.

There's a fine old Mason in the land, he's genial, wise, and true,
His list of brothers comprehends, dear Brothers, me and you;
So warm's his heart the snow blast fails to chill his generous blood,
And his hand is like a giant's when outstretched to man or God;—
Reproach nor blame, nor any shame, has checked his course or dimmed his fame—
      All honor to his name!

This fine old Mason is but one of a large family;
In every Lodge you'll find his kin, you'll find them two or three;
You'll know them when you see them, for they have their father's face,
A generous knack of speaking truth and doing good always;—
Reproach nor blame, nor any shame, has checked their course or dimmed their fame—
    Freemason is their name!

Ah, many an orphan smiles upon the kindred as they pass;
And many a widow's prayers confess the sympathizing grace;
The Father of this Brotherhood himself is joyed to see
Their works — they're numbered all in Heaven, those deeds of charity!
Reproach nor blame, nor any shame, can check their course or dim their fame—
      All honor to their name!

TRIBUTE TO ROBERT BURNS.

The sun is uprising on Scotia's far hills,
Day's labor is opening, the Grand Master wills,
But Lodge lights are gleaming in cheerfulness yet,
Afar in the West where we Masons are met.

There's song for the tuneful, kind words for the kind,
There's cheer for the social, and light for the blind.
But when we, uprising, prepare us to go,
With one thought and feeling we'll sing thy Adieu.

A melting farewell to the favored and bright,—
A sorrowful thought for the sun set in night,—
A round to the Bard whom misfortunes befell,—
A prayer that his spirit with Masons may dwell.
When freedom and harmony bless our design,
We'll think of thee, Brother, who loved every line;
And when gloomy clouds shall our Temple enshroud,
The voice of thy music shall come from the cloud.

Across the broad ocean two hands shall unite,
Columbia,— Scotia,— the Symbol is bright !
The world one Grand Lodge, and the Heaven above,
Shall witness the triumph of Faith, Hope, and Love;
And thou, sweetest Bard, when our gems we enshrine,
Thy jewel, the brightest, most precious, shall shine,
Shall gleam from the East to the far-distant West,
While morning shall call us, or evening shall rest.

MASONIC REMINISCENCES.

Where have we met, my boys?
  Let memory tell,
  She knows it well;
Beneath the Eye Divine,—
Before the ghostly shrine,—
Around the festive board,
Where wit and wine were poured,
  Bright wit and wine; —
  At silent graves,
  Where Acacia waves; —
There have we met, my boys;
Hands round, old friends, let's meet again!

When have we met, my boys?
  Let memory tell,
  She knows it well; —
At midnight and at noon,—
Beneath the crescent moon,—
Through festive winter-night,—
Through day-hours long and bright,
  Bright days of June;
  And all the year
  To us was dear;
Then have we met, my boys;
Hands round, old friends, let's meet again!

How have we met, my boys?
  Let memory tell,
  She knows it well;
In aprons blue and white,
And Tyrian scarlet bright,—
In funeral black arrayed,
Token of ONE who prayed

On Calvary's height;
With Gavel's aid,
Scepter and Blade; —
Thus have we met, my boys;
Hands round, old friends, let's meet again!

Why have we met, my boys?
Let memory tell,
She knows it well; —
To dry the widow's tear,—
The sorrowing heart to cheer,—
To keep our life's design
Within the unerring line
Of HIM so dear;
With mirth and song
Life to prolong,—
For this we've met, my boys;
Hands round, old friends, let's meet again!

Shall we not meet, my boys,
In Lodge above,
The Lodge of Love?
The MASTER waits us there,
With many a lost and dear,—
And wages of the best,—
And for our toilings, rest,—
Full end of care;
The Cross lay down,
Take up the Crown,
And in the spirit Lodge, my boys,
Hands round, old friends, let's meet again!

ONE HOUR WITH YOU.

One hour with you, one hour with you,
No doubt, nor care, nor strife,
Redeems a day of sin and woe,
And gives new zest to life.

One hour with *you*, and *you*, and *you*,
Bright links in mystic chain —
Oh may we oft these joys renew,
And often meet again!

Your *eyes* with love's own language free
 Your *hand grip*, strong and true,
Your *voice*, your *heart* do welcome me
 To spend an hour with you.

I come when morning skies are bright,
 To work my Mason's due —
To labor is my chief delight,
 And spend an hour with you.

I go when evening gilds the West,
 I breathe the fond adieu,
But hope again, by fortune blest,
 To spend an hour with you.

And if, perchance, the page is closed
 On which my life is given,
I would beseech the Mason's GOD
 That we may meet in HEAVEN!

In HEAVEN with *you*, and *you*, and *you*,
 To join the blissful strain;
Oh may we *there* these joys renew
 And meet in HEAVEN again!

These lines, wedded to *Auld Lang Syne*, are much used in the closing of American Lodges.

TO-DAY AS THEN.

CORNERSTONE, CHAMBER OF COMMERCE, PEORIA, ILL., JUNE 3, 1875.

How ever fresh and vigorous
 The tie that binds these men!
Three thousand years,— and yet as strong
 And true *to-day as then!*

The Sacred Hill, that owned the might
 And skill of Hiram's men,
Rears up its summit, gray and bold
 And grand *to-day as then!*

The tears, the sighs of broken hearts,
 The wails of dying men,
Appeal to sympathy as true,
 And strong *to-day as then!*

232

The arm Divine maintains its power.
The All-seeing Eye its ken,
As gracious and as wonderful
And wise *to-day as then!*

Lay deep the stone; apply the SQUARE,
The Level and the Plumb;
Happy the work and bright the day
When mystic craftsmen come.

THE LOVING TIE.

The loving tie we feel,
No language can reveal —
'Tis seen in the sheen of a fond Brother's eye.
It trembles on the ear
When melting with a tear,
A Brother bids us cease to sigh.

Behold how good and how pleasant
For Brothers in unity to dwell!
As Heaven's dew are shed
On Sion's sacred head,
The blessings of the Lord we feel.

'Twas at the sufferer's bed
Now moldering with the dead,
This *Bond*, ah, so fond, was discovered first to me!
I saw his dying eye,
Light up with speechless joy,
And I felt how fond that love must be

I ever will proclaim
With gratitude the name
Of Him, the DIVINE, who has granted this to me!
That weary tho' I stray
O'er nature's rugged way,
I never, never, alone can be.

There's some I know will smile
And others may revile —
'Tis so as we know with the evil heart alway —
But if I can but prove
Through life *a Mason's love*,
I little care what man may say!

SONG OF ST. JOHN.

How blest is the home
Where the Brotherhood come !
How charming the time and occasion !
The love that was born,
In the heart of St. John,
Now warms up the heart of the Mason.

It is you, Sir, and you,
Friendly Brothers and true,
No matter what may be your station,—
On the level our way,
We are equal to-day,
For I, Sirs, with you, am a Mason !

This love that was born
In the heart of St. John,
Is the bond of a charming connection;
Through good, and through ill,
It abides with me still,
And makes *me thank God I'm a Mason!*

When in the Lodge met,
And the officers set,
'Tis of duty and pleasure a season;
Ah ! gladly is given
The FATHER IN HEAVEN,
The praises devout of the Mason.

When labor is done,
And the Brotherhood gone,
Do you think that our secrets we blazon ?
No, no ! 'tis the joy
Of our mystic employ,
That we tell them to none but a Mason.

For 'tis this we do learn,
From our patron, St. John,
The pride of this charming occasion,
That the tongue that conceals,
And never reveals,
Is the very best thing for a Mason !

Then, Lady and Sir,
While we stoutly aver,
In our secrets we'll never work treason,
The rules we profess
Are the same that did grace
Our patron ST. JOHN, THE FREEMASON.

And while to his *name*
We may boldly lay claim,
To his *graces* we'll cling till death's season,
And then to the bourne,
Where his spirit has gone,
We'll hie us with every good Mason.

WALKING TOGETHER.

In thought, word and deed,
We, too, are agreed,
From the same FOUNT OF KNOWLEDGE instructed;
And by the same hand
We'll travel or stand,
To the same Goal of triumph conducted.

Through the same open door,
We lame, blind and poor,
Undertook the same mystic endeavor;
Through the same grave at last,
When death's trial is past,
We'll share the *forever and ever.*

Our *friends* are the same,
Whatever their name,
Whatever their nation or station;
The same are our *foes,*
Whose malice but shows
Their hearts black with coming damnation.

We too, then, can walk,
Sit, stand, work or talk,
In union make sign or give token,
And while life remains
With its losses and gains
Let's see that the tie be not broken !

NOT FAR FROM ME.

Not far from me, not far from me,
 When first on checkered floor
I bow in humble trust the knee,
 My Maker to adore ;
I bow, and fervently declare,
That God is all my portion there.

Not far from me, not far from me,
 In Middle Chamber led,
I pass the mystic portals three,
 And up the stairway tread ;
I pass before the MARK divine,
Whose light is Masonry's and mine.

Not far from me, not far from me,
 In holiest place betrayed,
When human hopes all fade or flee,
 And there is none to aid;
And there is none to hear me cry,
But Thee, all-pitying Deity!

Not far from me, not far from me,
 These mystic labors done,
My body 'neath the deathless tree,
 My soul before the Throne ;
O God, through blest eternity,
Be mine a place *not far from Thee*.

TRIBUTE TO GEORGE WASHINGTON.

O ! Brothers of the MYSTIC TIE,
 Come round me, if you please ;
Lay down the GAVEL and the SQUARE,
 And let the TROWEL cease ;
The work may stop a little while —
 The Master will not blame,
While I from memory sing of one
 Right worthy of the name,—
A true, old-time Freemason,
Whose name was WASHINGTON !

Of every superfluity
    His mind he did divest;
He would not set a timber up
    Unless it was the best;
He plumbed, and squared, and leveled well
    His BLOCKS, and set them true;
Then turned his apron MASTER-WISE
    And spread the mortar due,—
This true, old-time Freemason,
Whose name was WASHINGTON !

When bloody war at foreign hands,
    His country threatened sore,
He thought it *right* to take the sword,
    And guard his native shore;
He stood where bravest hearts are found,—
    He struck for liberty;
But when the white-winged angel flew,
    A man of peace was he,—
This true, old-time Freemason,
This glorious WASHINGTON !

Upon his Apron was no stain,
    His work had no defect ;
The OVERSEER accepted all,
    And nothing to reject.
He lived in peace with God and man;
    He died in glorious hope,
That CHRIST, the LION, JUDAH'S PRIDE,
    Would raise his body up,—
This true, old-time Freemason,
OUR BROTHER WASHINGTON,

CHEERFULNESS.

No, not a gloomy *look* to-night,
    To cloud the pleasant faces here ;
Our tapers burn, our walls are bright
    With emblematic cheer ;
Be every look a sunny smile,
    And let it speak of happier days,
When Mason songs did sweetly fill
    The Temple that we raise.

No, not a cruel *word* to-night,
  To mar the harmony that fills
And sanctifies this dear retreat,
  And every discord stills ;
Be every word a note of love,
  From that seraphic chorus heard
In the celestial Lodge above,
  Whose Master is the Lord.

Oh, not a painful *thought* to-night
  Of war ; are not we in God's hand?
Let's humbly follow in the light
  He gives the Mystic Band ;
Be every thought a ray divine,
  Prophetic of the days to come,
When holy peace shall smile again
  On each dear Mason's home.

Not often do we meet as now,
  Nor shall we all be here again ;
To-morrow each his path must go —
  To some a path of pain.
Then let to-night be doubly bright ;
  And when Low XII shall bid us part,
Its memories we will not forget
  While life blood warms the heart.

Written for a military Lodge, 1864.

FIRE OF FRIENDSHIP.

Men of the bright inheritance, oh, true and loving band,
Who, linked in chains of Masonry, around this altar stand,
Bright let THE FIRE OF FRIENDSHIP burn and warmly let it glow,
For a stranger from a distant land comes in your circle now.

THE ACACIA blooms in every clime, the BROKEN SHAFT doth rear
Its mournful form in mystic guise, and meets us everywhere ;
The GAVEL rings o'er land and sea, yon EMBLEM speaks the same
About the globe, as here it speaks, THE UNIVERSAL NAME.

And why? because ONE GOD we have, in whom alone we trust ;
He made us all, OUR FATHER made us all of kindred dust ;
The same green MOTHER EARTH, the broad, the generous, He gave
That feeds us while we live, and gives us when we die, a grave.

We build a common TEMPLE too, the lofty and the low,
We bring the same heart-offerings and in common homage bow;
Our TRACING BOARD the same designs in every clime has given,
And, serving the same MASTER, we expect the same bright Heaven.

Then let the stranger have a place within your mystic band,
Where eye responsive answers eye, and hand unites with hand;
He knows your WORD, He knows your SIGN, He asks no better grace
Than with you here to sit awhile and greet you face to face.

Peace in the Lodges where you work be Heaven's boon to-day;
Peace, Peace; it is the yearning prayer the stranger's heart would pray;
And could they hear it from the land and from the rolling sea,
From every Mason's lips would come the cry, So MOTE IT BE !

Nothing in the Masonic institution is more practical or more grateful to the sensibilities of the traveling brother than to find, as he will do in every Lodge in this country, an officer whose constitutional duty it is " to welcome and accommodate visiting brethren."

HAPPY HOUR.

Oh, happy hour when Masons meet !
Oh, rarest joys that Masons greet !
Each interwoven with the other,
And Brother truly joined with Brother,
In intercourse that none can daunt,
Linked by the ties of COVENANT.

See, ranged about the Holy Word,
The Craftsmen praise their common LORD !
See in each eye a love well proven !
Around each heart a faith well woven !
Feel, in each hand-grip, what a tie
In this whose scope is MASONRY.

Blest bond ! when broken, we would fain
Unite the severed links again ;
Would urge the tardy hours along
To spend the wealth of light and song,
That makes the Lodge a sacred spot ;
Oh, be the season ne'er forgot,
That takes us from a world of care
To happy scenes where Masons are !

THE TEST.

I never have denied —
I'm willing to be tried —
A call for sympathy from sorrowing man ;
My own hard griefs impel
My heart for such to feel,
And I am willing to be tried again.

The claim, so often made,
For shelter and for aid,
I never have refused, and never can ;
And though my purse is scant,
The poor did never want,
And I am willing to be tried again.

Is counsel craved, I give —
What pleasure to relieve
The doubts my neighbor's spirit that unman !
The wisdom given to me,
To him is offered free,
And I am willing to be tried again.

My brother goes astray,—
Ah, me, *I know the way*,
The slippery way that lures the thoughtless man !
I run to draw him back —
I point the dangerous track,
And I am willing to be tried again.

I've suffered many·a wrong,
From evil hand and tongue —
I've learned forgiveness from no common MAN !
Forgiveness I have shown,
As God to me has done,
And I am willing to be tried again.

Each night on bended knee,
The ALL-SEEING EYE doth see
My body suppliant at a THRONE DIVINE ;
And there for brothers' need,
As for my own I plead,
And I am willing to be tried again.

I'm dying fast and soon,—
My life is past its noon,—
I've had such premonitions as were plain;
My heart is strong in faith
That God will smile in death,
And I am willing to be tried again.

MASONIC VALEDICTORY.

When auld acquaintance closing round
    Our parting grips entwine;
What song awakes the tender sigh,
    Like auld lang syne!
'Tis auld lang syne, the voice
    Of other days divine!
Come, Brothers, now a parting word
    To auld lang syne.

From many a pilgrim pathway come,
    To work the grand design,
We've wrought, and praised the sacred bond
    Of auld lang syne.
Of auld lang syne, the bond
    Of auld lang syne;
Our fathers marked the sacred way
    In auld lang syne.

Though wintry blasts the flesh may chill,
    Though torrid suns may shine,
Our hearts' response unchanged will beat
    To auld lang syne.
To auld lang syne, they beat
    To auld lang syne;
Each pulse responsive, thrilling high,
    To auld lang syne.

Adieu, adieu! the falling tear
    To friendship we assign;
Your hand, your hand, my brother dear,
    For auld lang syne!
For auld lang syne, adieu
    For auld lang syne.
Ah! rent forever is the bond
    Of auld lang syne.

WINTER FESTIVAL.

Friends ever dear, begin the opening lay ;
 Chant ye of joys that none but Masons know ;
Heart answering heart, love's secret power display,
 Gain from our rites a blessing ere you go.
  Love reigneth here,— Love reigneth here ;
   Hate has the rule without,
   But love reigneth here.

Bleak blows the wind ; the sky with angry storms
 Glares on the traveler as he flits along ;
Here genial fire, the fire of Friendship warms ;
 Here gleams the eye, here tunes the jocund song ;
  Love reigneth here,— Love reigneth here ;
   Bleak storms may blow without,
   But Love reigneth here.

Sadness and care,— our life is full of these ;
 'Tis but a strife, a turmoil, at the best ;
Here all is calm ; our walls we build in peace ;
 Here one short hour the weary heart may rest.
  Love reigneth here,— Love reigneth here ·
   Sadness and care without,
   But Love reigneth here.

FESTIVAL ODE.

 Hark, from the lofty dome,
 Hark, from the Mason's home
  Comes a sweet song ;
 Words full of mystery,
 Virtue and charity,
 Tuned unto melody,
  Rise from the throng.

Joy, the Mason's year is ended,
  Freres of St. John !
Joys, which every month attended,
Pains with brightest pleasures blended,
  Ended and gone ;
Crafts of the temple, to your altar throng,
Children of light, upraise the festive song.

Come, oh ye newly made,
Late to our altar led,
    Hasten, oh youth ;
Gone is the gloomy night,
Sweet is the mystic light,
Broke on the dazzled sight,
    Glowing with truth.

Age, with your locks of snow,
Time's burden bending low,
    Fathers, oh come ;
Welcome the veteran here —
With every added year,
Dearer and yet more dear,
    To Masons' home.

Master, your toil is done ;
Brethren, the prize is won ;
    Hail the new year ;
Pledge every soul again,
Strengthen the mystic chain,
Long may the Lodge remain
    Without a peer.

THE GOODLY HERITAGE.

O, what a goodly heritage
    The LORD to us has given !
How blest the brotherhood that pledge
    Their Mason vows to Heaven !
We sing the mystic chain that binds
    These western realms in one;
Such loving hearts, such liberal minds,
    No other land has known.

Ten thousand lights in Mason halls
    Are gleaming on our eyes;
Ten thousand emblems on the walls
    Tell whence the gleaming is;
And when the portals ope, to pass
    The humble seeker in,
The *voice of prayer* pervades the place,
    And proves the light DIVINE !

On every hill our Brothers lie,
   And green sprigs deck the knoll;
Their fall brought sorrow to the eye,
   But triumph to the soul.
Our orphans sing in many a home,
   Our widows' hearts are glad,
And Mason light dispels the gloom
   And comfort finds the sad.

Thus link in link, from shore to shore,
   The mystic chain is wound;
Oh, blended thus forevermore,
   Be Mason spirit found !
And while the Heavens, on pillars sure,
   Of STRENGTH and WISDOM stand,
May Brotherhood like ours endure,
   Where Strength and Wisdom blend !

ODE FOR CORNERSTONE PLANTING.

CUSTOM HOUSE, CHICAGO, ILL., JUNE 24, 1874.

When the kindled wrath
   Of offended Heaven
Gave, in smoldering smoke and flame,
   The wealth that He had given ;
Though that day, in black dismay,
Saw our city melt away,
Yet we hoped, 'twas not in vain,
God would smile on us again.
   Then *deeply* lay the stone ;
     Plant it firm and true ;
   So shall distant ages own
     The work the Masons do.

In its deep recess,
   Set with mystic care,
Hark, our faithful witnesses,
   The Level, Plumb, and Square ! —
" Nations sink beneath the curse
As they deviate from us ;
In unerring truth may yours
Last while circling time endures ! "
   Then *strongly* lay the stone, etc.

Hear our prayer, O God,
　　Thou, the Nation's trust!
And may these walls majestic rise
　　When we are in the dust!
Humbly—we are but as one;
Hopeful—are we not Thine own?
Midst this mighty gathering
To Thy name we rise and sing,
　　And *grandly* lay the stone;
　　　　Plant it firm and true;
　　So shall distant ages own
　　　　The work the Masons do.

CENTENNIAL ODE.

Composed in 1855 for the Centennial of St. John's Lodge, No. 1, New York.

How the souls of friends departed
　　Brood around this joyful scene!
Tender, brave and faithful-hearted,
　　They have left their memories green.
　　　　Could we view them,
　　Smiles upon each face were seen.

As they scan our gladsome meeting,
　　It recalls a thousand joys;
As they list our cheerful greeting,
　　'Tis to them a glorious voice;
　　　　'Tis the echo
　　Of a hundred years of joys!

One by one those loved ones perished,
　　But they left the chain still wound;
Every virtue that they cherished
　　Here is found as here *they* found;
　　　　Thus in Heaven
　　Blessed souls with ours are bound.

Thus shall we, tho' long departed,
　　When a hundred years are sped,
Join the brave and faithful-hearted,
　　Who around this Lodge shall tread;
　　　　And our memories
　　Shall be cherished here, though dead.

HYMN FOR CONSECRATION.

Lo, God is here, our prayers prevail !
　In deeper reverence adore;
Ask freely now! he will not fail
　His largest, richest gifts to pour.

Ask by these Emblems old and true;
　Ask by the memories of the past;
Ask by His own Great Name, for lo,
　His every promise there is cast !

Ask Wisdom ! 'tis the chiefest thing;
　Ask Strength, such strength as God may yield;
Ask Beauty from His Throne to spring
　And grace the Temple we shall build.

Lord God most high, our Lodge we veil !
　'Tis consecrate with ancient care;
Oh, let Thy Spirit ever dwell,
　And guide the loving Builders here !

THE SCOTCH RITE.

Be ours to-night to sing,
　Be ours to-night to laugh,
And in these cups, no drunken bowls,
　The loving toast to quaff;
We consecrate this odorous wine
And drink to Love and Auld Lang Syne.

Now raise the generous flood,
　And drink to those who've gone;
Beyond the grave, beyond the sky,
　They seem to beckon on;
With tears of friendship we attest,
And drink *the Memory of the Blest.*

Now drink to sober age,
　To men in life's decline;
To eyes bedimmed and wrinkled front,
　The oldest, purest wine.
O brethren, give the loving toast
To Age and Worth and honest Frost.

Now drink the fond *farewell*,—
  Now drink the *come again;*
But not in song, and not in speech,
  We make this last refrain;—
With vision raised to God above
In silence drink —*Freemasons' love!*

TWELVE, HIGH TWELVE.

Now we hail the Junior Warden,
  Lo, his column crowns the South !
Drop the heavy tools of labor,
  Give the time to song and mirth.
Twelve, High Twelve, the hour is sounding,
  Noonday sun is in the sky;
Come, the Social Lodge surrounding,
  Filled with sympathy and joy.

Corn that feeds the soul in fatness,
  Oil in radiant truth to shine,
Wine that sparkles in love-promptings,—
  Come, ye weary ones, and dine !
Twelve, High Twelve, the hour is sounding,
  Noonday sun is in the sky;
Come, the Social Lodge surrounding,
  Filled with sympathy and joy.

How the Social Fire enkindles
  These true souls on every side !
Could we ask for richer wages
  Than OUR MASTER doth provide?
Twelve, High Twelve, the hour is sounding,
  Noonday sun is in the sky;
Come, the Social Lodge surrounding,
  Filled with sympathy and joy.

Lord Jehovah, bless our meeting,
  Thou this time of joy hath given !
'Tis for thee we toil and labor,
  Own our workmanship in Heaven !
When *High Twelve* by death is sounded,
  And eternal rest shall come,
Grant us bountiful refreshment
  In thine Upper Lodge at home !

LEANING TOWARD EACH OTHER.

There is an incident connected with these simple lines which is worth noting. They were first read at the banquet, following the inauguration of the Crawford Equestrian Statue of George Washington at Richmond, Virginia. Not long afterward, the writer, visiting President Buchanan at the White House, by invitation, was requested to repeat them again. He did so, having for his audience the president, the vice-president (John C. Breckenridge), the secretary of state (Lewis Cass), and the Hon. B. B. French, all four Freemasons!

The jolts of life are many,
As we dash along the track;
The ways are rough and rugged,
And our bones they sorely rack.
We're tossed about,
We're in and out,
We make a mighty pother —
Far less would be
Our pains, if we
Would *lean* toward each other!

Behold that loving couple,
Just mated for their life —
What care they for the joltings,
That happy man and wife!
The cars may jump,
Their heads may bump
And jostle one another;
They only smile,
And try the while
To *lean* toward each other!

Woe to the luckless pilgrim,
Who journeys all alone!
Well said the wise King Solomon,—
"Two better is than one!"
For when the ground's
Most rugged found,
And great's the pain and pother,
He cannot break
The sorest shake
By *leaning* toward another!

There's not one in ten thousand,
Of all the cares we mourn
But what *if 'twas divided*,
Might easily be borne!

If we'd but learn,
When fortunes turn,
To share them with a Brother,
We'd prove how good's
Our Brotherhood,
By *leaning* toward each other!

Then, Masons, take my counsel —
The Landmarks teach you so —
Share all the joltings fairly,
As down the track you go!
Yes, give and take
Of every shake,
With all the pain and pother,
And thus you'll prove
Your Mason's love,
By *leaning* toward each other!

THERE'S SOMETHING TRUE BELOW.

What years are gone since last we met,
What friends beloved are dead,
And frosty brow and failing eye
Confess the life that's fled!
But still our manly hearts deny
That time the soul can bow ;—
Oh, 'tis good to feel in a world like this
There's something true below!

The work goes on we loved so well,
In halcyon days of youth ;
And rising high upon the eye,
Behold the walls of truth!
The work we hope will still go up
Though we in death must bow :

For 'tis good, etc.

Th' Acacia blooms at silent graves,
The sorrowing Virgin weeps ;
The arm so strong in death is hung,
For lo, the Builder sleeps!
Yet they and we beyond the sea
Shall meet again, we know ; —

And 'tis good, etc.

Then raise the Mason song once more,
    Who meet so soon to part ;
The hands we clasped in days of yore
    Combine, and heart with heart ;
The MASTER lives, and at the close
    Good wages will bestow ;
For 'tis good to feel in a world like this
    There's something true below !

IF GOOD MEN ALL WERE MASONS.

There's never a tear would drop
    But some kind hand would steal it;
There's never a sigh would swell
    But some kind heart would feel it;
And never a widow sad,
    And never an orphan lonely,
But some one would make glad
    With smiles of joy, if only
        The good men all were Masons.

There's never a word profane
    By heedless mortal spoken,
And never a cruel blow,
    And never a law be broken;
There's never a man would die
    Away from loved ones, lonely;
There's never a shuddering cry
    Would mount to Heaven, if only
        The good men all were Masons.

But every heart would smile,
    And tongues break forth in singing,
And corn, and wine, and oil,
    The generous would be bringing;
And each would strive to make
    The path of life less lonely,
A green and flowery way,
    An Eden-walk, if only
        The good men all were Masons.

But since the good men all
    Are *not* in our connexion,
Let's try, what few we are,
    To be of one complexion;

Let's try, though few and frail,
And, maybe, poor and lonely,
To show what life would be
And men would do, if only
The good men were all Masons.

WELCOME TO THE VISITING BROTHER.

Oh welcome him from distant land
Who comes to bear his part ;
Give him the grasp of generous hand,
The warmth of trusting heart.

He sees the emblems on your walls,
And reads their light divine ;
Yon *hieroglyphic bright* recalls
His Master's Name and *thine.*

For well he knows the words you breathe,
Those sentiments of love,
And he can stand in form beneath
The All-Seeing Eye above.

Then welcome him from distant land,
No more a stranger now ;
Give him the grasp of generous hand,
A Mason's welcome show.

King Solomon, in his Dedication Prayer, that effort unparalleled in pathos, scope and religious trust, invoked a blessing upon the stranger who should visit the Temple. "Concerning the stranger," he said, " who is come from a far country for Thy great name's sake, if they come and pray in this house, then hear Thou from the heavens, and do all that the stranger calleth to Thee for." II CHRON. vi, 32. And this suggests that spirit of welcome which, in every Lodge of Masons, designates the officer, one of whose principal duties shall be " to welcome and accommodate visiting brethren."

PARTING HYMN.

Refreshed with angel food, we go
To serve Thee in Thy work below;
Trusting, when Sabbath rest is given,
To share Thy richer joys in Heaven.

Then bind our willing souls in one;
Confirm the COVENANTS here begun;
Each day these vows more sacred be,
Cemented in eternity.

251

HAPPY TO MEET, SORRY TO PART, HAPPY TO MEET AGAIN.

Happy to meet the sparkling eye,
　　The sinewy hand, the joyful tongue;
Happy to meet where never a sigh
　　Nor a cold word chills fraternal song;
Happy around the altar's base !
　　Happy beneath the All-seeing Eye !
Telling the glories of that place,
　　The happier LODGE beyond the sky.
　　　Happy to meet, sorry to part,
　　　　Happy to meet again, again;
　　　Happy to meet, sorry to part,
　　　　Happy to meet again.

Sorry to part, for who can tell,
　　As time goes by and changes come,
If those we have met and cherished so well,
　　Shall gather again in the Mason's home?
Sorry to part, we lingering stand;
　　Sorry to part, these loiterings prove;
But whisper the word along your Band:
　　" Meeting again in the LODGE above ! "

Happy to meet again, again;
　　Oh, hasten the joyful moment soon,
When, happily met, King Hiram's men
　　Shall measure again the Mason's tune !
The strong may bow, the hair grow white,
　　Mourners may go about the street;
But carol we will as we've sung to-night,
　　Happy again, again to meet !

HIGH XII.

There's Pillars II and Columns V
　　Support and grace our halls of truth,
But none such sparkling pleasure give
　　As the Column that adorns the S'.
" HIGH XII," the Junior Warden calls—
　　His Column grants the festive hour,
And through our antiquated halls
　　Rich streams of social gladness pour.

'Tis then, all toil and care forgot,
    The Bond *indissoluble* seems;
'Tis then the world's a happy spot,
    And hope unmixed with sadness, gleams.
HIGH XII ! I've shared the festive hour
    With those who realize the bliss,
And felt that life contains no more
    Than sparkles in the joys of this.

What memories hover round the time !
    What forms rise up to call it blest !
Departed friends ; why should it dim
    Our joys to know that they're at rest ?
HIGH XII! how they rejoice to hear !
    Quickly each implement laid down,
Glad to exchange for toil and care
    And heavy CROSS, a heavenly CROWN !

Then Comrades all, by 3×3,
    Linked in the golden chain of truth,
A hearty welcome pledge with me
    To the Column that adorns the S'!
HIGH XII ! and never be the hour
    Less free, less brotherly than now !
HIGH XII ! a rich libation pour,
    To joys that none but Masons know.

The custom of Lodge refreshment, time-honored and sanctioned by the example of the noblest and best of American Masons, might well be renewed. The Order with us has too much of the pulpit, and too little of the table. A due intermixture of both was what the Craft in the olden time regarded.

FERVOR OF AFFILIATION.

A place in the Lodge for me,
    A home with the free and bright,
Where jarring chords agree,
    And the darkest soul is light ;
Not here, not here is bliss,
    There's turmoil and there's gloom,
My spirit yearns for peace,—
    Say, Brothers, say, is there room ?

My feet are weary worn,
    And my eyes are dim with tears ;

This world is all forlorn,
　　A wilderness of fears;
But *there's one green spot below*,
　　There's a resting place, a home,
My spirit yearns to know,—
　　Say, Brothers, say, is there room?

I hear the orphan's cry,
　　And I see the widow's tear;
I weep when mortals die,
　　And none but God is near;
From sorrow and despair,
　　I seek the Mason's home,
My spirit yearns to share,—
　　Say, Brothers, say, is there room?

With God's own eye above,
　　With BROTHER-HANDS below,
With FRIENDSHIP and with LOVE
　　My pilgrimage I'll go;
And when, in death's embrace,
　　My summons it shall come,
Within your hearts' best place,
　　O, Brothers, O, give me room!

The privilege of association in a harmonious, strongly cemented band of Masons, is a thing to be coveted. Exiles from home, deprived of the long-accustomed pleasures of the Lodge, have been known to express their yearnings for reaffiliation in language not less forcible than this.

THE WIDOW AND THE FATHERLESS.

As on my road delaying,
　　The stream's cool waters by,
My thoughts in fancy straying,
　　I heard a plaintive cry:
"There may be hope in Heaven,—
　　For *us* no hope is here;
Oh, why was joy thus given,
　　So soon to disappear!"

Around the grave was weeping
　　A widowed, orphaned band;
Beneath their feet was sleeping
　　The husband, father, friend;

And as their sorrows swelling
    Broke forth midst sigh and tear,
Again these words are telling,—
    "Alas, no hope is here!"

The stream's cool waters flowing
    No longer sung to me,—
The soft spring sunbeams glowing
    Were cheerless all to see;
For still that widowed mother,
    And still those orphans dear,
Bewailed my buried BROTHER,—
    "Alas, no hope is here!"

MY BROTHER? yes, forsaken,
    These lov'd ones round thee mourn;
Too soon from friendship taken,
    Dear Brother, thou art gone!
Gone from a cold world's sighing,
    From sorrow and from fear,
But left these mourners crying,—
    "Alas, no hope is here!"

These tears, my heart, are holy!
    These sighs by anguish driven,
This mourning group so lowly,
    Are messengers of Heaven;
And so will I receive them,
    As God shall give me cheer,
Protect them and relieve them,
    And teach them HOPE IS HERE!

LET YOUR LIGHT SHINE.

"Let your light shine," the Master said,—
    "To bless benighted man!
The light and truth my spirits shed
    Are yours to shed again."

We come, O Lord, with willing mind,
    That knowledge to display;
Enlighten us, by nature blind
    And glad we will obey.

CONCERNING DEATH AND THE DEAD.

THRENODY, OR HYMN OF DEATH.

In the recitation of this piece (consecrate to the memory of Salem Town, of New York, 1864) a full set of Lodge emblems is employed as named in the poem, viz.: the square, level, plumb, green sprig, gauge, trowel, hour glass, and gavel.

So falls the last of the old forest trees,
Within whose shades we wandered with delight,
Moss-grown and hoary, yet the birds of Heaven
Loved in its boughs to linger and to sing.
The summer winds made sweetest music there;
The soft spring showers hung their brightest drops,
Glistering and cheerful on the mossy spray,
And to the last, that ancient, vigorous oak
Teemed with ripe fruitage.

Now the Masons mourn,
Through Temple chambers, their Grand Master fallen!
The clear Intelligence,— the genial Soul,—
The lips, replete with wisdom,— quenched and still.
The ruffian DEATH has met and struck his prey,
And from the Quarry to the Mount, all mourn!
Bind up with asphodel these mystic Tools
And Jewels of the Work; bind up, ye Crafts,
The SQUARE ; it marked the fullness of his life;
In truth's right angle all his deeds were true!
The LEVEL; lo, it leads us to the grave,
Where, in kind mother earth our veteran sleeps!
The PLUMB; it points the home his soul hath found ;
Did he not walk true to th' unerring Line,
Let down, suggestive, from the hand of God ?
Th' ACACIA SPRIG, type of the verdant life,
Bright and immortal in Celestial Lodge.

Bind up in mourning, dark and comfortless,
The GAUGE; he gave *one part* to God, and God,
In blest exchange, gave him *eternity*.
The TROWEL; in his gentle charge it spread
Sweet Concord, binding long estrangèd hearts;

256

The HOUR GLASS, whence his vital sands have sped,
But every grain denoted one good deed;
The GAVEL; in his master hand it swayed,
Through three score years, the Moral architects,
Quelling all strife, directing every hand,
And pointing us to the Great Builder, GOD !
Bind these with asphodel; conceal these Tools
And Jewels of the Work; let bitterest tears
Flow for the man who handled them so well,
But, overborne with death, hath, in ripe age,
His labor fully done, passed from our sight !

HONOR TO THE AGED.

Inscribed to Col. Moore, an aged and veteran Templar of Canada.

Who can without a sigh behold
   The bended form and furrowed face
   Of one we knew in manhood's grace,
Before he thought of growing old !

The memories of the joyous prime
   Come up with such a deep impress
   We make our dearest happiness
In calling back the parted time.

Dear friend ! our winter closes round,
   The summer gone ! the winter fled,—
   All objects bright and joyful dead,
And we just lingering on the ground.

How can we bear to live, if all
   Is but the phantom of the past ?
   We will believe, far o'er the waste,
There is a life beyond recall.

Aged and honored, when the cry
   Of death shall summon you away,
   Leave us to hope, in that bright day,
To meet our friend, and meet for aye.

A thousand hearts in sorrow sore,
   A thousand swords in mourning dressed,
   A thousand voices round thy rest,—
All honor to the gallant Moore.

OUR FUTURE MEETING.

Where types are all fulfilled—
　　Where mystic shades are real—
Where aching hands and hearts are stilled,
　　And death has set his seal—
In that bright land called *Heaven*,
　　Dear Friend, we'll meet once more!
The token in thy parting given,
　　Points to *a Heavenly shore*.

'Tis *this*, our signs have taught—
　　Our symbols old and true;
'Tis *this* upon our work is wrought,
　　Which every *frère* can view;
From the first line we traced,
　　On the foundation walls,
To that *bright stone*, the last, the best,
　　The glory of our halls.

Oh, what a land of joy
　　Hast thou beheld, my Friend!
Oh, what ineffable employ
　　Thy faithful heart has gained!
Thy Brother, weary, worn,
　　Longs for the same bright dome,
Where, all the week's hard service done,
　　He'll have thy welcome home.

YEARNINGS.

Brothers, when o'er my head,
　　The silent dust is spread,
And this poor heart its quiverings shall forbear,
　　Where'er my body lie,
　　Though far the grave away,
I would, dear Brothers, be remembered *here!*

Brothers, when tender sighs
　　Around me shall arise,
And speak of what I did, or fain would do,
　　Such honest, truthful words
　　As Mason's tongue affords,
I would, dear Brothers, have rehearsed by *you*.

HOW COLD WOULD BE THE TOMB.

How cold would be the tomb,
How desolate its gloom,
Were there no faithful tears to fall above!
Oh, who could bear to die,
Did not we know some sigh
Will move fond spirits in memorial love?

The gentle Jesus wept
Above his friend, who slept
Where sister-hands had laid him ; and His tear
Has hallowed every grief,
And yielded sweet relief,
And spread hope's brightest radiance round the bier.

The story told to-night
Of *Adah*, brave and bright,
And *Ruth* and *Esther*, gone to deathless home,
Proves how for love we burn,
And how our spirits yearn
To have some flower-wreaths laid upon our tomb

There's little here below
But misery and woe ;
But in yon realm there waits us an abode
"Of many mansions" framed,
THE LODGE ETERNAL named,
Its Master Builder, and its Master—GOD!

This sweet, sad story, fraught
With grand and noble thought,
Points us unerring to that Lodge afar ;
It guides the wandering eye,
As when, in days gone by,
Wise men were guided by the EASTERN STAR.

So let us read the tale,
And con its lessons well,
That we lose not the victory they won ;
But laboring in faith,
Inherit after death,
Eternal honor and the heavenly Crown.

MEMORIAL HYMN.

The Masonic membership is composed of two very unequal, yet homogeneous portions. One part consists of the comparatively small number who work in the Lodges of this life — build up the Temple of the Soul, and moralize upon emblems that can never fully satisfy the craving spirit; the other, of the innumerable host who throng the Celestial Lodge above, wearing robes of the same color as ours, and worshiping the same Deity, but purified, perfected, relieved of earthly burdens, stains and sins, and able to look face to face upon God. The following Hymn is supposed to be addressed by the laboring Few to the rejoicing Many.

We sing of those who've gone,
     The friends to memory nearest,
Who left our Lodge forlorn
     When youthful hopes were dearest;
We drop our voices low,
And tears in silence flow —
They're gone, they're gone, we know,
To the quiet place of death,
To the silent Lodge beneath,
Where the green sprigs ever bloom,
In the low, low tomb.
          Rest sweetly there !
          So mote it be !

Each mystic grace they had
     Our faithful souls have yielded
The types that made them glad,
     Our hearts on them are builded.
The Level, Plumb and Square,—
Th' Acacia, green and fair,
We dropped it gently there
In the quiet place of death,
In the silent Lodge beneath,
Where the green sprigs ever bloom,
In the low, low tomb.
          Rest sweetly there !
          So mote it be !

We deem not they are lost,
     To FAITH and HOPE no craven,
But, with the white-robed host
     Who look in LOVE to Heaven,
We raise our voices high,
And call them to the sky,
Who here in darkness lie;

From the quiet place of death,
From the silent Lodge beneath,
Where the green sprigs ever bloom;
From the low, low tomb,
    Rise, Brother, rise !
    So mote it be!

THE DARK DECREE.

'Tis done, the dark decree is said
    That called our friend away;
Submissive bow the sorrowing head,
    And bend the lowly knee;
We will not ask why God has broke
    Our Pillar on its stone,
But humbly yield us to the stroke,
    And say, " His will be done."

At last the weary head has sought
    In earth its long repose;
And weeping *frères* have hither brought
    Their chieftain to his close;
We held his hand, we filled his heart,
    While heart and hand could move;
Nor will we from his grave depart,
    But with the rites of love.

This grave shall be a garner, where
    We'll heap our golden corn ;
And here, in heart, we'll oft repair.
    To think of him that's gone;
To speak of all he did and said,
    That's wise, and good, and pure,
And covenant o'er the hopeful dead,
    In vows that shall endure.

Oh, Brother, bright and loving *frère*,
    Oh, spirit free and pure,
Breathe us one gush of spirit air,
    From off the heavenly shore,
And say, when these hard toils are done,
    And the GRAND MASTER calls,
Is there for every wearied one
    Place in the heavenly halls?

CONSECRATION OF A CEMETERY.

In each cold bed a mortal sleeps —
   The SILENT LODGE is here!
Pale death an awful vigil keeps,
   Through all the changing year.

What tears have wet these grassy mounds
   What sighs these winds have heard!
Oh, God, have not the piteous sounds
   Thy pitying bosom stirred?

Shall man thus die and waste away,
   And no fond hope be left?
Is there no sweet, confiding ray
   For bosoms all bereft?

From each cold bed a form shall rise
   When the great hour shall come ;
The trump shall shake the upper skies,
   And wake the lower tomb.

No weeping then, no tear nor groan,
   For these around us spread ;
A shout shall reach the very Throne
   From the long-silent dead.

Then hush our hearts, be dry each tear,
   Wake, oh, desponding faith!
And when our SAVIOUR shall appear,
   We too shall conquer death!

On these blest Graves let sunbeams pour
   Their balmiest influence;
On them let each reviving shower
   Its gracious pearls dispense.

O'er these blest Graves each gentle breeze
   Its heavenly whispers breathe ;
O'er them the foliage of the trees
   A crown of verdure wreathe.

Round these blest Graves at dead of night,
   May angel bands combine,
And from their Mansions ever bright,
   Bring something all Divine.

From these blest Graves may hope revive :
   May JUDAH'S LION tell
That we shall meet these dead alive,
   For oh, we loved them well !

Then come, sad hour, we lay us down
   And calmly wait his word :
Blest are the dead, our spirits own
   Who knew and served the LORD.

MONODY TO P. C. TUCKER.

The following Monody forms a part of the "Eulogy" pronounced by the writer in January, 1862, in the presence of the Grand Lodge of Vermont :

Dead ! and where now those earnest, loving eyes,
   Which kindled in so many eyes the light?
Have they departed from our earthly skies
   And left no rays to illuminate the night?

Dead ! and where now that heart of sympathy
   That welled and yearned, and with true love o'erflowed ?
Oh, heart of love, is the rich treasure dry?
   Forever sealed, what once such gifts bestowed?

Dead ! and where now that gen'rous, nervous hand
   That thrilled each nerve within its generous clasp?
Will it no more enlink the mystic band,
   Hallowing and strength'ning all within its grasp?

Heart, eyes, and hand, to dust are all consign'd —
   It was his lot, for he was born of earth ;
But the rich treasures of his master-mind
   Abide in Heav'n, for there they had their birth.

Abide in Heav'n ! oh, the enkindling trust !
   The record of his deeds remaineth here ;
The ACACIA blooms beside his silent dust
   To point unerringly to yon bright sphere.

Then, though the SHATTERED COLUMN mark his fate,
   And WEEPING VIRGIN tell th' unfinished FANE,
Not altogether are we desolate,
   For oh, departed friend, we meet again !

MOURNFULLY LAY THE DEAD ONE HERE.

Mournfully lay the dead one here,
    And silently gather nigh;
Lovingly yield your tribute tear,
    His dirge, a tender sigh.
Our chain is broke, and life can ne'er
    This fondest link supply;
Mournfully lay the dead one here,
    And silently gather nigh.

Ever his face was set to go
    Toward Jerusalem;
Ever he walked and lived as though
    He saw its golden beam;
That place whose emblem was so dear
    Is now his home on high;
Mournfully lay the dead one here,
    And lovingly gather nigh.

A piece of rich melody was composed to these lines, in 1866, by George F. Root.

TRUE SITE FOR MASONS' GRAVES.

In Shakespeare's *Timon of Athens* is a passage relating to the grave of one *who would be forgotten*. But the spirit of a Mason's interment suggests *eternal memory*.

Bury me on the hill top,
    Where sunbeams earliest come
And starlight longest lingers —
    Make there your Brother's home;
There, through the hours of darkness,
    The glittering hosts will pass,
And dewdrops weep my requiem,
    And night winds sigh, Alas! —
        When I am dead.

But not by ocean billow,
    Oh, not on briny shore,
This form consign to nature —
    I hate its hollow roar;
Cold weeds and sea things floating
    Above me, on the wave,
Would vex my spirit's slumber
    In that unquiet grave,
        When I am dead.

No stone to mark my resting —
    No gentle form to bow —
Oh, Brothers true and tender,
    Lay not your Brother so ;
Within my soul a yearning
    Impleads a Mason's home —
Bury me on the hill top,
    Where sunbeams earliest come,
        When I am dead.

FUNERAL SOUND.

Wreathe the mourning badge around —
Once again that funeral sound !
From his friends and from his home,
Bear him, Brothers, to the tomb !

While *they* journey weeping, slow,
Silent, thoughtful let *us* go;
Silent — life to him is sealed;
Thoughtful — death's to him revealed.

How his life-path has been trod,
Brothers, we will leave to God ;
Friendship's mantle, trusting faith,
Lends a fragrance, even to death.

Here, amidst the things that sleep,
Lay him down — his rest is deep ;
Death has triumphed — loving hands
Cannot raise him from his bands.

But the Emblems that we shower
Tell us there's a mightier Power ;
O'er the strength of death and hell,
JUDAH'S LION SHALL PREVAIL !

Dust to dust, the dark decree —
Soul to God, the soul is free !
Leave him with the lowly lain —
Brother, we shall meet again !

This hymn in many localities has taken the place of Vinton's " Solemn Strikes the Funeral Chime."

VIA CRUCIS, VIA LUCIS.

How *sad to the Grave* are our feet slowly tending,
    The cold form of one whom we loved, on the bier!
What sighs swell our hearts while above him we're bending,
    And shudder to think we must part with him here!
Ah, gloomy is life when our friend has departed!
    Ah, weary the pathway to travel alone!
There's little remaineth to cheer the lone-hearted
    Oppressed with the burden, "the loved one is gone!"

But *glad from the Grave* are our feet homeward tending,
    Though death's cold embraces our Brother restrain!
Hope springs from the hillock above which we're bending,
    And whispers, "Rejoice! you shall meet him again!
Death's midnight is sad, but there cometh the morning;
    The pathway is dark, but its ending is nigh."
Then patient we wait for the glorious dawning,
    That's told in our emblems of *life in the sky!*

GRAVE OF THE GRAND MASTER.

Over the grave of the Hon. Henry Gee, Past Grand Master of Masons in Florida, is a marble monument of rare beauty and propriety. The writer visited the spot January 24, 1858. The place of interment was selected by the deceased — a grove of oaks near the verge of a hill. The birds sing their sweetest through the Florida winters, and the evergreens, whose brightness is reflected upon the marble surface of the monument, give no indications of mortality.

"May I, when given to dust, be laid
In the o'erarching oak trees' shade!
Not midst the crowded ranks of those
In life commingled, friends or foes;
Not 'neath the dust of trampling feet;
Not where the mourners frequent meet;
But far from life's poor turmoil laid
In the o'erarching oak trees' shade."

'Tis done; this sweet, retired scene
Is nature's own delightful green;
No voice but the lamenting dove
That sighs and murmurs of her love;
No footsteps but the tender tread
Of those who loved, who love the dead;
No passion but the sigh subdued,
Breathed for the friend who's gone to God,

The pilgrim, dusty from a path
That circles round the weary earth,
Stands mutely pleased:—'Twas well to place
The MASTER on a couch like this!
The BUILDERS, scattered as they be,
Sleeping on plain, and mount, and sea,
Dispersed until the trumpet's blast—
Few of them have such fitting rest.

How searchingly that awful EYE
Reads the impress of memory!
Death cannot hide a brother dead,
But the OMNISCIENT EYE will read
Each act, each word, each secret thought,
Through a long life conceived or wrought;
Well for the sleeper if his life
Endure a scrutiny so rife!

But thou, oh MASTER of the Craft,
A spotless memory hath left;
The pitying heart, the loving soul,
The liberal hand to crown the whole,
And zeal in toils of mystic plan,
Which honor God and honor man —
These are thy jewels—they will try
The ken of the ALL-SEEING EYE.

Rest peaceful, then, while nature sighs,
And graces where thy body lies!
Lift high that column many a year,
To call the grateful BUILDERS near!
Wait patient for the mystic call
From out the depths of Heaven's hall;—
"Ye BUILDERS, MEN from many lands,
Come to the house not made with hands!"

TEARS AND SMILES.

The *tear* for friends departed,
The faithful and true-hearted,
Cast midst the rubbish of the silent grave,
Is changed to *smiles* of pleasure,
While trusting that our treasure
A glorious Resurrection day will have!

TWO VISITS.

I saw him *first* one snowy winter night,—
 But summer's fire glowed in his youthful breast,—
A humble seeker for Masonic light,
 A pilgrim journeying for Masonic rest;
 From the bright orient southward to the West,
Darkly he journeyed, while our eyes inquired
 If form, and heart, and garb fulfilled our test.
From the ordeal he came, as one inspired,
And glad amongst us stood, enlightened and attired.

Once more I saw him,— but his eyes were hid,
 Hoodwinked by death; as with an iron band
His limbs were fettered ; 'neath the coffin lid
 The strong man lay extended, and his hand,
 Whose grip had thrilled me, ah ! how dead it spanned
His pulseless breast ! yet 'round our Brother's head
 Thrice we encircled, though with grief unmanned,
And with respectful tenderness we spread
Upon his breast green sprigs, fit presents to the dead.

For he had journeyed further, learned a lore
 Profounder, drank in purer light than we,
And of desired treasure gathered more
 Than dwells in all the mines of Masonry!
 What unto us is veiled in mystery
Was real to him, and by his Master's side,
 Knowing as he was known, *the dead was free!*
Therefore we paid our homage to the dead,
And, "We shall meet again, our Brother dear," we said.

And we *shall* meet again, not as in quest
 Of light Masonic, nor as in that time
When last I saw him pallid in his rest,
 But in a Lodge transcendently sublime!
 Death there shall ring no funereal chime,—
No weeping band shall go about its dead,—
 But light and life inspire an endless hymn;
Ah, happy we, whose very grave may shed
Effulgent hope and joy as round its brink we tread !

The incident here versified occurred to the writer in western Tennessee in 1851.

RESURRECTION.

The Craft in days gone by
Drew from their Mystery
The mightiest truths God ever gave to men;
They whispered in the ear,
Bowed down with solemn fear,
"The dead, the buried dead, shall live again!"

Oh, wondrous, wondrous word!
No other rites afford
This precious heritage, this matchless truth!
"Though gone from weeping eyes,
Though in the dust he lies,
Our Friend, our Brother, shall renew his youth!"

And we, who yet remain,
Shall meet our dead again;
Shall give the hand that thrilled within our grasp,
The token of our faith,
Unchanged by time and death; —
And breast to breast his faithful form shall clasp!

But who, oh, Gracious God!
The power shall afford?
Who with Omnipotence shall break the tomb?
What morning Star shall rise
To chase from sealèd eyes
The long-oppressing darkness and the gloom?

Lo, at the Mystic shrine
The answer all Divine!
Lo, where the Tracing Board doth plainly tell;
"Over the horrid tomb,
The bondage and the gloom,
THE LION OF THE TRIBE OF JUDAH shall prevail!"

Then hopefully we bend
Above our sleeping friend,
And hopeful cast the green sprigs o'er his head;
'Tis but a fleeting hour —
The OMNIPOTENT hath Power,
And He will raise our Brother from the dead!

A MASON'S EPITAPH.

His epitaph, " a Mason true and good,
　　Sincere in friendship, ready in relief,
Discreet in trusts, faithful in Brotherhood,
　　Gentle in sympathy and kind in grief."

On grateful memories his name is writ;
　　His genial heart *our* hearts did kindle up;
We drew our inspiration from his light,
　　And buoyancy from his all-buoyant hope.

His toils are ended; *we* must labor on;
　　Our Master for a little longer calls
Our hands to *duty* at the rising sun,
　　Our hearts to *rest* when evening shadow falls.

But 'twill be ended soon; may our reward
　　Be upon hearts like his to lie secure;
Like him to enjoy the favor of the Lord,
　　Whose grace is boundless and whose promise sure.

WHEN GOOD MEN DIE.

This "song of death" was composed at the request of M.W. John W. Simon, of New York, a veteran in Masonic literature, and a life-long friend of the writer. It is arranged to the air of *Bethany.*

Better the day of death,
　　Life's evening nigh,
Better the parting breath,
　　When good men die.
Closed all the cares of life,—
Calm after toil and strife,—
O, in that *peaceful* hour
　　When good men die!

Sweet flow fond memories,
　　Life's evening nigh,
All bear a holy peace
　　When good men die.
Gently the fetters fall,
Softly the angel-call,
O, in that *happy* hour,
　　When good men die!

270

Sigh not by such a bed,
　　Life's evening nigh,
Let not a tear be shed
　　When good men die.
Better than day of birth,
Parting with sin and earth,
O, in that *joyful* hour,
　　When good men die!

Christ is the unerring hope,
　　Life's evening nigh,
He buoys the spirit up
　　When good men die.
He broke the darksome tomb,
He lights the dreaded gloom,
O, in that *blissful* hour,
　　When good men die!

THE DYING HOPE.

Algernon Sydney was executed on the scaffold, December 7, 1683. Having ended his devotions, he placed his head, unassisted, on the block. Being asked by the headsman, according to custom, "Sir, will you rise again?" he answered promptly and unfalteringly. "Not till the general Resurrection! Strike on!"

On the verge of Eternity, calmly surveying
　　The dark, rolling waters that threatened beneath,
The MARTYR OF LIBERTY ended his praying
　　And patiently waited the signal of death;
His head on the block, but his spirit away
In the land where the tyrant shall forfeit his sway.

The words of his lips, how undaunted and cheering!
　　They spoke of a victory grand and complete.
They told that this mortal, whom despots were fearing,
　　Though conquered by wrong, was the conqueror yet —
"The grave cannot hold me! the dust shall be won
From the worm and the darkness of nature! STRIKE ON!"

How mighty that hope, when the spirit departing,
　　Must sunder the ties that have bound it so long,
To feel that this tenement we are deserting,
　　Shall rise to new glories thro' JESUS, THE STRONG!
The grave cannot hold US! — the flesh shall be won
From the worm and the darkness of nature! STRIKE ON!

Ah, yes! and each flaw that the eye has detected,
   While occupied here, shall be covered above;
Renewed by the same glorious hand that erected,
   These Temples shall all be made perfect in love;
The grave shall not hold us — this flesh shall be won
From the worm and the darkness of nature! STRIKE ON!

Then cheer, Brothers, cheer! for why *should* death alarm us?
   A brief separation the monster will bring;
His pangs will afford, though a moment they harm us,
   A glorious reunion thro' Jesus, the King!
The grave shall not hold us — this flesh shall be won
From the worm and the darkness of nature! STRIKE ON!

VERY SOON.

Read before the Grand Lodge of Michigan, January, 1882.

There's a change will surely meet us
      Very soon;
Though our dearest friends may greet us,
And bewail us and entreat us,
Yet death's onset will defeat us
      Very soon, very soon.

Then these emblems, old and hoary,
      Very soon,
Will unfold their mystic story,
Making plain the allegory,
Blazing with a blaze of glory,
      Very soon, very soon,

Oh, the heartaches that will leave us
      Very soon;
Oh, the partings that bereave us,
And the traitors that deceive us;
They will lose their power to grieve us
      Very soon, very soon.

Soon the bedside of the dying,
      Very soon;
Soon the weeping and the sighing,
Soon th' Acacia, death defying,
And the clods above us lying,
      Very soon, very soon.

But in bright lands o'er the river,
Very soon,
Midst the treasures of the GIVER,
Who from sorrow will deliver,
We shall make our Lodge forever,
Very soon, very soon.

THE LAST DEBT OF NATURE.

When nature has paid her last debt,
And earth claims her lendings again,
When *soul* has no more a regret,
And *body* no longer a pain ;
Above the dark grave as we bend,
And cast the cold turf o'er his head,
We feel that *this is not our friend*,
It is not *our brother* that's dead.

We feel there is something that lives ;
The dust could but cover its dust ;
Fond memory faithful retrieves
The treasure we placed in her trust.
She rescues our friend from the gloom
That nature flings over his rest ;
She draws him with strength from the tomb,
And makes him eternally blest.

He lives in each comforting word
Once whispered in misery's ear ;
He lives in each bounty conferred
That lightened a sigh or a tear ;
He lives in those counsels so wise,
That point to the heavenly track,
A wisdom that comes from the skies
To guide all its votaries back.

His spirit still meets with us where
In mystic seclusion we group ;
Our emblems forever will bear
The perfect impress of his hope ;
His column is broken in twain,
Yet none will our brother forget,
Though earth claims her lendings again,
And nature has paid her last debt.

THE TYPE OF IMMORTALITY.

Green,— but far greener is the FAITH
That gives us victory over death;
    The waving woods of May,
        The meadows and the plain,
    This deathless hue display,
        Dispelling winter's reign;
    And grateful to the eye,
        And charming to the soul,
    Is that rich, grassy canopy
        That covers plain and knoll;
But greener is the hue of FAITH,
That gives us victory over death.

Fragrant,—more fragrant far the HOPE
That buoys the dying spirit up;
    This branch gave sweet perfume
        When from the Acacia rent,
    O'erhanging Mason's tomb,
        Its balsam tears were spent;
    No flowers bloom from the field,
        No spices from the East,
    An odorous breath like this can yield,
        That in the grave we cast;
But far more fragrant is the HOPE
That buoys the dying spirit up.

Enduring,— but the CHARITY
That Masons feel can never die;
    Faith may be lost in sight,
        Hope in fruition ends,
    And in Celestial light
        We meet departed friends;
    This mystic branch survives
        The tooth and touch of time,
    And till the Resurrection lives
        An emblem all sublime;
But yet more lasting CHARITY
That Masons feel, 'twill never die.

Faithful we cast the Acacia now,
Hopeful above our Brother bow;
    And when the dead shall rise,
        And emblems lose their power,—

And we within the skies
　　Shall view their forms no more,—
Blest Charity shall join
　　Our hands in endless chain,
And, glowing with the Love Divine,
　　Eternal shall remain.
Then *faithful* cast the Acacia now,
And　*hopeful* o'er the parted bow.

PILGRIM'S HOME.

Bear him home, his bed is made
In the stillness, in the shade;
Day has parted, night has come,
Bear the Brother to his home,—
　　Bear him home.

Bear him home, no more to roam,
Bear the tired Pilgrim home;
Forward! all his toils are o'er —
Home, where journeying is no more,—
　　Bear him home.

Lay him down, his bed is here;
See, the dead are resting near!
Brothers, they their Brothers own,
Lay the wanderer gently down,—
　　Lay him down.

Lay him down; let nature spread
Starry curtains o'er the dead;
Lay him down; let angels' eyes
View him kindly from the skies,—
　　Lay him down.

Ah, not yet for us the bed
Where the faithful Pilgrim's laid!
Pilgrims, weep, again to go
Through life's weariness and woe,—
　　Ah, not yet!

Soon 'twill come, if faithful here,
Soon the end of all our care;

Strangers here, we seek a HOME,
FRIENDS and SAVIOUR in the tomb,—
Soon 'twill come.

Let us go, and on our way
Faithful journey, faithful pray;
Through the sunshine, through the snow,
Boldly, Brother Pilgrims, go,—
Let us go.

In the "Life in the Triangle," is described a MASONIC BURIAL AT NIGHT, of which this Ode forms a part. Four members of the Fraternity, who resided in an intensely anti-Masonic community, had discovered the body of a man upon whose garments was seen the mystic emblem of the Order. This they had carefully enshrouded and provided with a coffin. At night, with every precaution against interruption, they took it to the village graveyard and interred it, with the songs and the signs and the circuits prescribed by the time-honored usage.

PLEDGE TO A DYING BROTHER.

We'll lay thee down when thou shalt sleep,
    All tenderly and brotherly;
And woman's eyes with ours shall weep
    The precious drops of sympathy;
We'll spread above thee cedar boughs,
    Whose emerald hue and rich perfume
Shall make thee deem thy resting place
    A balmy bed, and not a tomb.

That teeming breast which has supplied
    Thy wants from earliest infancy,
Shall open fondly, and supply
    Unbroken rest and sleep to thee;
Each spring the flower roots shall send up
    Their painted emblems to the sky,
To bid thee wait, upon thy couch,
    A little longer, patiently.

We'll not forget thee, we who stay
    To work a little longer here;
Thy name, thy faith, thy love shall lie
    On memory's tablet, bright and clear;
And when o'erwearied by the toil
    Of life, our heavy limbs shall be,
We'll come, and one by one lie down
    Upon dear mother-earth with thee.

And there we'll slumber by thy side;
    There, reunited, 'neath the sod,
We'll wait, nor doubt in HIS good time
    To feel the raising hand of GOD!
To be translated from the earth,
    This land of sorrow and complaints,
To the all-perfect Lodge above,
    Whose MASTER is the King of Saints.

DEATH, THE CELESTIAL GATE.

By the pallid hue of those
Whose sweet blushes mocked the rose,—
By the fixed, unmeaning eye,
Sparkling once so cheerfully,—
By the cold damps on the brow,
By the tongue, discordant now,—
By the gasp and laboring breath,
What! oh, tell us, what is death?

By the vacancy of heart,
Where the lost one had a part,—
By the yearning to retrieve
Treasures hidden in the grave,—
By the future, hopeless all,
Wrapped as in a funeral pall,—
By the links that rust beneath,
What! oh, tell us, what is death?

By the echoes swelled around,
Sigh and moan and sorrow-sound,—
By the grave that, opened nigh,
Cruel, yields us no reply,—
By the silent king, whose dart
Seeks and finds the mortal part,
We may know *no human breath*
Can inform us what is death!

But the grave *has* spoken loud!
Once was raised the pallid shroud;
When the stone was rolled away,—
When the earth, in frenzy's play,

Shook her pillars, to awake
HIM who suffered for our sake;
When the veil's deep fissure showed
All the mysteries of God !

Tell us, then, thou grave of hope,
What is He that breaks thee up?
"Mortal, from my chambers dim,
CHRIST AROSE, inquire of Him !"
Hark unto the answering cry
Notes celestial make reply!
"Christian, unto thee 'tis given,—
DEATH'S A PASSAGE UNTO HEAVEN !"

THE NOMENCLATURE OF LODGES.

ROBERT BURNS.

From Scotland's bard you have your honored name,—
　Master of song, bard of the social lyre;
Freemasonry has spread, world-wide, his fame,
　And Mason poets kindle at his fire.

He was the interpreter of bird and bee;
　The heather blossomed as he moved along ;
The streamlets down their beds rolled pleasantly,
　While Burns attuned their ripplings unto song.

And Masonry,— oh, who has sung like him ?
　Within his poesy our symbols glow;
The spirit warms, the tender eye grows dim,
　As we rehearse his " heart-warm, fond adieu."

Well named, then, Craftsmen ! sound it proudly forth,
　Kindle his genial flame within your band;
Like him, prize man for his intrinsic worth,
　And let the heart be wedded to the hand !

ORION.

In the Orient the Masonic star gazer is accustomed to accredit this brilliant to King Solomon.

Star of the canopy, oh, beaming star !
　The patriarch Job admired thy silver light
　Through the long courses of the Arabian night;
And worshiped God, seeing thy form afar.

The sailor marks thee in the glittering sky,
　Guiding his bark along the silent main,
　And names thee brightest of Celestial train,—
Good fortune follows him when thou art by.

Propitious star, star of King Solomon,
　Thy richest influence is o'er mystic toil,—
　We gain best wages of Corn, Wine and Oil
When through the glittering sky thou movest on.

Give light, Orion, to our gathering!
Guide us in paths of duty! move the heart
To do for suffering man the brother's part,
And honor give to the CELESTIAL KING!

LEXINGTON.

A fire was kindled on the plain
Of Lexington that gloweth yet;
Each blood drop from a patriot's heart
A lasting horror did beget,
Of tyrant's chain and despot's rule,
With which our sorrowing world is full.

Here on your altars glows the flame
Sacred to Truth and Charity;
Each Craft before the SACRED NAME
Bows low in mute sincerity;
And peace has, like a spirit, shone
Within the walls of LEXINGTON.

So mote it be till time shall end!
May circling ages bless the Band
That build the Mystic Temple here,
And round the Mystic Altar stand!
Eternity shall gild the flame
Of LEXINGTON's thrice-honored name!

CRESCENT MOON.

GROWING, GROWING still in NUMBERS,
Still in living stones of strength;
Some on earth and some in Heaven,
Where you may arrive at length;
While the Moon her horns shall fill,
"CRESCENT" be your motto still!

GROWING, GROWING still in WISDOM,
Light still breaking, day by day,
Sacred light from yonder volume
Leading to the perfect way!
While the Moon her horns shall fill,
"CRESCENT" be your motto still!

GROWING, GROWING still in HONOR,
  Still in all good men pursue;
Honest reputation gilding
  Every gracious deed you do;
While the Moon her horns shall fill,
"CRESCENT" be your motto still!

GROWING, GROWING still in GOODNESS,
  Drawing daily nearer Heaven;
All the emblems glowing 'round you
  For that very purpose given,—
While the Moon her horns shall fill,
"CRESCENT" be your motto still!

GROWING, GROWING:— Men of "Crescent,"
  May your growing never cease,
While there is a voice to chasten,
  Or a sorrowing heart to bless!
Till your fullness you shall see
Dawning on Eternity!

EASTERN STAR.

The Eastern Star that first arose
  And moved to where the Infant lay,
Though faint its beams, has since illumed
  The heathen world with perfect day;
And still, to all beneath the sun,
Its glorious light is moving on.

No holier name for Mason Lodge,
  No worthier thought than *Eastern Star!*
And may the knowledge here diffused
  Be spread o'er land and sea afar!
May each reflect the sacred ray
That moved to where the Infant lay!

Each perfect thought, each precept sure,
  That makes our Craft almost divine,
From the blest Altar rising here,
  In light and joy forever shine!
And in the world of bliss afar
Each Craftsman find the Eastern Star!

PLEIADES.

'Tis said that in the glittering Pleiades,
Now shining only *six* resplendent stars,—
There once were *seven* — one sweet astral's fled.

In every Lodge there should be virtues *seven ;*
First Brotherly Love, Relief and Truth, and then
Great Temperance,— lying at the base of all,—
And Fortitude and Prudence manifest,
And Justice, noblest attribute of God.

Brethren of Pleiades, is aught of these
Lacking to you? Is any dearth of Love
Or generous Relief, or Truth divine?
Say, is your glittering cluster incomplete?
In bonds of Temperance your workmen shine,
Bold unto Fortitude, they do not quail;
In laws of Prudence they are deeply versed;
And none deny to Justice her high claim.

When at the midnight hour you view the sky,
Radiant with lamps lit by the Hand divine,
Single your own, the pictured Pleiades!
And as you mourn the one bright astral fled,
And think how brighter were the former seven,
Rejoice that in your brotherly ranks there shines
The unbroken cluster.

SPRIG OF ACACIA.

It flourished in historic earth,
    Land long and greatly sanctified;
It had its proud and noble birth
    Among the hills where Hiram died;
It minds us of Masonic faith,
That knows no counterpart but death.

Though torn away from native dust,
    And faded from its mother tree,
Its leaves still whisper " sacred trust,"
    They still impart love's mystery;
They blend in one all thoughts of them
" Who last were at Jerusalem."

How many graves these leaves embower !
　　How many forms they lie above !
Mingled with tears, affection's shower,
　　And bursting sighs, and notes of love;
But oh ! *the comfort* they have given !
A balmy zephyr, straight from Heaven,

Telling of that not distant day
　　When parted love is joined again;
Bidding the storms of sorrow stay,
　　Affording antidote to pain;
Suggesting an all-powerful HAND
Will raise the dead and bid him stand.

Soon will these leaves be showered on thee —
　　Thy months are numbered, every one;
Soon the last solemn mystery
　　Above thy coffin will be done;
Once more thy requiem will be said,
Though thou, in silence, will not heed.

So live, that when these 'cacia leaves
　　Shall blend with thy forgotten dust,
Kind Mother Earth, who all receives,
　　Will yield, unchanged, her sacred trust;
While angels lead thee to the Throne,
And GOD, the MASTER, claims His own.

THE BEACON LIGHT.

A CITY set upon a hill
　　Cannot be hid;
Exposed to every eye, it will,
Over surrounding plain and vale,
　　An influence shed,
And spread the light of peace afar,
Or blight the land with horrid war.

Each Mason's Lodge is planted so
　　For high display;
Each is a BEACON LIGHT, to show
Life's weary wanderers, as they go,
　　The better way;
To show, by ties of earthly love,
How perfect is the Lodge above !

Be this your willing task, dear friends,
  While laboring here;
Borrow from Him who kindly lends
The HEAVENLY LADDER that ascends
  The higher sphere;
And let the world your progress see,
Upward, by FAITH, HOPE, CHARITY.

MYSTIC STAR.

The light your Lodge is blest to shed
  Is "mystic" and divine!
The radiance by its influence shed
  Each pious heart will win.

Its source is DEITY ; it comes
  Pure from the Eternal King,
And warm from those Celestial homes
  Whence all our blessings spring.

Its rays are FAITH and holy HOPE,
  And boundless CHARITY ;
Three steps by which the soul goes up
  To Immortality.

Its glory is the praise of God ;
  Join, Brothers in that praise;
And when these thorny walks are trod,
  To higher flights we'll raise.

SALEM.

Salem, peaceful city, blest,
Where the Ark of God did rest,—
Where the voice of prayer ascended,
With the silver trumpets blended,—
Where the incense, daily given,
Rose and reached the courts of Heaven,—
Peaceful city, home of love,
Type of better things above !

Here be peace, like that bestowed,
Salem, here from Israel's God !
Here the voice of daily prayer,
Sweetest music on the air,

From each angel hither come,—
Fill the chambers of our home;
Here be felt Jehovah's power,
Shielding in the dangerous hour !

Salem, in thy Lodge be love,
While the Orient Sun shall move !
May all strife and discord fail
As the fogs his rays dispel !
May the fruitage of the soul
Ripen 'neath his warm control !
And to all be heavenly grace,
Salem, seat of love and peace !

RISING SUN.

In dewy *Morn*, with day begun,
    The reddening East allures the sight;
We see the mild, the Rising Sun,
    And bless the invigorating light.

In radiant *Noon*, with day advanced,
    The sunny South attracts the eye;
We hail the luster thus enhanced,
    The larger glories of the sky.

In gentle *Eve*, with parting day,
    The painted West rewards the gaze;
And when her last beams fade away,
    We linger o'er the gorgeous rays.

So, Craftsmen of the Rising Sun,
    May all your working hours be past,
That when your temple toil is done
    Your brightest scenes may be your last.

CONCORD.

The song is set, the sweet accord
Of tuneful note to tuneful word —
    The Master and his men;
Thus do the Mystic brothers form,
With hand and heart and bosom warm,
    The rich, fraternal strain.

LINES CONGRATULATORY.

Read at the Public Ceremonial of Crowning Dr. Rob Morris as Poet Laureate of Freemasonry, at Masonic Temple, New York, December 17, 1884.

Composed by R. W. Daniel Sickels, P. G. J. Warden.

As we grow old, the world seems cold,
    When favors we ask of it ;
The word is " Walk ! no time to talk,
    Your business yields no profit ! "

'Tis thus we meet, as on the street
    We daily take our ramble ;
Man's busy life seems but a strife
    For fancied gains to scramble.

'Tis for *to-day* the game they play,
    Unmindful of the *morrow*,
And on the past no memory cast,
    Whate'er its joy or sorrow.

Thus the great mass of mankind pass
    On Time's unceasing river ;
As to life's goal they onward roll,
    Forgetful of the Giver.

*   *   *   *   *   *

Beside this throng, who rush along,
    A gentler stream is gliding,
Of men who feel for others' weal,
    By friendship's ties abiding ;

Whose every thought, with kindness fraught.
    Whose hands are ever open
To give relief, in hours of grief,
    And soothe the heart that's broken ;

To render praise to those whose days
    To aid mankind are given,—
To shield from cold those growing old,
    And make of earth a Heaven ;

Now such a Brother we have here,
And hold him in our hearts most dear ;
We name him with the good and great,
And crown him,— Poet Laureate !

PART THIRD.

MEMORIES OF HOLY LAND.

Much of the author's time prior to 1868 was spent in preparations for an Oriental journey. The journey itself and the public descriptions of his experience among the hills, valleys and plains of Palestine have occupied still more. A considerable number of his poetical productions referring to sacred localities were written for Sunday schools and religious conventions and cannot claim a place in the present volume, but the remainder are given, usually with reference to the places or circumstances of their authorship.

The volume "Freemasonry in Holy Land," published in 1872, and largely disseminated, gives the history of his explorations so thoroughly that nothing further is required here. One permanent result, among others, is that a broad and well traveled way has been opened between the Freemasons of the East and the West, and a solid foundation afforded for the traditions of Symbolical Masonry, before altogether mythical.

> We see not, know not; all our way
> Is night — with Thee alone is day.
> From out the torrent's troubled drift,
> Above the storm our prayers we lift,
>   THY will be done!
>
> We take, in solemn thankfulness
> Our burden up, nor ask it less,
> And count it joy that even we
> May suffer, serve or wait for THEE,
>   Whose will be done!
>   — *Whittier.*

MEMORIES OF HOLY LAND.

ACKNOWLEDGMENTS.

The flag named in the second stanza was displayed by the author on mountain, shore and plain in every sacred locality. It has been three times carried since through the same places by other Masonic explorers, viz.: in 1873, by John Sheville, and in 1880 and 1883 by Rev. Henry R. Coleman, Grand Chaplain of Kentucky.

Thanks, Brothers, thanks — a noble prize,
    The promptings of impulses high,—
Upon this altar of your sacrifice
    High heaped doth lie!
Earnings of honest, manly toil,
Winnings from your exuberant soil,
All consecrate with willing hand
To shed new light upon the Holy Land.

Thanks, Brothers, thanks! the fame of this
    Shall sound throughout the Orient
Where'er Freemasons work their mysteries,
    In homage bent.
This flag on many a sacred hill
The tale to every wind shall tell;
And echo gratefully prolong
Thro' holy caves my thankful song.

Aided by this, I cheerful go
    To do the work that God ordains;
My life and fate are in His hands, I know,—
    O'er all He reigns;
He'll guide me safely on my way,
Perfect my labors, day by day,
Nor leave me till my race is run
And the appointed work is done.

Praying and toiling I depart,
    Far eastward, over land and sea;
But let me ask each kind, fraternal heart
    To pray for me.

Yes, when within the Lodge you come,
The dear, delightful Mason's home,
One faithful, fervent prayer bestow
On him who'll never cease to pray for you.

Farewell,—farewell,—farewell,—farewell;
    My heart and voice would say adieu;
May the GRAND MASTER in great power dwell
    With you, and you;
Bright glow the Lodge fires kindled here;
Love to your home groups, fond and dear;
Prosperity your lives attend,
And each at last Heaven's ladder safe ascend.

THE GLORY OF LEBANON.

Written at the foot of Mount Lebanon after witnessing a terrific thunder storm.

O, charming Mount! thy flowery sides,
    Thy heights with cedars crowned,
Thy gushing springs, and painted wings,
    And birds of sweetest sound!
O, Lebanon! oh, roseate throne,
    The Church of God shall be,
In days to come, a flowery home,
    A roseate mount like thee!

O, fearful Mount! thy stormy Crown,
    Thy echoing tongues of flame,
Whose awful word proclaims its God,
    And bids adore His name!
O, Lebanon! oh, darkened throne,
    The Church of God shall be,
In days to come, an anchored home,
    A solid mount like thee!

O, mighty Mount! thy stony gates,
    Thy heights in walls secure,
Thy dizzy hills, and sheltered dales
    And guardians tried and sure!
O, Lebanon! oh, guarded throne,
    The Church of God shall be
In days to come, a castled home,
    A forted mount like thee!

THE GRATEFUL TESTIMONY.

COMPOSED ON THE AUTHOR'S RETURN FROM HOLY LAND, AUGUST, 1868.

There is no guiding hand so sure as HIS
    Who guided me, a weary pilgrim, home;
There is no utterance so true as this:
    "Go, trust in God, and you shall surely come,
    Though broad your pilgrimage, across the ocean foam."

In all my wanderings I met no harm;
    I could not go where God, OUR GOD, was not!
Though *weak*, I leaned on His Almighty arm;
    Though *ignorant*, on that Infinite thought,
    Which both on nature's page and in His Word is taught.

You sent me, Craftsmen, to the Holy Land —
    It was my dream from youth to manly age —
Birthplace and cradle of the mystic Band,
    Whose charities adorn earth's brightest page,
    Refuge of loving hearts, the Masons' heritage.

Receive now from that Orient land the tale
    Gathered for you on Lebanon's snow hills,
From Tyre's granite reefs, from sad Gebale,
    From Joppa's crowded slope, from Zarthan's rills,
    And from Jerusalem, the world's great heart that fills.

The spirit of our Craft is reigning yet
    Through every hill and dale of Palestine;
Strong hands, warm hearts, great sympathies I met,
    And interchanged around the ancient shrine,
    And brought my wages thence of corn, and oil, and wine.

I stood in silent awe beside the tomb
    Where Hiram, Prince of Masons, has his rest;
Its covering is the cerulean dome,
    So fitting one with Mason burial blest;
    His sepulcher o'erlooks his Tyre on the West.

I knelt beneath the cedars old and hoar
    That streak with verdure snowy Lebanon;
The mountain eagles o'er the patriarchs soar,
    The thunder clouds of summer grimly frown,
    Where large and strong they stand, those giants of renown.

I mused along the bay from whence the flotes
    Went Joppa-ward, in old Masonic days;
Its waters sing, as when the Craftsmen's notes
    Made the shores vocal with their hymns of praise;
    And fervent notes and true my grateful heart did raise.

I plodded midst the heaps of sad Gebale;
    Of all her glories not a trace is found,
Save here and there a relic, left to tell
    The School of Mystic lore, the holy ground,
    Where Hiram's matchless brows with laurel leaves were crowned.

I climbed the hill of Joppa, at whose foot
    The unceasing tide of stormy waters beats;
Though raftsmen's calls and gavel sounds are mute,
    The generous Ruler of the port repeats
    Our SACRED WORD in love, and all true Craftsmen greets.

From Shiloh's cap I overlooked the site
    Of Hiram's foundries, Zeredatha's plain;
Beyond, on Gilead's ranges swelled the fight
    When Jephthah drove the invading force amain,
    And Jordan tinged her waves with unfraternal stain.

Upon Moriah's memorable hill,
    And in the Quarries 'neath the city's hum,
And midst the murmurs of Siloam's rill,
    And in Aceldama's retired tomb,
    My Mason songs I chanted, fraught with grief and gloom.

For oh, in sadness sits Jerusalem!
    Queen of the earth, in widow's weeds she lies;
Shade of historic glory, low and dim,
    Thy Day star gleams upon our eager eyes;
    Oh, that from her decay loved Salem may arise!

Now homeward come, my Mission I return
    To this warm Brotherhood, dear Sons of Light;
My Testimony stands — my work is done,
    Yours be the honor, as is just and right!
    Be all your jewels bright, your aprons ever white.

Honor to those who bore this generous part,
    Writing their names upon the Holy Land!
Honor to every true and loving heart
    That makes Freemasonry such matchless Band;
    And may the Great I AM amongst you ever stand!

292

SALAAM ALEIKAM.

This is the common expression in Holy Land, signifying " Peace be with you."

Once, when a sorrowing group was met
    To weep their lord and master slain,
While every eye with tears was wet
    And every tongue made sad refrain;
Jesus Himself among them stood,
And "Peace be with you," said the Lord.

Now may your humble Craftsmen say
    Those words, so sweet, so sanctified?
Yes, for no other words portray
    The sacred bonds around him tied;
Hear, then, the message as I call
Salaam aleikam, one and all!

Salaam aleikam, peace to *you*
    Whose Square adorns and marks the East;
Though brightest honors are your due,
    Peace in the Lodge you prize the best!
Oh, let that Gavel never cease
Out of confusion to bring peace!

Salaam aleikam, peace to *you*
    Whose Level glitters in the West;
Your task at evening's close, you know,
    When weary Craftsmen go to rest,—
To give each laborer release,
His wages pay, and go in peace!

Salaam aleikam, peace to *you*
    Whose Plumb denotes the glowing South,
Where pleasure spreads her rosy hue,
    And social joy combines with truth;
The bond of Temperance ne'er release,
But make Refreshment yield to Peace.

Salaam aleikam, peace to *all*
    Good friends and true, around the Lodge,
Whatever fortune may befall,
    Be this the sentence of the judge,—
"In love and peace to pass away
And sleep beneath the Acacia spray!"

And when life's imagery shall fail,
    And closing eyes and ears no more
Tell of the friends we loved so well,
    And in our hearts their memories bore,
May the Great Master from His throne
Say, " Peace be with you, every one ! "

EMBLEMS IN THE HOLY LAND.

North, South, East, West, and everywhere,
    O'er hill and dale, in holy earth,
The emblems of the Masons are,
    Where Masonry itself had birth.

* * * * * *

I met them on the stony hills,
    Where olives yield the " oil of joy ";
I marked them by the sunny rills
    Where lilies hang their petals coy;
I found them on swift Jordan's shore;
    Upon the verge of Galilee
I read their " quaint and curious lore,"
    Those ancient types of Masonry.

Where *vines* upon Judea's fields
    Pour forth their sweet, refreshing juice;
Where Ephraim's *cornland* bounteous yields
    Its nourishment to human use;
Where the tall *cedars* glad the sight
    On high and snowy Lebanon;
And Hiram's *palm trees*, strong and bright,
    Hold forth their branches to the sun.

The *almond* taught me all its lore;
    On Joppa's beach the *scallop-shell*
Lit up the old historic shore
    With many a song remembered well;
By Junia's Bay, *the broken shaft*
    Recalled the fate of "Him that died ";
And far and near, the ancient craft
    Their *checkered pave* had scattered wide;
The fair *pomegranate's* scarlet flower
    Revived me in the noontide gleam,
Flaming through many a verdant bower
    That overhangs the murmuring stream.

In every *cave* I saw the print
    Of gavel marks and working band;
On every *hill* the skillful dint
    Of chisel in the working hand;
Each mighty *ashlar* bears a trace
    Indelibly inscribed, to show
That till old time those marks efface
    Freemasons have their work to do.

The *Parian marble* meets the eye
    In ruined shrines and palaces —
And yields its sacred purple dye,
    The *murex* of Sidonian seas;
The *salt* presents on Sodom's shore
    Its test of hospitality,
As though the patriarch at his door
    Stood yet, the coming guest to spy.

The *funeral lamp*, within each tomb,
    Speaks grandly of the ancient faith,
And burns and lightens up the gloom
    With its own doctrine, "life in death";
The *acacia* too, in bloom outside,
    Tells to the moldering form within —
"Not always shall the dead abide ;
    The morn will break, the sun will shine !"

All these I saw; and by the Sea
    Of Galilee, upon a stone
Of wondrous grace, appeared to me
    The *signet of King Solomon;*
The gentle *dews* that on me fell
    When midnight stars inspired the sky,
Told where the old historic hill
    Of Hermon soared in majesty.

'Twas like a vision thus to rove
    Amidst the emblems of the Art,
Which cheer the eye below, above,
    And with their wisdom fill the heart;
No wonder—'twas my frequent thought
    At noontide's stilly hour of ease—
No wonder Tyrian Craftsmen wrought,
    Inspired by emblems such as these !

MIZPEH.

This was the writer's farewell on his departure, February, 1868, for the Holy Land.

Mizpeh! well named the patriarchal stone,
 Once fondly reared in Gilead's mountain pass;
Doubtless the EYE ALL-SEEING *did* look down
 Upon that token of fraternal grace;
And doubtless HE who reconciled those men,
Between them *watched*, until they met again.

So, looking eastward o'er the angry sea,—
 The wintry blast, inhospitably stern,—
Counting the scanty moments left to me
 Till I go hence,— and haply *not* return,—
I would, oh! Brethren, rear a MIZPEH too,
Beseeching GOD to watch 'twixt me and you.

It was HIS providence that made us one,
 Who otherwise "perpetual strangers" were;
HE joined our hands in amity alone,
 And caused our hearts each other's woes to bear;
HE kindled in our souls fraternal fire,—
Befitting children of a common SIRE.

In mutual *labors* we have spent our life;
 In mutual *joys* sported at labor's close;
With mutual *strength* warred against human strife,
 And soothed with mutual *charity* its woes;
So, sharing mutually what GOD hath given,
With common *faith* we seek a kindred *Heaven*.

BRING stones, bring stones, and build a mound with me,—
 Rear up our Mizpeh, though with many tears,
Before I trust me to yon stormy sea,
 Hither, with memories of many years;
Come round me, mystic laborers, once more,
With loving gifts, upon this wintry shore.

Bring *prayer*,— the Watcher in the heavens will heed;
 Bring *types*,— significant of heavenly hope;
Bring *words*,— in whispers only to be said;
 Bring *hand-grasps*,— strong, to lift the helpless up; —
Bring all those reminiscences of light
That have inspired so many a wintry night.

Lay them on Mizpeh, and the names revered
    Of those who've vanished from our mystic band,—
Are we not taught, that with the faithful dead,
    In Lodge celestial we shall surely stand ?
Oh! crown the pile, then, with the good and blest,
Whose memories linger, though they are at rest.

    *   *   *   *   *   *   *

Finished,— and now I hope whate'er betide,
    Though wandering far toward oriental sun,
He who looked kindly on that mountain side,
    Will watch between us till my work is done.
Lord God Almighty, whence all blessings are,
Behold our Mizpeh and regard our prayer.

    *   *   *   *   *   *   *

Be my defender while in foreign lands,—
    Ward off the shafts of calumny accurst,—
My labors vindicate, while Mizpeh stands,
    And hold my family in sacred trust;
Should I no more behold them, fond and dear,
I leave them, Brothers, to Masonic care.

Finally, Brothers, if in careless mood,
    Forgetting pledges sealed on Word Divine,
I've injured any of the Brotherhood,
    Impute it not, this parting hour, a sin ; —
Forgive! lo, He by whom all creatures live
Grants *us* forgiveness,— *e'en as we forgive.*

SALUTATION TO H. E. MOHAMMED RESCHID, PASHA GENERAL OF SYRIA.

APRIL, 1868.

When God, propitious to his people's cry,
Directing to this suffering world his eye,
Would bless the earth with his most gracious boon,
He bends benignly from the Heavenly Throne,
And sends a Ruler from His presence down.

He takes the pattern best approved in Heaven,
One to whose *mind* the wisest views are given,
One to whose *heart* the law of truth is dear,
Who gives to vice a frown, to grief a tear,
And cherishes for all God's love sincere.

297

Happy the people whom God treateth so!
Happiest of all inhabitants below;
To them the teeming year incessant goes;
Greenness springs forth where yet no fountain flows;
And " desert lands do blossom as the rose."

So hath God blest this people in His love,
Hath granted them a Ruler from above,
Stern in integrity, in spirit pure,
Bounteous in charities, in justice sure,
His shadow in benignity and power.

May God prolong thy days! this ancient land
Needeth thy loving care and ruling hand;
God give thee " wisdom to contrive" the best,
And "strength to execute" each wise behest,
And " Beauty " in the radiance of the Blest !

PLINY FISK,

The first American missionary to the Holy Land, a Brother of the Mystic Tie. These lines
were conceived under the great cypress that overshadows his grave in the Protestant cemetery at
Beyrout, Syria.

'Neath our weeping, 'neath our weeping,
Lies the young disciple sleeping ;
    Jesus moved him with His story,
    Promised him the heavenly glory,
While his vows of service keeping.

Earnest spirit, earnest spirit,
How he did that fire inherit!
    How, to seek the lost, did wander,
    Rent his home-ties all asunder,
And his martyr's crown did merit.

O, to see him ! O, to see him,
When the stroke of death did free him !
    Burst the chains that long impeded,
    Quenched the sorrows he had heeded ;
Angels to his home convey him.

Blessed resting, blessed resting,
Not a jar of earth molesting ;
    Leaves of cypress sigh above him,
    Breathe the faith that once did move him,
Green and fragrant life attesting.

KABR HAIRAN.

Written April 15, 1868, at the tomb of King Hiram, five miles southeast of Tyre.

Eastward from Tyre, where the sun
　　First gleams above gray Hermon's side,
They brought thee, when thy work was done,
　　And laid thee here in royal pride;
They brought thee with the noblest rites
　　The wisest of our Craft enjoined ;
Before thee soared the mountain heights,
　　And thy loved ocean isle behind.

The cedars bowed their kingly tops
　　As Hiram, Chief of Masons, passed ;
O'er Lebanon's all-snowy slopes
　　The eagle screamed upon the blast;
Westward the foaming sea was crowned
　　With snow-white sails returning home;
Their Sea Queen glorious they found,
　　Where thou, their King, should no more come.

Where in thy lifetime thou hadst reared
　　This Tomb, befitting one so great,
They bore thee, monarch loved and feared,
　　And laid thee in thy bed of state.
They closed thee in with cunning art,
　　And left thee to thy well earned fame;
'Twas all the living can impart,—
　　A tomb, a pageant, and a name.

Loud was the wail on Zidon's hill,—
　　Her sages mourned thee as their own ;
Loud the lament on far Jebale,
　　Her wisest *Son of Light* was gone.
The ships of Tyre bore the word
　　On every wind across the main,
And white-robed Craftsmen wept their lord
　　And strewed the mystic leaves again.

Nor these alone,— on Zion too,
　　A Brother joins his tears with theirs ;
King Solomon, to friendship true,
　　The grief of Tyre fitly shares ;

His matchless pen such words indites
  Of true report and sacred woe,
That to this hour Freemasons' rites
  Within his wise direction go.

The centuries wore apace, and changed
  The kingdom of each royal sire;
Ephraim from Judah was estranged,
  And Zidon separate from Tyre;
Then swept the deluge over all —
  The conqueror came with sword and flame,
And templed shrine and kingly hall
  Are but the shadow of a name.

Yet here thy burial place is kept,—
  Still this MEMORIAL appears,
Though shadows of old time have crept
  Along these stones three thousand years.
The frost and rain have gently seared,
  The Orient sun hath kindly blessed,
And earthquakes shattering have spared
  Our *Kabr Hairan*, Hiram's rest.

Still warm thine eastern front the rays
  That call the Craftsmen to the wall;
Here let me chisel a device,
  The oldest, holiest of all!
And as the western sun goes down,
  To give the wearied Craft release,
His latest gleam, in smile or frown,
  These time-stained ashlars still doth kiss.

The lizard darts within thy walls,
  The Arab stalks indifferent by,
Vast relics once of lordly halls
  Around in mute suggestion lie;
The hyssop springs between the stones,
  The daisy blossoms at the foot,
The olive its peace lessons owns,
  Best moral where all else is mute.

Stand thou till time shall be no more,
  Great type of Masonry divine!
From eastern height, from western shore,
  Let Craftsmen seek this ancient shrine;

And from each pilgrim this be heard,
  As from one humble voice to-day:
"Honor to Hiram,—Masons' lord,
  Honor and gratitude we pay!"

FAREWELL TO JERUSALEM.

Planned upon Mount Seopus, the last point northward from which the Holy City can be seen.

Farewell, Jerusalem!—thy sun bends low,
And warns me with his parting beams to go;
One more fond look;—never again to me
On Moab's summit shall his *rising* be;
Never on flowery Sharon's westward plain
His *sunset* visage greet my eyes again;
Though other suns may lighten up my shore,
Sion, *thy sun* shall gladden me no more!

Farewell, blest city;—all thy sacred hills,
Thy winding valleys, thy historic rills,
Thy sepulchers that pierce the mountain's side,
Thy fragrant gardens 'neath Siloam's side,
With me I bear, by loving fancy's aid,
Inscribed in images that cannot fade;
Memory may forfeit many a precious gem,
But never *thee*, thou best Jerusalem.

Farewell, thou Mount beloved! can it be
The gracious KING in wrath abandoned thee?
There was no remedy; such clouds of sin
Polluted all thy courts, without, within,
That the fierce fire of vengeance, long withheld,
Kindled at last; His loving heart was steeled;
Then up those hills there surged such floods of flame,
They left thee but "a by word and a name."

Farewell! above the skies eternal wait
Glories transcending far thy best estate;
There gates and walls with precious jewels dressed,
And streets of gold allure the happy guest;
There flows the river and there grows the tree —
Water of life and endless fruits for me;
And God hath given to the place *thy name*,
The Holy City,— NEW JERUSALEM!

YEARNINGS FOR THE ORIENT.

WRITTEN IN 1867.

Before I go to death's dark shore
To meet the friends who've gone before,
I must survey that sacred earth
In which Freemasonry had birth.

I cannot lay this body down,
Until from snowy Lebanon
I trace the footsteps of that band,
Whose art ennobles every land.

I long to climb that sacred hill,
Once crowned with unexampled skill,
Where Hiram planned and Hiram wrought
Perfection of Masonic thought.

To sleep where wearied Jacob slept,
To glean where Ruth, the widow, wept;
To kneel at Lazarus' rocky tomb —
These are the charges I assume.

To stand by Jordan's rushing flood,
That once in meek submission stood;
To watch the stars' mysterious gleam,
Upon the plains of Bethlehem.

To scale the walls of Joppa's height,
And hear those solemn sounds by night,
Which from the waves below he hears
Who contemplates three thousand years.

To walk o'er Zeredatha's plain;
At Sinai's base to list in vain
For that long-silenced voice, that broke
The stillness when Jehovah spoke;

To search the quarries deep and vast, —
Dark caverns of the buried past,
Whence block and pillar fitly came —
This is the privilege I claim.

Since all those strangers passed away
Who hailed the Dedication Day,

No Mason's foot in search has trod
The Shore, the Plain, the Mount of God.

My foot shall tread them ; and *my eye,*
Though dim, those landmarks shall espy
Which from our fathers' lips we took,
Or gathered from God's holy book.

Around Moriah's walls I'll go;
Each sure foundation-stone I'll know;
And not a relic shall elude
My search through Sion's solitude.

Then home returned, I will rehearse
To you, in faithful prose and verse,
My journeyings through the Holy Land,
Where worked the first Masonic band.

CRYPT IN THE CORNERSTONE.

It is a legend in Masonry that the Cornerstone of Solomon's Temple, sunk firmly in the northeast corner of the holy Mount, contains many objects strange and curious. Among them is a collection of all the vices and passions that were found in the hearts of the Temple builders when they came up from Phœnicia to undertake the work. These King Solomon was enabled, by his wisdom, to detect, and by his power to withdraw from their working places, and to confine them securely as already stated. Since that period, whenever a Mason-brother exhibits any passion or impropriety repugnant to his Covenants, he may correctly be charged with having "robbed the Cornerstone of King Solomon's Temple !"

Build up, ye Crafts, the Sacred Fane —
Raise up its walls as high as Heaven —
But *shape your blocks* and lay them there,
        Upon the pattern given.
Our MASTER bade us labor so —
He marked the years, three score and ten,
And gives us many a noon-tide hour,
        To cheer his toiling men.
We build no walls for time to gnaw,
No halls for men who yield to death ; —
Our *pattern* is the perfect LAW,
        And God our service hath !

He reined the passions' evil train ;
He quenched the fires within the breast ;
He sunk them deep beneath the earth,
        And *there* we bid them rest.

He laid in love the CORNERSTONE,—
A firm, unshaken ROCK 'tis found,
Our fathers built on this alone,
    For this is holy ground !
We build no walls for time to gnaw,
No halls for men who yield to death ; —
Our *pattern* is the perfect LAW,
    And GOD our service hath !

THE KENTUCKY STYLE.

If it were only that you hold within
    Such faithful breasts the secrets of the Craft;—
If only that the Mystery divine
    In your devoted spirits is engraft,—
We would extend to each of you the hand,
And welcome to *the Dark and Bloody Land.*

For here Freemasonry we prize above
    All other gifts the Gracious Lord bestows.
Where first our fathers with the savage strove,
    They reared her altars, they exchanged her vows,
And taught us, as we love each parted sire,
To keep alive, undimmed, the Sacred Fire.

And we have done it; until now, no more
    A *dark and bloody ground*, Kentucky stands;
The light and love our fathers did adore,
    Refulgent, in six hundred Mason bands,
From mountain height to river,— east to west,—
The gavel falls, our mystic toils to attest.

But what best welcome *shall we offer you,*
    Masters and leaders in the sacred quest ?
What fitting salutation shall we show
    To Masonry's thrice-honored, worthiest, best ?
Take, Brothers, *take our hearts!* words are too weak
To express the sentiment we fain would speak.

Shape your own welcome in Kentucky's home;
    Find at each vestibule the latch string out;
As conquerors within our dwellings, come;
    Abide in peace, nor harbor fear nor doubt;
Ours the honor,— give us but to know
Our guests are happy, we are happy, too !

SOLOMON'S MIDNIGHT VISIT.

It is one of the most charming traditions that past generations have intrusted to the present, this of *King Solomon's Midnight Visit*. The legend is that the Mighty Sage, weary with protracted waiting for the Resurrection Day, is permitted an hour each night to roam over the earth. Naturally looking up Masonic Lodges, he hears the gavel sounds of those that are working past midnight, enters them, though invisible, and infuses a spirit of wisdom and love into every bosom. Thus it has long been observed of the Brethren returning home at so late an hour, that they are fraught with a peculiarly brotherly spirit, explained best by this hypothesis of the *Midnight Visit of King Solomon!*

In a deep, rocky tomb great King Solomon lies,
Sealed up till the judgment from all prying eyes;
The SQUARE on his breast, and his kingly brow crowned —
His GAVEL and Scepter with filletings wound;
At midnight, impatient, his spirit comes forth,
And haunts, for a season, the places of earth.

He flits, like a thought, to the chambers of kings, —
To the field where red battle has shaken his wings, —
To the cave where the student his late vigil keeps, —
To the cell where the prisoner hopelessly weeps;
But most, where Freemasons their mystical round
Continue past midnight, King Solomon's found!

Oh, then, when the bell tolls Low XII do we hear
A rustling, a whispering, startling the ear!
A deep, solemn murmur — while Crafts stand in awe
At something the eye of a mortal ne'er saw!
We know it, we feel it, we welcome the KING
Whose spirit takes part in the anthems we sing!

And then, every heart beats responsive and warm —
The ACACIA blooms freshly — we heed not the storm
Our tapers are starlit, and lo! from above,
There seems as descending the form of a dove!
'Tis the EMBLEM OF PEACE which King Solomon sends,
To model and pattern the work of his friends.

His Friends, loving Brothers, as homeward you go,
Bear Peace in your bosoms, let Peace sweetly flow!
In Concord, in Friendship, in Brotherly Love
Be faithful, — no Emblem so true as the dove!
The world will confess, then, with cheerful accord,
You have met with King Solomon at midnight abroad!

THE LAND OF MILK AND HONEY.

"A good land and a large. . . . a land flowing with milk and honey." — DEUT. vi, 3; xi, 9, etc.

O, land of wondrous story, old Canaan bright and fair,
Thou type of home celestial, where the saints and angels are;
In heartfelt admiration we address thy hills divine,
And gather consolation on the fields of Palestine.

In all our lamentations, in the hour of deepest ill,
When sorrow wraps the spirit as the storm clouds wrap the hill,
Some name comes up before us from thy bright, immortal band,
As the shadow of a great rock falls upon a weary land.

The dew of *Hermon* falling yet, revives the golden days;
Sweet *Sharon* lends her roses still, to win the poet's lays;
In every vale the lily bends, while o'er them wing the birds
Whose cheerful notes so marvelously recall the Saviour's words.

From *Bethlehem* awake the songs of Rachel and of Ruth;
From *Mispah's* mountain fastness mournful notes of filial truth;
Magdala gives narration of the Penitent thrice blest,
And *Bethany* of sister-hosts who loved the gentle Guest.

Would we retrace the pilgrimage of Jesus Christ, our Lord,
Behold His footsteps everywhere, on rocky knoll and sward;
From Bethlehem to Golgotha, His cradle and His tomb,
He sanctified old Canaan and accepted it His home.

He prayed upon thy mountain side, He rested in thy grove,
He walked upon thy Galilee, when winds with billows strove;
Thy land was full of happy homes, that loving hearts did own,
Even foxes and the birds of air — but Jesus Christ had none.

Thou land of milk and honey, land of corn, and oil, and wine,
How longs my hungry spirit to enjoy thy food divine !
I hunger and I thirst afar, the Jordan rolls between,
I faintly see thy paradise all clothed in living green.

My day of life declineth, and my sun is sinking low;
I near the banks of Jordan, through whose waters I must go;
Oh, let me wake beyond the stream, in land celestial blest,
To be forever with the Lord in Canaan's promised rest !

LAST WORD OF SOLOMON.

With true and ardent grasp,
A strong and mystic clasp,
In fond farewell the Mason monarchs bent;
Briefly upon the tongue
The *word of parting* hung,
But hand and eye and face were eloquent.

The servant of the Lord
Gave them a *parting word ;*
From mouth to ear the whispering farewell passed;
The world can never know
That sound, conveyed so low,
But 'tis the Mason's fondest and his last.

Hand answered hand, and tongue
Moved the Great Word along;
It kindled up each Mason's bosom there,—
As you have seen the rain
Moistening the barren plain
And making green the hillocks, lately bare.

It banished all the pain
Of parting from those men;
It left a glow fraternal in each breast;
And though no brother's eye
Beneath its power was dry,
Their tears were holy dewdrops, soft and blest.

And then, all silently
The Builders moved away,
And turned forever from the Mount of God;
But never to the end
Did friend forget the friend
Who wept that farewell morning 'neath the Word.

And never to this day,
And never while the sway
Of time shall roll the mighty spheres around,
Can one who owns the tie
Of holy Masonry
Refuse to melt before that mystic sound.

SALUTATION TO AN ORIENTAL BROTHER.

These lines were directed to Hon. E. T. Rogers, now the chief commissioner of public instruction in Egypt.

How sweet is friendship in a foreign land !
How warm the pressure of fraternal hand,
When every other voice upon the ear
Falls cold and meaningless, or insincere !

Dear Friend, I swear your hospitable creed
Embodies all that Mason's heart can heed ;
The courtesy, unwearied kindness, love —
The ruling principle in things above —
A genial manner, grateful to the soul,
And dignity of mien, to grace the whole.

Is this the work of Masonry ? why then
Honor to Masonry, we'll shout again !
But no ; 'tis the Great Master Builder's Craft,
Intent on shaping one exquisite shaft.
God makes the good man ; ours the humbler part,
To indorse the work, and polish it with Art.

Around thee let me, with prophetic eye,
A band of Moral Architects espy —
Warm with thy fervor, in thy wisdom wise,
Seeking through Masonry a goodly prize ;
Bounteous in charities, in honor true,
Yielding to man and God the guerdon due ;
Brave in the truth as to each one 'tis shown,
And bold with justice, fearing God alone.

Thus circled, honored, blest by old and young,
Thy years shall pass as one continued song ;
The Temple, rising 'neath thy Master care,
Golden inscriptions in thy praise shall bear.
Jew, Christian, Moslem, blent in one by thee,
Shall show the world how Masons can agree ;
And influenced by thy wise and timely thought,
Blood feuds and hatreds shall be all forgot.

Then shall this epitaph as thine be given:
"Faithful and true, *his wages* are in Heaven."

LINES AT SAREPTA, APRIL 14, 1868.

Composed at the place where the miracle occurred of the healing of the daughter of the Syro-
Phœnician woman. Matthew xv, 21-28.

Led by a hand invisible,
    I come at length to view the place
Where Jesus broke the power of hell,
    And gave the tortured child release.

And can it be my wearied feet
    Press the same earth that Jesus trod?
O, happy hour, O, bliss complete,
    O, promises fulfilled of God!

These mountains looked on Christ that day;
    This fountain murmured in His ear;
The sky serene, the glassy bay,
    The charming flowerets all were here.

How looked the Saviour? O, to see
    His face divine! Was it in grief
At human pain, and misery,
    And want, and sin, and unbelief?

Beneath this tamarisk tree I muse;
    Grant me to drink the spirit in
Of that great hour, nor let me lose
    One feature of the wondrous scene.

The mother clamorous with her plea,
    The apostle's cold, impatient word,
Faith's trial and sure victory,
    And O, the utterance of the Lord!

Cease, murmuring fountain, cease thy flow,
    And let His utterance reach my soul:
"Great is thy faith, O, woman, go!
    Already is the child made whole!"

The chain of evil power released,
    The demon's fetters broke at last;
The very crumbs of Jesus' feast
    Better than all the world's repast.

No longer to restrain my tears,
    Such gratitude these drops recount;
'Tis surely worth my fifty years,
    This noontide at Sarepta's fount!

Sing, murmuring waters, lulling streams;
    Roar, foamy breakers, on the shore;
Broken Sarepta's fleeting dreams,
    The vision will return no more.

Far o'er the western sea my heart
    Wanders from lone Sarepta's shrine;
I rise, and on my way depart,
    Never to view these scenes again.

But *I shall meet Him!* yes, I know,
    My inmost being this assures,
Where founts celestial smoothly flow,
    And perfect blessedness allures.

Onward and onward moments fly,
    My sands of life make haste to run;
Lord, grant me favor ere I die,
    To leave no appointed task undone!

THE INSCRIPTIONS NEAR GEBAL.

Thoughtfully gazing on this wall,
    By Egypt carved for Egypt's glory,
I strive to call before me all
    The sum of this symbolic story;
It is, that in the human breast
    There ever is a deathless longing
For life eternal; from death's rest
    The immortal soul expects returning.

These conquerors, in blood and flame,
    Wrote on earth's history their hope
To have eternity of fame!
    Traveler upon these mountains, stop
And pay obeisance! 'twas a good
    And worthy hope,— the same that fires
And animates your generous blood,
    And to all noble deeds inspires!

AN INITIATION.

Within this sacred chamber, where in still
And awful solitude, great Peace abides,
Where Hiram fell and taught the Craft to die
In solemn testimony to their faith;
Where lies the WORD OF GOD, out of which speaks
The *Voice* that broke from Sinai, we have brought
One from the outer world and made him ours.

With solemn vows,— JEHOVAH witnessing;
In mystic methods,— ancient and complete;
With quaint devices,— teaching truth divine;
Here in tyled portals,— all the world shut out;
A faithful friend to brother is transformed!
New birth and wondrous! not from ties of blood,
But spirit-born, his mother, *this our Lodge!*

What have we done? how will our mysteries
Bear fruitage on this new and untried stock?
Alas, so many barren plants appear
Within our vineyard, shall we look in vain
To Him? A hope prophetic fills my soul
That *here*, at least, our choice has fallen well.

From Sion's temple there were two escapes
For offerings made by pious worshipers;
One through pure burnings *upward to the skies*,
One by foul conduit *to Kedron's Vale;*
His be the upward flight!

                Bring now the tools,
The mystic Implements that Hiram loved,
And place them on this Ashlar, newly set;—
How beautiful, how beautiful the sight!
As Boaz and as Jachin see him stand!
Lo, in what narrow bounds of truth he moves,—
His virtues, how they gratify the Square!

It needs but that we ask the MASTER's gift
To endow him with all grace in life, in death;
That when his work is ended here, a seat
May wait our Brother in the Lodge above!

THE OLIVE LEAF.

And the dove came to him in the evening; and lo, in her mouth was an olive leaf pluckt off. So Noah knew that the waters abated from off the earth.— GENESIS viii, 11.

The author, upon his arrival at Beyrout, Syria, March, 1868, gathered olive leaves, then just in maturity, and sent, inclosed in printed copies of the above poem, to a very large number of Masonic patrons and friends. throughout the three continents.

Like wandering Dove, whose restless feet
   Could find no solid landing place,
   I pluck this Olive leaf, to grace
A memory ever pure and sweet.

This was the ancient type of peace;
   The wrathful flood was overpast,—
   The gladsome sun beamed forth at last,—
The ark on storm-tossed waves did cease

Then from the Olive bough the bird
   Cropt this green leaf with mystic care;
   And to the patriarch's hand she bare
The missive with its high accord.

Dear Friend, to you this Olive spray
   I send, the messenger of love;
   It speaks a sentiment above
All other language to convey.

The Olive,—glory of this land,—
   Our ancient Craft from this expressed
   The Oil of joy that shone and blessed,
In hours of rest, the laboring band.

The deadliest hands, upraised in hate,
   Before this gentle missive drop;
   The direst discords quickly stop;
The Olive speaks,— the floods abate.

All this and more I fain would teach,
   From this bright, ancient, verdant text;
   Take it with all the words annexed,—
Be yours the sermon that they teach!

WHO IS WORTHY?

Into whatsoever city or town ye shall enter inquire in it *who is worthy*, and there abide till ye go hence.— MATTHEW x, 11.   During my stay in Beyrout, in 1868, my good fortune led me to the house of *the worthy*, viz.: *Samuel Hallock*, with whom I "abode" for two months.

It was a happy day
That brought my feet this way,
And stopped me at this hospitable door;
Parting, I'll not forget
T' acknowledge friendship's debt,
Now that I go, to see these walls no more.

There is no such thing as chance,
God rules the circumstance,—
HE guided me, a stranger in this land;
Intending good that day
HE led my feet this way,
And joined my hand with this fraternal hand.

With Christian courtesy stored,
Gentle in deed and word,
Generous with all the MASTER doth bestow,
Modest and kind and true,—
This eulogy is due
To him whose roof-tree gives me welcome now.

A blessing on him rest!
I seek the distant West;
But I can never sail so far, or fast,
But that my instant prayer
Shall find him even there,
And crown him with good wishes to the last.

THE PALM TREE.

Best type that teeming nature gives
    Of the accepted man;
Lofty and large, the palm tree thrives,
    And where no other can,
Stands crowned with glorious fruit, and lives
    Its whole allotted span.

FAREWELL TO AMERICA.

Composed at the Narrows in sight of the sea, July 3, 1878, and sung by Prof. Wm. H. Slack,
on the steamer next day in celebration of the national anniversary.

Low, low, sing low; the surge is hoarsely murmuring;
Sighs the sad wind, the cold, reproachful blast;
Hark, 'tis the sea bird, on pursuing wing,
Bearing words from home, the tenderest and the last,
Sweet home, good bye! sweet friends and true,
Love breathes the prayer — the fond, the last *adieu*.

O, in this hour, when memory claims the whole,
What tears, what sighs, to us are fondly given;
Christ heed them all ! and give the praying soul
Hopes, bright and strong. the gleaming star of Heaven.

Lands yet untrod await our eager feet;
Skies all untried will lend their radiance soon;
Hand joined in hand, the chain fraternal greet,
Notes, strange and weird, the mystic chords attune.

Swift roll the months; and oh, ye seasons fleet,
Bring the best morning on returning track;
Wait, sweet, sweet Home, your pilgrim friends to greet,
Bear, ye sad sea bird, this fond message back.

CROWN THE SACRED HILL.

CROWN the Sacred Hill !
  Raise the Golden Shaft !
God doth bless the cheerful will,
  Oh, Brothers of the Craft !
Long in sleep Moriah lay,
Mourned her desolation day;
Now awake, in accents clear,
Speak, and willing Masons hear,
To crown the Sacred Hill, etc.

Bring each mystic tool,—
  Old and worn they are,
Trowel, Gavel, Line and Rule,
  And Level, Plumb and Square.

Spirits of the ages gone,
Guide us to the cornerstone;
Strangers wait, a loving band.
Westward gazing, yearning stand,
To crown the Sacred Hill, etc.

Lo, the ruined shrine !
    Ours that mighty pile;
See on every stone the sign,
    We know and love it well !
Though in dust the builders lie,
Though their works in ruin sigh,
Yon device, in whispers read,
Give the lesson earnest heed,
To crown the Sacred Hill, etc.

GRAY WITH THE FROSTS OF AGE.

Gray with the frosts of age,
Dim o'er the midnight page,
Bowed toward the earth, where soon my rest must be,
I give my closing years,
With all its sighs and tears,
O land of holy mysteries, to thee !
Hills, over which our Brotherhood have trod,
Dales, in whose shadows Masons worshiped God !

No nobler work at hand,
It is our fatherland,
There first JEHOVAH breathed his awful name;
In that historic earth
Our customs had their birth,
Our emblems from the land of Hiram came;
Eastward they rose, where Orient suns enrobe,
Westward they moved, encircling all the globe.

Then, Craftsmen, work with me !
Freemasons, come, and see
The sacred mountain where our Temple stood;
Join your right hand with them
Who, at Jerusalem,
Have linked anew the Mason brotherhood;
Help us to kindle up the hidden flame
That on Moriah gilt the Holy Name.

315 .

MEMORIES OF GALILEE.

Each cooing dove and sighing bough
    That makes the eve so blest to me,
Has something far diviner now —
    It bears me back to Galilee.

CHORUS.

Oh, Galilee, sweet Galilee,
    Where Jesus loved so much to be;
Oh, Galilee, blue Galilee,
    Come, sing thy song again to me.

Each flowery glen and mossy dell
    Where happy birds in song agree,
Thro' sunny morn the praises tell
    Of sights and sounds in Galilee.

And when I read the thrilling lore
    Of Him who walked upon the sea,
I long, oh, how I long once more
    To follow Him in Galilee.

Dr H. R Palmer, of New York, has composed music to these lines that received an instant and national fame.

CONSIDER THE LILIES.

Consider how the lilies grow,
    Perfume shedding, widely spreading,
How the scarlet blossoms blow !
Broad in Galilee their fame,
Jesus called them by their name.

Consider how the lilies thrive,
    Beauteous ever, toiling never,
Only need to smile and live;
Father has them in his care,
Makes the scarlet blossoms fair.

Consider what the lilies say:
    " All is given us from Heaven,
Father keeps us every day !
He who makes the lilies grow,
Will He not provide for you ? "

Consider how the lilies die —
  Loved and cherished, lost and perished.
We are for eternity !
He who gives the flowerlet bloom,
He will snatch us from the tomb !

THE LODGE FAR AWAY.

Composed for a most happy occasion at Hopkinsville, Kentucky, June 24, 1877.

In the Lodge far away, where the work is completed,
  The temple in glory, exalted, sublime,
And the Masons are met 'round the Grand Master seated,
  In one grand accord swell the jubilant hymn :
"All hail, MASTER GRAND, from our labors terrestrial,
  Thou raisest Thy workmen when labor is past !
All hail on Thy throne with a glory celestial,
  Thy promise is sure, for we meet Thee at last,
Where the weary at rest have an ample reward,
And the praises we hear are the word of the LORD ! "

For the Lodge far away how the spirit is yearning !
  In low lands of sorrow we labor forlorn ;
To the East, whence its sunrise, the eye will be turning ;
  We wait and we long for the coming of dawn.
We know we must pass by the fords of the river,
  And nature will shudder in view of the grave;
But " the Strong Hand " we feel, and 'tis strong to deliver,
  " The Lion of Judah " will conquer the grave,
And the weary at rest have an ample reward,
And the praises we hear be the voice of the LORD ! "

THE VOICE OF THE TEMPLE.

The Voice of the Temple ! the tidings of Love,
That speak of the MASTER who reigneth above ;
" HIS GLORY, HIS GLORY, in the Highest who dwells
And GOOD WILL TO MAN " is the burden it tells !
  Come, Brothers, in chorus
  Prolong the glad tidings,
No duty so sweet as the hymning of God ;
  His faith each professing,
  His knowledge possessing,
Exalt each the blessing His grace hath bestowed.

317

THE DEATH OF KING HIRAM; AND HOW IT CAME TO SOLOMON.

Traditions embodying the remarkable friendship that existed between King Solomon and King Hiram abound in the East. The tie that connected those neighboring potentates of Israel and Phœnicia was intimate and enduring beyond the custom of kings. After the completion of the celebrated Temple on Mount Moriah, the Royal Brothers used often to visit each other at their respective capitals, *Jerusalem* and *Tyre*, to exchange friendly sentiments. Embassies were continually passing. Costly presents were given and received. Bonds of amity were established between the two nations, which it took the events of five centuries to weaken and destroy.

The death and obsequies of King Hiram were accompanied by incidents extremely curious. It being announced to King Solomon that his venerable friend was in the last extremity, he ordered chosen men placed as sentinels upon every prominent peak in the interval of one hundred miles that separates Jerusalem from Tyre. These were provided with signal flags and torches, so that the news of the calamity came to Solomon in the space of *thirteen seconds;* and thus he was enabled to join, in due time, the obsequies of King Hiram.

'Twas told me by a Troubadour,[1] a singer of Jebail,[2]
Part prose, part song, on thrumming strings, this Oriental tale;
The bard had learned it from his sires with whom, with some arrears,
This story of King Solomon had lived three thousand years.
Around us the Fellaheen[3] sat with flashing eyes and teeth,
And swore by Allah it was true, upon an Arab's faith!
I wrote it then and there, lest time the legend should efface,
And bring it accurately here, our interview to grace.

"Be not afraid of sudden fear!" thus Solomon did write;
"Thou shalt lie down in glorious rest, nor dread eternal night
Sound wisdom and discretion all thy busy life have blest,
And God is now thy confidence and thy eternal rest."
For was not Hiram dying? was there not a wail of dread
Moving along the Tyrian shores, the palm trees overhead?
Therefore the Royal Comforter his words of parting said.

Then thrums my bard the strings;
His slave the coffee brings;
Each Fellah draws upon his pipe the while;
Till with my pencil swift
I catch the gusty drift,
And wait another portion to beguile.

[1] Traveling singers, resembling the troubadours of the Middle Ages, abound in the East. Seating themselves in the corner of a coffee shop, in the center of a crowd of natives, or walking through the villages, they ply their art and sing, to the accompaniment of a rude guitar, legends of the olden time.

[2] This is the ancient Gebal of the Freemasons, the place from whence the *Ghiblimites* or Stone-squarers of Solomon were derived. The word is now pronounced as in the text. Jebail is twenty-five miles north of Beyrout.

[3] The Fellaheen are the *village* Arabs, in distinction from the Bedaween or *desert* Arabs.

318

On every mountain peak between Jerusalem and Tyre,
A sentinel was set alert, supplied with flag and fire,
Each facing to *the Northward*, where the dying monarch lay,
Prepared to pass the intelligence, who knows, by night or day;
And "death to him that slumbers," the relentless Captains say!

The King on Sion waited, midst a bright and gallant throng,
Five thousand steeds begirt beneath five thousand horsemen strong;
Ten score and seven chariots, in gold and silk arrayed,
And twice twelve thousand footmen, armed with Hebrew spear and blade.
Oh, who, of all the sons of earth, in grace and glory can
Complete in royal pageantry with *Melek Suleyman?*[1]

> *Tyeeb, Tyeeb,*[2] aloud
> Screams forth the enraptured crowd;
> The bard thrums all his strings in ecstacies;
> While round the Hakeem[3] stand
> The wild and motley band,
> And watch his pencil as it deftly flies.

Was it a meteor darting down from lofty Lebanon?
Was it the fox fire of the marsh that lures the traveler on?
Or meant that little flash to say, *The Royal race is run?*

The sentinel by Scandaroon[4] a faithful vigil bore,
And with quick torch the message sent, *King Hiram is no more!*
While thunderous lamentation mocked the surges on the shore.

The sentinel at *Nazareth*[5] took up the fatal word;
The sentinel on *Carmel*[6] saw, and passed it to his lord;
A flash on *Ebal*[7] followed, and high *Gerizim*[8] replied,
And *Bethel*[9] told to *Sion* of the Monarch who had died!

[1] This is the Arabic equivalent of the expression, "King Solomon."

[2] *Tyeeb* means *good, excellent, first rate.*

[3] *Hakeem* is the Arabic for *Doctor.* The author was styled Melican Hakeem, or the *American Doctor.*

[4] The mountain pass, ten miles south of Tyre. The word means *Alexander*, and the construction of the military road there is attributed to that enterprising mona.ch.

[5] The high mountain behind Nazareth is in sight of that above Scandaroon.

[6] Mount Carmel is in plain view of the mountain near Nazareth.

[7] I am not quite positive that Mount Ebal is in sight of Mount Carmel, but such is my impression.

[8] Mount Gerizim is but half a mile south of Ebal.

[9] The high ground near Bethel was equally in view of Gerizim on the North, and of a sentinel standing on the towers of Jerusalem on the South.

Oh, was there ever wisdom like the wisdom of the plan
By which, in *thirteen seconds* came the news to Suleyman?
Oh, was there ever King like him, who, over earth and hell,[1]
Could make his power felt, and yet be loved so long and well?
Now let my strings be vocal, and resound in every chord
The praises of great SULEYMAN, the matchless Hebrew Lord!

   At this, th' excited wretch
   Was wrought to such a pitch,
  He sprang aloft and led a fiendish dance;
   The Arabs joined apace,
   And for a little space
  It seemed my Legend would no more advance.
   They circled round and round,
   They spurned the very ground,
  They danced lascivious measures at my feet,
   Till, weary, faint and sore,
   The bard returned once more,
  And thus his ancient story did complete:

As Bethel told to Sion of the Monarch who had died,
The body guards of Solomon were buckled for the ride,
Five thousand shining cavaliers, in military pride,
Ten score and seven chariots, in silk and gold arrayed,
And twice twelve thousand footmen, armed with Hebrew spear and blade.
The horses neighed, the lances flashed beneath the starry dome,
And the procession answered to the message that had come.

Up *Scopus* rode they, as *Low Twelve* struck the attentive ear;
Up *Ebal*, when on *Gilead* the sunrise did appear;
By nine at *Nazareth* they drank, that thirsty morn of June,
And through the portals of old *Tyre* they entered at *High Noon!*
Oh, was there ever such a ride, since horsemanship began?
And was there ever as our guest so great and good a man?
And who of all the sons of earth so liberal and free
As this our *Hakeem*, who will give *good Backskeesh* unto me?

   The Legend thus was done;
   The begging then begun.
  My ears were deafened with the horrid yell;
   I fled the crowd, aghast,
   But ere I went to rest
  Wrote down the narrative which now I tell.

[1] All Oriental traditions credit King Solomon with *power over demons*, and they attribute the getting out and removal of the enormous ashlars yet seen around Mount Moriah and elsewhere, to the aid of supernatural hands.

AN HOUR IN GETHSEMANE.

Recited in the Grand Consistory of Kentucky (Scotch Rite), at Louisville, May 2, 1868.

The sun had sunk beneath the western slope,
The deepening shades of eve were gathering in,
The sounds were of the closing hours of day ;
When 'neath an olive tree I, musing, sat
Within Gethsemane.

I sat and mused
Upon the awful scene that opened there.
Here, said my heart, here JESUS knelt and prayed,—
Here, at my feet, those drops of sorrow fell
Like blood drops to the ground ; *here*, with sad voice
He prayed : "O Father, if it be Thy will, this cup,
O, let it pass ! but yet Thy will be done ! "
And *here* the Father, yearning for His Son,
A strengthening Angel sent right from the Throne.

My answering tears fell 'neath that olive tree,
And in that darkening hour my spirit cried :
"O, Father, who didst give sustaining Grace
Unto the suffering Son, give strength to me !
I know not what's before me,— be my stay !
I cannot see before me,— give me light !
My burden is too heavy,— give me power !
My enemies are mighty,— be my shield ! "

Ten years have passed, I see that place no more,
The olive tree still blooms in fatness there;
But down life's slope my rapid steps have trod,
Near to that bourne whence man cannot return.
But He who heard me in Gethsemane
Hath followed still my prayer ; I have not been
One moment from His presence ; never once,
In all my sorrow, all my burdens, stood
Alone, but always knew Emmanuel !
And come what may, my soul hath confidence
That He will guide and bless me to the end.

Brethren, this was the very night He prayed
Within that garden ! pray ye now to Him,
The reascended Saviour ! by the lights
And tokens of your Faith, light up your souls
This night to follow through Gethsemane
And Golgotha and Olivet, *to Heaven*.

LINES UPON CROWNING BRO. ROB MORRIS POET LAUREATE.

Contributed by R.W. HIRAM N. RUCKER, Junior Grand Warden, Merced, California.

All hail to the Chief! thus in harmony meeting
    To crown thee with laurels so gallantly won;
Thy sphere is *the world*, but we come with a greeting,
    Proclaiming thee, proudly, Columbia's son.

With heart pure and warm, with fraternity beaming,
    With banners Masonic unfurled to the breeze,
A rare signal of truth in foreign lands gleaming,
    Bearing tidings of love far over the seas.

At home and abroad there was ever devotion
    To cause fondly cherished, enshrined in the heart;
Reviewing thy life work we, thrilled with emotion,
    Are pledging this token ere now we must part.

You labored and builded without ostentation,
    With will never tiring, with zeal ever free;
You taught us that spirit "of true emulation"
    Of Craftsmen who wrought best and best to agree.

You gave to the world rich gifts without measure,
    Gems sparkling like dew drops and teeming with lore;
You gave them, we took them with exquisite pleasure,
    As fresh from the wealth of thy bountiful store.

O, Brother, thy songs breathe a new inspiration;
    The bright scintillations from diamond most rare,
Thy mystical wand yields a rich delectation,
    By such gifts to the Craft as "The Level and Square"!

O, sweet to reflect upon life's busy morning,
    Which brings us at noontime those halcyon hours;
Time, swift in his flight, rings out the glad warning,
    Evening replete and resplendent with dowers.

Great Author and Ruler, attend our petition,
    And fill us with thoughts of Thine infinite love;
Vouchsafe to our BROTHER a full recognition,
    And bring him at last to Thy temple above!

322

PART FOURTH.

MELODIES OF ADOPTIVE MASONRY.

No one will begrudge to the friends of ADOPTIVE MASONRY the few pages given its melodies here. So strong a hold has the Order of the Eastern Star secured in this country through its General Grand Chapter, its sixteen Grand Chapters and its four hundred and thirty constituent Chapters, that the present volume would be notably incomplete without it, especially as Dr. Morris himself was the originator of the entire system, and the father of its literature.

Many of these pieces were written for music, and this explains the irregular forms of the stanzas. The best compositions to which they are attached are those of Brother M. H. Morgan, of Chicago, Illinois, who has given to some twenty of them the advantage of his talented and experienced genius as a musical writer.

MELODIES OF ADOPTIVE MASONRY.

MARTHA.

Yea, I believe, although death's cloud
　　Enwrap my soul in gloom;
Thou art the Christ, the Son of God,
　　The Saviour that should come;—
　　　　Yea, Lord, I *do* believe!

Yea, I believe; what though the grave
　　Hath won my love from me?
I felt that Thou hadst power to save,
　　And still do trust in Thee;—
　　　　Yea, Lord, I *do* believe!

Yea, I believe; through ages past
　　Thy coming voice was heard;
The promised King hath come at last,
　　My Saviour and my God;—
　　　　Yea, Lord, I *do* believe!

Yea, I believe; Lord, let this hour
　　Some gracious token give!
O, grant a sweet, reviving power,
　　That others may believe;—
　　　　Yea, Lord, I *do* believe!

Wildly her hands are joined in form of love,
　　As at the Saviour's feet the mourner lies;
Beseechingly she raises them above,
　　While showers of tear drops blind her languid eyes;
Then looks, and pleads, and supplicates His aid
In words that win her brother from the dead.

Raise thy hands above, sweet mourner,
　　Higher, higher, toward the throne!
Ah, He sees thee, hears thy story,
　　Hears and feels that plaintive moan.

He has wept for human sorrow,
　　Let thy sorrows with Him plead;
Raise thy hands in faith, and doubt not,
　　He hath power o'er the dead.

ESTHER.

See, O, King, the suppliant one,
Pale and trembling at the throne!
See the golden crown she bears,
And the silken robe she wears;
Whiter, brighter than their sheen,
Is the woman's soul within!

Mercy's golden wand extend,
While her gentle head shall bend
Meekly o'er Thy scepter now,
Pardon, favor, bounty show;
Naught in all Thy broad domain,
Like the woman's soul within!

Must we perish, O my nation,
　　With the light of ages crowned?
Surely there is yet salvation
　　With our great Deliverer found;
Cry aloud, then, Sion's Daughter,
　　Rend with sorrowing groans the sky;
Blunt with prayer the sword of slaughter,—
　　Haste, my people, ere we die!

Thou, who shone our Nation's glory,
　　Mark this time of deep distress!
Hear, with pitying ear, our story,
　　See our anguish, Lord, and bless!
But if thus our sins to chasten
　　Thou refuse Thy children's cry,
All submissive, I will hasten
　　With my people, Lord, to die.

Nobly she stands, a Queen; the glittering band,
Mark of a royal state, beneath her hand;
She points the silken robe with peerless grace,
Pure as her soul and pallid as her face;
Then reaches to the Scepter, whence is drawn
The kingly pardon she has bravely won.

THE FATHER TO THE DYING DAUGHTER.

JUNE 15, 1876.

No apology is needed for the introduction of lines that have entered so deeply into the acceptance of sisters of the Eastern Star. The gentle spirit to whom they were addressed passed from earth July 29, 1877, at the age of twenty. She was known among us as Ella Wilson Morris.

Dear Ella, as you watch the flowers of June,
   And wear away the summer days in pain,
Do you not often think of seasons gone,
   And wish that childhood's days were back again?

I know you do,—they were such sunny days;
   Your happy girlhood never knew a care;
Sisters and brothers shared your merry plays,
   Your parents took of all your pains the share.

How sweet the moments fled! we used to sing
   Such joyful melodies! when evening fell
To father's knee your little hand would cling,
   And prayers went up to HIM we loved so well.

We sang sweet "Mary at the Saviour's tomb,"—
   We sang "Thus far the Lord hath led us on,"—
And in dear mother's own domestic room
   We kissed *good night*, and then to bed were gone.

Ah, Ella, there is nothing left like this!
   In womanhood there dwell such woe and pain;
Had we but known it was our time of bliss,—
   Oh that my children were but young again!

Gray-haired and sad, I meditate to-day,
   My tears fast dropping through the lonely hour;
Is there not somewhere, somewhere, far away,
   A home where bitter memories come no more?

We *do* believe there is, we *will* believe,—
   You learned such faith, my daughter, at my knee;
The Holy One, who never can deceive,
   Assures us of a blest eternity.

Read it again,—"All tears are wiped away,"
   The saints with crowns and harps all radiant stand,
The LAMB sits on the throne, and endless day
   And jubilant song pervade the happy Land.

Then bow with patience, Dearest, 'neath your load;
A mighty Saviour waits to be your Guide;
JESUS the painful pilgrimage hath trod,
Eternal life and light with Him that died.

TARRYING IN THE SHADE.

Official Ode in the Oriental Order of The Palm and Shell. Inscribed to Sir Knight the Rev. Henry R. Coleman, Supreme Chancellor.

From the foamy billows won,
To the sands of Joppa thrown,
    From the darkness of the salt, salt wave,—
In the cooling shadows brought,
With Masonic lessons fraught,
    As we journey to the far-off grave.

O, the burning of the sun
When his middle course is run,
    As the pilgrimage of life we haste!
But a sympathetic calm
In the cooling of the palm,
    Is the glory of the weary waste.

As we tarry in the shade,
'Neath the drooping foliage laid,
    How the grateful heart to God doth rise,—
Unto God, supremely good,
Who will crown the weary road
    With the resting of the quiet skies.

Then, ye Pilgrims of the Shell,
Con the mystic lessons well,
    With the Signet and the tie so blest,—
For the burning of the noon
Will be changed to glory soon,
    And the Pilgrim find a long, long rest.

CHORUS.

For we journey o'er the dust,
In a fond and loving trust,
    To the City where our dead are laid ;
And we con the lessons well,
Mystic lessons of the Shell,
    As we tarry, as we tarry in the shade.

328

LOVE AND LIGHT.

Where lies the maid — the Mason's Daughter;
  Where is her tomb?
Down by the softly flowing water —
  There is her long, long home.
Sounds of the flowing water breathing
  Peace o'er her bed;
Vines in a tender sorrow wreathing
  Bowers for the early dead.

CHORUS.

Sister, oh, farewell forever!
  None are left like thee;
Weep, Brothers! o'er the dark, dark river
  Fades love and light far away!

Oft, when the mystic toils were ended,
  True hearts among,
What joys the evening hours attended,
  Blest with her matchless song!
Thence, when the midnight hour resounded,
  Rapt with her lay,
Each from the circle that surrounded
  Parted in gloom away!

When, through the haunts of sorrow straying
  At duty's call,
We, every sign of grief obeying,
  Bore friendly aid to all;—
How with us on the holy mission
  Fervent was she!
How, like a bright and blissful vision,
  'Twas her delight to be.

Death called the Mason's Daughter early,—
  Far, far too soon;
Blight nipped the tender flower unfairly,
  Faded her light at noon.
Doubtless in mercy it was given,
  Mercy divine,
That in the love and light of Heaven
  She might forever shine.

Sing, every little bird around her,
      Sing o'er her tomb!
Forms from the better world have found her
      Here, where we made her home.
Grief to this sacred scene forbidden,
      Vanish afar!
Only a little time she's hidden,
      Christ will the maid restore.

JEPHTHAH'S DAUGHTER.

On the hills of Mizpeh bloomed the mountain maid;
Blue the skies above her where she strayed;
As the light gazelle she scaled the rocky slope,
Adah, child of love and hope.

CHORUS.

Gone from the mountain,— lost to her home,—
Called in life's beauty to the tomb;
Wake the wild lamenting in the lonely glen,
She will never come again.

Glad was her uprising, when, with maiden mirth
And the merry timbrel, she came forth;
But, alas! the death march! day of utter gloom!
'Twas the signal of her doom.

O, the grand deliverance of the mountain maid!
"Keep the vow, my father,"— thus she said;
"Shall a Mason's daughter fear for truth to die?
There's a home beyond the sky!"

From the hills of Mizpeh let the story rise,—
"Death before dishonor,"— to the skies;
While the seasons blossom on the mountain free,
Adah, we will weep for thee!

She will not die as thief or murderer dies,
    Whose fate but expiates his horrid crime;
She will not veil her pure and loving eyes,
    As fearing death, for hers is death sublime;
Lo, with determined heart and eye she stands,
Her face upturned toward Celestial lands!

See midst the multitude the VICTIM stands!
　Dauntless, serene, though terror palsies them!
And she must die by her own father's hands!
　And she must die, a sacrifice of shame!
Of shame? ah, no! she flings the veil abroad,
Once, twice, yea thrice; looks hopefully to God;
Fixes the noonday sun with earnest eyes,
Then crowned with innocence, the Maiden dies.

Lament for JEPHTHAH, ye who know his fate,
　Weep and lament; "Broken the beautiful rod,
And the strong staff; Mizpeh is desolate!"
　But for sweet ADAH weep not; let the word
Be: "Joy to the Captive, freed from earthly dust,
Joy for one witness more to woman's trust,
And lasting honor, Mizpeh, be the strain
To HER WHO DIED IN LIGHT without a stain!"

THE SUMMARY.

Fairest of Souls above
　Are those who suffered here;
They gave the sacrifice of Love,
　To prove their hearts sincere.

Among the pearls of earth
　Most cherished, Constancy;
Maid of a high, celestial birth,
　Child of eternity!

Ten thousand anxious thoughts
　Do oft our prayers oppress;
But He who reigns in heavenly courts
　Will surely hear and bless.

And altogether blest
　Are those who know the LORD;
The grave will kindly yield its guest
　To His resistless word.

Lovely upon the shore
　Of Jordan's streams she stands,
Who gave her life for CHRIST, and bore
　His witness in her hands.

331

RUTH.

From Moab's hill the stranger comes,
    By sorrow tried, widowed by death;
She comes to Judah's goodly homes,
    Led by the trusting hand of faith.

CHORUS.

Ye friends of God, a welcome lend
    The fair and virtuous Ruth to-day;—
A generous heart and hand extend.
    And wipe the widow's tears away.

She leaves her childhood's home, and all
    That brothers, friends and parents gave;
The flowery fields, the lordly hall,
    The green sod o'er her husband's grave.

She leaves the gods her people own,—
    Soulless and weak, they're hers no more;
Jehovah, HE is God alone,
    And HIM her spirit will adore.

At Bethlehem's gates the stranger stands,
    All friendless, poor, and wanting rest;
She waits the cheer of loving hands,
    And kindred hearts that God hath blest.

Entreat me not, dear friend, to go,
    Or leave thy cherished side;
The Lord hath called me here, I know,
    And here I will abide.

CHORUS.

There is a place beyond the sea,
    Where sisters meet again ;
Ah! let me journey there with thee,
    And with thee still remain.

The haunts of girlhood, once so dear
    My soul doth prize no more;
I yearn, my Love, far off to hear,
    And find the better shore.

I leave the mansions of the dead,—
　Farewell the grassy mound ;
The flowery plains we soon will tread,
　Where all the lost are found.

I'll go with thee, do not deny;
　I'll make with thee my home,
Where'er thou diest I will die,
　And there shall be my tomb.

Pity the widow, desolate and poor ;
Those little parcels are her only store;
Meekly upon her breast she crosses them,
Prophetic of the Cross of Bethlehem ;
Then looks, imploringly, into the sky,
Where sits enthroned the pitying Deity.

Widow, mourning for the dead,
　Midst the golden harvest mourning,
Beats the sun thy aching head,
Burns the stubble 'neath thy tread?
　No kind look thy gaze returning ?
These poor parcels all thy store?
Surely God will give thee more.

Stand, then, mournfully and sigh ;
　Raise thy hands in meek submission ;
Thy Redeemer, RUTH, is nigh,—
Marks thee with a gracious eye,
　Knows thy lonely, sad condition ;
All thou'st given Him, and more,
Shall be rendered from His store.

RESIGNATION.

Pure and holy resignation,
　Honor high and faith undimmed,—
Gentleness in every station,
　Christian lamp alight and trimmed;
Charity from fount unfailing,
　Sweet forgiveness of all wrong —
These the Eastern Star is telling —
　These the burden of its song.

333

MASONIC TRAINING.

Oh, Ladies, when you bend above
The cradled offspring of your love,
And bless the child whom you would see
A man of truth and constancy,—
Believe there is in Mason's lore,
A fund of wisdom, beauty, power,
Enriching every soul of man
Who comprehends the mystic plan.

Then train your boy in Mason's truth;
Lay deep the cornerstone in youth;
Teach him to walk by virtue's line,
To square his acts by SQUARE DIVINE;
The cement of true love to spread,
And paths of Scripture truth to tread;
Then will the youth to manhood grow
To honor *us* and honor *you.*

BID THEM COME IN.

Bid them come in — the loving, the beloved —
They whose fidelity we've fondly proved;
Throw wide the doors, ye sentinels alert —
Admit them, they're *the Tylers of the heart!*
Conduct them through our imagery, and tell
The lessons that those emblems teach so well.

Open yon *Book* — it is divinely good,
For in it are best types of womanhood;
Heroic Adah — golden Ruth are there —
Truest in sorrow, noblest in despair —
And Esther, Queen — and Martha crowned in faith —
And brave Electa, glorious in death;
It is our First Great Light, whose rays inspire
The soul of woman with celestial fire.

Show them the Orient, whose *Sacred Name*
Bespeaks God's presence unto us and them;
The ripened *Sheaf*, the fruitful South above,
Yields its best nourishment for those we love;
Display the *Square*,— of all beneath the sky
Woman can best resolve its mystery;

The *Level*,— on our passage to the tomb,
No voice like hers dispels the thickening gloom;
The *Plumb* — her walk is virtue's ways sublime,
And the best model of the passing time;
The *Trowel* — she delights to calm and please,
Smooth our asperities and teach us peace;
Show them these ancient mystic monitors,
They testify the jewels that she wears.

Now point the Imagery that graces high
The *Brazen Pillars* in their majesty;
The ripe Pomegranate's shell, the Lily's leaf,
The Net whose meshes such fond counsels weave;
Her delicate taste will best combine the thought,
Of Plenty, Peace and Unity inwrought;
Thus the whole Lodge, from furthest West to East,
Will yield its treasures to our gentle guest.

Now lead them forth unto the abode
Where Masons labor in the works of God;
Go to the desolate home, the darkened door,
The scanty table of God's sorrowing poor;
Behold the sick, groaning on beds of pain;
List to the orphans, lonely they complain;
See the pinched face of poverty; go in
Where haunt the fiends intemperance and sin;
Observe the midnight candle, by whose light
The widow toils for bread through half the night;
See, rioting in sinful ways, the youth,
Lost to all discipline and lost to truth;
See the unburied dead, who wait to gain
The last sad rites that man bestows on man;
See the whole earth in crime and sorrow hid,
And drop the pitying tear as Jesus did.
Now let them learn what Masons teach and do,
The spirit and the limit of our vow;
To soothe the sorrowing, dry up the tear,
Visit the sick, attend the sable bier,
Rear up the desolate in virtue's way,
Check the intemperate who go astray;
Make God's name honored through his Volume bright,
And guide men out of darkness into light.

So all our purposes they'll understand,
And give us loving voice, and heart, and hand.

335

THE SWEET NOW-AND-NOW.

As we glide down the soft-flowing wave,
   And the stars in the sky all aglow,
Let us prize every joy that we have,
   And be glad in the sweet *now-and-now.*

O ye hearts that despair can forget,—
   O ye souls that can drown every woe,
There's a bright-shining hope for us yet,
   And a bliss in the sweet *now-and-now.*

When the dear ones around us are gone,
   And the cypress above them we strow,
'Twill be time for the dirges forlorn,—
   Let us sing in the sweet *now-and-now.*

CHORUS.

In the sweet *now-and-now*
   Oh, to drive every care far away;
In the sweet *now-and-now*
   Let's rejoice, let's rejoice while we may!

LODGE WELCOME TO LADIES.

It is in our heart, dear Sisters,
   While the Mason chain is bright,
To give our warmest welcome
   To the best beloved, to-night;
To the wife, so fondly cherished,
   To the daughter, sister, true,
To the faithful, tender-hearted,—
   Shall I say the word?—*to you.*

We acknowledge countless blessings
   From the Bounteous Hand above;
Our bond was first cemented
   By Divine assent and love;
We are grateful, truly grateful,
   For all gifts He doth bestow,
But our warmest thanks are given,—
   Shall I say the word?—*for you.*

The woes of life are many,
  Thronging dark on every side,
In tears, and sighs, and broken hearts,
  And sorrows far and wide ;
The Mason's hand is generous,
  But most freely we bestow
When the appeal is made us,—
  Shall I say the word ?—*by you.*

Our Brotherhood is countless,
  From the East unto the West ;
In every land, and clime, and tongue,
  They rank among the best ;
And every man a hundred miles
  On frosty sod will go,
To give you help, or win a smile,—
  Shall I say the word ?—*from you.*

Then hail! Adoptive Masonry,
  That brings us here together ;
May manly arms 'round lovely forms
  Protect from stormy weather ;
And when, adown the hill of life,
  Our tottering feet shall go,
May our weary steps be comforted,—
  Shall I say the word ?—*by you.*

ELECTA.

Land far away,— home of the blest,—
Mansion Celestial, O, give her sweet rest !
With her belovèd, crowned with His crown,
Bathed in His glory, whose Cross she has borne;
No failing tongue,— no fading eye,—
No worldly scorn, or heart-rending sigh,—
    Land far away, etc.

Found with the saved, she who was lost,
Raised in His likeness to dwell with His host;
Clothed all in white, spotless as snow,
Henceforth with Jesus the MASTER to go.
Ah, who would stay on this cold shore,
When she has gone to joys evermore?
    Land far away, etc.

THE ORIENT.

Light from the East, 'tis gilded with hope;
STAR OF OUR FAITH, thy glory is up!
Darkness apace, and watchfulness flee;
Earth, lend thy joys to nature and me.
See, Brothers, see yon dark shadows flee;
Join in His praise, whose glories we be!
Now, let these Emblems ages have given,
Speak to the world, blest SAVIOUR, of Thee.

Lo, we have seen, uplifted on high,
STAR IN THE EAST, thy rays from the sky!
Lo, we have heard, what joy to our ear—
Come, ye redeemed, and welcome Him here!

Light to the blind, they've wandered too long—
Feet to the lame, the weak are made strong—
Hope to the joyless, freely 'tis given—
Life to the dead, and *music to Heaven!*

Praise to the Lord, keep silence no more!
Ransomed, rejoice from mountain to shore!
Streams in the desert, sing as ye stray!
Sorrow and sadness, vanish away!

SHE WOULD BE A MASON.

The funniest thing I ever heard,
The funniest thing that ever occurred,
Is the story of Mrs. Mehitable Byrde,
    Who wanted to be a Mason!

Her husband, Tom Byrde, is a Mason true,
As good a Mason as any of you;
He is Tyler of Lodge Cerulean Blue,
And tyles and delivers the summons due,
And she wanted to be a Mason too.
    This ridiculous Mrs. Byrde!

She followed round, this ridiculous wife,
And nabbed him and teased him half out of his life;
So to terminate this unhallowed strife,
    He consented at last to admit her.

And first, to disguise her from bonnet to shoon,
This ridiculous lady agreed to put on
His breech — ah ! forgive me, I meant pantaloon,
 And miraculously did they fit her !

The Lodge was at work on the Master's degree ;
The light was ablaze on the letter G ;
High soared the pillars J and B ;
The officers sat like Solomon wise ;
The brimstone burned amid horrid cries ;
The goat roamed wildly through the room ;
The candidate begged them to let him go home ;
The devil himself stood up in the East,
As bold as an alderman at a feast,
 When in came Mrs. Byrde!

O, horrible sounds ! O, horrible sight !
Can it be that Masons take delight
In spending thus the hours of night ?
Ah, could their wives and daughters know
The unutterable things they say and do,
Their feminine hearts would burst with woe !
 But this is not all my story : —

Those Masons joined in a hideous ring,
The candidate howling like everything,
And thus in tones of death they sing
 (The candidate's name was Morey):
" Blood to drink, and bones to crack,
Skulls to smash, and lives to take,
Hearts to crush, and souls to burn —
Give old Morey another turn,
 And make him all grim and gory."

Trembling with horror stood Mrs. Byrde,
Unable to utter a single word;
She staggered and fell in the nearest chair,
On the left of the Junior Warden there ;
And scarcely noticed, so loud the groans,
That the chair was made of human bones.

Of human bones ! On grinning skulls
That ghastly throne of horror rolls,
Those skulls, the skulls that Morgan bore ;
Those bones, the bones that Morgan wore ;

His scalp across the top was flung,
His teeth around the arms were strung;
Never in all romance was known
Such uses made of human bone.

The brimstone gleamed in lurid flame
Just like —, the place I will not name;
Good angels, that inquiring came
From blissful courts, looked on with shame
    And solemn melancholy.
Again they dance, but twice as bad,
They jump and sing like demons mad
    (The tune was *Hunkey Dorey*) :
"Blood to drink, and bones to crack," etc.

There came a pause — a pair of paws
Reached through the floor, up sliding doors,
And grabbed the unhappy candidate!
How can I without tears relate
The lost and ruined Morey's fate?
She saw him sink in fiery hole,
She heard him scream, "My soul! my soul!"
While rolls of fiendish laughter rolled,
    And drowned the yells of Morey,
"Blood to drink," etc.

The ridiculous woman could stand no more;
She fainted and fell on the checkered floor,
Midst all the diabolical roar;
What, then, you ask me, did befall
Mehitable Byrde? Why, nothing at all —
She dreamed she had been in a Mason's hall!

TO THE GENTLER SEX.

To win the love of women to our cause,
    The love of mother, sister, daughter, wife,—
To gain her admiration of our laws,—
    This were the greatest triumph of our life;
For this " we well may work and well agree ";
    No emblem on our Trestle board so rife,
But would the brighter shine could we but see
    On woman's breast its rays, that fount of purity.

Ladies, the hearts of Masons are sincere;
　　For you and yours we cheerful meet and toil;
We plan, in mystic gloom and silence here,
　　That which doth make the widow's heart to smile;
　　That which the mourner's sorrow doth beguile;
That which brings bounty to the fatherless,
　　And rescues innocence from plottings vile;
Your God and ours these charities do bless,—
Then lend your brightest smiles Freemasonry to grace.

THE MANIAC SISTER.

It is reported that during the Civil War a Mason, returning from the Lodge, was waylaid by guerrillas at his own gate, and hung upon one of the trees that sheltered his dwelling. His wife at once lost her reason. Her infant died. And while she lingered for a few months she was observed always on the evening of new moon to simulate the nursing of the infant, and to talk as though its father would soon "come home from Lodge."

It was a nursing mother singing low,
　　Singing as though her baby crowned her knee;
The sobbing winds of winter murmur so,
　　But nature has no sight so sad as she;
For oh, her little one lies in the earth,
　　Its murdered father by the baby's side,
And she who gave the tender floweret birth
　　Sings crazy lullabies since baby died.

She thinks her husband to the Lodge has gone ;
　　At Gavel's fall, with smiling, she will meet;
And she will wait, if need be, till the morn
　　To greet with baby his returning feet;
And sighing.— oh, heart-broken one so sad !
　　And rocking, mother-like, as if to sleep,
Her plaintive lullabies are ceaseless made,
　　Which whoso heareth, let him turn and weep.

She saw him murdered,— heard the murderous shout;
　　Saw him with gasping horror swing and die;
Then went from that poor girl her reason out,
　　Her mind with Jamie's soul made haste to fly;
Her baby died,—'twas well, we felt it so,
　　And laid the blighted bud in peace away;
We dared above it bright green sprigs to strew;
　　We'll meet it on the Resurrection Day.

341

Why should she live?—this world is not her home
    Her babe and husband wait beyond the sky;
Her heart and hopes already in the tomb,
    Better, far better, the poor girl should die;
Not long to wait,—her gentle cheek is pale;
    Her lullabies grow fainter, day by day;—
Hark, hark! I hear the loving Masons tell,
    "Our much tried sister soon will pass away."

THE COMPLETION OF THE EASTERN STAR.

A poem composed for and inscribed to the Illustrious Sisters of the Four Chapters of the Order of EASTERN STAR, at Chicago, Ill., assembled August 31, 1881, on the Annual Festival Day decreed by the general Grand Chapter of the Order.

If there be lacking anything within this starry group,—
If there is place for other grace amidst the radiant troupe,—
I'll not go back on history's track to find a model clear,—
But crave *your* light, dear ladies bright, who grace my birthday here ;
    And so I'll fill the measure of the EASTERN STAR !

The sparkling eye, the fairy form, they shall my muse inspire;
The singing tongue, the sacred song, awake my humble lyre;
The tripping feet in mazes fleet their mystic spell shall cast,
And all shall say, "The present day is better than the past!"
    And so I'll add new splendor to the EASTERN STAR !

From mothers here and maidens dear I'll borrow many a grace,—
In all this earth there is no worth like that a woman has;
Last at the Cross,—in lingering hope by Jesus, the adored;
First at the Grave,—in eager haste to magnify their Lord;
    From these I'll take fresh brilliance for the EASTERN STAR !

In each home circle, where the wife keeps household lamp alight,—
From sister's vigilant eye that guides the brother's steps aright,—
From mother's knee where childhood learns its one effectual prayer,—
If I indeed a lesson need I'll find that lesson there,
    And it will give rare glory to the EASTERN STAR.

Lastly, I'll seek the happy dead,—that grave, I know it well,
How fondly loved my Ella was, ah me, no words can tell,—
I know the answer that will come from yon bright maiden blest,
"They who with JESUS suffer here shall have eternal rest."
    This overfills the radiance of the EASTERN STAR.

No more than this is earthly bliss,— but might I dare look up,
If in the immortal mansions I might place one daring hope,
'Tis that th' All-wise will realize this fond attempt of mine
With beaming LIGHT ineffable, with endless LIFE divine,
And so unto His glory I devote the EASTERN STAR.

THE SISTER'S FUNERAL

Bear her softly, Brothers, softly,
　　Slowly tread and lightly move;
Little children walk beside her,
　　Weeping for the one they love,
　　　　And they cannot walk so fast.
　　Hurry not, support her gently,—
　　　　This sad march is mother's last.

Are these raindrops falling on us,
　　Tears of angels, dropped from Heaven?
Well they may be; never sorrow,
　　Tribute more sincere, was given!
　　　　Softly, Brothers;— let them fall;
　　" Blest the dead the rain rains on,"—
　　　　Angels weep o'er mother's pall.

Softly,— softly,— 'tis the graveyard,
　　And her husband's grave is here;
Right it was *her* grave to open,
　　By the man she loved so dear;
　　　　Now her widowhood is past,—
　　All her yearnings now are over,—
　　　　Let the lovers meet at last!

Slowly give her form interment,
　　Mother unto mother earth;
Death,— thy victory was never
　　Over more transcendent worth!
　　　　Never one more pure than she;
　　O, how can we, Brothers, spare her,
　　　　From this world of misery?

Lightly lay the sods above her,
　　Hiding from her children's eyes;
Ah, those hapless sons and daughters,—
　　Pity them above the skies!

343

All this world cannot afford
   Unto them a friend so faithful;
      None so faithful *save the Lord!*

Brothers, yet a moment longer,—
   Hand in hand about her grave;
She, in fullness of our virtues,
   Mason's eulogy shall have.
      Ere we leave this sacred heap,
      Join in tender reminiscence,—
         Then in silent parting, weep.

That influence that warms the earth
   In spring time, waking trunks and roots,
Moved on her spirit, giving birth
   To Heaven's fairest flowers and fruits;
She *bloomed* in spiritual grace,
   In Christian light, and love, and song;
Her *fruitage* was to cheer and bless
   The sorrowing, as she passed along.

Her pilgrimage was made with God,
   His seal divine was on her brow;
His truth inspired her every word —
   That truth which Masons chiefly know.
Each precept in our emblems taught
   Was in her life exemplified;
Freemason's *works* in her were wrought
   And in Freemason's *faith* she died.

Therefore we make those ancient signs,
   Which, living, she so deftly made.
Through them a mystic glory shines
   Like that which gilt the Saviour's head.
In them we read of conquering faith,
   And hope as free and bright as hers,
Which made immortal in their death
   Five of the Old World's worshipers.

(The next stanza is recited with esoteric accompaniments.)

Like *Adah*, she expired in light —
   Like *Ruth*, adored the widow's friend —
Like *Esther*, chose the crown most bright —
   Like *Martha*, did in meekness bend —

Like blest *Electa* bore her cross
    As one who scorns its weight and pain,
Laid down life's richest gifts as dross,
    Believing she would rise again.

Fairest of earthly daughters, she
    Among the angelic hosts doth fly;
Ten thousand forms around her be,
    And all together mount the sky.
Lovely their forms; their joyous tongues
    Go thrilling up to Heaven's gate,
Where cherub-shouts and seraph-songs,
    Their ransomed sister's spirit wait.

Silently, silently turn away,
Patiently yield to death the sway,
Hopefully leave her in the tomb,
Until her Lord shall come.

FAITHFUL FRIENDSHIP.

Abide thou with me; fear not. For he that seeketh my life, seeketh thy life, but with me thou shalt be in safeguard.— I SAMUEL xxii, 23.

Abide thou here with me !
    Our arms in covenant twine;
Whoever seeks thy life to harm,
    Shall reach thy life through mine.
My heart thy heart secure shall guard,
Or, blend its current with thy blood.

Confide thy name with me,
    No slanderer shall upbraid;
Each harmful utterance shall recoil
    Upon the slanderer's head;
Traitor to friendship as to truth,
And perjured in a double oath.

Name every want to me !
    Art poor? lo, here's my store !
Though scanty, it is offered free,
    And God will give us more.
Who formed this covenant of us twain,
Will never hear us cry in vain.

Thy slumbers leave to me!
　Thy last and dreamless rest;
I'll lay thee in earth's sunniest glade,
　A spot by angels blest.
And when my hour shall come to die
My choice shall be with thee to lie.

SONG AND FREEMASONRY.

Addressed to a lady who had written various Masonic productions of merit.

Rich is song when tuned to passion,
　Love, benevolence, or joy—
Vast its power, and blest its mission ; —
　Saints in Heaven the notes employ ;
Heaven itself resounds with song,
Tuned by an unnumbered throng.

But its power is best extended,
　When, to bless the SONS OF TOIL,
Masons' joys with songs are blended,
　Rhyming Corn and Wine and Oil ;
Then it thrills the inner sense,
Driving gloomy shadows hence.

Sister, from your heart are welling
　Thoughts attuned to sweetest song !
But the sweetest yet are telling
　Of the ancient Mason-throng ;
Telling of its TENETS three,
FAITH, and HOPE, and CHARITY !

Still to us your muse be given —
　Ours the genial spirit-birth ;
Sing the Sabbath rest of Heaven,
　Sing the six days' toil of earth,
Festive joys, and sacred grief,
Love fraternal, truth, relief.

Then, when death his object gaining,
　Stills the answer of your lyre,
These the gems of song remaining,
　Other genius shall inspire,
And the Craft, in deathless lays,
Shall embalm their Poet's praise.

THE BLISSFUL MEETING.

Referring to the meeting between Martha and Jesus in the pleasant little wady below Bethlehem.

Where should she go, if not to Him ?
  Her home was cold and desolate,
  For there the sorrowing Mary sate,
Her eyes with ceaseless weeping dim.

She went and met Him ; met her Lord,
  As up the rocky slope He came,—
  His pardoning spirit will not blame
The faithful girl, her hailing word.

In fond rebuke, she kneeling said,—
  " Master, we sent Thee timely word,
  Thou wert our own, our saving Lord,—
Thou didst not come, and he is dead ! "

Life flows in Jesus ; soon her grief
  Was past, her brother raised from death ;
  To us who meet the Lord in faith,
His presence *is* eternal life.

A VALEDICTORY.

Good night ! the spirits of the blest and good
  From these dear walls go with you and abide ;
In hours of sorrow, hours of solitude,
Or when the hosts of melancholy brood,
  And cloud your mind, may angel spirits glide
From the WHITE THRONE and give you great delight ;
    Dear friends, good night !

Good night ! good night ! and joy be with you all ;
  May sickness never blight, nor poverty ;
May slanderous breath your spirits ne'er appall ;
May no untoward accident befall,
  But all things prosperous and happy be ;
May morning suns rise on you fresh and bright ;
    Dear friends, good night !

Good night! in dreams may faithful *Martha* come
　To tell of her beloved, high in Heaven;
And *Ruth*, the gleaner, from her harvest home,
And *Adah*, maid immortal, from her tomb,
　　Esther and true *Electa*, spirits bright,
　　　And say, good night!

Good night! and when the shadows of the grave
　Close in around you,— when the laboring breath
Draws heavily, and unto Him who gave,
You yield the spirit, be HE strong to save,
　Who is our GUIDE and SAVIOUR unto death!
Then may dear friends and heavenly hopes unite
　　To say, good night!

COME, VIEW THE HOLY LAND.

Come, view the Holy Land, indeed!
　Come, see the place wnere Jesus lay!
The rock, the tree, the flower, the seed
　Are all there as they were that day
　When heartless thousands heard him pray,
When pitiless thousands saw him bleed.

Behold, this is the Holy Land!
　From Jordan's wave these pure drops come;
This shell, that glittered on the strand,
　Bears witness with its ocean foam,
　And this from its high mountain home,
That all the words of Jesus stand.

Now read the Gospel of these things,—
　On this poor stone perhaps Christ trod!
And so, a Monitor, it brings
　Our clay-bound spirits nearer God,
　Because it represents the sod
Whence his humanity took wings.

With fervent tongue each little thing
　Its words of testimony says;
You, who Christ's truths are gathering,
　These tokens from His land address,
　For tree, mount, river chant his praise,
And "they that dwell in dust do sing."

348

ELECTA.

When cares press heavy on the heart,
    And all is gloom around,
Where shall we fix the heavy eye
    In all this mortal bound?
What emblem hath the mourner here?
What love to warm, what light to cheer?

Thine, true ELECTA, thine which tells,
    Of His distress and thine!
The Cross upon whose rugged limbs
    Ye both did bleed and pine!
The Cross by heavenly wisdom given
To raise our thoughts from earth to Heaven.

Dying, as JESUS died, upon the tree,—
    Was ever worthier sacrifice than hers?
Sacred the Cross, the nail, the thorn; for He
    Who suffered has redeemed them from the curse;
Just as she passed to blest eternity
    She plead forgiveness to her murderers.

THE ANGEL OF MERCY.

Composed for a called session of the Grand Chapter E.S. of California, May, 1876.

The angel of mercy to-night is abroad;
There gleams from her finger the signet of God;
Her work in beneficence all is designed—
The sad to console and give light to the blind.
Oh brightest of beings that nestle above
The angel of mercy, the angel of love!

The sound of her wings rustles light on the air;
She bends her bright course to th' abodes of despair
Her features entrance the dull vision of pain,
And the joyless are kindled with rapture again.
Oh sunniest object that sparkles above,
The angel of mercy, the angel of love!

To lips of the fevered she tenders the cup;
The head of the drooping her hand beareth up;
The friendless she points to the land far away,

And the dying makes hopeful with visions of day.
Oh, nearest divine of the powers above,
The angel of mercy, the angel of love!

Dear Sisters, to you is her mission consigned,
To you she, departing, leaves duty behind;
In errand Celestial she bids you go forth,
And be the beneficent angels of earth!
Yes, each of you prove on the model above,
An angel of mercy, an angel of love!

TALITHA CUMI.

This is the story of "the daughter of Jairus" and her resurrection, as told me in Galilee in 1868. The Scriptural passages are these: He took her by the hand and the maid arose.— MATTHEW ix, 25. He took the damsel by the hand, and said unto her *talitha cumi*, which is, being interpreted, Damsel, I say unto thee, arise.—MARK v, 41. He took her by the hand and called, saying, Maid, arise.—LUKE viii, 54.

By the sea her memory dwelleth,
    Maiden well beloved and fair;
And each loving mother telleth
    How the child lay dying there;
How she lay, that sweet one, dying,—
    Only child, there was no more,
While the Oriental crying
    Swelled the murmurs of the shore;
        So they tell it by the Sea
        Of the placid Galilee.

How the anxious father hastened
    Jesus, present help, to meet,
And, with awful sorrow chastened,
    Fell imploring at His feet;
"Master, oh, my little daughter,—
    Only child,—about to die!"
While the plashing of the water
    Mocked at his despairing cry.
        So they tell it by the Sea
        Of the storm-tossed Galilee.

How the Lord, no tarry making,
    Through the thronged and narrow street,
Hastened to a wondrous waking,
    Such as every saint shall meet;

Matters not though servant coming
  Told him that the child was dead,
And the breakers hoarsely booming,
  All the mournful message spread.
    So they tell it by the Sea
    Of the dirge-like Galilee.

How He found the stricken dwelling;
  Clasped the clay-cold little hand,—
Needless is the further telling,—
  Death obeyed the Lord's command;
While those waters roll, the story
  Of the maiden will remain,
Promise of the greater glory
  When the Christ shall come again.
    So they think along the Sea
    Of this much-loved Galilee.

THE STAR.

Where the bright acacia waving
  Tells of life forever green,
Lo, yon starry-pointed graving
  The emblem of Faith is seen.

CHORUS.

Star that gleamed in heavenly story,
  Oh, whisper tender hope in every ray,
Shine with the light of perfect glory,
  And lead to eternal day.

Lo, that star that went before them,
  Stood above the gentle guest!
Oh, for the mighty faith that bore them
  So far in the holy quest!

Guide us up among the mountains,
  Where true Adah smiled at death;
Lead us down beside the fountains,
  By the scene of Ruth's great faith.

Land of Persia's queen immortal,
  Star of matchless wonder, show;
Thence with Martha to the portal,
  As a guide to our glad feet go.

Where the rose of Sharon bloometh,
  By the martyr's grave afar,
There in mighty glory cometh
  So gently the Eastern Star.

EXORDIUM.

Here is a story of the grand old time.
A tale of virtues tender, yet sublime,
Inscribed on sacred page to give us faith
In woman's constancy in life and death.
Here in God's Book the bright narration see,
And five brave hearts make up the history!

Adah, great Jephthah's daughter, soul of truth;
Ruth, flower of Moab, humble, pious Ruth;
Esther, the crowned, the worthiest of a crown;
Martha, His friend whom saints and angels own;
Electa, strong the martyr's cross to bear,—
These are the heroines of the EASTERN STAR!

Fairest among ten thousand deathless names,
  How altogether lovely do they glow!
Time's annals yield no brighter, nobler themes,
  No purer hearts the ranks immortal show.
Come then, oh, sisters, sister-virtues trace,
And light anew from them your lamps of grace.

THE LADIES' WELCOME.

A welcome and a greeting now,
  To gentle friends and sisters true,
Around the place where Masons bow,
  And pay their homage due;
On CHECKERED FLOOR, 'neath STARRY SKY,
Welcome, kind friends of Masonry!

To her who finds a FATHER here;
  Or BROTHER'S strong and trusty hand;
To her who mourns the lost and dear,
  Once cherished in our band;
To her who HUSBAND'S love doth own,
Greeting and welcome, every one!

Welcome the *light* our emblems shed ;
Welcome the *hopes* yon Volume gives,—
Welcome the *love* our Covenants spread,
The *wages* each receives ;
And when is past life's toilsome week,
Welcome the HOME that Masons seek.

In the bonds of Mason's *duty,*
Seek ye now the Mason's *light,*
Forms of Wisdom, Strength, and Beauty
Teach us what is good and right;
Far be every sinful passion,
Near be every gentle grace;
And so at last this holy mission
Shall reveal our MASTER'S face.

THE DOUBLE SCORE.

Contributed by Rev. HENRY G. PERRY, M.A., of Chicago, Illinois, to the laureation cere-
monies of Bro. ROB MORRIS, December 17, 1884.

For two score years the brain and pen
Of one of our own noblemen
Have graced the Trestle Board;
Treasures of prose and poetry,
Peculiar for the Masons free,
Their precious yield outpoured.

If from them all but *few* be sought,
From them then *best* the wreath be wrought
To deck the writer's head;
It needs not volumes to compose
A scroll of soulful worth that goes
To show where merit led.

The " tried and true " of forty years
Experienced ! what hopes and fears
Inspired the Craftmen's mind !
" The Master Cometh " to afford
" The Utterances of the Sword "
And " Masons' Auld Lang Syne."

In that he gave " One Hour with You,"
" Five Points of Fellowship " all true,
With " Level, Plumb and Square,"

Frame but the CROWN from these alone,
It serves, within the secret zone,
  His honor to declare.

Prove then such DOUBLE SCORE in sooth
His, both in point of Time and Truth,
  Who labored long and hard;
Recount his trophies hundreds o'er,
The Poet Craftsman's "double score";
  God bless, God bless the Bard!

THE TWO ROBS.

Lines contributed by Brother Joseph Robbins, Quincy, Illinois, P.G. Master, for the Laureate Testimonial, at New York, December 17, 1884.

'Tis meet that Masonry should twine anew
  For the sweet singer of her later days
The LAUREL WREATH, that on *his* brow she threw,
  Her earlier ROB, who mid ".the banks and braes"
Of her first mountain home, on living strings
  Of human hearts, so waked the minor chords,
Attuned to that sweet sadness which still sings
  The while it weeps, transmuting into words
Tears that slake our spirits as the earth the dew,
  That scarce we know if most of joy or pain
Swells when his " Heart-warm, fond adieu " thrills through
  The later minstrel's " Bright Fraternal Chain!"
Twin ROBS are these; when either strikes the lyre
The other's heart throbs trample on the wire.

354

PART FIFTH.

A SELECTION OF

POETICAL PIECES FROM OTHER AUTHORS.

It is but justice to others who have written detached pieces upon Masonic themes, to present a few of their best productions here. Much care has been taken in making selections, and it is thought that no partiality can be charged either in the choice of authors or works.

SELECTION OF POETICAL PIECES FROM OTHER AUTHORS.

AH, WHEN SHALL WE THREE?

By JOHN H. SHEPPARD, late of Boston, Mass.

Ah, when shall we three meet, like them
Who last were at Jerusalem?
For three there were, but one is not,—
He lies where Acacia marks the spot.

Though *poor* he was, with kings he trod;
Though *great*, he humbly knelt to God;
Ah, when shall those restore again
The broken link of friendship's chain?

Behold, where mourning beauty bent
In silence o'er his monument,
And widely spread in sorrow there
The ringlets of her flowing hair!

The future Sons of Grief will sigh,
While standing round in mystic tie,
And raise their hands, alas! to Heaven,
In anguish that no hope is given.

From whence we came, or whither go,
Ask me no more, nor seek to know,
Till three shall meet who formed, like them,
The GRAND LODGE at JERUSALEM.

THE SPRING HAS LESS OF BRIGHTNESS.

By ALBERT PIKE, of Washington, D. C.

The Spring has less of brightness
        Every year,
And the snow a ghastlier whiteness
        Every year;
Nor do Summer flowers quicken,
Nor Autumn fruitage thicken,
As they once did,—for we sicken
        Every year.

It is growing darker, colder,
 Every year,—
As the heart and soul grow older
 Every year;
I care not now for dancing,
Nor for eyes with passion glancing,
Love is less and less entrancing,
 Every year.

Of the loves and sorrows blended,
 Every year,—
Of the charms of friendship ended,
 Every year,—
Of the ties that still might bind me,
Until time of death resigned me,
My infirmities remind me
 Every year.

Ah, how sad to look before us
 Every year,—
While the cloud looks darker o'er us
 Every year!
When we see the blossoms faded,
That to bloom we might have aided,
And immortal garlands braided,
 Every year.

To the past go more dead faces
 Every year,—
As the loved leave vacant places
 Every year;
Everywhere the sad eyes meet us,
In the evening's dusk they greet us,
And to come to them entreat us,
 Every year.

You are growing old, they tell us,
 Every year;
You are more alone, they tell us,
 Every year;
You can win no new affection,
You have only recollection,
Deeper sorrow and dejection,
 Every year.

Yes, the shores of life are shifting
  Every year;
And we are seaward drifting
  Every year;
Old places changing fret us,—
The living more regret us,—
There are fewer to regret us,
  Every year.

But the true life draweth nigher
  Every year;
And its Morning Star climbs higher
  Every year;
Earth's hold on us grows slighter,
And the heavy burden lighter,
And the DAWN IMMORTAL brighter,
  Every year.

PARAPHRASE OF JOB XIV.

By GEORGE P. MORRIS, late of New York.

Man dieth and wasteth away,
 And where is he? hark, from the skies
I hear a voice answer and say,
 "The spirit of man never dies.
His *body*, which came from the earth,
 Must mingle again with the sod ;
His *soul*, which in Heaven had birth,
 Returns to the bosom of God ! "

The sky will be burnt to a scroll,
 The earth, wrapped in flames, will expire;
But, freed from all shackles, *the soul*
 Will rise in the midst of the fire;
Then, Brothers, mourn not for the dead
 Who rest from their labors, forgiven ;
Learn this from your Bible instead,—
 "The grave is the gateway to Heaven ! "

O, Lord God Almighty! to THEE
 We turn as our solace above;
The waters may fail from the sea,
 But not from thy fountains of love.

O teach us thy will to obey,
 And sing with one heart and accord,—
"The Lord gave, He taketh away,
 And blest be the name of the Lord!"

KING SOLOMON'S TEMPLE.

By Brother A. J. H. DUGANNE.

PART I.

It is told, in a quaint old nursery tale,
 That perchance you have often read,
How a castle lies hid in some charmèd vale,
 Remote from the usual tread;
And within an enchanted Princess lies,
 Asleep in her silken bed;
Whilst round about, under slumberous charms,
 Lie the forms of her lordly train —
And their squires, and archers, and yeomen-at-arms,
 As valiant as ever drew rein;
But with helmets, and bucklers, and lances,
 All clouded with mildew-stain.

All corroded and mildew'd with rust of time,
 They are lying in court and hall;
Every young knight's beard bears a frosty rime —
 Like the beard of the Seneschal
Who awaits, in his chair, at the postern gate,
 The sound of a trumpet call;
While below, in the crypts of this castle strange
 O'erbrooded by self-same spell,
There are shapes like friars, in cloister'd range,
 Lying each at the door of his cell,
And awaiting, in motionless slumber,
 The stroke of a summoning bell!

For whenever a Knight who is tried and true
 Rides late o'er the haunted wold,
And peals a loud summons the trumpet through,
 That hangs at the postern old,
Then, in all the crypts of this castle
 A bell is solemnly toll'd —

And the Princess arises, in royal gear,
    From the couch of her charmèd rest,
And her knights and her nobles take shield and spear,
    At their beautiful lady's behest;
And they hie to the gate of the postern
    To welcome their midnight guest !

Then afar through the cloisters and corridors
    Sounds a monotone stroke of the bell;
And each friar steals forth, o'er the marble floors,
    From the door of his darksome cell;
And he creepeth away to the postern gate —
    His marvelous story to tell;
While the bell of the castle is ringing amain,
    And the wondering guest comes in;
And the Seneschal leading his ghastly train
    Away through the ghostly din;
Then the friars rehearse to the stranger knight
    Their stories of sorrow and sin.

With a patter of prayers and a dropping of beads,
    They recount, to the shuddering man,
How their souls waxed heavy with sinful deeds
    In the days of their mortal span;
And how Heaven's avenging sentence
    Their earthly years o'erran !
And the Princess reveals to the stranger knight
    How she needs must slumber alway,
Till a Prince of the Temple, in valorous fight,
    Shall a Saracen sorcerer slay —
And the spell of his midnight magic
    Disperse under morn's sweet ray !

But alas ! for that guest of the haunted grange,
    If no Templar Knight he be;
And woe, when he listeth that story strange,
    If no memories pure hath he !
To the spell of the sorcerer's magic
    He must bow his powerless knee;
He must sink into sleep, with the shape he sees,
    And his buckler and helm will rust !
He must lie in the cloisters and crypts, with these
    Who have risen, to greet him, from dust !
And await, with them, an awakening
    By hero more pure and just !

Like that charmèd castle, in haunted vale,
    Is the wondrous Masonic Past !
Where the heroes and yeomen of History's tale
    Are reclining in slumbers fast;
With the spell of an indolent seeming
    Over all their memories cast !
But the Princess, who sleeps in her silken bed,
    Is the spirit of ancient Truth;
Lying evermore shrouded with tatter and shred,
    But for evermore fresh with youth —
And awaiting the pure-hearted Seeker
    To come, with his valor and truth !

Like the knights and the nobles in slumber profound,
    Are our riddles and fables of old;
In their rust and their dust they incumber the ground,
    And abide in their garments of mold —
Keeping truth, like a charmèd Princess,
    Asleep in their ghostly hold.
'Mid the haunted cloisters of History's script,
    In the House of the Past they dwell;
Like the souls of the friars, they hide in each crypt,
    And emerge from each darksome cell—
At the blast of a summoning trumpet,
    Their wonderful stories to tell !

In the volumed marvels of Grecian mind,
    And the records of Roman lore,
There are riddles of wisdom for human kind,
    To ponder a lifetime o'er ;
And to all of their mystical meanings
    Each heart is an open door !
Every human heart is a postern gate
    To the house of the wondrous Past,
Where the heroes and sages of History wait
    The sound of a trumpet blast,
That shall break the enchanted slumbers
    For ages around them cast !

How the voices of song, out of Dorian aisles
    With their Iliad and Odyssey swell !
How they roll'd from the shadows of Tuscan piles,
    Where the Florentine chanted of Hell !
And how grandly, through Gothic chancels,
    Of Paradise Lost they tell !

And the whispers of hearts, and responses of souls,
  Flow around, like the west wind kind,
When the song of the Singer of Avon rolls
  Through the gates of our listening mind,
And the plaint of the pilgrim Harold
  Sounds fitful and strange behind !

All the climes of the earth are as Holy Lands
  To the feet of the children of Song ;
Every realm hath its Mecca, where pilgrim bands
  To some Kaäba of Poesy throng ;
And the homes and the tombs of the poets
  To the whole wide world belong.
In the paths of their minstrels the nations tread,
  And the king on his bard awaits ;
For Ulysses is dumb, and Achilles is dead,
  Until Homer their soul creates ;
And 'tis Tasso who frees Jerusalem,
  Though Godfrey wins her gates.

Through the twilight of oaks and of mistletoe bowers,
  The hymns of the Druids I hear ;
And the Fairie Queene, through lab'rinths of flowers,
  Lures me with her melodies clear,
From the echoes of " woodly Morven,"
  To the murmurs of sweet Windermere ;
And I hear the old Norsemen chanting their tunes,
  Under arches of boreal fires,
And the Troubadours singing, through long, rich Junes,
  To their soft Provencal lyres ;
And the bards of the Cambrian mountains,
  O'ersweeping their 'wildered wires.

O ! those voices of Song, how they ebb, how they flow !
  How they swell, like the tides of the main !
Every age, every clime, hath its life-giving throe,
  And its utterance of generous pain —
Till its master-thought leapeth, full armor'd,
  From out some Jove-like brain !
O ! the heroes and kings have no story to tell,
  In the dust of their funeral urns ;
But the songs of the poets immortally dwell
  Wheresoever a true heart yearns —
In the halls of the royal David,
  Or the cottage of Robert Burns !

PART II.

But the house of the past hath its tongues of stone,
  Yea, its voices of marble and brass —
From the sands of the desolate desert up-thrown,
  And the mold of the wilderness grass !
Though the myth of their awful meanings
  Too often we idly pass !
Where the Nile flows down by its pyramid tombs ;
  Where the ruins of Tadmor lie ;
Where the Petræan cities, from cavernous glooms,
  Like sepulchers, startle the eye —
O ! the voices of granite and marble
  To our souls make audible cry !

Every crumbling plinth, every prostrate shaft,
  Hath a murmur of moldering years ;
From each column and cornice the low winds waft
  A dirge to our listening ears ;
And each frieze, from its sculptured tablet,
  Seems weeping with stony tears ;
Where the gardens of Belus o'er Babylon hung,
  And where Nineveh's walls were raised ;
Where the hundred portals of Thebes swung,
  And old Tyre over ocean gazed ;
And where high upon Mount Moriah,
  King Solomon's Temple blazed !

Oh ! that mountain of God, in the realms of my love,
  Hath a marvelous glory and worth ;
And the Temple that rose its high places above,
  Covers more than Jerusalem's girth ;
For its aisles are the highways of ages,
  And its courts are the zones of earth.
O'er its mythical meanings and parabled sense
  I have pondered, in childlike mind,
Until, back through the ages, with yearnings intense,
  My unsatisfied heart hath inclined —
Longing still for the word of the Master —
  The Word that no mortal may find !

In the dreams and the visions of fervent desire,
  I have mingled with Levite and Priest ;
With the widow's son, Hiram, and Hiram of Tyre,
  Sitting down at Meridian feast ;
And beholding King Solomon's glory
  Arising, like morn in the East !

With mine ancient brethren in Masonry's craft —
    When my soul the lambskin wore —-
I have stood by the mystical corner shaft,
    And knelt on the tesselate floor ;
With the glorious roof of the Temple,
    Like Heaven's roof, arching me o'er !

Under all the rude noises of battling thrones,
    And of realms that jar and strive,
Flows the voice of our Master, whose tender tones
    Overbrooded the Hebrew hive.
When he spake three thousand proverbs,
    And his songs were a thousand and five ;
When he sang of Mount Lebanon's cedar tree,
    And of hyssop that springs from the wall ;
Of the fowls of the air, of the fish of the sea,
    And of things in the dust that crawl ;
Till the words of his love and his wisdom
    Enlighten'd and beautified all.

To the ruler of Sidon — the lord of the seas —
    Flies the word of Jerusalem's king,
Saying, "Bid thou thy servants that Lebanon's trees
    To Judean borders they bring ;
And between us shall peace be alway,
    And blessings around us cling.
From his wars and his sorrows King David hath rest,
    And he sleeps under Sion's sod ;
But, with trembling and awe, at his high behest,
    I abide in the paths he trod ;
And I build on the MOUNT of Moriah
    A house to the Lord my God !"

Then, from far-away forests of Lebanon come
    Great floats unto Joppa's strand ;
And from Tyre and Sidon arises a hum,
    As of bees, overswarming the land ;
And it swells through the Valley of Jordan,
    In chorals of industry grand !
Under manifold halos of column and arch,
    Through the soundless courts and aisles,
At the word of their Master the Craftsmen march
    To their labors, in lengthening files ;
While the Temple arises before them,
    From portal to golden tiles !

365

From the echoless earth, through the motionless air,
　　How that beautiful fabric upgrows !
From the heart of the King, like a voiceless prayer,
　　How it mounts, in its fragrant repose ;
Bearing upward King Solomon's worship,
　　As incense ascends from the rose !
In their brass and their silver, their marble and gold,
　　All noiseless the Crafts have wrought,
Till, in grandeur of silence, their works unfold,
　　As with life everlasting fraught.

By the glow of the greater and lesser Light,
　　And the power of the Master's Word —
By the Plummet of Truth, and the level of Right,
　　And the Square that hath never err'd —
Through the work of a Master Mason,
　　King Solomon's prayer was heard.
At the fragrant morn, 'neath the golden moon,
　　And the eventide's hour of balm,
All the hearts of his Craftsmen were lifted in tune,
　　Like the mingling of harmonies calm ;
And the Temple arose on Moriah,
　　A mighty Masonic Psalm !

Oh ! that Temple of God, from the house of the past,
　　Shineth down o'er the centuried years ;
And my heart, through the veil of its mysteries vast,
　　The voice of King Solomon hears,
Asking me, with the sign of a Master,
　　Why my spirit no Temple rears.
With the Three Great Lights ever shining above,
　　And the tools of the Craft at hand,
Why I build up no fabric of prayerful love,
　　With the arch of a lifetime spann'd ;
And the wings of embracing cherubs
　　Overbrooding its yearnings grand.

Oh ! the house of the Lord that our lives might raise,
　　How it gleams from our fair youth-time !
How its manifold arches and architraves blaze,
　　Through the wilderness-dust of our prime ;
Yet our years, when they molder to ashes,
　　Behold us but wrecks sublime !

For the house that we build in a lifetime's length,
   From the midst of our worldly din,
Hath no Jachin and Boaz, established in strength,
   And no Holy of Holies within;
And we bear up no Ark of the Covenant,
   From out of our Desert of Zin!

There's a mountain of God in each human heart
   For that glorious Temple's base;
And the lines of each loyal Mason's art
   May its grand foundations trace;
And within it, the wings of cherubs
   May the Holy of Holies embrace!
Through the beautiful aisles of the charmèd past,
   How its wonderful harmonies swell!
When their meanings arise, at the Templar's blast,
   From the mold of each darksome cell;
And the soul of the true no longer
   With the dust of the false shall dwell!

When the thoughts of our morning shall royally plan,
   And the deeds of our day shall build;
And the arch of perfection eternally span,
   With the measure our Master hath will'd;
And the depths of our Holy of Holies
   With incense of prayer be filled!
When the pillars of strength in our porch shall abide,
   With the lilies of beauty above;
And the veil of the Presence, encompassing wide,
   Overshadow the ark of our love;
And the peace of the blessed Shekinah
   Enfold, like the wings of a dove!

Oh! the cedars of Lebanon grow at our door,
   And the quarry is sunk at our gate;
And the ships out of Ophir, with golden ore
   For our summoning mandate wait;
And the word of a Master Mason
   May the house of our soul create!
While the day hath light, let the light be used,
   For no man shall the night control!
" Or ever the silken cord be loosed,
   Or broken the golden bowl,"
May we build King Solomon's Temple
   In the true Masonic soul!

DIRGE OF GEORGE WASHINGTON.

Written December, 1799, by OLIVER HOLDIN, a celebrated musical composer of the day. He was the author of the immortal air, "Coronation."

What mortal strains invade our ears?
Whence those sad plaints, those copious tears?
This solemn silence, awful pause,
All, all bespeak some deep-felt cause;
A deep-felt cause! a nation weeps!
In dust Columbia's Guardian sleeps.

A nation's prayers his life to save,
To Heaven, in clouds of incense rose;
A nation's tears bedew his grave,
And angels guard his sweet repose.
The Patriot's dead! a nation weeps!
In dust Columbia's Guardian sleeps.

When Albion, proud, insulting foe,—
Aimed our best rights to overthrow,
His arm, outstretched in conquering might
Their veteran armies put to flight.
The Hero's dead! a nation weeps!
In dust Columbia's Guardian sleeps.

The peace obtained so long desired,
To Vernon's shade the Chief retired;
But faction's hateful feuds arose,
And broke the Farmer's hoped repose.
Our Friend is dead! a nation weeps!
In dust Columbia's Guardian sleeps.

His country's voice once more he hears,
And in its councils he appears.
The mighty charter of our land
Is sanctioned by our Moses' hand.
Our Chief is dead! a nation weeps!
In dust Columbia's Guardian sleeps.

With equal laws he rules the State,
Supports the weak, directs the great;
Then yields the helm, retires to rest,
By all his country loved and blest.
The Sage is dead! a nation weeps!
In dust Columbia's Guardian sleeps.

Again his ready sword he draws;
Unmoved he stands in freedom's cause;
Nor shrinks to hear the marshaled band,
Should hostile foes invade the land.
Our General's dead! a nation weeps!
In dust Columbia's Guardian sleeps.

Thy ways, O King of Kings, are just,
Or when we live or turn to dust!
Then cease from man, look up on high,
Our only hope's above the sky.
We all must die and turn to dust;
Though man is mortal, God is just.

TO STRETCH THE LIBERAL HAND.

ANONYMOUS.

To stretch the liberal hand,
   And pour the stream of gladness
O'er misery's withered strand,—
   To cheer the hearth of sadness,—
To dry the orphan's tear,
   And soothe the heart nigh broken,—
To breathe in sorrow's ear
   Kind words in kindness spoken,—
    This is the Mason's part,
     The Mason's bounden duty,
    This rears the Mason's heart
     In wisdom, strength and beauty.

To practice virtue's laws
   With fervency and freedom,
And in her noble cause
   Advance where'er she lead 'em,—
To curb the headlong course
   Of passion's fiery pinion,
And bend its stubborn force
   To reason's mild dominion,—
    This is the Mason's part,
     The Mason's bounden duty,—
    This rears the Mason's heart
     In wisdom, strength and beauty.

> To shield a brother's fame
>   From envy and detraction,
> And prove that truth's our aim
>   In spirit, life and action,—
> To trust in God, through all
>   The danger and temptation,
> Which to his lot may fall,
>   In trial and probation,—
>   This is the Mason's part,
>   The Mason's bounden duty,
>   This rears the Mason's heart
>   In wisdom, strength and beauty.

LET THERE BE LIGHT.

By Thomas Smith Webb.

> *Let there be light*, th' Almighty spoke,—
> Refulgent streams from chaos broke
>   T' illume the rising earth ;
> Well pleased the Great Jehovah stood,—
> The Power Supreme pronounced it good,
>   And gave the planets birth.
> In choral numbers, Masons, join,
> To bless and praise this Light divine !
>
> Parent of Light, accept our praise,
> Who shed'st on us thy brightest rays,
>   The light that fills the mind !
> By choice selected, lo ! we stand,
> By friendship joined, a social Band,
>   That love to aid mankind !
> In choral numbers, Masons, join,
> To bless and praise this Light divine !
>
> The widow's tear, the orphan's cry,
> All wants our ready hands supply,
>   As far as power is given;
> The naked clothe, the prisoner free,—
> These are thy works, sweet Charity,
>   Revealed to us from Heaven.
> In choral numbers, Masons, join,
> To bless and praise this Light divine.

THE ELEGY OF THE DUKE OF SUSSEX.

By HERCULES ELLIS, a British poet of celebrity.

Linger no voices in our island home
    Which Sussex, by his virtues, long adorned,
To raise the grateful song above his tomb,
    And praise our Prince so loved, so deeply mourned !

Ye Masons whom he led so long and well,
    Ye sons of Science whom his goodness raised,
Widows and orphans fed by him, O tell
    How shall your patron worthily be praised?

His kindness, truth, his worth and wide-spread fame,—
    O, words are vain, when hearts by grief are riven ;
But write upon your hearts his grief and name,
    And let them shine as stars in memory's Heaven.

Ye loved him for the love that was his life,
    The gentleness that round his glory grew,
And as he parted from the world's dark strife,
    Fell o'er his spirit, soft as evening dew.

ADIEU, A HEART-WARM, FOND ADIEU.

By ROBERT BURNS, first Masonic Poet Laureate.

Adieu, a heart-warm fond adieu,
    Dear brothers of the mystic tie!
Ye favored, ye enlightened few,
    Companions of my social joy!
Tho' I to foreign lands must hie,
    Pursuing fortune's sliddery ba',—
With melting heart and brimful eye,
    I'll mind you still, though far awa'.

Oft have I met your social band,
    An' spent the cheerful, festive night;
Oft, honored with supreme command,
    Presided o'er the sons of light ;
And by that Hieroglyphic bright,
    Which none but Craftsmen ever saw,
Strong memory on my heart shall write
    Those happy scenes, when far awa'.

May freedom, harmony and love
　　Unite you in the grand design,
Beneath th' Omniscient Eye above,
　　The glorious Architect divine ; —
That you may keep th' unerring line,
　　Still guided by the plummet's law,
Till order bright completely shine,
　　Shall be my prayer when far awa'.

And you farewell, whose merits claim
　　Justly that highest badge to wear, —
Heaven bless your honored, noble name,
　　To Masonry and Scotia dear !
A last request, permit me here ;
　　When yearly ye assemble a',
One round, — I ask it with a tear,
　　To him, the Bard, that's far awa'.

THE SENIOR WARDEN.

By J. WERGE, of Glasgow, Scotland.

Of a' the seats within our ha'
　　I dearly lo'e the West;
For here the Brethren, great and sma',
　　At parting ha'e been blest;
And memory lends her ready aid
　　Recalling all the past;
The many times we've met, and prayed
　　It might not be the last.

Each time we're Brothers, Brothers a',
　　And every worthy guest,
For here we to the Level fa',
　　E'en Kings are like the rest;
They may be great in Church and State,
　　Or any other sphere; —
The poor, the rich, the low, the great,
　　Are on a level here.

Assembled in our Sacred ha'
　　We're with our Order blest,
For by the great unerring law,
　　We're lowly in the West.

372

Before us we have *Wisdom's* light
    And *Beauty* shining there,
Here *Strength* to keep the work aright
    By acting on the Square.

This symbol tells us once and a'
    Who with the light are blest,
How grand and mighty structures fa'
    And mingle in the West.
When faith must be our password on
    To the Celestial goal,
Where Kings and peasants stand as one
    On the GRAND MASTER's roll.

THE EBONY STAFF OF SOLOMON.

By OWEN MEREDITH.

King Solomon stood in his crown of gold,
    Between the pillars, before the altar,
In the House of the Lord.   And the King was old
    And his strength began to falter,
So that he leaned upon his ebony staff,
Sealed with the seal of the Pentagraph.

And the King stood still as a carven king,
    The carvern cedarn beams below,
In his purple robes, with his signet ring,
    And his beard as white as snow ;
And his face to the Oracle where the Hymn
Dies under the wings of the Cherubim.

And it came to pass as the King stood there,
    And looked on the house he had built with pride,
That the hand of the Lord came unaware,
    And touched him so that he died,
In his purple robe, with his signet ring,
And the crown wherewith they had crowned him King.

And the stream of the folk that came and went,
    To worship the Lord with prayer and praise,
Went softly over in wonderment,
    For the King stood there always ;
And it was solemn and strange to behold
The dead King crowned with a crown of gold.

For he leaned on his ebony staff upright,
  And over his shoulders the purple robe,
And his hair and his beard were both snow-white,
  And the fame of him filled the globe ;
So that no one dare touch him, though he was dead,
He looked so royal about the head !

And the moons were changed and the year rolled on,
  And the new King reigned in the old King's stead,
And men were married and buried anon,
  But the King stood stark and dead ;
Leaning upright on his ebony staff,
Preserved by the sign of the Pentagraph.

And the stream of life, as it went and came
  Ever for worship and praise and prayer,
Was awed by the face and the fear and the fame
  Of the dead King standing there ;
For his hair was so white and his eyes were so cold
That they left him alone with his crown of gold.

So King Solomon stood up, dead in the house
  Of the Lord, held there by the Pentagraph,
Until out from the pillar there came an old mouse,
  And gnawed through his ebony staff ;
Then flat on his face the King fell down,
And they picked from the dust a golden crown !

OLD TUBAL CAIN.

Words by CHARLES MACKAY; Music by HENRY RUSSELL.

Old Tubal Cain was a man of might,
  In the days when earth was young;
By the fierce red light of his furnace bright,
  The strokes of his hammer rung;
And he lifted high his brawny hand
  On the iron, glowing clear,
Till the sparks rushed out in scarlet rout,
  As he fashioned the sword and spear.
And he sang,—" Hurrah for my handiwork !
  Hurrah for the spear and sword !
Hurrah for the hand that shall wield them well,
  For he shall be king and lord !"

To Tubal Cain came many a one,
    As he wrought by his roaring fire,
And each one prayed for a strong steel blade,
    As the crown of his own desire;
And he made them weapons, sharp and strong,
    Till they shouted loud for glee,
And gave him gifts of pearl and gold
    And spoils of the forest free.
And they sang,—"Hurrah for Tubal Cain,
    Who hath given us strength anew !
Hurrah for the smith ! hurrah for the fire !
    And hurrah for the metal true !"

But a sudden change came o'er his head,
    Ere the setting of the sun;
And Tubal Cain was filled with pain,
    For the evil he had done;
He saw that men with rage and hate
    Made war against their kind;
And the land was red with the blood they shed,
    In their lust for carnage blind;
And he said, "Alas, that ever I made,
    Or that skill of mine should plan,
The spear and the sword, for the man whose joy
    Is to slay his fellow man !"

And for many a day old Tubal Cain
    Sat brooding o'er his woe,
And his hand forebore to smite the ore,
    And his furnace smoldered low!
But he rose at last with a cheerful face,
    And a bright, courageous eye,
And bared his strong, right arm for work,
    While the quick flames mounted high;
And he sang, "Hurrah for my handiwork";
    And the red sparks lit the air;
"Not alone for the blade, was the bright steel made,"
    And he fashioned the first plowshare !

And men, taught wisdom from the past,
    In friendship joined their hands,
Hung the sword in the hall, the spear on the wall,
    And plowed the willing lands;
And they sang,—"Hurrah for Tubal Cain,
    Our stanch, good friend is he !

And for the plowshare and the plow,
    To him our praise shall be ! ''
But while oppression lifts its head,
    Or a tyrant would be lord,
Though we may thank him for the plow
    We'll not forget the sword !

BENEATH A ROYAL ARCH.

By Hon. Charles Scott, late of Memphis, Tennessee.

Beneath a Royal Arch, I see
A Thrice Illustrious Deity;
And Faith, and Hope, and Charity
Whisper the Sacred Name to me.

Their mystic hands were raised on high,—
The white-robed multitude stood by;
In syllables I heard the Word,
Eternal Word,— Almighty God.

Masons should love their Master's name,
Jesus, the Spirit, God's the same,
The Holy Being, making three,
Th' Eternal One,— ah, can it be?

When raised, exalted, I shall hear
The Living Word I love so dear,
Beneath an arch of heavenly light
Where day ne'er sings a song of night;

The Word,— how good, how great, how free !
Accepted it shall ever be !
While Faith, and Hope, and Charity
Revere Thy name, O, Deity.

HYMN.

By Fay Hempstead, of Little Rock, Arkansas.

Sung at the Opening Services of Christ Church Chapel, Little Rock, Arkansas, November 5, 1876.

O, Father, bless this sacred place,
    Which for thy glory now we rear;
And may the riches of Thy grace
    Be on Thy people gathered here !

376

Here would we seek the Church, Thy bride,
    In this fair fane of bright array;
O, draw us, Saviour, near Thy side,
    That we may see Thou art the way.

Incline our hearts to seek Thine aid,
    And turn our thoughts to things above;
May numbers at this shrine be made
    To feel the sweetness of Thy love!

So teach us, Lord, our faith to cast
    Upon Thy Word which firmly stands,
That we may gain, when life is past,
    A home with Thee, not made with hands.

PRAISE HYMN OF THE ROSE CROIX.

By J. S. REEVES, M.D., of Niles, Michigan.

God said, "Let there be light," and there was LIGHT!
    Light for a world,— dark night was rolled away;
The sullen, solemn gloom was put to flight,
    As burst upon the earth the light of day.
A holy stillness reigned, as o'er the earth
    The silvery radiance spread its cheering beam;
Then angel voices to the shout gave birth:
    "Light for the world!" for angels fit the theme.
And earth was bathed in glory, Eden bloomed,
    The garden-home of man to whom 'twas given;
The Tempter came, man fell and, falling, doomed
    His race to exile from his God and Heaven.

Light for the world! O great and glorious day,
    The Son of God came down, a world to save;
On Calvary the curse was washed away,
    And many triumph over death, the grave:
Praise to the ALMIGHTY Architect, who willed
    Form to the void profound, great FIRST and LAST!
Praise to our MASTER great, that HE did build
    The glorious structure of Creation vast!
Praise for the Immortal Spirit breathed in man;
    All kindreds, climes and tongues your voices raise;
But higher praises for the Gospel Plan,—
    Let all Creation join the work of praise!

HOW SHALL WE RAISE OUR DEAD?

By Thomas W. Davis, of Waverly, Massachusetts.

How shall we raise our dead?
   Bring from their worldly store
Treasures unlimited,
   To give them life once more?
With these the realms of death invade?
Perchance a ransom may be paid ; —
Ah no! skin slips from flesh ; ye know
We cannot raise the body so.

How shall we raise our dead?
   Their dear ones join the cry ;
Our tears with theirs are shed
   In fruitless agony.
Shall love have power to vanquish death,
And summon back the fleeting breath ?
Ah no! flesh cleaves from bone ; ye know
We cannot raise the body so.

How shall we raise our dead?
   O, God, relieve our pain!
Help in the hour of dread,
   For mortal help is vain.
When dust returns to kindred dust,
In Judah's Lion fix the trust ;
For by His strength, and only so,
Our dead eternal life shall know.

THE PRAYER OF A MASON.

By Brother Joseph Covell, late of Jay Bridge, Maine.

Parent of all, Omnipotent,
   In Heaven and earth below,
Through all Creation's bounds unspent,
   Whose streams of goodness flow,—

Teach me to know from whence I rose
   And unto what designed ;
No private aims let me propose,
   Since linked with human kind.

But chief to hear fair virtue's voice
    May all my thoughts incline ;
'Tis Heaven's law, 'tis wisdom's choice,
    'Tis Nature's call and Thine.

Me from our Sacred Order's cause,
    Let nothing e'er divide;
Grandeur, nor gold, nor vain applause,
    Nor friendship's false misguide.

Teach me to feel a Brother's grief,
    To do in all that's best ;
To suffering man to give relief,
    And blessing, *to be blest.*

THE HEAD AND HEART.

By John G. Saxe.

The Head is stately, calm and wise,
    And bears a princely part,
While down below in secret lies
    The warm, impulsive heart.

The lordly Head that sits above,
    The Heart that beats below,
Their several office plainly prove,
    Their true relations show.

The Head erect, serene and cool,
    Endowed with reason's art,
Was set aloft to guide and rule
    The throbbing, wayward Heart.

And from the Head as from the higher,
    Comes all-directing thought,
And in the Heart's transforming fire,
    All noble deeds are wrought.

Yet each is best, when both unite
    To make the man complete ;
What were the Heat without the Light?
    The Light without the Heat?

TO LIVE BEYOND THE GRAVE.

By JAMES G. PERCIVAL, a poet of rare powers.

To live beyond the grave,— to leave a name
That like a living sun shall hold its way
Undimmed through ages,— to be hailed hereafter
As first among the spirits who have gifted
Their land with fame,— to dwell amid the thoughts
Of all sublimer souls or deities,
As treasures in their shrines,— to lead the tongues
Of nations, and be uttered in the songs
And prayers of millions,— he who bears *such hope*
Fixed in his heart, and holds his lonely way,
Cheered by this only, and yet keeps himself
Unwavering in the many shocks that push
His purpose from its path,— he was not cast
In nature's common mold. *Such hope itself
Is greatness.*

SACRED ASYLUM.

By JOSEPH ROBBINS, M.D., of Quincy, Illinois.

Sacred Asylum! here we meet
   And tell our vows at Friendship's shrine ;
FATHER! guide Thou our wandering feet,
   And make the hearts before Thee THINE.

Beneath the bannered Cross we stand,
   From worldly noise and strife apart,
And, trusting, grasp the offered *hand*,
   That holds within its palm the *heart*.

From off our pilgrim sandals brush
   The dust of busy, toiling day,
And here, in evening's quiet hush,
   Bending before the MASTER, pray —

That in our hearts, without alloy,
   May dwell the love that Christ hath shown,
Responsive to a Brother's *joy*,
   And making all his *griefs* our own.

380

With firm reliance on Thy name,
  May we the path of duty tread
O'er frozen ways, or through the flame,
  Whence Molay's martyr-spirit fled

And when at last, this mortal dust
  Shall put on Immortality;
O, grant us then serenest trust
  In Thine unending verity.

AN OLD MASON'S DREAM.

By Hon. John P. Brown, late Official Dragoman to the American Embassy, Constantinople.

Ah, yes, indeed, I'm the children's friend,
  Though my limbs are weak and my pulses slow;
From their homes above this word they send,—
  "How that old man loved us here below;"

When I hear the sound of their voice at play,
  It seems to come from the far-off sky;
Its tones are not of life's rugged way,
  And I think of my age with a gentler sigh.

A glimpse of Heaven I catch in their smile,
  It frees my heart of all earthly cares;
I feel me away from this earth awhile,
  And my breast is free from the load it bears.

In their merry eyes there are angel forms,
  When they look in each other, so pure and bright;
In their small blue orbs are no sinful storms,
  But they seem resplendent with Heaven's light.

How often I sit with my old eyes closed,
  And am carried away, far away from this,
To that peaceful abode, where it is supposed
  The children dwell in the kingdom of bliss.

Yes, then indeed, I'm the children's friend,
  Though my limbs are weak and my pulses slow!
From their homes above this thought they send,—
  "How that old man loved us here below!"

STABILITY OF MASONRY.

ANONYMOUS.

Amid this life of change how glorious the thought
That one bright link survives the wreck,
By warring nations wrought;
This Mystic Tie doth proudly scorn
The touch of change and blight,
And, like the pinions of the morn,
Spreads o'er the world her light.

Six thousand years of wingèd flight,
Have chased the hopes of man away
Like withered leaves in tempest's might;
But this one fabric nobly braves
The tooth of time, the papal power,
The traitor's fang, the trick of knaves,
Sublime, immutable, unchanged its tower.

And each successive age has taught
How weak the venom of her foes;
In God's right arm her strength she sought,
Hope, Charity, and Holy *Faith,*
A garland woven for her brow;
Love's pure cement the fabric hath,
And crowned with youth's eternal glow.

THE TEMPLE OF LIVING STONES.

By LAWRENCE M. GREENLEAF.

The temple made of wood and stone may crumble and decay,
But there's a viewless Fabric which shall never fade away;
Age after age the Masons strive to consummate the Plan,
But still the work's unfinished which th' immortal THREE began;
None but immortal eyes may view, complete in all its parts,
The Temple formed of LIVING STONES,—the structure made of hearts.

'Neath every form of government, in every age and clime;
Amid the world's convulsions and the ghastly wrecks of time,—
While empires rise in splendor, and are conquered and o'erthrown,
And cities crumble into dust, their very sites unknown,—
Beneath the sunny smiles of peace, the threatening frown of strife,
Freemasonry has stood unmoved, with age renewed her life.

She claims her votaries in all climes, for none are under ban
Who place implicit trust in God, and love their fellow man;
The heart that shares another's woe beats just as warm and true
Within the breast of Christian, Mohammedan or Jew;
She levels all distinctions from the highest to the least,—
The King must yield obedience to the Peasant in the East.

What honored names on history's page, o'er whose brave deeds we pore,
Have knelt before our sacred shrine and trod our checkered floor !
Kings, princes, statesmen, heroes, bards who square their actions true,
Between the Pillars of the Porch now pass in long review;
O, Brothers, what a glorious thought for us to dwell upon,—
The mystic tie that binds our hearts bound that of WASHINGTON!

Although our past achievements we with honest pride review,
As long as there's Rough Ashlars there is work for us to do;
We still must shape the LIVING STONES with instruments of love
For that eternal Mansion in the Paradise above;
Toil as we've toiled in ages past to carry out the plan,—
'Tis this;— the Fatherhood of God, the Brotherhood of Man !

THE TEMPLE OF MASONRY.

By W. SNEWING, London, England.

Lo, where yon structure rears its ample dome!
'Tis light's abode, 'tis Masonry's high home;
See where its walls, by love cemented, rise,
Till their bright turrets pierce the brighter skies :
From where the East pours forth the ruddy ray,
To where the West receives its fading ray;
From the mild South to where the gelid North
Marshals its storms and sends them hurtling forth.

In form symmetrical the pile extends,
Nor with earth's center or earth's concave ends.
Three pillars high their polished fabrics rear
And with united force the structure bear.
This Wisdom called, *that* Strength, *that* Beauty named,
Emblems of those whose hands the Temple framed ;
Of work mosaic wrought with matchless skill,—
The pavement formed, designed the mind to fill
With truthful images of man's estate,
To curb proud scorn and suffering truth elate.

A blazing sun in liquid azure glows,
And o'er the starry roof its luster throws;
While all around bright hieroglyphics gleam
Like Heaven's jewels to a slumbering stream.
Between the pavement and the starry spheres,
Of many steps a rising way appears;
Pleasing the path to him by *faith* inspired,
By *hope* sustained, by *charity* attired.

But effort impotent and labor vain
To him who strives with carnal steps to gain;
From out the Temple, flashing with light's beams,
Three rivers gush, then mix their crystal streams;
Still as they roll, their limpid waves expand,
Bless every shore and gladden every land,
With the full tide of sweet fraternal *love*,
Relief and *truth*, all hallowed from above.

A GREETING.

By R. H. TAYLOR.

My Brother of the Mystic Tie
    Wherever you abide,
Or on Nevada's mountain high,
    Or by the ocean tide,—
Whate'er your station, rank or fame,
    Where'er your native land,
Because you bear a Mason's name,
    Here is a Mason's *Hand*.

As you and I our journey take
    Along life's rugged way,
No adverse fate our *faith* may shake,
    Or turn our *love* away;
The bond between us, triple strong,
    No power on earth may part;—
To you this tribute of a song,
    Goes with a Mason's *Heart*.

While in the quarries of the Craft
    We work with one accord,
A Mason's blessing let me waft
    To all who keep the *Word;*

384

With *charity* to all mankind,
And *faith* in God above,
And these with gentle *hope* entwined
Accept a Mason's *Love!*

FALLEN IS THY THRONE.

By Thomas Moore.

Fallen is thy throne, O, Israel!
Silence is o'er thy plains;
Thy dwellings all lie desolate,
Thy children weep in chains;
Where are the dews that fed thee
On Etham's barren shore?
That fire from Heaven which led thee
Now lights thy path no more.

Lord, Thou didst love Jerusalem!
Once she was all thy own;
Her love Thy fairest heritage,
Her power Thy glory's throne;
Till evil came and blighted
Thy long-loved olive tree,
And Salem's shrines were lighted
For other gods than Thee.

Then sunk the star of Solyma,
Then passed her glory's day,
Like heath that in the wilderness
The wild wind whirls away;
Silent and waste her bowers,
Where once the mighty trod,
And sunk those guilty towers
While Baal reigned as God.

"Go," said the Lord, "ye conquerors,
Steep in her blood your swords,
And raze to earth her battlements,
For they are not the Lord's!
Till Sion's mournful daughter
O'er kindred bones shall tread,
And Hinnom's vale of slaughter
Shall hide but half her dead!"

OPENING ODE.

By S. M. CALKINS.

Come, Brothers, assemble, the pleasures to share,
Where we meet on the Level and part on the Square,
Where the watchword is *love*, and strife is unknown,
Save striving to honor the widow's lone son.

Where the poor and the rich unite on the Plumb,
Inviting and welcoming others to come ;
Come, place on the altar a sprig that is green,
To mark the loved spot where a Brother has been.

If we meet in our place and live by the rule,
And walk by the lights which encircle the soul,
We'll all find a Lodge and a temple of rest,
Where the GRAND MASTER rules o'er the loved and the blest.

Come, then, with the Trowel and spread the cement
Of Brotherly Love with the common intent,
Presenting the CHIEF of the Grand Lodge above
With richest of jewels all brightened with love.

MASONRY IN ASIA MINOR.

Written in 1745, at Smyrna, by ALEXANDER DRUMMOND, British Consul at Aleppo, Syria.

" I cannot help congratulating myself upon the opportunity I enjoyed here, of making so many worthy Brethren at Smyrna, and of forming the only Lodge that is in the Levant."

For ages past a savage race
  O'erspread the Asian plains,
All nature wore a gloomy face,
  And pensive moved the swains;
But now Britannia's generous sons
  A glorious Lodge have raised,
Near the famed banks where Meles runs,
  And Homer's cattle grazed,

The briery wilds to groves are changed,
  With orange trees around,
And fragrant lemons, fairly ranged,
  O'ershade the blissful ground.

Approving Phœbus shines more bright,
  The flowers appear more gay,—
New objects rise to cheer the sight
  With each revolving day.

While safe within the sacred walls
  Where heavenly friendship reigns,
The friendly Mason hears the calls
  Of all the needy swains;
Their generous aid, with cheerful soul,
  They grant to those who sue,
And while the wholesome precepts roll,
  Their smiling joys pursue.

THE RED CROSS DEBATE.

By Thomas Smith Webb.

Which is the greatest, the strength of wine, or of the king, or of woman?

How STRONG IS WINE! it causeth all to err,
Who to calm temperance excess prefer;
Under its influence the mind's undone,
The poor man and the rich become as one;
Their thoughts are turned to jollity and mirth,
Sorrow and debt despise, and pride of birth;
The miserable man forgets his woes,
Neglects his kindred, mingles with his foes;
The virtuous heart a vicious course defends,
And draws its sword against its truest friends;
How strong is Wine, that forceth to these things!
Is it not greater than the power of Kings?

The GREAT CREATOR, when He formed our race,
To all His creatures each assigned a place,
And man ordained the master of the whole,
To rule and govern them without control.
But man himself by man must be restrained,
And Kings and Princes this great power attained;
Now those who rule all sublunary things
No earthly power controls, and such are Kings!

The strength of Wine is not to be denied,
It lightens poverty and humbles pride;
Neither is that of Kings, whate'er its source,
Which binds so many men by will and force;

387

But yet the frown of Woman far excels
The force of Wine and Kings; with magic spells
She captivates her votary by her charms,
And he's content to die within her arms.

Though Wine by *strength* should rule, by *wisdom* Kings,
Though Woman's *beauty* partial durance brings,
Yet all their power shall fail and fade like youth,
And wisdom, strength and beauty dwell with Truth.
For neither Beauty, mighty Kings, nor Wine,
Hath power and majesty, fair Truth, like thine.

Thy judgments just, thy precepts ever pure,
In all vicissitudes shall still endure;
Thy fruits are not the pleasures of an hour,
And ages yet unborn shall own thy power;
For neither Beauty, mighty Kings, nor Wine,
Hath power and majesty, fair Truth, like thine.

All else is evanescent, false and frail,
All else deceives, but thou shalt never fail;
At thy approach hypocrisy shall flee,
For wisdom, strength and beauty dwell with thee;
Thou still shall blossom in immortal youth,—
Forever blessed be the God of Truth!
For neither Beauty, mighty Kings, nor Wine,
Hath power and majesty, fair Truth, like thine!

A SIGNAL FROM THE OUTER GATE.

By Benjamin B. French, late of Washington, D. C., a pillar of Masonry in the last generation.

A signal from the outer gate
    Has passed within the wall,
The Master from his Orient throne
    Surveys the Brethren all ;
Each, duly clad, is in his place,
    Where truth stands ever by,—
Falsehood would quail beneath the frown
    Of the All-seeing Eye.

The Tyler stands with naked blade,
    To guard the sacred door;
None but true men must ever tread
    The tesselated floor.

There the great lesson,—*how to live*,
    The greater,—*how to die*,
Are taught beneath the symbol grand,
    The All-beholding Eye.

But joy and love and sympathy
    Burn bright in every soul,—
'Tis human bliss to worship God,
    And seek Heaven's happy goal ;
This bliss within the Lodge is found,
    Beneath its azure sky,
Whence, ever watchful from above,
    Looks God's All-seeing Eye.

The gavel falls, the Lodge is closed,
    Each wends his several way,
But the great lesson he has learned
    Within his heart shall stay;
And as he walks his worldly walk,
    Whatever work he ply,
He ne'er forgets that o'er him still
    Is God's All-seeing Eye.

GREAT SOURCE OF LIGHT AND LOVE!

By Brother THADDEUS MASON HARRIS, of Massachusetts, a Masonic writer of eminence.

Great Source of light and love,
    To Thee our songs we raise !
Oh, in Thy temple, Lord, above,
    Hear and accept our praise !

Shine on this festive day !
    Succeed its hoped design ;
And may our Charity display
    A ray resembling Thine !

May this fraternal Band,
    Now consecrated, blest,
In Union, all distinguished, stand,
    In Purity be dressed !

May all the Sons of Peace
    Their every grace improve,
Till discord through the nations cease,
    And all the world be Love !

MASON MARKS.

Anonymous.

They're traced in lines on the Parthenon,
    Inscribed by the subtle Greek;
And Roman legions have carved them on
    Walls, roads and arch antique;
Long ere the Goth, with vandal hand,
    Gave scope to his envy dark,
The Mason craft in many a land
    Has graven its *Mason mark.*

The obelisk old and the pyramids,
    Around which a mystery clings,—
The hieroglyphs on the coffin lids
    Of weird Egyptian kings,—
Syria, Carthage and Pompeii,
    Buried and strewn and stark,
Have marble records that will not die,
    Their primitive *Mason mark.*

Upon column and frieze and capital,
    In the eye of the chaste volute,—
On Scotia's curve, or an astrogal,
    Or in triglyp's channel acute,—
Cut somewhere on the entablature,
    And oft, like a sudden spark,
Flashing a light on a date obscure,
    Shines many a *Mason mark.*

These craftsmen old had a genial whim,
    That nothing could e'er destroy,
With a love of their art that naught could dim,
    They toiled with a chronic joy;
Nothing was too complex to essay,
    In aught they dashed to embark ;
They triumphed on many an Appian Way,
    Where they'd left their *Mason mark.*

Crossing the Alps like Hannibal,
    Or skirting the Pyranees,
On peak and plain, in crypt and cell,
    On foot or on bandaged knees;—

From Tiber to Danube, from Rhine to Seine,
    They needed no "letters of marque ";—
Their art was their passport in France and Spain,
    And in Britain their *Mason mark.*

The monolith gray and Druid chair,
    The pillars and towers of Gael,
In Ogham occult their age they bear,
    That time can only reveal.
Live on, old monuments of the past,
    Our beacons through ages dark!
In primal majesty still you'll last,
    Endeared by each *Mason mark.*

THE GREAT LIGHTS.

By Captain SAMUEL WHITING, late of New York.

O, HOLY BIBLE, book of truth,
    Full of rich love on every page,
"Our rule and guide of faith" in youth,
    Our help and comforter in age!
Let thy clear beacon shine afar,
    Dispelling all the gloom of night,
And prove a guiding Bethlehem Star
    To all inquiring Sons of Light.

The SQUARE upon the Bible place,
    To rule our actions day by day,
May we, while on life's eager race,
    Ne'er from its line of duty stray,
Though Beauty's line may be the curve,
    And angles seem, perchance, less fair,
From rectitude let no man swerve
    Who ever parts upon the Square.

The COMPASS let us keep at hand,
    To circumscribe our daily life;
If we within its limits stand
    We shall escape all worldly strife.
These three GREAT LIGHTS our path will cheer,
    And guide to Heavenly Mansions fair,
If "meeting on the Level" here,
    At last "we part upon the Square!"

WHEN FIRST ETERNAL JUSTICE.

By Michael Hodge, Jr., late of Newburyport, Massachusetts.

When first Eternal justice bade
    Life's varied ills untempered flow,
'Twas then Almighty Goodness said
    "Go, Pity ! cheer the realms of woe !
Go, mild Compassion ! Go, Charity and Love !
Tell man there's mercy yet above."

Scarce fled from Heaven the high behest
    That whelmed in light the smiling earth,
Ere wide creation, doubly blest,
    Hailed Masonry's propitious birth;
With strains majestic ye Masons lift the skies !
Let grateful hallelujahs rise !

Hail, royal Art ! in humble zeal
    The Mason greets thy gladdening sway;
'Tis thine to teach *his heart* to feel,
    'Tis thine to bid *his hand* obey;
'Twas Wisdom fashioned, 'twas Strength thy Temple raised,
And beauty o'er the fabric blazed.

Sweet Charity, whose soothing art
    Can bid all apathy adore,
Come, sweep the chords of every heart,
    Primeval harmony restore.
Come, lovely Sister, come smooth life's rugged way,
And lead our souls to realms of day !

HAVE FAITH IN ONE ANOTHER.

By W. W. Fernie, of South Shields, England.

Have faith in one another,
    When you meet in friendship's name;
For a true friend is a brother,
    And his heart shall throb the same;
Though your paths in life may differ,
    Since the hour when first ye met,
Have faith in one another,—
    Ye may need that friendship yet.

Have faith in one another
   When ye whisper faith's fond vow;
It may not be always summer,
   Nor always bright as now;
And when winter time comes o'er ye,
   If some kindred heart ye share,
Have faith in one another,
   And ye ne'er shall know despair.

Have faith in one another;
   For should doubt alone incline,
It would make this world a desert,
   And the sun would cease to shine;
We have all some transient sorrow
   That o'ershadows us to-day,
Yet have faith in one another,
   And it soon will pass away.

Have faith in one another,
   And let honor be your guide,
Let the truth alone be spoken,
   Whatever may betide;
The false may reign a season,
   And we doubt not but it will,
But have faith in one another,
   And the truth will triumph still.

ORARE, LABORARE, CANTARE.

By JOHN STUART BLACKIE.

Three blissful words I name to thee
   Three words of potent charm,
From carking care thy heart to free,
   Thy life to shield from harm.
Whoso these blissful words may know,
A bold, bright-fronted face shall show,
And, shod with peace, shall safely go
   Through fire and wild alarm.

First, ere thy forward foot thou move,
   And wield thine arm of might,
Lift up thy heart to God above
   That all thy ways be right,

To the prime source of life and power
Let thy soul rise, even as a flower,
That skyward climbs in sunny hour,
   And seeks the genial light.

Then gird thy loins to manly toil,
   And in the toil have joy;
Greet hardships with a winning smile
   And love the stern employ.
Thy glory this,— the harsh to tame
And by wise stroke and technic flame
In God-like labors fruitful name
   Old Chaos to destroy.
Then mid thy workshop's dusty din,
   Where Titan stream hath sway,
Croon to thyself a song within,
   Or pour the lusty lay;
Even as a bird that cheerily sings
In narrow cage, nor frets its wings,
But with full-breasted joyance sings
   Its soul unto the day.

For *lofty things* let others strive
   With roll of vauntful drum;
Keep thou thy heart, a honeyed hive,
   Like bee with busy hum.
Chase not the bliss with wistful eyes
That ever lures and ever flies,
But in the present joy be wise,
   And let the future come!

TABLE OF CONTENTS.

[The selections from other authors are distinguished by a *.]

TABLE OF CONTENTS.

TABLE OF CONTENTS.

398

399

Printed in the United States
123876LV00004B/13/A